China's Second Capital

This book is a study of the dual capital system of Ming dynasty China (1368–1644), with a focus on the administrative functions of the auxiliary southern capital, Nanjing. It argues that the immense geographical expanse of the Chinese empire and the poor communication infrastructure of pre-modern times necessitated the establishment of an additional capital administration for effective control of the Ming realm. The existence of the southern capital, which has been dismissed by scholars as redundant and insignificant, was, the author argues, justified by its ability to assist the primary northern capital better control the southern part of the imperial land. The practice of maintaining auxiliary capitals, where the bureaucratic structures of the primary capital were replicated in varying degrees, was a unique and valuable approach to effecting bureaucratic control over vast territory in pre-modern conditions. Nanjing translates into English as "southern capital" and Beijing as "northern capital".

Jun Fang is Professor of History at Huron University College, Western University, Canada.

Asian States and Empires

Edited by Peter Lorge, Vanderbilt University

The importance of Asia will continue to grow in the twenty-first century, but remarkably little is available in English on the history of the polities that constitute this critical area. Most current work on Asia is hindered by the extremely limited state of knowledge of the Asian past in general, and the history of Asian states and empires in particular. *Asian States and Empires* is a book series that will provide detailed accounts of the history of states and empires across Asia from earliest times until the present. It aims to explain and describe the formation, maintenance and collapse of Asian states and empires, and the means by which this was accomplished, making available the history of more than half the world's population at a level of detail comparable to the history of Western polities. In so doing, it will demonstrate that Asian peoples and civilizations had their own histories apart from the West, and provide the basis for understanding contemporary Asia in terms of its actual histories, rather than broad generalizations informed by Western categories of knowledge.

1. The Third Chinese Revolutionary Civil War, 1945–49
An Analysis of Communist Strategy and Leadership
Christopher R. Lew

2. China's Southern Tang Dynasty, 937–76
Johannes L. Kurz

3. War, Culture and Society in Early Modern South Asia, 1740–1849
Kaushik Roy

4. The Military Collapse of China's Ming Dynasty, 1618–44
Kenneth M. Swope

5. China's Second Capital
Nanjing under the Ming, 1368–1644
Jun Fang

China's Second Capital
Nanjing under the Ming, 1368–1644

Jun Fang

LONDON AND NEW YORK

First published 2014
by Routledge
2 Park Square, Milton Park, Abingdon, Oxon, OX14 4RN

and by Routledge
711 Third Avenue, New York, NY 10017

Routledge is an imprint of the Taylor & Francis Group, an informa business

© 2014 Jun Fang

The right of Jun Fang to be identified as author of this work has been asserted by him in accordance with the Copyright, Designs and Patent Act 1988.

All rights reserved. No part of this book may be reprinted or reproduced or utilised in any form or by any electronic, mechanical, or other means, now known or hereafter invented, including photocopying and recording, or in any information storage or retrieval system, without permission in writing from the publishers.

Trademark notice: Product or corporate names may be trademarks or registered trademarks, and are used only for identification and explanation without intent to infringe.

British Library Cataloguing in Publication Data
A catalogue record for this book is available from the British Library

Library of Congress Cataloging in Publication Data
Fang, Jun, 1962-
China's second capital : Nanjing under the Ming, 1368-1644 / Jun Fang.
  pages cm. – (Asian states and empires ; 5)
Summary: "This book is a study of the dual capital system of Ming dynasty China (1368-1644), with a focus on the administrative functions of the auxiliary Southern Capital, Nanjing. It argues that the immense geographical expanse of the Chinese empire and the poor communication infrastructure of pre-modern times necessitated the establishment of an additional capital administration for effective control of the Ming realm. The existence of the Southern Capital, which has been dismissed by scholars as redundant and insignificant, was, the author argues, justified by its ability to assist the primary Northern Capital better control the southern part of the imperial land. The practice of maintaining auxiliary capitals, where the bureaucratic structures of the primary capital were replicated in varying degrees, was a unique and valuable approach to effecting bureaucratic control over vast territory in pre-modern conditions. Nanjing translates into English as "Southern Capital" and Beijing as "Northern Capital""– Provided by publisher.
  Includes bibliographical references and index.
1. Nanjing (Jiangsu Sheng, China) 2. China–Politics and government–1368-1644. I. Title.
  DS797.56.N365F358 2014
  951'.136–dc23
                    2013047540

ISBN: 978-0-415-85525-9 (hbk)
ISBN: 978-1-315-73794-1 (ebk)

Typeset in Times New Roman
by Taylor & Francis Books

Printed and bound by CPI Group (UK) Ltd, Croydon, CR0 4YY

For Lifang and Tina

Table of Contents

List of illustrations	ix
Acknowledgements	xi
Explanatory Notes	xii
Major Epochs of Chinese History	xiii
Table of Ming Emperors and Their Reigns	xiv
Ming Weights and Measures	xv

	Introduction	1

1. Why the Southern Capital of Ming China 1
2. The Southern Capital, Nanjing 2
3. Previous studies of the Southern Capital 6
4. The Southern Capital and state control in Ming China 9
5. The sources 11

1	The Secondary Capital System in Imperial China	18

1. The pre-Sui dynasty period 19
2. The Sui, Tang, and Five dynasties 20
3. The Song, Liao, and Jin dynasties 24
4. The Yuan, Ming, and Qing dynasties 27

2	Ministers and eunuchs: the Southern Capital administration	44

1. The civil bureaucracy 44
2. The military apparatuses 50
3. The eunuch establishment 52
4. The leadership of the Nanjing administration 55
5. The reduction and restoration of the Nanjing offices 56

3	Patronage, proving ground, and punishment: the political functions of the Southern Capital	64

1. Wang Shu and his posting to the Southern capital 64
2. A training ground for the junior officials 66

viii *Contents*

3. *A source of specially appointed task-force central officials*   *71*
4. *A place of exile for disfavored officials*   *74*
5. *A sinecure for superannuated officials*   *80*
6. *Concluding remarks*   *84*

4   Center of wealth: the financial functions of the Southern Capital   92

1. *Regional roles*   *92*
2. *Collection of tax grain*   *94*
3. *Transport of tribute grain*   *98*
4. *Role in the state salt monopoly*   *101*
5. *Collection of miscellaneous taxes*   *104*
6. *The storage and verification of the Yelow Registers*   *110*

5   Southern Stronghold: The military functions of the Southern Capital administration   121

1. *Military forces under the command of the Southern Capital administration*   *121*
2. *Maintaining stability at the second political center*   *124*
3. *Suppression of piracy along the southeast coast*   *128*
4. *The suppression of aboriginal rebellions in the south*   *131*
5. *Non-combat functions*   *133*

Conclusion   142

1. *The Southern Capital: an auxiliary implement of state control in Ming China*   *142*
2. *The relationship between Beijing and Nanjing*   *145*

Bibliography   148
Glossary   168
Index   207

List of illustrations

Figure

I.1   A section of *Nandu fanhui tujuan* (scroll painting
of the prosperous southern capital) attributed to Qiu Ying
(1498–1552)   3

Maps

Map of Ming Provinces   xvi

Tables

2.1	The civil offices and the staffing levels of officials (*guan*) in the Beijing and Nanjing administrations (late Ming)	46
2.2	The staffing levels of the lesser functionaries (*li*) in the Beijing and Nanjing administrations (1587)	47
2.3	The army stationed in the cities of Beijing and Nanjing	51
2.4	The 24 eunuch departments in both Beijing and Nanjing in the Ming	53
3.1	The composition of ministers of the Nanjing administration appointed during the 1522–66 period	67
3.2	The composition of ministers of the Beijing administration appointed during the 1522–66 period	67
3.3	Promotion patterns of Beijing vice ministers appointed to be Nanjing ministers during the 1522–66 period	70
3.4	Transfer patterns of Nanjing ministers appointed to be Beijing ministers during the 1522–66 period	70
3.5	Nanjing officials appointed to supreme commandership in the Ming	72
3.6	Nanjing officials appointed to grand coordinatorship in the Ming	73
4.1	Estimated land tax collection and distribution in piculs of grain, *c.* 1578	95

x *List of illustrations*

4.2   The bureaus which administered the tax grain   97
4.3   The tribute grain delivered via the *duiyun* system   99
4.4   The tribute grain delivered via the *gaidui* system   100
4.5   Salt certificates issued by the Nanjing Ministry of Revenue in 1549   104
4.6   The transit duties and local business tax collected from the seven major customs houses (early Ming)   106
5.1   The number of officers and soldiers in 48 Nanjing guard units (*c.* 1615)   125

Acknowledgements

I would like to thank many people who have helped to make the publication of this book possible. I must thank Peter Lorge for inviting me to contribute a volume on Ming Nanjing to the Asian States and Empires series. My thanks are also due to Timothy Brook, Chen Dezhi, Raymond Chu, Edward Farmer, Richard Guisso, Hsiao Ch'i-ch'ing, Yuan-chu Lam, Bernard Luk, Frederick Mote, Qiu Shusen, Michael Szonyi, Frederick Wakeman, and Yamane Yukio. They generously supported me in many ways: provided inspiration and guidance, supplied bibliographical questions, read the whole or parts of the book in its earlier forms and offered valuable suggestions for improvement. I am also delighted to have the opportunity to thank my friends and colleagues for their encouragement and assistance over the years: Amy Bell, Charles Chan, Fan Jinmin, Lai Ming-chiu, Geoff Read, Wang Shuanghuai, Wang Zhenping, Simon Wong, and Zhu Bangwei. I wish to single out James Flath, who has been always generous with his time and expertise in proofreading my manuscripts. This time is no exception. I am, of course, solely responsible for the deficiencies and errors that remain.

The helpful staff at the libraries of the following institutions were contributory to the completion of this book as well: the Academic Sinica (Fu Ssu-nien), the Chinese University of Hong Kong, Harvard-Yenching, Huron University College, Nanjing University, Toyo Bunko, and the University of Toronto (Cheng Yu-tung). I am grateful to *Ming Studies* and *Monumenta Serica* for publishing early versions of Chapter Three and Chapter Five respectively. I am also fortunate to have been able to work with Peter Sowden, Paola Celli and Helena Hurd at Routledge who provided warm encouragement at every step from manuscript to book.

To the end I reserve a special debt of thanks to my wife and daughter for their love and care. This book is dedicated to them.

The publisher believes the cover image 'A Section of Nandu fanhui tujuan (Scroll Painting of the Prosperous Southern Capital) Attributed to Qiu Ying (1498–1552)' to be in the public domain. Please contact us if this is not the case.

Explanatory Notes

1. In this book Beijing and Nanjing are generally used to indicate the Northern Capital and the Southern Capital of the Ming dynasty, and occasionally to denote the cities of Beijing and Nanjing. Governmental departments in the primary Northern Capital are referred to without the prefix "Beijing", whereas those in the secondary Southern Capital are prefixed with "Nanjing".
2. In general, offices and official titles in this book follow Charles O. Hucker's *A Dictionary of Official Titles in Imperial China*.
3. The Ming emperors are referred to by their reign titles rather than by their posthumous honorific temple names.
4. Only the modern page numbers are cited for those modern reprints of Ming source materials which have both the new page numbers and the old ones. For those reprints which have only old page numbers, the original chapter (*juan*) and page numbers are cited. The letters *a* and *b* are used to denote the first and second halves of a double page.

Major Epochs of Chinese History

c. 2070–1600 BCE	Xia
c. 1600–1050 BCE	Shang
c. 1050–256 BCE	Zhou
–	Western Zhou (*c.* 1050–1771 BCE)
–	Eastern Zhou (*c.* 771–256 BCE)
221–206 BCE	Qin
206 BCE–220 CE	Han
–	Western (206 BCE–9 CE)
–	Xin (9–25 CE)
–	Eastern Han (25–220 CE)
220–65	Three Kingdoms
–	Wei (220–65)
–	Shu (221–63)
–	Wu (222–80)
265–420	Jin
–	Western Jin (265–316)
–	Eastern Jin (317–420)
420–589	North-South Dynasties
581–618	Sui
618–907	Tang
907–60	Five Dynasties and Ten Kingdoms
960–1279	Song
–	Northern Song (960–1127)
–	Southern Song (1127–1279)
–	Liao (907–1125)
–	Western Xia (1038–1227)
–	Jin (1115–1234)
1271–1368	Yuan
1368–1644	Ming
1644–1912	Qing
1912–49	Republican period
1949–Present	People's Republic period

Table of Ming Emperors and Their Reigns

Reign Name	Duration	Personal Name	Temple Name
Hongwu	1368–1398	Zhu Yuanzhang	Taizu
Jianwen	1399–1402	Zhu Yunwen	Huizong
Yongle	1403–1424	Zhu Di	Taizong, Chengzu
Hongxi	1425	Zhu Gaozhi	Renzong
Xuande	1426-1435	Zhu Zhanji	Xuanzong
Zhengtong	1436–1449	Zhu Qizhen	Yingzong
Jingtai	1450–1456	Zhu Qiyu	Daizong
Tianshun	1457–1464	Zhu Qizhen (again)	Yingzong
Chenghua	1465–1487	Zhu Jianshen	Xianzong
Hongzhi	1488–1505	Zhu Youtang	Xiaozong
Zhengde	1506–1521	Zhu Houzhao	Wuzong
Jiajing	1522–1566	Zhu Houcong	Shizong
Longqing	1567–1572	Zhu Zaihou	Muzong
Wanli	1573–1620	Zhu Yijun	Shenzong
Taichang	1620	Zhu Changluo	Guangzong
Tianqi	1621–1627	Zhu Youjiao	Xizong
Chongzhen	1628–1644	Zhu Youjian	Sizong

Ming Weights and Measures

Chinese Unit		English Unit	Metric Unit
Area			
1 *mu*	=	.14 acre	5.803 acre
1 *qing*	=	100.0 *mu*	5.803 hectares
Capacity			
1 *sheng*	=	.99 quart	1.0737 liters
1 *dou* = 10 *sheng*	=	9.9 quart	10.737 liters
1 *dan* = 10 *dou*	=	99.0 quarts	107.37 liters
Length			
1 *chi* = 10 *cun*	=	12.3 inches	31.1 cm
1 *bu* = 5 *chi*	=	61.5 inches	1.555 meters
1 *zhang*= 10 *chi*	=	123.0 inches	3.11 meters
1 *li*	=	1/3 mile	559.8 meters
Money			
1 *liang* (tael) = 1/16 *jin* (of silver)			
1 *qian* (copper cash) = .1 *liang*			
1 *guan* (string of cash) = 1,000 cash			
Weight			
1 *liang*	=	1.3 ounces	37.3 grams
1 *jin* (catty) = 16 *liang*=		1.3 pounds	.5968 kg

Map of Ming Provinces

Introduction

1. Why the Southern Capital of Ming China

This is a study of the secondary Southern Capital of Ming China, with a focus on the various functions of its administration and the reasons why the Ming court retained it for more than two centuries. The book also attempts to solve, by using the Ming case, the enigma of why imperial Chinese rulers were interested in establishing secondary capitals, and to further reveal the relationship between this secondary capital and state control in imperial China.

My interest in the subject matter stems from time spent in the city of Nanjing. While attending university there, I was struck by the fact that two national capitals simultaneously existed during the Ming empire,[1] and also that the Southern Capital (Nanjing) possessed a set of bureaucratic apparatuses which were identical to those in the primary Northern Capital (Beijing). The similarities in the governmental apparatuses of Nanjing and Beijing were displayed not only in the civil and military agencies but also in the eunuch household departments. Almost all the government departments in Beijing – civil, military, and eunuch – had their counterparts in Nanjing, with the staff of officials and functionaries exceeding 1,000. Furthermore, the ranks and emoluments of the Nanjing officials were identical to those of Beijing bureaucrats. My curiosity was further piqued as I tried but failed to find satisfactory answers to my questions regarding the Southern Capital, owing to the absence of thorough study on the subject.

As my interest in the topic developed, three sets of questions began to take shape. The first concerns the Southern Capital itself. How large was the bureaucracy in the Southern Capital and how was it structured? What were the administrative responsibilities of the capital in general and those of individual departments in particular? How did this capital administration operate? What was the composition of the leadership of the Nanjing administration? Were there dignitaries in Nanjing who supervised the officials in Nanjing? If there were, who were those officials? What was the background of those officials who served in the Southern Capital? Did the careers of Nanjing officials follow any pattern?

The second group of questions concerning the Southern Capital deals with its relationship with the Northern Capital. For instance, was there a division

2   *Introduction*

of labor between the two capitals? What was the relationship between the Nanjing officials and their counterparts of equal rank in Beijing? Was there competition between the officials of the two capitals? Was the Ming emperor ever worried about any increase in the power of the Southern Capital? Was there any time when the court in Beijing felt threatened by the Nanjing administration?

The third and last group of questions concerns the rational basis of the Ming's retention of a secondary capital. What were the functions of the Southern Capital administration? Why did the Ming emperors keep an auxiliary capital with such a large number of bureaucrats? What can we learn from this institutional arrangement about state control in the Ming dynasty and possibly in late imperial China more generally?

Consisting five chapters, this book attempts to solve some of the puzzles I have posed above. Chapter One probes the early historical origins of the Chinese secondary capital system and reviews the various auxiliary capitals in imperial China. Chapter Two discusses the bureaucratic apparatuses of the Southern Capital administration and their major responsibilities. The remaining three chapters analyze respectively the political, financial, and military functions of the Nanjing administration. This book argues that the immense geographical expanse of the Chinese empire and the inadequate communications infrastructure of pre-modern times necessitated the establishment of additional capitals for an effective control of the realm. The existence of the Southern Capital of Ming China, which was regarded previously by many as redundant and insignificant, was largely justified by its ability to assist the primary Northern Capital in better controlling the southern half of the Ming realm. The practice of creating auxiliary capitals, as the Ming case testifies, was a workable way of effecting bureaucratic domination over a vast territory under pre-modern conditions.

2. The Southern Capital, Nanjing

Before proceeding further, it is necessary to note the multiple statuses of Nanjing as the Southern Capital of the Ming, the capital of the Southern Metropolitan Area (Nan Zhili), and the seats of government for Yingtian Prefecture as well as Shangyuan and Jiangning counties. It is also important to establish the basic properties of the city of Nanjing.

The city of Ming Nanjing consisted of three parts, or four if we count the first two separately. They were, from center to periphery, the Forbidden City and the Imperial City, the Inner City, and the Outer City. Each of them was protected by high walls with access gates. The square-shaped Forbidden City (*zijincheng, gongcheng, neigong,* or *danei*), located in the east of Nanjing, was the residential area of the emperor and his imperial family. Accessed by six gates, the Forbidden City consisted of two sections. The front section housed the three most important imperial buildings in the capital: the Fengtian Hall, where the emperor conducted grant ceremonies and received his court

Figure 1.1 A section of *Nandu fanhui tujuan* (scroll painting of the prosperous southern capital) attributed to Qiu Ying (1498–1552)

4 *Introduction*

officials; the Huagai Hall, where the emperor met his cabinet ministers and other senior officials before receiving all the court officials at Fengtian on the special occasions of the Spring Festival, the Winter Solstice, and the emperor's birthday; and the Jinshen Hall where the palace examination was held. The rear section of the Forbidden City was the residential area of the emperor and his imperial consorts.[2]

The Forbidden City was surrounded by a similarly square-shaped Imperial City (*huangcheng*), which was in essence the extension of the former. The Imperial City was primarily an area where the imperial family and its entourage performed their religious and ceremonial activities. More than a score of sacrificial altars were constructed here by the founding emperor. Among them, the Altar of Heaven and Earth (*yuanqiu*), the Ancestral Temple (*taimiao*), and the Altar of Soil and Grain (*shejitan*) were the most frequently mentioned in the Ming historical records. Imperial offices rendering services largely to the imperial family, such as the eunuch departments, the Court of Imperial Entertainment, and the Seal Office, were also stationed in the *huangcheng*.[3]

Further from the center was the Inner City (*jingcheng* or *neicheng*),with a circumference of 70 *li*.[4] This was where the officials and the general public lived. Most of the central government offices (the Southern Capital offices after 1421), both military and civil, were concentrated in the east of the city. Among them were five of the six ministries,[5] the five chief military commissions, and other minor offices.[6] The prefectural government of Yingtian, which administered the city of Nanjing (except for the Forbidden City and Imperial City) and the county *yamen* of surrounding counties of Shangyuan and Jiangning, were seated in the south of the city. Many of the military guards were stationed in the north of the city. Generally speaking, the eastern segment of the Inner City was a political area, the northern part was a military area, and the southern part an area of business and handicraft industries. Possibly due to its pleasant environment, the city's south was also the residential area of both central and local officials.[7]

The periphery of Nanjing was the Outer City (*waiguocheng*), with a circumference of some 180 *li*.[8] Strictly speaking, it was a suburb of Nanjing. The only government departments located in *waiguocheng* were the so-called Three Judicial Offices (*san fasi*): the Ministry of Justice, the Censorate, and the Court of Judicial Review.[9] They were situated in the north because that was the direction of winter, the season of punishments and death. It was also the site of the execution ground, which was a sparsely populated area adjacent to the Three Judicial Offices.[10]

Nanjing remained one of the two largest cities in the Ming throughout the dynasty.[11] It was the most populous city in the Hongwu era with an estimated population ranging from half a million to one million.[12] When Emperor Yongle relocated the primary capital to his former fief in 1420, he ordered 27,000 civilian and artisan households to be moved from Nanjing to Beijing, resulting in a drastic decrease in Nanjing's population.[13] The number

Introduction 5

rebounded gradually and, according to one estimate, by the middle of the dynasty the population in the Southern Capital had jumped to some 1,200,000, making it the second largest metropolis in the empire, if not the largest.[14] A city of great wealth and ease in the post-1421 years, Nanjing was a center of inland water transportation and a center of fine silk and brocade production in the late years of the dynasty. It was also famous for its elaborate facilities for entertainment and its concentration of artists, writers, and wealthy book collectors.[15] The following excerpt from Wu Jingzi's (1701–54) *The Scholars* (*Rulin waishi*), a great classic Chinese novel depicting intellectual life during the Ming, vividly reflects the dynamic city life of Ming Nanjing:

> Nanjing was the capital of the Hongwu emperor and its inner wall has thirteen gates, its outer wall eighteen. More than ten miles across and forty miles in circumference, the city has several dozen large streets and several hundred small alleys which are thronged with people and filled with gilt and painted pavilions. The Qinhuai River which flows through Nanjing measures over three miles from the east to the west ford; and, when its water is high, painted barges carrying flutists and drummers ply to and fro on it day and night. Within and without the city stand monasteries and temples with green tiles and crimson roofs. During the Six Dynasties there were 480 temples here, but now there must be at least 4,800! The streets and lanes house six or seven hundred taverns large and small, and over a thousand tea-shops. No matter what small alley you enter, you are bound to see at least one house where a lantern is hung to show that tea is sold; and inside the shop you will find fresh flowers and crystal-clear rain water on the boil. The tea-shops are always filled.[16]

The observation of Nanjing by Matteo Ricci (1552–1610), a noted Jesuit missionary who resided in China for almost three decades (1583–1610),[17] offers a European view of this Ming city:

> In the judgment of the Chinese this city [Nanjing] surpasses all other cities in the world in beauty and in grandeur, and in this respect there are probably very few others superior or equal to it. It is literally filled with palaces and temples and towers and bridges, and these are scarcely surpassed by similar structures in Europe. In some respects, it surpassed our European cities ... There is a gaiety of spirit among the people, who are well mannered and nicely spoken, and the dense population is made up of all classes; of hoi-polloi, of the lettered aristocracy and the Magistrates. These latter are equal in number[18] and in dignity to those of Pekin [Beijing], but due to the fact that the king [emperor] does not reside here, the local Magistrates are not rated as equal with those of the Capital City [Northern Capital Beijing]. Yet in the whole kingdom of China and in all bordering countries, Nankin [Nanjing] is rated as the first city. It is surrounded by three circles of walls. The first and innermost

6 *Introduction*

of these, and also the most decorative, surrounded by a triple wall of the arches, and of circling moats, filled with circulating water. This palace wall is about four or five Italian miles in length. Considering the whole structure, rather than any particular feature of it, there is probably no king in the world with a palace surpassing this one. The second wall, encircling the inner one, which contains the king's palace, encloses the greater and the most important part of the city. It has twelve gates, which are covered with iron plates and fortified by cannon from within. This high wall is almost eighteen Italian miles in circumference. The third and exterior wall is not continuous. At places that were judged to be danger spots, they scientifically added to natural fortifications. It is difficult to determine the full length of the circuit of this particular wall. The natives here tell a story of two men who started from opposite sides of the city, riding on horses toward each other, and it took a whole day before they came together.[19]

In a nutshell, Nanjing was one of the most important cities throughout the Ming. Politically, it was the primary capital from 1368 to 1420 and the secondary capital from 1421 to 1644; economically and culturally, it operated the largest government-sponsored handicraft production and most prosperous publishing businesses; and militarily, its share of guard units and troops were second only to Beijing.

3. Previous studies of the Southern Capital

While there is a small body of published work on the secondary capital system ad the Southern Capital of the Ming, most do not address the issues raised at the beginning of this chapter. Edward Farmer's book, *Early Ming Government: The Evolution of Dual Capitals*, is a pioneering study of the origins of the Ming dual-capital system during the Hongwu-Yongle eras, but it does not examine the actual working of the Southern Capital in particular and the dual-capital system in general in the middle and late Ming. A number of articles published in China in the past two decades on the origins of the Ming two-capital system largely repeat Farmer's conclusions.[20]

Wang Tianyou's (1944–2012) work on the bureaucratic apparatuses of the Ming state devotes one chapter to the Nanjing administration, in which he concludes: (1) the number of officials in the Nanjing government were fewer than in the Beijing administration; (2) the administrative responsibilities of the Nanjing government were less than those of the Beijing administration since, according to Wang, the jurisdiction of the central agencies in Nanjing were restricted to the city of Nanjing and the Southern Metropolitan Area; (3) some of the Nanjing offices existed in name only and did not have any duties to perform. The duties of the non-nominal offices were also moderate.[21] While these observations are not unreasonable, the study does not touch upon the functions of the Southern Capital administration, and most conclusions are based on a general description of the various apparatuses and staffing levels of the Ming bureaucracy, not on concrete and detailed analysis, Wang's findings are therefore open to question.

Huang Kaihua's 1972 article is a major Chinese study devoted completely to the Southern Capital administration. After presenting a brief historical survey of the origins and development of the two-capital system in the Ming period, Huang compares the staffing levels of the six ministries and censorates in both Nanjing and Beijing and examines the pattern of transfer of ministerial officials between the two national capitals. The pattern, in which junior Beijing officials were sent to assume higher positions in Nanjing, confirms the obvious, which is that the real power center in the post-1421 Ming was Beijing. However, he argues that the appointment of officials to either Nanjing or Beijing was not without bureaucratic purpose. The Southern Capital performed a function as the transfer station of the Ming bureaucracy. It is wrong to assume that officials dispatched to Nanjing were elderly and physically infirm or had suffered demotion. Although Huang examined only one of the many bureaucratic functions of the Southern Capital, his argument that Nanjing was training ground for junior Ming officials is persuasive.[22]

Of the recent studies of Ming Nanjing published in China, Zhang Yingpin's articles on the administrative functions of Nanjing stand out. Her 2001 article, exploring the administrative functions of the six ministries and censorate of Nanjing, argues that the administrative role of Nanjing declined considerably after it was downgraded to be the secondary capital, yet it did not lose its status as the governing center of southern China in the post-1420 years.[23] Her 2005 article presents a complete list of the heads of the six ministries and censorate of the Southern Capital during the years from 1424–1645, which shows that Nanjing was not only a refuge for Ming officials who were forced out of Beijing but also a sanctuary for those who wanted to escape the atrocious power struggles taking place in the Beijing court.[24] Hu Mengfei's 2013 article on the roles of the Nanjing Ministries of Revenue and Works, while failing to mention Zhang's earlier research, nevertheless largely repeats what Zhang has concluded.[25]

The Southern Capital of the Ming dynasty is also mentioned indirectly by many scholars without much elaboration. For example, before his untimely demise during the Cultural Revolution, the late Ming specialist Wu Han (1909–69)[26] summarizes the two roles played by the Southern Capital in one of his introductory essays on the Ming dynasty: to protect the communication line between the north and south along the Grand Canal and to strengthen the government's grip over the people in the south.[27] F. W. Mote's (1922–2005) study of Nanjing during the 1350–1400 period focuses on how Nanjing was transformed from an insignificant prefectural city of the Yuan into an extensive imperial city of the Ming. Some of his observations on the Southern Capital are nonetheless pertinent: the two-capital system in Ming China was different from that of previous dynasties because Nanjing, as the secondary capital, retained a full complement of administrative posts at the highest levels that duplicated the structures of the government in Beijing; also, these

8 *Introduction*

posts were equal to Beijing's in rank and emolument; and the supplementary activities maintained at the secondary capital were essential and not just of formal and ritual significance.[28]

In summary, most studies have either dealt with the Southern Capital indirectly or used incomplete descriptions and paid insufficient attention to bureaucratic features. None have adequately addressed the question of how the secondary capitals actually functioned or elaborated on its various functions and its relationship with the Northern Capital.

Owing to the absence of thorough investigations and consequent lack of knowledge about the Southern Capital, there are many misunderstandings about this institution, even among historians of late imperial China. For instance, in his monumental work on the Ming-Qing transition, Frederic Wakeman (1937–2006) writes inaccurately that "although a skeleton bureaucracy duplicated most of the capital structure in Beijing, *Nanjing lacked the capital guard system* as well as the energetic vitality of the northern seat of state."[29] Ping-ti Ho (1917–2012) comments that as the second capital, Nanjing "*maintained a separate smaller central government and a larger and more important Imperial Academy.*"[30] Charles Hucker (1919–94) conflates the grand commandant (*shoubei*) with the eunuch grand commandant (*shoubei taijian*) as one dignitary, whereas they were two separate and powerful figures in the Southern Capital,[31] dubbed unofficially "outer grand commandant" (*waishoubei*) and "inner grand commandant" (*neishoubei*) respectively.[32]

The incomplete picture has also been instrumental in sustaining the popular portrayal of the Southern Capital as a wasteful and useless institution. The following is an exaggerative accusation quoted by Xie Bin (fl. 1550), a bureau director at the Nanjing Ministry of Revenue and vigorous defender of the Southern Capital administration, before he refuted it:

> The Nanjing Ministry of Personnel does not bear responsibilities for evaluating and selecting officials; the [Nanjing] Ministry of Rites does not know how to organize and administer the civil service recruitment examination; the [Nanjing] Ministry of revenue has no duty to collect taxes; and the [Nanjing] Ministry of War possesses no power to deploy troops.[33]

Many contemporary scholars still take a dim view of Ming Nanjing. Wu Han writes that most of the officials at Nanjing were political failures or the superannuated who could no longer achieve anything prominent. They were sent to Nanjing to hold down a sinecure.[34] Wei Qingyuan (1928–2009) remarks that "the central governmental agencies in the auxiliary Southern Capital were in fact mere foils and ornaments (*beishe*)."[35] This perception is also shared by a few historians in the West. For example, in a number of writings, Lynn Struve repeatedly dismisses the Southern Capital as an essentially worthless institution. In *The Southern Ming*, she describes Nanjing as a "skeleton administration consisting largely of sinecures."[36] The Nanjing

Introduction 9

Ministry of Revenue "had never operated on a grand scale. In late Ming years, it had handled annually only about 1,400,000 taels in silver and payments in kind, and in 1643–44 it had seen serious shortfalls."[37] In the chapter on the Southern Ming regime for the *Cambridge History of China, The Ming Dynasty*, she writes in the same vein that the ministry posts that remained in the "moribund" [southern] capital administration were "generally considered to be unprestigious transitional positions, and they often went unfilled."[38] She continues to depict the Southern Capital in this unfavorable light in her 1993 book, *Voices from the Ming-Qing Cataclysm*.[39]

My own research had led me to conclude that these views are simplistic and unsubstantiated. This book is intended to demonstrate that the Southern Capital can be dismissed no longer and that its existence was largely justified by its ability to assist the primary capital to better control the southern portion of the Ming empire.

4. The Southern Capital and state control in Ming China

During the two centuries that extended from 1421 to 1644, the Southern Capital was occasionally ridiculed by officials in their memorials to the court and its bureaucratic size trimmed a number of times, but no single attempt was made to abolish it. That fact raises an important question: if the Southern Capital of the Ming dynasty was valueless and unserviceable, why did nobody propose abandonning it? Why did the Ming court retain it throughout the dynasty? This book argues that the establishment of the Southern Capital of the Ming was significant in a number of ways; foremost being its role in state control over the Ming empire.

China in imperial times had one of the most elaborate systems of state control in the world.[40] Some of the techniques of Chinese state control are familiar to students of Chinese history but nonetheless bear repeating for the sake of my argument. The most famous feature of the Chinese state control system was the sophisticated, centralized administrative hierarchy created after the first unification of China under the Qin.[41] At the centre, directly under the emperor, there were a variety of major and minor government offices or *yamen*; the ranking officials of these *yamen* advised the emperor on important matters, helped him to reach decisions, and carried out his orders or transmitted them to lower administrative levels. The local territorial administration was divided into between two and four levels, which varied from dynasty to dynasty. In Ming times it consisted of three echelons of province, prefecture, and county. All local government officials were dispatched by the central government, their performance regularly evaluated, and their tenure centrally determined.[42]

Below the county level, the population was subdivided into two to four tiers of residential groupings. In the Ming, the standard subcounty structure, common in central and southern China, had three levels: cantons (*xiang*), townships (*du*), and wards (*tu*).[43] In addition to this subcounty administrative

10 *Introduction*

system, some other control devices were also put into effect to varying degrees: the hundred-tithing system (*lijia*) for assessing and discharging fiscal obligations as well as imposing comprehensive control over local society; the watch-tithing system (*baojia*) for mutual security and village defense; and the rural covenant system (*xiangyue*) for moral exhortation, instruction, and the dissemination of government policies.[44] Timothy Brook's research suggests that by building up an increasingly dense structure of subcounty units, the imperial state was able to keep pace with, and perhaps reverse, other trends toward the dissipation of its power at local level. As long as these systems were extended, even if only formally, down to household level, their officers stood as proxies of state power. Thus, although "heaven is high and the emperor far away," the presence of the state administration could be felt in every settlement of the empire.[45]

Another mode of state domination in imperial China was ideological control, which was in no way looser than that exerted over central and local government. Since the first century BCE, Chinese government had consistently adopted Confucianism as the state ideology. The virtues taught by Confucianism were enthusiastically embraced by the state: respect, humility, docility, obedience, submission, and subordination to elders and betters. Especially welcome was its idea of social hierarchy, which regarded society as an organism composed of different members. Each member has its own function. Each must receive the means suited to its station and must claim no more. Within classes there must be equality, and between the classes there must be inequality.[46] Under the later dynasties, the position of Confucianism was further consolidated and regularized through the system of civil service examination. Instituted by the Sui and elaborated to perfection in the Tang and based primarily on the Confucian classics, the system eventually became the principal avenue for entry into government service. It instilled the Confucian state ideology in the minds of scholars and officials as well as commoners. Politically, it produced well-trained and loyal officials. It allowed the government to select men of loyalty and real talent from the numerous competitors for the office. Socially, it contributed to the formation of the local gentry. Culturally, it promoted Confucian ideals. The government-sponsored examinations tended to create a uniformity of thought among those taking examinations.[47]

This concept of state control is well established and widely disseminated, but it overlooks the role of secondary capitals, a noteworthy component of state surveillance. Since the Shang dynasty, the practice was employed by virtually every major dynasty. This book argues that the secondary capital system was created by the imperial rulers as a complement to the well-organized administrative hierarchy, to facilitate the state's grip over the empire where the geographical expanse was vast and the facilities for communication and transportation limited. These secondary capitals, with functions varying from dynasty to dynasty, assisted the primary capitals control the various parts of the imperial realm. The Southern Capital of the Ming is an exemplary case.

Introduction 11

The symbolic values of the secondary capitals, which furnished a source of legitimacy for the reigning emperor, also contributed to the state's rule. To secure a stable, peaceful, and enduring reign, Chinese monarchs needed to mobilize a variety of sources to bolster their image as legitimate rulers.[48] The usage of the capital of previous dynasties (especially those that were highly regarded) as the secondary capital of the present regime could render its ruler extra legitimacy. By associating himself closely with the great dynasties or wise rulers of the past, the reigning emperor could borrow some of the prestige of the previous rulers to buttress his own status. As Arnold Toynbee (1889–1975) has rightly pointed out in his study of global capital cities, "a *ci-devant* imperial capital may retain its prestige long after it has ceased to perform its function."[49] The symbolic value of secondary capitals helps explain why dynastic rulers granted the status of secondary capital, rather than some other form of administrative units, to major urban centers. In the Ming case, the Southern Capital was chosen by the founding emperor as the seat of court. After usurping the throne from his nephew and the second ruler of the dynasty and moving the primary capital to Beijing, the Yongle emperor retained Nanjing's capital status in part to ward off criticism that his actions were a violation of his father's will, but also because of its efficacy in governing the southern half of the empire.

5. The sources

In this book I make extensive use of official publications, which are of two types. The first, largely unexplored by historians of China, are departmental gazetteers, which were compiled by bureaucrats at the Southern Capital in the sixteenth and seventeenth centuries. The second type, mainly compendia of official regulations, is better known. Included in this group are the *Veritable Record of the Ming Dynasty* (*Ming shilu*), the *Statutes of the Ming Dynasty* (*Da Ming huidian*), and the *Official History of the Ming Dynasty* (*Mingshi*). These sources reflect the official version of the history and institutions of the Ming dynasty. A few words of explanation may be necessary.

My utilization of official sources has something to do with the nature of this study, which is about the organization, responsibilities, and functions of an official institution in the Ming. Regarding the bureaucratic apparatus and government regulations, as well as the history and administrative responsibilities of governmental departments, I find that officially sponsored and printed publications provide more information than private sources. This is especially the case with the departmental gazetteers compiled by the bureaucrats in the Nanjing administration.

The gazetteer (*zhi*) is a unique genre in Chinese historiography, recording important information about a particular place or administrative unit. Depending on the subject matter, Chinese gazetteers can be classified into three main groups: administrative, topographical, and institutional. Best known to historians are gazetteers with the history and geography of an

12   Introduction

administrative unit, such as a county, subprefecture, prefecture, province, or even the entire country. Topographical gazetteers concern natural features such as mountains, and institutional ones deal with man-made structures, like monasteries and academies.[50] Less known are the "departmental gazetteers" (*bumen zhi*) that record the history, administrative responsibilities, precedents, and major officials of a department. During the Ming dynasty many gazetteers of this type were compiled and published, especially in the secondary capital, Nanjing.[51]

It is indeed an unusual phenomenon, in both Ming bureaucracy and Ming historiography, that almost all government agencies in the Southern Capital compiled and printed their own departmental gazetteers,[52] while only a few departments in the Northern Capital administration ever published such works.[53] My search for these Nanjing gazetteers indicates that eleven such works are extant.[54] Of them, the *Gazetteer of the Nanjing Ministry of Revenue* (*Nanjing hubu zhi*), the *Gazetteer of the Nanjing Ministry of Personnel* (*Nanjing libu zhi*), and the *Gazetteer of the Nanjing Censorate* (*Nanjing duchayuan zhi*), are the three most informative.

A number of factors justify my frequent use of these gazetteers. First, they preserve a rich record of regulations, administrative responsibilities, and precedents of the departments concerned. Although varying in their contents and writing style, these gazetteers share some commonalities. A Nanjing departmental gazetteer normally included the imperial decrees and the general regulations of the Ming government, which were relevant to the department concerned, the history of the department (including the early period when the primary capital was still in Nanjing), the responsibilities of the principal officials and functions of the related offices (e.g. in the case of a ministry it includes the responsibilities of the ministry and its subordinate bureaus), the list of officials who had served in the department, and the biographies of the principal officials. In the case of a ministry, the officials recorded include the ministers, the vice ministers, the bureau directors, the vice bureau directors, and office managers. A gazetteer also contains a collection of notable memorials submitted by the department's officials on various subjects, and the congratulatory essays (*timingji*) written by them. The information regarding the history, organization and administrative responsibilities of the Nanjing departments in these gazetteers is much more detailed and richer than that contained in the relevant sections of comparable sources such as the *Collected Statutes of the Ming Dynasty* and the *Official History of the Ming Dynasty*, and the complete list of officials who had served in the department and the biography of principal officials contain information which is often recorded nowhere else. These largely untapped departmental gazetteers compiled by Nanjing officials are a valuable source for the study of the Southern Capital administration in particular and the Ming bureaucracy in general.

Second, all of these gazetteers were compiled and edited by those who were familiar with the departments, and the compilation was usually conducted under the auspices of the department head. For example, Tao Shangde and

Introduction 13

Pang Song were the minister and Shandong Bureau director of the Nanjing Ministry of Justice respectively when they compiled the *Gazetteer of the Nanjing Ministry of Justice*; Xu Bida, author of the *Gazetteer of the Nanjing Censorate*, was the assistant censor-in-chief of the Nanjing Censorate; Xu Daren was the chief minister of the Nanjing Court of Imperial Entertainments when he composed the *Gazetteer of the Nanjing Court of Imperial Entertainments* in 1590s.[55] As officials working for the same department, they had easy access to departmental archives and files.

Third, although these gazetteers have been occasionally cited by a few historians, they have not received enough attention. Huang Zhangjian (1919–2009) uses some material from the *Gazetteer of the Nanjing Ministry of Justice* in his study of early Ming legal regulations; Liang Fangzhong (1908–70) cites one piece from the *Gazetteer of the Nanjing Ministry of Revenue* in his article on the Yellow Registry system of the Ming, but it is unclear whether he read the gazetteer in person or only cited the piece from Japanese scholars; Ray Huang (1918–2000) had noticed that some Japanese scholars had used materials from the *Gazetteer of the Nanjing Ministry of Revenue*, but he was unable to locate the gazetteer.[56] In his fascinating account of commerce and culture in Ming China, Timothy Brook cites numerous times from the *Gazetteer of the Nanjing Ministry of Revenue*.[57]

This is not to say that there is no weakness in these gazetteers, one fault being the tendency of the compilers to glorify the office holders in the Nanjing departments. One of the aims of compiling these gazetteers was to provide readers with information about what the agencies in the Southern Capital were doing. As with other types of gazetteer used by the authors to exalt the subjects about which they were writing, these departmental gazetteers were also exploited by the Nanjing officials to bolster the status of their offices and to justify the very existence of the Southern Capital administration. However, while an author might be extravagant in praise, they could not fabricate the administrative duties of their offices, nor claim administrative powers that were not conferred to them. It is the section that concerns the bureaucratic responsibilities and the evolution of the departments that is of greatest interest to this book.

Notes

1 In fact five if we include the two nominal capitals, the Middle Capital at Fengyang, Anhui, and the Flourishing Capital at Chengtian (Anlu), Hubei, as well as the transitory first Northern Capital Kaifeng. For more on Fengyang and Anlu, see Wang Jianying, *Ming Zhongdu yanjiu*, 29–205; Ding Haibin, *Zhongguo gudai peidu shi*, 569–76.

2 Chen Yi, *Jinling shiji*, 12–13; Zhu Xie, *Jinling guji tukao*, 177–8; Yang Guoqing, *Nanjing Mingdai chengqiang*, 77–81.

3 Wenren Quan et al., *Nanji zhi*, 1.5a; Yang, *Nanjing Mingdai chengqiang*, 84.

4 This figure was taken from aerial survey photographs taken by the United States Army in 1945. The length of the Inner City wall recorded in the *Ming yitongzhi*

14   Introduction

(6.1b) and *Nanji zhi* (1.2a) was 96 *li*. The modern *Capital Gazetteer* (*Shoudu zhi*), compiled in 1935, holds that the correct figure was 61 *li*. The discrepancies for the figures cited in Chinese sources are difficult to explain. F. W. Mote tends to doubt the accuracy of the traditional measurements. See "The transformation of Nanking, 1350–1400," 136.

5 They were the ministries of Personnel, Revenue, Rites, War, and Works.

6 They included the Imperial Clan Office, the Court of Imperial Sacrifices, the Office of Transformation, the Directorate of Astronomy, the Court of State Ceremonial, and the Passenger Office. Li Xian et al., *Ming yitong zhi*, 6.2b–3b.

7 Jiang Zanchu, *Nanjing shihua*, 124–5.

8 Li Xian, *Ming yitong zhi*, 6.1b.

9 Wenren, *Nanji zhi*, 1.5a.

10 For more details on the history and physical layout of Nanjing, see Mote's "The transformation of Nanjing, 1350–1400," 126–47; Edward Farmer, *Early Ming Government: The Evolution of Dual Capitals*, 51–6; Yang, *Nanjing Mingdai chengqiang*, 76–107.

11 Jiang, *Nanjing shihua*, 108.

12 Fan Jinmin, *Guoji minsheng: Ming Qing shehui jingji yanjiu*, 433; Jiang, *Nanjing shihua*, 123–34. The estimation of Ming Nanjing population varies among scholars. Mote believes that Nanjing's population in the late 1370s was around one million, while Farmer estimates that Nanjing's population in the early Hongwu period may have exceeded 300,000 and approached one million at the end of the fourteenth century. Based on his lengthy study, Xu Hong concludes that Nanjing's population during the early and late Hongwu era were respectively 330,000 and 550,000. See Mote, "The transformation of Nanking," 132; Farmer, *Early Ming Government*, 57; Xu, "Mingchu Nanjing de dushi guihua yu renkou bianqian," *Shihuo yuekan*, Vol. 10, No. 3 (1980), 27–35.

13 Gu Qiyuan, *Kezuo zhuiyu*, 64. Gu states that as a result of the removal of the civilian and artisan households Nanjing's population dropped by more than half. Si-yen Fei and Fan Jinmin take this claim at its face value without questioning its validity. See Fei, *Negotiating Urban Space: Urbanization and Late Ming Nanjing*, 64–5; Fan, "Mingdai Nanjing de lishi diwei he shehui fazhan," *Nanjing shehui kexue*, No. 11 (2012), 146.

14 According to Gao Shouxian's study, the population of Beijing in 1375, 1425 and 1621 approximated respectively 100,000, 800,000, and 1,200,000. See "Mingdai Beijing chengshi renkou shu'e yanjiu," *Haidian zoudu daxue xuebao*, No. 4 (2003), 35.

15 For more on the economic and cultural aspects of Ming Nanjing, see Mote, "The transformation of Nanking," 148–52; Fei, *Negotiating Urban Space: Urbanization and Late Ming Nanjing*, 212–38.

16 Wu Jingzi, *Rulin waishi*, 243. This translation is from Yang Hsien-yi and Gladys Yang, *The Scholars*, 312, with a slight alteration.

17 For more on Ricci, see Jonathan Spence, *The Memory Palace of Matteo Ricci*; Po-chia Hsia, *A Jesuit in the Forbidden City: Matteo Ricci, 1552–1610*; Michela Fontana, *Matteo Ricci: A Jesuit in the Ming Court*.

18 The number of Nanjing officials was fewer than that of Beijing bureaucrats. For details on the Nanjing bureaucracy, see Chapter Two.

19 Louis J. Gallagher, trans., *China in the Sixteenth Century: The Journal of Matthew Ricci, 1583–1610*, 268–9.

20 Wan Yi, "Lun Zhu Di yingjian Beijing gongdian qiandu de zhuyao dongji ji houguo," *Gugong bowuyuan yuankan*, 3 (1990), 31–36; Wan Ming, "Mingdai liangjing zhidu de xiangcheng jiqi queli," *Zhongguoshi yanjiu*, No. 1 (1993), 123–32.

21 Wang Tianyou, *Mingdai goujia jigou yanjiu*, 212. For his description of the Nanjing offices, see Chapter Five, "Liangjing zhi he Nanjing jigou," 199–212.

Introduction 15

22 See his "Ming zhengzhi shang bingshe Nanjing buyuan zhi tese," in *Mingshi lunji*, 1–51.
23 Zhang Yingpin, "Mingdai Nanjing xingzheng gongneng chutan," *Mingshi yanjiu*, No. 7 (2001), 39–57.
24 Zhang Yingpin, "Mingdai Nanjing qiqing bianbiao jianshu," *Ming Qing luncong*, No. 6 (2005), 28–82.
25 Hu Mengfei, "Mingdai Nanjing liushou jigou jingji zhineng chutan: Yi Nanjing hubu he gongbu wei zhongxin," *Hexi xueyuan xuebao*, Vol. 29, No. 1 (2013), 72–6.
26 Wu Han and his Beijing opera play, *Hai Rui Dismissed from Office*, was attacked in November 1965 by Yao Wenyuan (1931–2005), later one of the notorious Gang of Four, on grounds that he equated Hai Rui (1515–87) with former Defense Minister Peng Dehuai (1898–1974), and therefore Mao Zedong (1893–1976) with the despotic Jiajing emperor (1507–67). He was jailed in March 1968 and died in prison in October 1969. For more on his last years, see Su Shuangbi and Wang Hongzhi, *Wu Han zhuan*, 315–35.
27 Wu Han, *Mingshi jianlun*, 37.
28 Mote, "The transformation of Nanking, 1350–1400," 130–1, 151–2.
29 Wakeman, *The Great Enterprise*, Vol. 1, 320, note 2. Emphasis added.
30 Ho, *The Ladder of Success in Imperial China*, 232. Emphasis added.
31 See his "Governmental Organization of the Ming Dynasty," in *Studies of Government Institutions in Chinese History*, 130–31; *A Dictionary of Official Titles in Imperial China*, 433, entries 5393 and 5394. This mistake is repeated in F. W. Mote and Denis Twitchett, eds, *Cambridge History of China*, Vol. 7, part 1, 643.
32 For a discussion on the two positions in Nanjing, see Jun Fang, "Mingdai Nanjing de neiwai shoubei," *Zhongguo yanjiu*, No. 36, 42–4.
33 *NJHBZ*, 1.5b.
34 Wu Han, *Mingshi jianshu*, 37; Su Shuangbi, ed., *Wu Han xuanji*, 364.
35 Wei Qingyuan, *Mingdai huangce zhidu*, 90.
36 *The Southern Ming, 1644–1662*, 211, note 101.
37 *The Southern Ming*, 43.
38 Mote and Twitchett, *Cambridge History of China*, Vol. 7, part 1, 643.
39 Struve writes that Nanjing "had been maintained as the auxiliary capital by a skeleton staff, largely composed of sinecure holders," See *Voices from the Ming-Qing Cataclysm: China in Tigers' Jaws*, 55.
40 I prefer the term "state control" to either "imperial control" or "bureaucratic control" in this book, as I take "state control" to mean the combined efforts of the two institutions, the imperial monarch and his bureaucracy. It seems to me that "imperial control" connotes the supervision the imperial monarchs excised over their bureaucracy in particular and the populace in general, and that "bureaucratic control" denotes the power held by the bureaucracy and used by them to counterbalance imperial power.
41 Max Weber had noticed this when he queried why, in China, bureaucracy, a central element of capitalist states in Europe, failed to propel it in the direction of capitalism. The "culprit" he found was the "pacification of a unified empire." See Weber, *The Religion of China*, 61.
42 For a succinct description of the evolution of the central and local governments in imperial China, see Hucker, *A Dictionary of Official Titles in Imperial China*, introduction, 3–96.
43 In north China and other areas of lower population density, two subcounty levels existed: cantons and wards. In certain parts of central China, there was a sub-canton (*li*) between the canton and the township.
44 For a detailed study of the various subcounty administrative systems in the Ming, see Timothy Brook, "The Spatial Structure of Ming Local Administration," *Late*

16 Introduction

Imperial China, Vol 6, No. 1 (June 1985), 1–55. The article is reprinted in *The Chinese State in Ming Society*, 19–42.

45 Brook's findings also show that, although all these various subcounty systems were structured according to strict principles, they were implemented with considerable flexibility and never disrupted existing communities. In other words, although local communities were not autonomous, they did have sufficient internal cohesion to prevent them from being completely subject to government authority. As long as the minimum requirements imposed by the state were met and the forms of the administrative systems implemented, local communities were free to organize themselves as they or other elite chose. See "The Spatial Structure of Ming Local Administration," 46–9.

46 Etienne Balazs, *Chinese Civilization and Bureaucracy*, 18; Derk Bodde, *China's Cultural Tradition*, 49–50.

47 For excellent studies of the Chinese civil service examination, see Miyazaki Ichisada, *China's Examination Hell*; Benjamin A. Elman, "Political, Social, and Cultural Reproduction via Civil Service Examination in Late Imperial China," *The Journal of Asian Studies*, Vo. 50, No. 1 (Feb. 1991), 7–28.

48 The other sources of legitimacy in imperial China, according to Hok-lam Chan, included the adoption of a cosmic patron, endorsement of Confucianism as the state ideology, promotion of Confucian studies via civil service examinations, codification of the law, compilation and revision of state statutes, historical works, and classical literary works, as well as the designation of an appropriate dynastic title, an era name, and imperial capital. For his survey on the theories and practices of legitimization in imperial China, see *Legitimation in Imperial China*, Chapter One.

49 Toynbee, *A Study of History*, Vol. 7, 230. Although Toynbee's observation regarding the "exploitation of the prestige" of the previous regimes' capital by a "usurper" ("an interloping empire builder") refers to the usurper's inheritance or adoption of his victim's capital, the statement also applies well to the Chinese case, where an empire-builder used the capital of a previous dynasty as the secondary capital of his own.

50 For a detailed discussion of these three types of gazetteers, see Timothy Brook, *Geographical Sources of Ming-Qing History*, 49–66.

51 For discussions of the origin and development of departmental gazetteers in China, see Jun Fang, "The *Gazetteer of the Nanjing Ministry of Revenue*: The Record of an Auxiliary Capital Department in the Ming Dynasty," *East Asian Library Journal*, Vol. 7, No. 1 (Spring 1994), 77; Fang Jun, "Song Yuan shiqi de guanshu zhi," *Yuanshi luncong*, Vol. 7 (1999), 54–6.

52 It is unclear whether or not the following minor offices compiled their departmental gazetteers: the Nanjing Imperial Academy of Medicine (*Taiyiyuan*), the Nanjing Buddhist Registry (*Senglusi*), and the Nanjing Daoist Registry (*Daolusi*). For discussions of the compilation, printing, and historical value of the departmental gazetteers of the Nanjing offices, see Fang Jun, "Ming Nanjing guanshuzhi gaishu," *Nanjing shida xuebao*, No. 4 (2000), 104–9. An earlier version of the article, in the form of a conference paper, was published in 1999 in the *Diqijie Mingshi guoji xueshu yantaohui lunwenji* (588–94) without the author's knowledge.

53 The Northern Capital gazetteers are: *Huang Ming libu zhigao* (*Gazetteer of the Ministry of Personnel of the Imperial Ming*) in 40 *juan*, *Libu zhigao* (*Gazetteer of the Ministry of Rites*) in 100 *juan*, both printed in 1620, and the 20-*juan Taichang xukao* (*Supplementary Notes on the Court of Imperial Sacrifices*) issued in 1643. The word "*xu*" in the last work was used in the sense that it supplements the record of the relevant part in the *Da Ming huidian*. It is worth noting that the three Beijing gazetteers were not published until the end of the Ming dynasty. Si-yen Fei mistakenly classifies *Libu zhigao* as one of the departmental gazetteers compiled by Nanjing officials and translates it as *Gazetteer of the Nanjing Ministry of Rites*. See, *Negotiating Urban Space: Urbanization and Late Ming Nanjing*, 302, note 61.

Introduction 17

54 They are: *Nanjing hubu zhi* (*Gazetteer of the Nanjing Ministry of Revenue*), *Nanjing libu zhi* (*Gazetteer of the Nanjing Ministry of Personnel*), *Nanjing duchayuan zhi* (*Gazetteer of the Nanjing Censorate*), *Nanjing xingbu zhi* (*Gazetteer of the Nanjing Ministry of Justice*), *Nanjing guanglusi zhi* (*Gazetteer of the Nanjing Court of Imperial Entertainments*), *Nanjing taipusi zhi* (*Gazetteer of the Nanjing Court of the Imperial Stud*), *Nanjing zhanshifu zhi* (*Gazetteer of the Nanjing Household Administration of the Heir Apparent*), *Nanyong zhi* (*Gazetteer of the Nanjing National University*), *Nanyong xuzhi* (*Supplementary Gazetteer of the Nanjing National University*), *Jiujing ciling zhi* (*Gazetteer of the Nanjing Hanlin Academy*), and *Jingxue zhi* (*Gazetteer of the Nanjing Capital School*). See Jun Fang, "The *Gazetteer of the Nanjing Ministry of Revenue*," 73–97; Fang Jun, "Xiancun Mingchao Nanjing guanshuzhi shuyao," *Shaanxi shifan daxue jixu jiaoyu xuebao*, Vo. 17, No. 1 (2000), 79–82.

55 For a more complete list of the compilers of the Nanjing departmental gazetteers, see Jun Fang, "Mingdai Nanjing guanshuzhi gaishu," *Nanjing shida xuebao* (shehui kexue ban), No. 4 (2000), 142.

56 Huang Zhangjian, "Ming Hongwu Yongle chao de bangwen junling," in *Ming Qing shi yanjiu conggao*, 237–86; Liang Fangzhong, *Liang Fangzhong jingji lunwenji*, 280; Ray Huang, *Taxation and Governmental Finance in Sixteenth-Century Ming China*, 332.

57 *The Confusions of Pleasure: Commerce and Culture in Ming China*, 271, note 50; 272, note 77.

1 The Secondary Capital System in Imperial China

Before proceeding further, it is necessary to define the various types of capitals which will be discussed in this book. The term "primary capital" is used to denote the seat of the central government, the residence of the emperor and the city where political authority was concentrated. Capitals other than the primary one are considered as secondary and are of two types: auxiliary capitals and nominal capitals. The former type was an institutionally developed imperial capital. Administratively it supported a complement of central or high-level government agencies, and physically, in most cases, it contained palaces, temples, altars, and imperial tombs. The latter, in contrast to both primary and auxiliary capitals, lacked the essential elements of a major political center. It possessed no central or high-level administrative bodies and was not essential as a focal point for economic or political activity. The only criterion by which the nominal capital transcended other great cities of the empire was its symbolic status.[1] Owing to a lack of significant records in the source materials, it is often difficult to distinguish auxiliary from nominal capitals in many dynasties and in such cases the term "secondary capital" is employed to describe the non-primary capitals.

The two Chinese terms, "*jing*" and "*du*", are also worth discussing before we begin the overview of the Chinese secondary capital system. The two were interchangeably used to denote capitals throughout Chinese history.[2] It is uncertain which term appeared first in the historical documents, but it seems clear that when referring to a capital, neither denotes a superior or inferior status. For example, all of the capitals in the Northern Song, the Liao, and the Qing were named *jing*, while all the capitals in the Yuan dynasty were called *du*. In the Later Han dynasty, the primary Eastern Capital and auxiliary Western Capital were designated as Dongjing and Xijing respectively, while the nominal Southern Capital was named Nandu. In the Tang dynasty, all of the capitals except the auxiliary Eastern Capital, Luoyang, were designated *jing*.[3] In the Jin dynasty, the term *du* was reserved for the primary Middle Capital, while the five secondary capitals were known as *jing*. In the Ming, the primary Northern Capital and auxiliary Southern Capital were termed *jing*, while the nominal Middle Capital and Flourishing Capital were called du. *Jing* and *du* were also interchangeably used by scholars to designate the

The Secondary Capital System 19

national capital. For example, Zhang Heng (78–139) mentions Chang'an and Luoyang as Xijing and Dongjing, while Ban Gu (32–92) refers to them as Xidu and Dongdu.[4] Kaifeng in the Northern Song was referred to as either Dongjing or Dongdu. In short, the terms *du* and *jing* do not indicate the higher or lower status of a capital *per se* in imperial Chinese history and could both describe capitals.

1. The pre-Sui dynasty period

When the practice of a secondary capital system first started is debatable. Zhang Guoshuo believes that it dates back to the Xia dynasty.[5] This view, however, is not well received by most of the scholars on early China. Some hold that it originated from the Shang dynasty, when the Shang ruling elites, during the reign of its second king (*c.* 1709–1706 BCE), brought many of their followers from Yanshi, the first Shang capital, to the present-day east Zhengzhou and converted it to the dynasty's new political, economic, and cultural center. The smaller Yanshi was made a secondary capital, rendering primarily military support to the defense of the larger primary capital.[6]

The succeeding Western Zhou dynasty continued the Shang practice. The founder of the dynasty, King Wu (*r. c.* 1046–1043 BCE), built palaces at Luoyi (present-day Luoyang), east of the dynasty's main capital, Gaojing (in modern Chang'an County on the east bank of the Feng River). His son and successor, King Cheng (*r.* 1042–1020 BCE), completed the construction of Luoyi and made it the Zhou state's secondary capital with the assistance of dukes Zhou and Zhao.[7] According to Cho-yun Hsu and Katheryn M. Linduff, the establishment of an eastern capital in the Luoyang area was aimed at strengthening Western Zhou control over the east-west route along the Yellow River and assuring its grip over the region previously under the Shang.[8]

Some historians argue that the Qin and Western Han established secondary capitals as well. Their evidence is found in two paragraphs in Gu Yanwu's (1612–82) *Imperial Capital of the Previous Dynasties* (*Lidai zhaijing ji*), which state that "there were southern and northern palaces (*gong*) during the Qin," and "from Gaodi (i.e. Han founder Liu Bang, 256–196 BCE) to Wang Mang (45 BCE–23 CE), the southern and northern palaces [of the Qin] and the military depot, all existed in Luoyang."[9] This interpretation is questionable. Palaces are not tantamount to secondary capitals. Students of imperial China know well that palaces, especially palaces serving as lodges for the travelling emperor (*xinggong*), were built in many places in imperial China. These palaces can hardly be regarded as secondary capitals.[10]

By contrast, the establishment of secondary capitals by the Eastern Han dynasty is fairly certain. The founder of the dynasty, Liu Xiu (*r.* 25–57 CE), for the purpose of projecting an image as a legitimate successor of the Western Han imperial house, chose Chang'an, the capital of the previous dynasty, as the Western Capital of his dynasty, in addition to his primary capital Luoyang.[11] He went even further, and designated Nanyang, his birthplace, as

20 *The Secondary Capital System*

the Southern Capital of the dynasty, as indicated by Zhang Heng's three rhapsodies.[12]

When Chancellor Cao Pi (187–226) finally replaced the Eastern Han with his own Wei Kingdom in 220, he created five capitals. While retaining Luoyang as his primary capital, Cao Pi granted capital (*du*) status to four other places: Qiao (present-day Boxian, Anhui), Xuchang (present-day Xuchang, Henan), Chang'an and Ye (present-day Anyang, Henan).[13] Of the four, Qiao was the ancestral place of the Wei where Cao Pi's father, Cao Cao (155–220), was born. Xuchang, where Emperor Xiandi (*r.* 190–220) of the Eastern Han was held hostage by his ambitious general Cao Cao, was the headquarters of the Cao forces for unifying northern China and was a favorite place for the Wei rulers to visit during the reigns of Cao Pi and Cao Rui (226–39). Chang'an was the capital of the Western Han and the Eastern Capital of the Eastern Han. Ye was Cao Cao's power base and the site where he defeated his chief rivals and rose to prominence. Prior to 229, when the Ancestral Temple of the Wei imperial family was completed in Luoyang, the ancestral tablets of Cao Pi, his great grandfather, grandfather, and father were all housed in the Ancestral Temple at Ye.[14]

Zhu Shiguang and Ye Xiaojun hold that the Northern Wei (398–534), established by the Tuoba (Tabgach) tribe during the north-south dynasties period, was the first nomadic regime to adopt more than one capital. Zhu and Ye note that after Xiaowendi (*r.* 471–99) ordered that the main capital be moved from Pingcheng (present-day Datong, Shanxi) to Luoyang, Pingcheng was renamed Beijing (northern capital) and thus served as the secondary capital of the Northern Wei. However, the source that they cite, the "imperial annals of Gaozu (i.e. Xiaowendi)" of the *Weishu* does not contain such information, and only records that in 494, Xiaowendi expressed his intention to transfer the capital to Luoyang, doing so two years later. Ding Haibin holds a similar view on the secondary capital status of Pingcheng, but his sources simply regard Pingcheng as Jiujing (old capital), Daidu (replaced capital), or Beijing.[15]

Judging from the currently available sources, it is clear that most of the dynasties in early China adopted dual- or multi-capital systems for political, military, and symbolic considerations; but it is uncertain what kind of governmental structure existed in the secondary capitals or how effective the practice of creating and maintaining secondary capitals was. It is also unclear how long they existed. This uncertainty becomes less acute with the availability of more written sources in the later period.

2. The Sui, Tang, and Five dynasties

The secondary capital of the Sui dynasty was created in the reign of Sui Yangdi (604–18). In 605 the emperor ordered his chief administrators, Yang Su (d. 606) and Yuwen Kai (556–612), to build Luoyang as the Eastern Capital (Dongdu) of the dynasty.[16]

The Secondary Capital System 21

Various considerations led Yangdi to build his Eastern Capital at Luoyang. In the first place, the geographical location of Luoyang could help the Sui court control its realm politically. East of Luoyang lies the Gu River and the Xiao Mountains. Building the Eastern Capital at Luoyang enhanced the government's control of the entrance to the Xiao Mountains and eventually helped in the defense of the primary capital Daxingcheng (as Chang'an was called in the Sui). The eight passes surrounding Luoyang, set up during the reign of Lindi of the Eastern Han (168–89), were all strategically vital.[17] Luoyang's geographical advantage is well reflected in Sui Yangdi's decree of 604, in which he declared that "commanding the Sanhe (Henan, Hedong, Hebei) region, it (Luoyang) is safeguarded by the four mountain passes. With excellent land and water transportation, it provides a full range of taxes and tribute."[18]

Second, Luoyang was easily accessible by water and land transportation. Three rivers, the Gu, Chan, and Luo, pass through the city. The construction of the Grand Canal in the Sui, which turned Luoyang into the hub of the Grand Canal, further increased its accessibility.[19] The transportation of tax grain from other parts of the country, especially the southeast, became much easier. This was in contrast to Chang'an, for which all grain transported had to pass the dangerous Sanmen Gorge along the Yellow River.[20] After the founding of the Sui dynasty in 581, the population boom in the Guanzhong and Sanhe areas strained local resources, and Chang'an became especially vulnerable to famines. The granaries of the capital area were inadequately prepared for a natural disaster. Even after a number of granaries were set up from east to west along the Yellow River, their capacity to relieve the capital from drought was limited. In fact, Sui Wendi (r. 581–604), founder of the dynasty, was twice forced to lead his starving subjects and court officials eastward to Luoyang in search of food.[21]

The construction of the Sui Eastern Capital took less than one year to complete.[22] During this period, the inhabitants of the neighboring Yuzhou subprefecture were ordered to move to Luoyang, along with "tens of thousands of rich merchant households (shuwan jia fushang dagu)."[23] Soon after the construction was completed in 606, Yangdi, together with court officials and palace ladies, moved to the city and state affairs in Chang'an were delegated to the heir apparent.[24] In 609 the emperor issued an edict designating Luoyang the dynasty's Eastern Capital.[25]

The administrative structure of the Sui Eastern Capital was that of a local administration. During the Sui, the rank of a governor (taishou) of a Commandery (jun) was grade 3b, whereas the rank of the head of Luoyang, like that of Chang'an, was grade 3a. He was assisted by an administrative aide (zanwu).[26] No central government departments were established at the Eastern Capital of the Sui.

The status of Luoyang as the Eastern Capital of the Tang dynasty was not granted until 657, when the court decided to renovate the city. The official status of Luozhou Prefecture, of which Luoyang was the seat, was raised one

22 The Secondary Capital System

rank higher (as in the Sui) to match that of Yongzhou Prefecture, whose seat was also Chang'an.[27] Imposing buildings, including the Shangyang Palace, were built. Starting from the Xiangqing reign (656–60), Tang Gaozong (r. 649–84) frequently travelled to Luoyang and held court audiences at the Shangyang Palace, where he could also attend to his manipulative empress, Wu Zetian (624–705).[28] During his absence, the heir apparent handled state affairs at Chang'an. In 682, when the Guangzhong region was once again struck by drought, Gaozong moved his court to Luoyang, where he stayed until his death in 684.[29]

Luoyang became the permanent site of the court during the twenty-odd-year regime of Empress Wu (first as Empress Dowager [684–89] and then as monarch of her self-proclaimed Zhou dynasty [690–704]). She designated the city "Divine Capital" (Shendu) in 684, when she became the de facto ruler of the empire after the death of her husband. Chang'an remained the Western Capital and was placed in the immediate charge of one of the princes of the Wu family.[30] Many noted buildings such as Shangqing Palace and the Hall of Enlightened Rule (*mingtang*), an institution and a form of architecture serving as a symbol of dynastic legitimacy and sovereignty,[31] were constructed in Luoyang during this time in order to create the necessary "imperial air" (*wangqi*) of the Divine Capital. Upon the completion of the Hall of Enlightened Rule, Empress Wu carried out in it various functions considered to have been characteristic of the ancient *mingtang*: promulgation of edicts, nourishing of the aged, banqueting of officials, rewarding of the meritorious, and the reception of emissaries.[32] In transferring the seat of government to Luoyang Empress Wu was attempting to dissociate herself from the loyalist clans of the Tang who had been drawn by official posts to settle in Chang'an.[33] Luoyang was deprived of its "Divine Capital" title and named "Eastern Capital" in 705 when Emperor Zhongzong (r. 684, 705–9) restored the Tang dynastic title and moved the court back to Chang'an after the deposition of Wu Zetian.[34]

Six of the twenty Tang emperors resided on occasion in Luoyang and had the court moved there for approximately 40 years in total.[35] There were two central institutions in Luoyang: the auxiliary Censorate (*Dongdu liutai*) and the National University (*Guozijian*). Both were operated on a smaller scale than their counterparts in Chang'an. The former had a seven-member staff, which included one vice censor-in-chief (*zhongchen*), one attendant censor (*shiyushi*), two palace censors (*dianzhong yushi*), and three investigating censors (*jiancha yushi*).[36] The latter, created in 662,[37] was composed of a variety of specialized schools.[38]

In addition to the primary capital Chang'an and auxiliary capital Luoyang, there were also four nominal capitals in the Tang period, if we include the temporary Western Capital at Fengxiang,[39] the Middle Capital at Hezhong,[40] and the Southern Capital at Jiangling.[41] The only nominal capital that lasted throughout the dynasty was the Northern Capital Taiyuan. The city, which had been both the rebel base of the dynastic founder, Gaozu (r. 618–25), and the hometown of Empress Wu, was made the Northern Capital in 690, the

The Secondary Capital System   23

first year of the Tianshou era, and abolished in 705 when the empress was dethroned. In 723, its capital status was restored by Emperor Xuanzong (r. 713–55). It is not clear why Xuanzong, who suffered imprisonment during the reign of Wu Zetian, decided to restore Taiyuan's capital status. In 761, together with the three other existing secondary capitals, it was abolished by Emperor Suzong (r. 757–62),[42] and one year later, restored as the Northern Capital of the dynasty.[43] One plausible explanation is that the retention of Taiyuan's capital status was largely due to its having been the base of the Tang founder's uprising against the Sui. A number of imperial buildings, such as the Jinyang Palace and Qiyi (uprising) Hall, were erected in Taiyuan at this time.[44]

It appears that each of the Tang secondary capitals was administered by a regency (*liushou si*), which in later years became a standard administrative unit for the auxiliary capitals. Notices of information regarding the official appointment of the Northern Capital regent and the Eastern Capital regent are scattered throughout the imperial annals section of the various Tang emperors. The regency was often staffed by high officials, who were concurrently ministers or censors-in-chief. For instance, in 755, Li Guangpi (708–64), the Fengyang military commander, was appointed by Suzong as minister of revenue and prefect of Taiyuan, as well as regent of the Northern Capital.[45]

The semi-nomadic Bohai (Parhae in Korean) Kingdom (698–926) of the Mohe (Malgal in Korean) tribe[46] was a major non-Han regional regime in north and northeast China which established a multiple capital system. At its zenith, Bohai divided its territory into five capitals (Upper, Central, Eastern, Western, and Southern), 15 prefectures and 62 subprefectures.[47] Of the five capitals, the location of three is agreed upon by historians. Its Upper Capital Shangjing was Longquan (present-day Dongjingcheng, Ning'an County, Heilongjiang), its Middle Capital Xiande (present-day Xiguchengzi, Helong County, Jilin), and Eastern Capital Longyuan (present-day Baliancheng, Huichun County, Jilin). The exact locations of the Western Capital, Yalu, and the Southern Capital, Nanhai, are disputed. North Korean scholars argue that the Southern Capital of Bohai was located in Pukchong, South Hamgyong, North Korea, and many Chinese researchers believe that the seat of Bohai's Western Capital was in the present-day Baishan of Jilin.[48] Archeological excavations indicate that the design of Bohai's Upper Capital was modeled after Chang'an and that of the Middle and Western capitals were patterned after both Chang'an and Luoyang.[49] However, owing to the scarcity of historical records, the government structure at each of the five capitals is not known.[50]

During the Five Dynasties period, the five ephemeral regimes all had more than one capital. The Later Liang (907–23) and Later Zhou (951–60) had their Eastern and Western capitals at Kaifeng and Luoyang respectively. The Later Tang (923–36), Later Jin (936–46) and Later Han (947–50) established their Eastern, Western, and Northern capitals at Luoyang, Chang'an and Taiyuan respectively.[51] Following the Tang system, all of the capitals in this period were managed by regencies.[52]

24 *The Secondary Capital System*

If the practice of multiple capitals in the Eastern Han and the Wei Kingdom was still rudimentary, and many minor regimes during the period from the third to tenth century did not adopt multiple capitals,[53] it appears that a clear precedent had been established by the end of the tenth century. After the Sui and Tang, the two major dynasties of the medieval age, the practice of creating more than one capital seems to have been widely accepted. The unanimous adoption of multiple capitals by the short-lived regimes of the Five Dynasties period serves as an illustrative example.

Why was it necessary for the dynastic rulers to build more than one national capital? There are perhaps two main motives. First, they were compelled to do so by the relatively inadequate communications existing in premodern times. The auxiliary capitals, scattered throughout the various parts of the empire, could assist the central government in the primary capital in controlling the imperial realm. To a certain extent, Chang'an in the Eastern Han and Luoyang in the Sui and Tang assumed this role. Second, the consideration of legitimacy played a part in establishing nominal capitals. Qiao of the Wei, the Southern Capital of the Eastern Han, and the Northern Capital of the Tang were all the hometowns of imperial monarchs who attempted to increase their legitimacy by granting capital status to their birthplaces. By claiming that they came from prominent localities with an imperial character, not ordinary or humble areas, dynastic founders could assert their legitimacy as sovereigns. The reverse cause and effect would be easily overlooked, especially with the passage of time.

3. The Song, Liao, and Jin dynasties

There were four capitals in the Northern Song dynasty, with the primary capital at Kaifeng, Henan. The city was the capital of the Later Liang and Later Zhou during the Five Dynasties period, and the power base of Emperor Song Taizu (*r.* 960–76), who established his own dynasty by staging the famous bloodless putsch at Chenqiao, 40 *li* northeast of the dynastic capital. Kaifeng underwent considerable expansion during the Later Zhou, and by the time of the early Song its population had reached one million. The city's infrastructure enabled it to assume the function of seat of government. Also, most of Song Taizu's followers who had rallied around him in the Chenqian coup were former officials of the Later Zhou, who, having settled in the Kaifeng area for a certain period of time, were reluctant to move to a new and unfamiliar location. Although not as vital in the strategic sense, Kaifeng was geographically better situated than Chang'an and Luoyang in terms of receiving the transported tribute grain from the southern part of the empire.[54]

Luoyang, the Eastern Capital of the Sui and Tang dynasties, was made the Western Capital of the Northern Song due to its location west of Kaifeng, which in turn was designated Eastern Capital.[55] Even years after settling his primary capital at Kaifeng, Taizu still felt attraction to Chang'an and Luoyang, as the two cities were closely associated with the great dynasties of

The Secondary Capital System   25

the past. In 976 he made an imperial trip to Luoyang and refused to leave. The action sparked a heated argument between the emperor and his senior officials. Taizu justified his reluctance to depart from Luoyang by stressing the city's "superior strategic environs" (*shanhe zhixian*) and his resolve to "follow the precedents of the Zhou and Han" (*xun Zhou Han gushi*), while the remonstrators among his entourage cited Kaifeng's unobstructed accessibility to the grain supply of south China as the main reason to reject his move. Eventually practical considerations prevailed over ritual ones, and the emperor was persuaded.[56]

Of the other two capitals, which existed largely in name only, Yingtian (modern Shangqiu, Henan) was designated Southern Capital in 1014. It was the former Song subprefecture where Taizu once served as military commissioner (*jiedu shi*) before he launched the Chenqiao coup to capture the throne. In fact, the dynasty derived its name from this subprefecture, which in 1007 was upgraded to become Yingtian Prefecture.[57]

Daming (present-day Daming, Hebei) was made the Northern Capital in 1042 following the proposal of Prime Minister Lü Yijian (979–1044). His biography in the *History of the Song Dynasty* (*Songshi*) has it that in 1042 when the Khitan Liao assembled a massive force around the Youji (modern Beijing) area and planned to make an immediate assault on the Song, many court officials suggested the dispatch of troops to Luoyang for defense. Lü dismissed the suggestion by arguing that if the Khitans were able to cross the Yellow River, even a fortified Luoyang could not defend the Song. Instead he proposed the establishment of a Northern Capital at Daming, to "show that the emperor was determined to command the Song troops in person to counterattack the Liao" (*yishi qingzhen*). Lü's advice was accepted by the Renzong emperor, and as a result, the Northern Capital was created.[58] This act, together with the displayed vigilance and combat readiness of the Song army, forced the Khitans to the negotiating table. Peace between the two was eventually restored after the Song court promised to increase its annual payments to the Liao.[59]

Each of the three secondary capitals in the Northern Song was administered by a regency, which was responsible for the defense and renovation of the capital city and its palaces. Grain supplies and other civil and military affairs within the capital region were all under its jurisdiction.[60] Another known department in the three capitals was the Regency Censorate (*liushousi yushitai*), which presumably assumed the usual functions of the traditional Chinese censorate with its jurisdiction restricted to the respective capital. It was run by a court official appointed as "currently managing the censorate" (*guangou taishi*).[61] A Repair Office (*bazuosi*) was kept in the Western Capital, Luoyang, for the maintenance of the old palace buildings.[62]

When the Northern Song court was captured by the troops of the Jurchen Jin in 1126, Zhao Gou (*r.* 1127–62), the younger brother of the last Northern Song emperor, was enthroned in Yingtian, the Southern Capital of the defunct Northern Song. His enthronement ushered in the era of the Southern

26   *The Secondary Capital System*

Song. After numerous escapes from the relentless pursuit of the Jurchens, the Southern Song court finally settled in Lin'an (present-day Hangzhou) in 1129. Still claiming that Kaifeng was its capital and would be recaptured in due time, the Southern Song court named its functioning capital as "the temporary imperial abode" (*xingzaisuo* or *xingzai*). To show its determination to recover lost territory and return to the north, the palace compounds in Lin'an were all modestly built.[63] For its own protection, the Southern Song government, also in 1129, designated Jiangning (renamed as Jiankang, modern Nanjing) as its "temporary auxiliary capital" (*xinggong*). The palace buildings of the Southern Tang (937–76),[64] a small, short-lived dynasty of the tenth century, were used as the palaces for the temporary auxiliary capital. A regency was consequently established in Jiankang.[65] The east, west, and north of the city were heavily garrisoned with troops in order to protect both the city and the main capital.[66] In a sense, the temporary auxiliary capital was created to provide a buffer for the Southern Song court in Lin'an to secure its safety. A number of Southern Song emperors resided in Jiankang from time to time.[67]

The two major non-Han rivals of the Song dynasty, the Khitan Liao and Jurchen Jin, also adopted a multiple capital system. During the period extending from 918 to 1044, the Khitans established five capitals in their realm:[68] Upper Capital Linhuang (present-day Balin Zuoqi County, Inner Mongolia),[69] Eastern Capital Liaoyang (modern Liaoyang, Liaoning), Middle Capital Dading (present-day Damincheng, in the west of Ningcheng, Liaoning),[70] Southern Capital Youdu (later renamed Xijing Prefecture; modern Beijing),[71] and Western Capital Datong (present-day Datong, Shanxi).[72] Of the five capitals, the Upper Capital was the primary capital, the other four were auxiliary.[73]

Each of the five capitals of the Liao was administered by its own capital officials (*jingguan*). In the primary Upper Capital, in addition to the capital officials, there were also court officials (*chaoguan*) from the Southern and Northern offices of Grand Councilors (*nanbei zaixiang fu*) which governed the whole Liao realm.[74] At the capital administration level, the Eastern, Middle, and Southern capitals were supervised by the office of the Grand Councilors (*zaixiang fu*).[75] Other capital-level offices at the four secondary capitals included: Regency, Chief Area Command (*zongguan fu*), fiscal agency,[76] and a half dozen minor offices.[77]

The administrative responsibilities of each of the four auxiliary capitals were not identical. Generally speaking, there were more officials for frontier defence in the Western Capital, in the occupied political and military center known as the Sixteen Prefectures.[78] For their part, the Southern and Middle capitals were mainly staffed by officials for finance and taxation,[79] while the officials in the Eastern Capital were more concerned with ruling over the territory the Liao had annexed from Bohai in 926.[80]

The Jurchen Jin dynasty had an unprecedented number of capitals in its territory, a total of six.[81] Of the six, the primary capital was the Middle Capital (Zhongdu) (present-day Beijing). The five secondary capitals were:

Upper Capital (Shangjing) Huining (present-day Baichengzhi in the south of Acheng, Heilongjiang), where the Jin court of the first three rulers (r. 1115–49) was located,[82] Eastern Capital Liaoyang,[83] Northern Capital Dading,[84] Western Capital Datong,[85] and Southern Capital Kaifeng.[86]

Each of the five secondary capitals of the Jin was administered by a regency.[87] The rank of the regents in the Jin was equal to that of area commander-in-chief (*zhongguan*) in the other fourteen commands since the status of the five secondary capitals of the Jin was not as high as that of the Liao secondary capitals, and yet the number of graded officials in the secondary capital was larger than that in the route;[88] it is consequently difficult to place these non-primary capitals into either the category of auxiliary capital or that of nominal capital. It appears that they were closer to the auxiliary model.

The multiple-capital system matured considerably and became almost a standard practice of the imperial dynasties by the early thirteenth century. The number of secondary capitals reached its apex at this time, ranging from the four of the Northern Song to the six of the Jurchen Jin. Most capitals bore a directional designation and were located in the corresponding parts of the empire. Thus we see the Eastern, Southern, Western, and Northern capitals of the Northern Song; the Upper, Eastern, Southern, Middle, and Western capitals of the Liao; and the Upper, Eastern, Southern, Western, Northern, and Middle capitals of the Jin. The other noteworthy development was the establishment of bureaucratic apparatuses other than the regency in the secondary capitals. This was particularly the case in Liao times.

4. The Yuan, Ming, and Qing dynasties

a. The Yuan

The Mongol Yuan had two permanent capitals and one temporary one. In 1260 when Khubilai (r. 1260–95) ascended to the Mongol throne by claiming his rulership in Kaiping (around 20 kilometers northeast of Huangqi dayingzi, the seat of Zhenglan County, Inner Mongolia), he named the city the Upper Capital of the Yuan dynasty. Meanwhile he designated Beijing as his Middle Capital. Four years later he made it the primary capital which in 1272 was renamed Grand Capital (Dadu). The Upper Capital consequently became auxiliary.[89]

There was a short-lived effort to build a Middle Capital during the Wuzong reign era (1307–11). In 1307, the newly-enthroned Wuzong emperor ordered the building of palaces in Wangwuchadu, Longxing Route. A branch ministry of works (*xing gongbu*) was established there to supervise the construction, which consumed a large amount of money and involved the conscription of many laborers.[90] When the palace was completed there, the emperor designated it Middle Capital. A capital regency, a court of imperial entertainments, a supervisorate of silver smelting, and an imperial storehouse were subsequently established.[91] The capital was, however, immediately abandoned

28   The Secondary Capital System

by the succeeding Renzong emperor in 1311 and the regency was replaced by the Longxing Route Command.[92] From its creation to abolition, the Middle Capital lasted for less than three years.

The post-1264 Upper Capital enjoyed great prominence in the Yuan. Every year the Yuan emperor and his large entourage of officials made their "tour of the northern frontier inspection" (*beixun*) to the city, where they spent a few months and handled important political and military matters.

There are a number of reasons why the Upper Capital remained popular during the Yuan. Firstly, the area surrounding it was of strategic importance. It provided a crucial link between the Northern Mongolia area where the Mongols had risen to power and the traditional Chinese region. To its east and west lay the fiefs of the Mongol princes and nobles who, by holding large appanages, had substantial economic, political, and military sway.[93] Winning over their loyalty became the constant concern of Yuan emperors after Ogodei Khan (r. 1229–41).

For that purpose, when the Yuan emperor was in Kaiping, most of the Mongol princes and nobles were received in audience by the khan and this practice gradually became fixed.[94] Also, upon arrival at the Upper Capital, the Yuan emperor held various events such as holding banquets, hunting, and sacrificing to heaven, earth, and the ancestors in the traditional Mongol manner.[95] Holding a banquet was a good opportunity for the Yuan ruler to reward the Mongol nobles and show his concern for them, thus enhancing the connection between the court and the nobles. As to the hunting activities, the emperor's involvement helped to build the image of military prowess, even though now he spent most of his time acting in a civil capacity in Beijing.

The Yuan emperor held various sacrifices in the Upper Capital as well. After the founding of the Yuan, the government built an Altar of Heaven and an Ancestral Temple in southern Dadu where the ceremonies of the sacrifices to Heaven and to the ancestors were conducted in accordance with the Tang ritual system. But at the Upper Capital, these ceremonies were carried out in the traditional Mongolian way.[96]

Secondly, the Upper Capital had a variety of roles to play in the political life of the dynasty. In the early Yuan period, important Mongol affairs were decided at a tribal conference commonly known as the *khurilitai*. The election of new chieftains and matters related to battles and conquests were all deliberated and decided at the *khurilitai*. In theory, this was obligatory for all Mongol Khans and Yuan emperors in post-Chinggis Khan times (though this in the later years became more or less a formality) and most of the *khurilitai* ratifying the enthronement of the new Mongol ruler were held at the Upper Capital.[97]

Lastly, the summer weather in the Upper Capital area was much favored by the early Mongol leaders who had spent most of their lives on the steppes, and the Upper Capital became a favorite place for the Mongol rulers to escape the summer heat in Beijing. Yuan sources record that the climate in the sixth month of the year in Kaiping was similar to the autumn weather in Beijing.[98]

The length of the Yuan emperor's sojourn in the Upper Capital varied: on average, it was between four to six months. For example, Khubilai began this northern inspection practice in 1263 when he left for Kaiping in the second month and returned to Beijing in the eighth month. This schedule was basically followed in the later years of the dynasty. Wuzong (r. 1328; 1330–31) fixed the time of his temporary residence in the Upper Capital from the third to ninth month. Emperors Yingzong (r. 1320–23) and Taidingdi (r. 1323–28) all followed this schedule. The last Yuan emperors Renzong (r. 1311–20), Wenzong (r. 1329–32), and Shundi (r. 1333–68) tended to shorten their time in Kaiping, for they were raised in Beijing and were not accustomed to the cold steppe climate.[99]

When the Yuan emperor was in the Upper Capital, almost all of the central governmental offices had branches temporarily set up there.[100] Most of the government officials, both civil and military, from top prime ministers down to low-ranking secretaries, were among the imperial entourage.[101] For example, at the Secretariat, only a very few junior officials were left to take care of routine affairs in Beijing.[102] All the senior officials accompanied the emperor.[103] As for the Bureau of Military Affairs only one official was ordered to stay; all other high ranking officials from the bureau, such as the military affairs commissioner (*shumi shi*), associate commissioners (*tongzhi*), and deputy military commissioners (*shumi fushi*), travelled with the emperor.[104] As with the Censorate, only the vice censor-in-chief and a small number of officials stayed in Beijing to oversee state affairs.[105]

Some central governmental agencies were permanently established in the Upper Capital. These could be classified into four types: agencies responsible for taxation and production in the Upper Capital;[106] bureaus charged with administering the state artisans; offices related to the administration of the postal relay station households (*zhanhu*) in the Upper Capital;[107] and units administering the various ordo (camps of tribal chiefs) and the appanages.[108]

The other regular government apparatus in Shangdu was the Upper Capital Regency.[109] Its chief responsibilities included safeguarding the palaces, administering the supplies of the Shangdu Route, and constructing and renovating the palaces, imperial gardens, and storehouses.[110] The staffing level at the Upper Capital Regency did not become permanent until the reign of Wenzong. Since then it was administered by six regents, two associate administrators (*tongzhi*), two vice-regents (*fu liushou*), and a few administrative assistants (*panguan*). Its subordinate offices numbered more than a dozen.[111]

Compared with those in the previous dynasties (with the possible exception of the Liao), the official apparatuses established in the Yuan Upper Capital were more comprehensive. In addition to the standard administrative office for secondary capitals, regency, a number of government offices were set up permanently in the Upper Capital. On the other hand, they were still not comparable with those in the primary capital. Most of the branch offices of the central government were created and used only when the emperor and his entourage were in the Upper Capital. This practice reflects the vestige of the Mongol nomadic tradition.

30 *The Secondary Capital System*

b. The Ming

There was a total of five capitals in the Ming dynasty, if we include three nominal ones: the Middle Capital at Fengyang, the Flourishing Capital (Xingdu) at Chengtian, and the transitory first Northern Capital, Kaifeng. The primary and auxiliary capitals of the post-1421 Ming were Northern Capital Beijing and Southern Capital Nanjing, seated at the prefectures of Shuntian and Yingtian respectively.

Of the three nominal capitals, the Middle Capital enjoyed relatively more prestige. Attempting to turn his hometown into the primary capital of the empire, the dynasty founder, the Hongwu emperor, established a Middle Capital at Fengyang in 1369, one year after the founding of the Ming.[112] Several institutions were created there: an observatory (*guanxing tai*) in 1372, a temple to honor past emperors (*lidai diwang miao*) in 1373, and a national university (*guozixue*) in 1375.[113] The Middle Capital performed a number of services for the Ming regime. The most distinctive was its role as a training ground for imperial princes. In the early years of the dynasty, especially in the 1370s, the emperor's sons were dispatched to Fengyang to familiarize themselves with government affairs and responsibilities. In 1377, the Hongwu emperor arranged to have all government affairs routed through the heir apparent to let him practice managing state affairs and learn firsthand the burden resting on the Son of Heaven.[114] However, due to its unfavorable geographical location and the immense costs of building a capital from scratch, the Ming court eventually abandoned the attempt to turn it into the primary capital. One sign of this was that by 1394 the Middle Capital National University was reduced to the status of being merely the Fengyang Prefectural School.[115] As with most of the secondary capitals, the so-called Middle Capital was also administered by regency.[116]

The other nominal capital, which lasted from its founding through to the end of the dynasty, was the Flourishing Capital at Chengtian. When the Zhengde emperor died without leaving an heir in the early sixteenth century, the throne was passed to Jiajing, son of the prince of Xing and a grandson of the Hongzhi emperor. In 1531 the Jiajing emperor raised his father's old fief to the prefecture of Chengtian (literally "succeeding to heaven"), a name on the same pattern as Shuntian (submitting to heaven) and Yingtian (responding to heaven). It was this Chengtian Prefecture that was known as the Flourishing Capital. A regency (*Xingdu liushou si*) was created in 1539 for this nominal capital, which commanded four guards.[117] The official rank of the regency was identical to that of the Middle Capital regency.[118]

The first Northern Capital of the Ming, Kaifeng, was created in 1368. The adoption of the former Northern Song capital as the auxiliary capital of the dynasty was designed for better control of the northern part of the empire. It would also appeal both to the popular anti-Mongol forces who championed the slogan "restore the Song" and to the Confucian scholars who identified the Song with the Chinese cultural tradition.[119] However, there is no evidence

The Secondary Capital System 31

to indicate that any effort was made to rebuild Kaifeng as a capital city. Edward Farmer speculates that the Hongwu emperor might have seriously intended to make a capital in the north (he made two trips to Kaifeng in 1368) but was discouraged by the conditions he found, the expense of the restoration, and the problems of grain transportation. As a result, Kaifeng was abandoned as the Northern Capital in 1369, when Fengyang was made the Middle Capital.[120]

The primary capital and auxiliary capital of the Ming moved between the Southern Capital (Nanjing) and the Northern Capital (Beijing) in the post-1369 Ming period. The city of Jinling, historically also known as Jiankang, Jianye, and Jiqing, served as a base for Zhu Yuanzhang's expansion from 1356 when it was captured by the Ming forces. In 1367, a year before the Ming was formally proclaimed, it was designated the capital of the dynasty.[121] Besides being the power base of the Ming forces, the other attraction of the city was its proximity to the rice supply of south China. In the eyes of the first Ming emperor, the adoption of the major Northern Capital site would have imposed too heavy a burden on the populace of south China.[122]

A few months after his investiture in 1368, Zhu Yuanzhang named Jinling the Southern Capital when he decided to designate Kaifeng the Northern Capital. Early in 1378, the name Nanjing was dropped in favor of Jingshi (capital city), as Zhu had now concluded it should be his main seat of government.[123] In 1402, the army of the Prince of Yan, later the Yongle emperor, overthrew the reigning Jianwen emperor. Sensing that his real power base was his princely fief and considering the various advantages it possessed, Yongle in 1402 ordered the primary capital to be moved to Beiping, which had been given the name on its capture in 1368, and renamed it Beijing.[124] The primary capital was consequently deprived of the title of the Jingshi and called Nanjing again.[125] From 1402 until 1421, Beijing served as an auxiliary capital of the Ming. During this period, Yongle spent most of his time in the north. In his absence, state affairs in Nanjing were overseen by the crown prince.[126]

The transfer of the primary capital to Beijing took eighteen years to complete. A branch ministry (*xingbu*) was established in 1402 in Beijing to manage the affairs of the Northern Capital.[127] Under the ministry were six bureaus: personnel, revenue, rites, war, justice, and works, which were later on expanded to become six ministries. An affix "*xingzai*" (temporary capital) was attached to each of the Beijing departments.[128] When the construction work of the Northern Capital was finally completed in 1420, the Yongle emperor selected the first day of the nineteenth year of his reign (1421) to inaugurate Beijing formally as the new primary capital of the dynasty. Nanjing was retained as the auxiliary capital. All the governmental agencies were moved to the north and only the ministries of rites, justice, and works had their offices in Nanjing. The affix "*xingzai*" associated with the Beijing departments since 1403 was deleted and the remaining agencies at Nanjing had the affix "Nanjing" added to them to distinguish between the two capitals. The ministerial affairs of each of the three remaining agencies in Nanjing were administered by a vice minister.[129]

32 *The Secondary Capital System*

The Yongle emperor died in the autumn of 1424. His son, the succeeding Hongxi emperor, who had assisted his father in governing state affairs for almost twenty years in Nanjing,[130] had a certain attachment to the city, and in the spring of 1425 he decided to transfer the primary capital of the dynasty back to Nanjing. He ordered all the Beijing agencies redesignated "*xingzai*" as they had been in the 1402–20 period,[131] and he also established all the other governmental agencies in Nanjing (plus the original remaining three ministries) at the same time. The affix "Nanjing" was deleted from the Nanjing administration.[132]

However, the plan to transfer the primary capital back to the south died as the result of the sudden passing of the Hongxi emperor. The emperor's son and successor, the Xuande emperor, the imperial grandson since 1410, had spent most of his time with his grandfather, the Yongle emperor, in the north while his father resided at Nanjing to supervise state affairs.[133] Xuande retained Beijing as the seat of court and government for his ten-year reign.

Although Beijing continued to be the primary capital during the Xuande reign, the affix "*xingzai*" remained attached to it until 1441 when the Zhengtong emperor decided to restore all practices of the Yongle emperor. In that year, Zhengtong finally ordered the deletion of the affix "*xingzai*" from the Beijing administration and attached "Nanjing" to the Nanjing administration. From 1441 until the end of the dynasty in 1644, for more than two centuries, Beijing remained the primary capital and Nanjing maintained its status as auxiliary capital.[134]

The existence of the two active administrative capitals was seemingly an accidental outcome of the Yongle usurpation. However, had there been no such coup and had the court remained in Nanjing, the Ming might still have had two functioning capitals. The fact that the Ming founder first tried to establish a northern capital in Kaifeng and then a middle capital in Fengyang indicates that the Ming court was serious in wanting to establish an additional capital, although eventually Kaifeng was deserted and Fengyang did not become a functioning capital. When Beijing was formally designated as the primary capital in 1421, officials from the Nanjing ministries of Rites, Justice, and Works were ordered to stay. The duplication of the central governmental agencies in Nanjing was not completed in the Yongle region but only in 1425 when the Hongxi emperor came to the throne. Although we do not know what was in Hongxi's mind when he decided to move the court back to Nanjing, one thing is certain: he did not want to abandon the Northern Capital; otherwise there would have been no need to create a complete shadow government in Nanjing. In other words, the functional two-capital system of the Ming was not a historical accident. Had there been no Yongle usurpation, the Ming could have chosen another northern city as an auxiliary capital in the course of time, for the idea of having secondary capitals and using them to aid the governance of the imperial realm was deep-rooted in the minds of traditional Chinese rulers.

The secondary capital system of the Ming dynasty was the most elaborate in Chinese history. The primary Northern Capital and auxiliary Southern

The Secondary Capital System 33

Capital were almost completely parallel in the power structure and installation of their bureaucratic apparatuses.[135] As we shall see, almost all the government agencies that existed in the Northern Capital had their equivalents in the Southern Capital. Even offices closely associated with the emperor, the heir apparent, and the imperial family found counterparts in Nanjing. Moreover, the ranks and remuneration of Nanjing officials were identical to those of their counterparts in Beijing.[136] Since the focus of this book is the Southern Capital of the Ming, the various functions of the auxiliary administration will be discussed in detail in the following chapters.

c. The Qing

The last dynasty of imperial China, the Manchu Qing, had two national capitals: the primary capital, Beijing, and the auxiliary capital, Shengjing.[137] After crushing Li Zicheng's (1606–45) rebel army which toppled the Ming in 1644, the Manchus established their own dynasty and relocated their seat of government to Beijing. The former capital of the Manchu imperial house (present-day Shenyang, Liaoning) was retained as the Grand Capital, Shengjing.

In terms of the size of the bureaucratic apparatus and structure of power, the Qing auxiliary capital was second only to the Southern Capital of the Ming. Like Ming Nanjing, Shengjing also possessed a set of bureaucratic agencies similar to those of the primary capital, notably the Five Shengjing Ministries (*Shengjing wubu*) and the Department of the Imperial Household,[138] although the size of the Qing auxiliary capital was considerably smaller than that of the primary capital. For example, other important central government agencies in Beijing, such as the Ministry of Personnel, the Court of Colonial Affairs (*lifanyuan*), the Censorate, the Office of Transmission, the five major courts,[139] and the two major directorates[140] found no counterparts in Shengjing. Moreover, each of the five ministries in Shengjing was only headed by a vice minister.[141] The number of functional bureaus under the ministry was fewer as well. There were two bureaus under the Shengjing ministries of War, Rites, and Works, whereas the bureaus under the three Beijing ministries all numbered four. The bureaus under the Shengjing ministries of Revenue and Justice numbered three and four respectively, whereas the counterparts of the two ministries in Beijing had 14 and 18 subordinate bureaus respectively.[142] The bureau in Shengjing was typically run by one director, two vice directors, one or two secretaries, one or two headquarter secretaries (*tang zhushi*), and a number of clerks (*bitieshi*).[143]

The five ministries at Shengjing were the highest civilian authorities in Manchuria until 1905 when they were abolished by the late Qing political and military reforms. They were directly under the control of the emperor and his chief governing office, first the Grand Secretariat (*neige*) and later the Grand Council (*junjichu*), and were not subordinated to the six ministries in Beijing.[144]

The Ministry of Revenue took charge of all financial affairs in the Shengjing area. Of the five ministries, its official duties were comparably heavy.

34 *The Secondary Capital System*

Under the ministry were 126 state farms (*guantun*). The grain produced from these farms and the grain supplies transported from Tianjin were supervised and stored by the ministry. It also took charge of collecting miscellaneous taxes, allocating the land (especially wasteland under the control of government) to the officials and soldiers and ordinary bannermen at Shengjing, paying for the expenses incurred at various sacrificial ceremonies, as well as supplying the payroll of the officials and soldiers at Shengjing, Ningguta, and Shanhaiguan.[145]

The Ministry of Rites was charged with administering the ceremonial and sacrificial activities that took place in Shengjing, which included sacrifices to the tombs of the early Manchu rulers and their ancestors,[146] the temples, and various mountains and river deities. It had one other duty as well: receiving and seeing off officials from neighboring Korea.[147] The focus of the Shengjing Ministry of Justice was similarly local: it was charged with handling judicial matters among the bannermen population in the Shengjing region.[148]

The Ministry of Works took charge of all the construction projects in the Shengjing area. It was responsible for the maintenance and renovation of the imperial palaces in Shengjing, the ancestral temple, Confucian temple, and the temples of other lesser deities. The construction and renovation of the imperial tombs, the residence of Shengjing officials, as well as the construction and repair of the transport vehicles in Manchuria was also handled by the ministry.[149]

The Qing government maintained a sizeable military presence in Manchuria, where approximately 25,000 soldiers and more than 1,000 naval personnel were stationed.[150] The Ministry of War in Shengjing, in cooperation with the offices of the Fengtian, Ningguta and Heilongjiang generals, was responsible for administering military equipment and personnel in the Shengjing area, operating the postal relay system, and coordinating frontier defense.[151]

Shengjing received close attention from the Qing emperors. To visit these mausoleums and make sacrifices to their ancestors became a prominent event of the Manchu emperors in the high Qing. During the period extending from the Kangxi reign (1662–1772) to the Qianlong reign (1736–95), Qing monarchs frequently made imperial tours to Shengjing. These widely publicized and lavishly displayed trips provided them with an opportunity to show their filial piety toward their ancestors and inspect frontier defenses and the development of the region, as well as practice horse-riding and hunting in order to maintain their military prowess.[152]

Shengjing was also regarded by the Qing emperors as the imperial rear base. Although the Manchus had conquered the whole of China proper and established a solid national regime by the time of the Kangxi emperor, the Manchu rulers always maintained a certain degree of vigilance against the Han Chinese. In their eyes, Manchuria was an ideal place to retreat to in case of a massive Han Chinese revolt. For this purpose, the Qing rulers made every effort to strengthen their control over Manchuria and keep the region purely Manchu by prohibiting Han Chinese settlement. As a result of this policy, all chief Shengjing offices were reserved for the Manchus. Only some minor positions were filled by Mongols and Chinese bannermen. For example, in the Shengjing Ministry of Justice, two vice-directorships, two secretary posts, and two clerkships were assumed by the Mongols; one headquarter secretary, five clerks, and one warehouseman were Chinese bannermen.[153]

The period extending from the Yuan to the Qing saw a decrease in the number of capitals. Except for the Ming, which still maintained two nominal capitals, the Yuan and Qing had only two capitals respectively, the primary capital and the secondary capital. Although the number of capitals dwindled, the functions assumed by the auxiliary capitals increased. One noticeable phenomenon was that all the auxiliary capitals during this period had previously been primary capitals.[154] The administrative departments in the auxiliary capitals became more complete and even comparable to those in the primary capitals. The areas under the jurisdiction of the auxiliary capitals were all of strategic importance and were the power bases of the imperial houses of these dynasties. The responsibilities of these auxiliary capitals consequently increased, and the Ming case is the most illustrative.

In conclusion, the secondary capitals in imperial China were essentially of two types: nominal and auxiliary, each assuming different functions. The nominal capitals were created primarily for their symbolic value.[155] One of the major considerations of the Ming founder for designating Kaifeng as his first Northern Capital was to use its association with the Northern Song dynasty to attract both the popular anti-Yuan forces and Confucian scholars. A number of nominal capitals were the emperors' hometowns, notably Qiao of the Wei, the Southern Capital of the Eastern Han, the Northern Capital of the Tang, and the Middle Capital of the Ming. The other two related cases were the Flourishing Capital of the Ming and the Southern Capital of the Northern Song. The former was the fief of the Jiajing emperor's father, the latter the power base of Song Taizu. The main purpose of designating these places imperial capitals was to honor the emperors and help them to project the image of legitimate sovereigns. The converting of Daming into the Northern Capital of the Northern Song was intended as an appeal to the troops, for what they were defending was an imperial capital, not an ordinary city.

Auxiliary capitals were established mainly to assist the primary capitals in controlling the empire more effectively. The auxiliary capitals of the Liao and Jin, scattered across their realms, aided the primary capitals in governing various parts of the empires and as a result reduced the burden of the central governments. Luoyang, the Eastern Capital of both the Sui and Tang, helped the primary capital alleviate shortages of grain supplies when natural calamities struck. Its ideal geographical location also provided a shield for Chang'an at the time of nomadic marauding. The establishment of the Upper Capital in the Northern Mongolian region enabled the Yuan court to keep a firm hold on the powerful Mongol princes and nobles. By spending a few months there every year and holding various political and ritual events, the Yuan emperors greatly strengthened their ties with the conservative Mongol

36 *The Secondary Capital System*

nobles and stabilized the situation in the north. The Grand Capital of the Qing contributed significantly to the defense of the empire's northern frontier and maintenance of Manchuria as a pure Manchu homeland. It provided the Qing court with a safe rear base and peace of mind. The Southern Capital of the Ming, as the following chapters of this book will further confirm, played a variety of political, financial, and military roles in imposing state control over the Ming empire.

Notes

1 In defining the various capitals in imperial China, I have basically followed Edward Farmer's classification with slight modification. For his classification, see *Early Ming Government*, 174–82.

2 Like most of the Chinese characters, *du* and *jing* also have many other meanings. Victor Cunrui Xiong holds that *du* in pre-Wei (22–260) was used to mean "urban center" instead of "capital". See his "Sui Yangdi and the building of Sui-Tang Luoyang," *Journal of Asian Studies*, Vol. 52, No. 1, 77.

3 Luoyang retained the title of Dongdu in most of Tang times except for the period from 741–61 when it was termed Dongjing and for the reign of Empress Wu Zetian when it became the seat of the court and government and was renamed Shendu (divine capital). Ouyang Xiu, *Xin Tangshu*, 981–82.

4 See Xiao Tong, ed., *Wenxuan*, 3, 15, 25, 47.

5 Zhang Guoshuo, *Xia Shang shidai ducheng zhidu yanjiu*, chapter two.

6 Zhang Guoshuo, "Zhengzhou Shangcheng yu Yanshi Shangcheng bingwei Bodu shuo," *Kaogu yu wenwu*, No. 1 (1996), 36–7; Pan Mingjuan, "Cong Zhengzhou Shangcheng he Yanshi Shangcheng de guanxi kan zao Shang de zhudu he peidu," *Kaogu*, No. 2 (2008), 58–61.

7 Gu Yanwu, *Lidai zhaijing ji*, 6; Ding Haibin, *Zhongguo gudai peidu shi*, 64–7; Zhu and Ye, "Shilun woguo lishi shang peidu zhi de xingcheng yu zuoyong," 61–2; Hsu and Linduff, *Western Chou Civilization*, 123–4; Li Xueqin, *Eastern Zhou and Qin Civilizations*, 16–17.

8 Hsu and Linduff, *Western Chou Civilization*, 124. Xiong Cunrui dismisses the view that Luoyi was established as the Eastern Capital of the Western Zhou as lacking clear evidence. See "Sui Yangdi and the building of Sui-Tang Luoyang," 77.

9 Gu, *Lidai zhaijing ji*, 116. See also Zhu and Ye, "Peidu zhi de xingcheng yu zuoyong," 62.

10 Li Jiuchang, in his book-length study of the history of Luoyang, explicitly states that the Qin and Western Han did not employ Luoyang as secondary capital. See *Guojia kongjian yu shehui*, 98.

11 In the mid-Jianwu reign (26–55 CE), the famed intellectual Tu Du (d. 78) argued in his famous memorial, "Lun du" (On Capital), that the capital of the Eastern Han dynasty, strategically located, was the source of imperial power, and thus should not be abandoned. The Eastern Han court even considered to move the main capital back to Chang'an. Xu Tianling, *Dong Han huiyao*, 533–4.

12 Zhang Heng, *Dongdu fu*, *Xijing fu*, and *Nandu fu*, in *Wenxuan*, 25–81.

13 In his notes to *Sanguo zhi*, Pei Songzhi (372–451) writes that "Yu Huan's *Wei lu* records that [in the second year of the Huangchu reign era (e.g. 220)], [Cao Pi] 'ordered that Chang'an, Qian, Xucheng, Ye, and Luoyang be designated as the five capitals [of the dynasty].'" Chen Shou, *Shanguo zhi*, 77; Gu, *Lidai zhaijing ji*, 14.

14 Chen, *Sanguo zhi*, 96–7; Gu, *Lidai zhaijing ji*, 14.

15 See Zhu and Ye, "Peiduzhi de xingcheng yu zuoyong," 63; Wei Shou, *Weishu*, 178; Ding, *Zhongguo gudai peidu shi*, 141–2.

The Secondary Capital System 37

16 Wei Zheng et al., *Suishu*, 63.
17 For the importance of those passes and their relevance to Luoyang being chosen as the Eastern Capital, see Cao Erqin, "Luoyang cong Han Wei zhi Sui Tang de bianqian," in Zhongguo gudu xuehui, ed., *Zhongguo gudu yanjiu*, Vol. 3, 223–7.
18 *Suishu*, 60–2; Han Guopan, *Sui Yangdi*, 23–4.
19 In 605, Sui Yangdi ordered the excavation of the Tongji Canal which connected the Gu and Luo River with the Yellow River. The Langdang Canal at Xingyang linked the Yellow River to the Huai River. After the completion of these two canals, Yangdi ordered the dredging of the Han Ditch (Hangou) which linked the Yangzi River and the Huai River. In 608 a decree ordering the digging of the Yongji in the north was issued. In 610 the Jiangnan Canal was constructed from Jingkou (present-day Zhenjiang) to Hangzhou, and the completion of these two canals made the linkage between Hangzhou and Zhuojun (modern Beijing) possible. Cao, "Luoyang de bianqian," 227–9.
20 Prior to the Han dynasty, Guanzhong, where Chang'an was located, was a comparatively prosperous area. However, by the early Han period, the grain produced in Guanzhong could no longer feed the rapidly increased population of Chang'an and the government began to ship grain from the Shandong area to supply Chang'an residents. During the reign of Han Xuandi (74–49 BCE), grain transported from the east of the Guanzhong area to the capital reached 4 million piculs (*hu*). Ban Gu, *Hanshu*, 1141.
21 Xiong, "Sui Yangdi and the building of Sui-Tang Luoyang," 67–8.
22 *Suishu*, 65.
23 *Suishu*, 63.
24 *Suishu*, 66; Li Jianren, *Luoyang gujin tan*, 123.
25 *Suishu*, 72.
26 Li, *Luoyang gujin tan*, 136.
27 Liu Xu, *Jiu Tangshu*, 77.
28 *Xin Tangshu*, 76–87, 89–113.
29 *Jiu Tangshu*, 111–12.
30 Sima Guang, *Zizhi tongjian*, 6473.
31 For a detailed discussion of *mingtang* and its functions, see Antonio Forte, *Mingtang and Buddhist Utopias in the History of the Astronomical Clock: the Tower, Statue and Armillary Sphere Constructed by Empress Wu*.
32 Howard J. Wechsler, *Offerings of Jade and Silk: Ritual and Symbol in the Legitimation of the Tang Dynasty*, 210.
33 R. W. L. Guisso, *Wu Tse-T'ien and the Politics of Legitimation in T'ang China*, 129.
34 Sima, *Zizhi tongjian*, 6606; *Xin Tangshu*, 982.
35 They were Empress Wu, Zhongzong (*r.* 683–84 and again 705–10), Xuanzong (*r.* 712–56), Zhaozong (*r.* 888–904) and Aizong (*r.* 904–7). Li, *Luoyang gujin tan*, 171.
36 Wang Fu, *Tang huiyao*, 1408.
37 *Jiu Tangshu*, 82.
38 They included the School for the Sons of the State (*guoziguan*), the School of the Four Gates (*simenguan*), the Institute for the Extension of Literary Arts (*guangwenguan*), the Calendar School (*lüguan*), the Calligraphy School (*shuguan*) and the Mathematics School (*suanguan*). Wang, *Tang huiyao*, 1160.
39 It served as the restoration base of Emperor Suzong during the An Lushan Rebellion. It was established in 757, abolished in 761, re-established, and re-abolished around 762. *Xin Tangshu*, 966.
40 It was established and abolished in the same year (720), later restored on an unspecific date and finally abolished in 808. *Xin Tangshu*, 999; *Jiu Tangshu*, 1470.
41 The first Southern Capital of the Tang was Shujun (Chengdu) which was granted the status in 757 when the fleeing Tang court settled there temporarily. In 760 Chengdu was replaced by Jiangling as the Southern Capital. *Jiu Tangshu*, 250, 259.

38 *The Secondary Capital System*

42 *Xin Tangshu*, 1003.

43 *Xin Tangshu*, 164–5, 1003.

44 Gu, *Lidai zhaijing ji*, 219.

45 *Jiu Tangshu*, 243.

46 Chinese scholars almost unanimously regard the Bohai Kingdom as a regional regime (*difang zhengquan*) of China, while many Korean historians view it as a Korean kingdom, as it was established by a former Koguryo general and its people consisted of Koguryoans and the Tungusic tribes. See, for example, Wanne J. Joe, *Traditional Korea: A Cultural History*, 67; Sohn Pow-key et al., *The History of Korea*, 66–8. In any case, the territory of the Bohai state occupied most of the present-day northeast China and parts of Korea.

47 *Xin Tangshu*, 6182.

48 See *Liaoshi*, 462; Song Yubin and Qu Yili, "Bohai guo de wujing zhidu yu ducheng," *Dongbei shidi*, 6 (2008), 2–6. Some Chinese historians hold that the archaeological findings in the North Korean county of Pukchong do not sufficiently support the argument of the existence of a capital city in the area, while a few Korean historians argue that the seat of Bohai's Western Capital was located in the Korean side of the Yalu River. For a detailed discussion of the possible location of the five Bohai capitals and their respective functions, see Toriyama, *Bokkai shijo shomondai*, 107–76; Ding Haibin, *Zhongguo gudai peidu shi*, 258–70.

49 Su Bai, "Sui Tang Chang'an cheng yu Luoyang cheng," *Kaogu*, No. 6 (1987), 423.

50 Song Yubin and Qu Yili argue that only two (i.e. the Upper Capital and Eastern Capital) of the five *jing* of the Bohai state possessed the capital status; the other three were merely administrative units of the ethnic kingdom. See "Bohai guo de wujing zhidu yu ducheng," *Dongbei shidi*, 6 (2008), 5.

51 Xue Juzheng et al., *Jiu Wudai shi*, 48, 146, 351, 404, 419, 421, 997, 1005, 1013, 1323, 1324, 1332, 1335, 1468, 1481. Zhu and Ye, "Peidu zhi de xingcheng yu zuoyong," 64.

52 *Jiu Wudai shi*, 94, 404, 421, 1005, 1006, 1323, 1331, 1335, 1468, 1474.

53 They include the Wu Kingdom and Shu Kingdom, the Jin dynasty, and a number of regional regimes in the Period of Disunion.

54 Zhou Baozhu, *Songdai Dongjing yanjiu*, 20–21.

55 *Songshi*, 2103–5.

56 Bi Yuan, *Xu zizhi tongjian*, 202–3; Zhou Cheng, *Song Dongjing kao*, 7–8.

57 Zhou Cheng, *Song Dongjing kao*, 6–8; *Songshi*, 155.

58 *Songshi*, 2105, 10209.

59 Wang Mingsun, *Song Liao Jin Yuan shi*, 32.

60 *Songshi*, 3959–60.

61 Deng Guangming, ed., *Zhongguo lishi dacidian: Songshi*, 16. I have not found any source on the Western Capital Censorate. The Southern Capital Censorate and the Northern Capital Censorate were established in 1045 and 1047 respectively. See *Song huiyao jigao*, Vol. 15, 7331–32.

62 *Song huiyao jigao*, Vol. 15, 7330.

63 *Songshi*, 2105.

64 For a complete history of the Southern Tang dynasty, see Johannes Kurt, *China's Southern Tang Dynasty, 937–976*; Ren Shuang, *Nan Tang shi*.

65 The head of the regency was first a supervisor (*gongshi*) and then a regent (*liushou*). *Songshi*, 2186.

66 Jiang, *Nanjing shihua*, 98.

67 Mote, "The Transformation of Nanking," 131.

68 Karl Wittfogel and Feng Chia-sheng write that the *Liaoshi* relates that the Liao five-capital system was modeled upon that of the Bohai Kingdom, but there is no such a record in the source they cite (37.2). See Wittfogel and Feng, *History of*

The Secondary Capital System 39

Chinese Society: Liao (907–1125), 448. However, it seems reasonable to suppose that the Liao was influenced by the five-capital system of Bohai.

69 Before it received its present name in 938, the capital city, established by Liao Taizu in 918, was called "imperial Capital" (Huangdu). *Liaoshi*, 438.

70 The Middle Capital of the Liao was established in 1007. *Liaoshi*, 481–82.

71 The capital status of the city was established during the reign of Liao Taizong (928–46). *Liaoshi*, 493–94.

72 The Western Capital was created in 1044. *Liaoshi*, 506.

73 *Liaoshi*, 438.

74 Capital officials were those whose responsibilities were restricted to the capital city itself, whereas the court officials were those whose jurisdiction was the whole country.

75 It was composed of left grand councilors (*zuoxiang*), right grand councilors (*youxiang*), a left manager of government affairs (*zuo pingzhang zhengshi*) and a right manager of government affairs (*you pingzhang zhengshi*). Wittfogel and Feng, 488. It is not certain whether or not the Western Capital also had the office of the Grand Councilors. The wording of the record in *Liaoshi* (802–3) is unclear. Yang Shunfa holds that the three capitals (which had the office of the Grand Councilors) were Upper, Western, and Eastern Capitals. See his "Liao Jin difang zhengzhi zhidu zhi yanjiu," in Songshi zuotanhui, ed., *Songshi yanjiu ji*, Vol. 11, 362–8.

76 They were the Tax Commission (*hubushi si*) at the Eastern Capital, Revenue Commission (*duzhishi si*) at the Middle Capital, Finance Commission (*san si*) and Fiscal Commission (*zhuanyun si*) at the Southern Capital, and Accounting Commission (*ji si*) at the Western Capital. *Liaoshi*, 803.

77 They were the Palace Visitors Bureau (*neikesheng*), Visitors Bureau (*kesheng*), Palace Service Office (*neishengsi*), offices of Inspector-in-chief (*du yuhou si*), Police Commission (*jingxun Yuan*), Supervisory Commission (*chuzhi si*), and Capital School (*jingxue*). *Liaoshi*, 802–3.

78 *Liaoshi*, 802–3; Jagchid Sechin, *Essays in Mongolian Studies*, 27.

79 *Liaoshi*, 801.

80 Sechin, *Essays in Mongolian Studies*, 26.

81 Many tend to accept the explanation from the *Jinshi* (549) that "following the Liao government system, the Jin established five capitals (*xi Liao zhi, jian wu jing*)." The compilers of *Jinshi* said so because they did not include the primary capital of the dynasty, the Central Capital (Zhongdu). It seems odd that the same writers who accept and state that the Jin had five capitals do count both the primary and secondary capitals or both *jing* and *du* when they calculate the number of the capitals of other dynasties, such as, the five capitals of the Liao dynasty. See, for example, Chen Gaohua and Shi Weimin, *Yuan Shangdu*, 10.

82 The city was made the Upper Capital of the Liao in 1138. When Prince of Haining (*r.* 1149–61) moved the court to Beijing and established the Central Capital there in 1153, the Upper Capital was deprived of its title. Twenty years later in 1173 it was renamed Upper Capital. *Jinshi*, 555.

83 It was the Eastern Capital of the Liao. *Jinshi*, 555.

84 The Middle Capital of the Liao retained that title in the early years of the Jin. In 1153 it was renamed the Northern Capital, *Jinshi*, 557.

85 It was also the Western Capital of the Liao. *Jinshi*, 564.

86 Bianjing, as it was called in the early years of the Jin, was made Southern Capital in 1153. *Jinshi*, 587.

87 The regency officials included one regent who was concurrently the military commandant of the capital route (*bingma duzongguan*), one associate regent (*tongzhi liushoushi*) who also held the position of military commandant, one assistant regent (*fuliushou*) who was concurrently the deputy military commandant, one administrative assistant (*liushou panguan*), one administrative assistant of the chief

40 *The Secondary Capital System*

area command, one Judge (*tuiguan*) who was charged with handling judicial matters, and one warder(*siyu*). Under these major officials were a certain number of Jurchen and Han Chinese warden clerks, two to three interpreters (*yiren*), two interpreter-clerks (*tongshi*) for each of the five capitals, two law clerks (*zhifa*, one Jurchen and one Chinese), one copyist clerk (*chaoshi*) and 100 ordinary clerks (*gongshi*) for each of the five auxiliary capitals. *Jinshi*, 1035–6.

88 The staff of a route normally included a fiscal commissioner (*zhuanyun shi*), who was in general charge of fiscal affairs, and a judicial commissioner (*tixing shi*) or surveillance commissioner (*ancha shi*) or agricultural development commissioner (*quannong shi*). See *A Dictionary of Official Titles in Imperial China*, 55–6.

89 *Yuanshi*, 1347, 1350.

90 For example, in the first month of 1307, 18,500 soldiers were dispatched to build the palaces. *Yuanshi*, 484.

91 *Yuanshi*, 480, 484, 500, 502, 503, and 525; Chen Gaohua, "Zhongdu de xingfei," *Wenwu chunqiu*, 3 (1998), 17–18.

92 *Yuanshi*, 537.

93 For the granting of appanages to the imperial family members during the period of Ginggis and Ogodei Khans, see Zhou Liangxiao, "Yuandai touxia fenfeng zhidu chutan," in *Yuanshi luncong*, No. 2, 53–76; Elizabeth Endicott-West, *Mongolian Rule in China: Local Administration in the Yuan Dynasty*, 89–90.

94 Emperor Renzong decreed that "the princes and imperial relatives should come to the Upper Capital to be admitted in audience. They should not frequently come down to the capital (i.e. Beijing). If they have urgent matters to be dealt with, they should send envoys to (Kaiping to) report." *Yuanshi*, 565.

95 According to Wang Yun (1227–1304), in the Yuan period, three activities were essential to the life of the Mongol ruling class: conquest, hunting, and banquetting. After conquering China and its neighboring countries, the Mongol emperors paid special attention to the holding of banquets and hunting. Wang Yun, *Qiujian xiansheng daquanji*, 580.

96 Zhou Boqi, *Jinguang ji*, 1.8; Chen and Shi, *Yuan Shangdu*, 133–34.

97 Exceptions were: the khurilitai for Taidingdi was held at the Longju River in the northern Mongolian area; for Wenzong at Beijing; for Mingzong (*r*. 1329), Wenzong's brother, at Khorakorum (Helin). Chen and Shi, *Yuan Shandu*, 54–56.

98 Zhang Yanghao, *Guitian leigao*, 18.1a. Modern meteorological observation indicates that the average temperature in July in the Kaiping area is 18.5 Celsius, whereas that in Beijing is 26 Celsius. Beijing ribao, ed., *Beijing zhinan*, 59–60.

99 Xiong Mengxiang, *Xijin zhi jiyi*, 204 and 221; Chen and Shi, *Yuan Shangdu*, 59–60.

100 To name a few: offices such as Secretariat (*zhongshu sheng*), Bureau of Military Affairs (*shumi yuan*), Censorate (*yushi tai*), Grand Agricultural Administration (*daisinong si*), Hanlin and Historiography Academy (*hanlin guoshi yuan*), Academy of Scholarly Worthies (*jixian yuan*), Commission for Buddhist and Tibetan Affairs (*xuanzheng yuan*), Palace Provisions Commission (*xuanhui yuan*). Chen and Shi, *Yuan Shangdu*, 85.

101 Huang Jin, *Jinhua Huang xiansheng wenji*, 8.87; Wang Shidian and Shang Qiweng, *Mishujian zhi*, 56.

102 Such as, managers of government affairs (*pingzhang zhenshi*) or right councilors (*youcheng*) and left councilors (*zuocheng*).

103 Such as, director (*zhongshu ling*), right grand councilor, left grand councilor, manager of government affairs, right councilors, and left councilors.

104 *Yuanshi*, 3637.

105 Chen and Shi, *Yuan Shangdu*, 61–62.

106 They included the Upper Capital Fiscal Commission (*Shangdu zhuanyunsi*), the Upper Capital Herds Office (*Shangdu qunmu du zhuanyunsi*), and the Upper Capital Supervisorate of Mining (*Shangdu yinye tijusi*).

The Secondary Capital System   41

107 For example, the branch office of the Bureau of Transmission (*tongzhengyuan*).

108 Such as the Upper Capital Supervisorate of All Classes of Artisans (*guanling Shangdu quelinkou zhuse renjiang tijusi*). For the details of the establishment of official apparatuses in the Upper Capital, see Ye Xingmin, "Yuan Shangdu de guanshu," *Nei Menggu daxue xuebao*, No. 1 (1983), 85–92.

109 The predecessor of the regency was the Kaiping prefecture, which in 1260 was staffed by one overseer (*daluhuachi*) and one general administrator (*zongguan*). In 1281 the capital itself was placed under the control of the Upper Capital Regency. *Yuanshi*, 1347–50.

110 *Yuanshi*, 2297–98.

111 They included the Chief Military Commission of the Brave as Tigers Imperial Guards (*huben qinjun du zhihuishisi*), the Upper Capital Warden's Office (*Shangdu bingmasi*), the Upper Capital Police Commission (*Shangdu jingxunyuan*), the Imperial Regalia Office (*yiluanju*), the Commercial Tax Supervisorate (*shuike tijusi*) and another ten or so offices. Ye, "Yuan Shangdu de guanshu", 79–85. For more on the Upper Capital, see Chen Gaohua and Shi Weimin, *Yuandai Dadu Shangdu yanjiu*, 142–295; Ye Xinmin, *Yuan Shangdu yanjiu*, 1–280.

112 *MS*, 912.

113 Farmer, *Early Ming Government*, 49.

114 Farmer, *Early Ming Government*, 180–81.

115 Farmer, *Early Ming Government*, 50.

116 *MS*, 912. For a complete history of the creation, construction, and abandonment of the Ming Middle Capital, see Wang Jianying, *Ming Zhongdu yanjiu*, 18–441.

117 *DMHD*, 1705; *MS*, 1076, 2216; Tan Qian, *Guoque*, 3578.

118 *DMHD*, 1705; Sun Wenlong, *Chengtian fuzhi*, 2.21a.

119 Farmer, *Early Ming Government*, 44.

120 Farmer, *Early Ming Government*, 45.

121 Farmer, *Early Ming Government*, 33.

122 Farmer, *Early Ming Government*, 42.

123 Carrington Goodrich and Chaoying Fang, eds, *Dictionary of Ming Biography*, xiv.

124 For a detailed discussion of the considerations on the move of the primary capital to the north, see Farmer, *Early Ming Government*, 148–72.

125 Goodrich and Fang, *Dictionary of Ming Biography*, xiv.

126 *MSL: Taizong*, 2229.

127 For a detailed study of the Beijing Branch Ministry, see Xu Hong, "Ming Beijing xingbu kao," *Hanxue yanjiu*, 2:2 (Dec. 1984), 569–96.

128 *MS*, 1738–39.

129 *MS*, 1836.

130 Li Xu, *Jie'an laoren manbi*, 68.

131 *MS*, 111.

132 *MS*, 1836.

133 *MS*, 115.

134 *MS*, 312.

135 Since the Middle Capital and the Flourishing Capital existed largely in name only and did not play significant roles in the political, military and financial affairs of the dynasty, I exclude them from further discussion.

136 *MS*, 1832.

137 The Manchus established three capitals in 1634: Flourishing Capital (Xingjing) in Hetuala, Eastern Capital (Dongjing) in Liaoyang, and Grand Capital (Shengjing) in Shenyang. Although the Qing government did not renounce Hetuala's auxiliary capital status after 1644, it did not maintain a capital administration there either. See Ding Haibin, *Qingdai peidu Shengjing yanjiu*, 12–13.

138 The central offices in Shengjing were established in 1657. At the beginning there were only ministries of Revenue, Rites, Justice, and Works. The Ministry of War in

42 The Secondary Capital System

Shengjing was created in 1691. *Qingchao xu wenxian tongkao*, 84.5614. In the late Qing reforms of 1905 all five ministerships in Shengjing were abolished and ministerial affairs were placed under the supervision of the Shengjing General. Two years later the position of Shengjing General was abolished and replaced by the newly created post of Governor of Northeast Provinces. Liu Jinzao, *Qingchao xu wenxian tongkao*, 129.8896; Jin Yufu, *Fengtian tongzhi*, 1077.

139 I.e., the Court of Judicial Review, the Court of Imperial Entertainment, the Court of Imperial Sacrifices, the Court of State Ceremonial, and the Court of Imperial Stud.

140 I.e., the Directorate of Astronomy and the Directorate of Education.

141 In 1730, a minister was appointed to supervise the bureaucratic operation of all the five ministries, but this position was soon abolished. See Liu, *Qingchao xu wenxian tongkao*, 129.8895.

142 Liu, *Qingchao xu wenxiao tongkao*, 79.5588.

143 Liu, *Qingchao xu wenxiao tongkao*, 79.5588.

144 *Da Qing huidian*, 17.19a.

145 *Da Qing huidian*, 215.1a–21a; Liu, *Qingchao xu wenxian tongkao*, 5588.

146 They were the tombs of Nurhachi (r. 1616–26), his son Huang Taiji (r. 1626–43) and Nurhachi's ancestors.

147 *Da Qing huidian*, 216.1a–3b. Under the ministry were two bureaus: the Left Bureau (*zuo si*) and the Right Bureau (*you si*), each of which was staffed with one director and two vice directors. Liu, *Qingchao xu wenxian tongkao*, 5588. The other staff in the ministry included one secretary, eight prayer readers (*duzhuguan*), sixteen ceremonial assistants (*zanlilang*), two officials with the rank of grade 6 and grade 7 respectively, four instructors second class (*zhujiao*), three Korea Affairs officials, and ten clerks. The total number of the ministry bureaucrats was 51. Of the various yearly sacrificial activities, the most important were four sacrifices to the three tombs during the Qingming Festival, the Zhongyuan Festival (mid-seventh month), the Winter Solstice, and at the end of the year. Smaller-scale sacrifices were held on the first day of the tenth month and the birthday of the reigning emperor. There were also other kinds of sacrifices to deities such as the deity of Mount Changbai and guardian deity Guandi. *Da Qing huidian*, 216.1a–5a.

148 *Da Qing huidian*, 218.1a. It consisted of four bureaus: bureaus of the Rear, Front, Left, and Right. *Qingchao xu wenxian tongkao*, 5588.

149 *Da Qing huidian*, 219, 1a–7b. Its subordinate bureaus were the Bureau of the Left and the Bureau of the Right. Liu, *Qingchao xu wenxian tongkao*, 5588.

150 The calculation is mine. For the detail of the distribution of the military personnel in Manchuria, see *Da Qing huidian*, 217.13a–15b. The account in *Shengu* is different from that in the *Da Qing huidian*. It records that around 13,000 cavalrymen, 1,750 foot soldiers, and 540 naval personnel were garrisoned in Manchuria. See Yang Tonggui, ed., *Shengu*, 1.10b.

151 *Da Qing huidian*, 217.1a. Under it were two functional bureaus: the Left Bureau and the Right Bureau, each of which was supervised by one director, two vice directors and one secretary. Liu, *Qingchao xu wenxian tongkao*, 5588.

152 For details of the Qing imperial tours to Shengjing, see Wang Peihuan, *Qingdi dongxunn*; Ding Haibin and Si Yi, *Qingdai peidu Shengjing yanjiu*, 228–54.

153 Liu, *Qingchao xu wenxian tongkao*, 5588. Other well-known measures included the building of the Manchu Great Wall, the "Willow Palisade" (*liutiaobian*), to prevent the migration of Han Chinese. The border was built on an earthen dike one meter wide and one meter high. Willow trees were planted on top of the dike. Outside the willow tree dike was a ditch of eight Chinese inches (*chi*) deep, with a width of five *chi* and at the bottom and eight *chi* at the top. The western end of the Willow Palisade started from Fenghuangcheng (present-day Fengcheng, Liaoning) and ended at Weiyuanbo. Its eastern end began at Weiyuanbao and stopped at

Shanghai Pass, with a total length of more than 1900 *li*. See Yang Shusen, *Qingdai liutiaobian*, 31–4.

154 One of the possible reasons is that the retention of the previous capital would ward off criticism of those who were against the change of capital locations.

155 Ding Haibin classifies non-primary capitals of pre-modern China into six groups. See "Lun Zhongguo gudai peidu xianxiang," *Shehui kexue zhanxian*, No. 1 (2011), 81–4.

2   Ministers and Eunuchs
The Southern Capital administration

As suggested in the preceding chapter, the secondary capital system of the Ming dynasty was the most elaborate in imperial China. Almost all of the government departments belonging to the Beijing administration existed in Nanjing. This chapter examines the bureaucratic apparatuses and staffing levels for the civil and military offices, as well as for the eunuch household departments in Nanjing, and briefly explores the principal administrative responsibilities of the various Nanjing agencies. It also discusses the leadership of the Nanjing administration and reviews the reductions and restorations of the various Nanjing offices in the post-1421 Ming dynasty.

1. The civil bureaucracy

Like the military and eunuch establishments in Nanjing, the civil bureaucratic apparatuses in the post-1421 Southern Capital were almost identical to those of the Northern Capital, as shown by tables 1 and 2.

The tables make two points clear. First, the Southern Capital administration retained almost all of the bureaucratic departments that existed in the Northern Capital. Although the "Monograph on Offices" (*baiguanzhi*) in the *Official History of the Ming Dynasty* (*Mingshi*) does not mention the Nanjing Directorate of Imperial Parks (*shanglinyuan*), the Nanjing Music Office (*jiaofangsi*), or the Nanjing Central Drafting Office (*zhongshuke*), records in other Ming sources testify to the existence of the three, at least prior to the seventeenth century. The Nanjing Music Office and the Nanjing Central Drafting Office were noted in the *Collected Statutes of the Ming Dynasty*.[1] A blaze which occurred in the Nanjing Music Office in 1523, and which was recorded by the late Ming historian Tan Qian (1594–1657), provides an additional piece of evidence as to the existence of the agency.[2] The *Gazetteer of the Nanjing Directorate of Imperial Parks* (*Nanjing Shanglinyuan zhi*), compiled and published in the Ming, also indicates the existence of an office in charge of imperial parks and gardens in Nanjing.[3]

Second, although the bureaucratic apparatuses of the Northern and Southern Capital administrations were generally identical, the staffing levels in the two capitals were not symmetrical. As shown in the tables, the number of graded officials and functionaries in Nanjing was fewer than in Beijing. Table 2.1 reveals that the number of administrative officials at the various Nanjing offices was approximately one third of that in the Beijing departments, and Table 2.2 indicates that the number of clerks in Nanjing was close to half of that in Beijing. Unlike in Beijing, where a ministry was supervised by one minister (*shangshu*) and two vice ministers, a senior vice minister of the left (*zuoshilang*) and junior vice minister of the right (*youshilang*), a ministry in Nanjing was administered by only one minister and one vice minister of the right.[4] As for the bureaus under a ministry, in Beijing they were normally administered by one director (*langzhong*),[5] one vice director (*yuanwailang*),[6] and a number of secretaries (*zhushi*),[7] whereas in Nanjing, in most cases a bureau was staffed by one director and one to three secretaries.[8] The vice directorship was only retained in certain bureaus.[9] Similarly, the number of administrative officials and clerks in the other Nanjing departments was, in most cases, reduced to half of that in Beijing.

For obvious reasons, the governmental agencies that were closely associated to the emperor, the heir apparent, the royal family, and their activities had only nominal staffing levels in the Southern Capital. Agencies such as the Court of the Imperial Clan (*zongrenfu*), the Seal Office (*shangbaosi*), and the Office of Princely Affairs (*zhanshifu*) each had one official administering its affairs in Nanjing.[10] The Hanlin Academy, an agency providing literary and scholarly assistance of all kinds to the emperor and the court, had – owing to the absence of the emperor – only two officials in Nanjing.[11] It appears that the retention of these offices was primarily for the purpose of maintaining a bureaucracy for the Southern Capital equivalent to that of its northern counterpart.

The other similarity between the two capital administrations was the identical substructure of the governmental departments. For example, the Nanjing ministries of Revenue and Justice, like their counterparts in the Beijing administration, were comprised of thirteen bureaus named after the thirteen provinces in the empire. The ministries of Personnel, Rites, War, and Works in Nanjing were all constituted of four subordinate bureaus like those in Beijing.

The official ranks and emoluments at the two capitals were identical as well. For instance, a minister at both capitals enjoyed the same rank of grade 2a, a vice minister the rank of grade 3a, a director and vice director of a bureau the same rank of grade 5a and 5b respectively. This was applicable to the rest of the governmental departments at Nanjing and Beijing.[12] In theory, the remuneration and benefits enjoyed by the officials of identical rank in both capitals were the same. In practice, the Nanjing officials, at least at certain periods, were treated less favorably. As revealed in a memorial of 1435 by Zhang Ying (1375–1436), grand secretary and minister of rites, after the Yongle era, Nanjing officials with the ranks of grade 6 and below received 20 percent of their salary in rice and 80 percent in paper money, whereas officials in Beijing with the same ranks received 40 percent in rice and 60 percent in currency. Considering the unstable monetary system of the dynasty, the treatment of lower-ranking officials in Beijing was preferential.[13]

46   Ministers and Eunuchs

Table 2.1 The civil offices and the staffing levels of officials (*guan*) in the Beijing and Nanjing administrations (late Ming)

Agency	No. of officials (Beijing)	No. of officials (Nanjing)
Imperial Clan Court	5	1
Ministry of Personnel	19	9
Ministry of Revenue	103	52
Ministry of Rites	23	13
Ministry of Wars	26	17
Ministry of Justice	61	36
Ministry of Works	64	26
Censorate	123	37
Office of Transmission	8	4
Court of Judicial Review	15	9
Office of Princely Affairs	30	1
Hanlin Academy	29+	2
National University	40	17
Court of Imperial Sacrifices	131	26
Court of Imperial Entertainments	22	7
Court of Imperial Stud	10	4
Court of State Ceremonial	69	17
Seal Office	6	1
Offices of Scrutiny	55	7
Central Drafting Office	22+	?
Messenger Offices	40	1
Directorate of Astronomy	22	8
Imperial Academy of Medicine	27	4
Directorate of Imperial Parks	19	?
Registry of the Nanjing Guards	10	48
Warden's Offices of the Five Wards	30	15
Central Buddhist Registry	8	8
Central Daoist Registry	19	8
Music Office	7	?
Total	1043	378

Notes: (a) *MS* is the preferred source in this chapter because it was compiled in 1679 and printed in 1736 and reflects the vicissitudes of the central bureaucracy that occurred in the late Ming. *DMHD*, published in 1587, and *NJLBZ*, in print in 1587 and revised in 1622, lack information on the Ming bureaucracy after 1587 and 1622 respectively. It should be noted that the accounts in the three sources often are not identical. I shall point out the discrepancies later in the discussion of each individual office. (b) Throughout the Ming there were a number of efforts by the central government to reduce its bureaucracy, especially in the two national capitals. The figures listed here are the final ones (which exclude all of the abolished positions). (c) "+" indicates that the number was not precisely fixed; the actual figure was often higher than that shown in the table. (d) Officials from the two prefectures (Shuntian and Yingtian) where Beijing and Nanjing were located and the two Capital Guard military schools (*jingwei wuxue*) are excluded from this table. (e) *MS* contains no information about the Central Buddhist Registry and Central Daoist Registry in Nanjing; the figures of these two offices are from *DMHD* and *NJLBZ*.

Table 2.2 The staffing levels of the lesser functionaries (*li*) in the Beijing and Nanjing administrations (1587)

Agency	No. of clerks (Beijing)	No. of clerks
(Nanjing)		
Imperial Clan Court	3	1
Ministry of Personnel	43	18
Ministry of Revenue	238	127
Ministry of Rites	48	21
Ministry of Wars	238	83
Ministry of Justice	187	105
Ministry of Works	118	55
Censorate	179+	103
Office of Transmission	24	12
Court of Judicial Review	37	15
Office of Princely Affairs	6	1
Court of Imperial Sacrifices	7	5
Court of Imperial Entertainments	17	13
Court of Imperial Stud	23	12
Court of State Ceremonial	8	4
National University	4	4
Hanlin Academy	1	1
Directorate of Astronomy	4	3
Imperial Academy of Medicine	9	4
Directorate of Imperial Parks	21	?
Messenger Office	1	1
Total	1216	587

Notes: (a) *MS* does not contain information on the functionaries in the two capitals. Although *DMHD* cannot provide the changes that occurred in the late Ming, it does provide a clue to the distribution of the functionaries in the two capitals. (b) "+" means that the number was not exactly fixed; the actual figure was often higher than that shown in the table. (c) Shuntian and Yingtian prefectures are excluded from this table.

The territorial jurisdiction of many Southern Capital offices was restricted to the Southern Capital and the Southern Metropolitan Area. For example, the Nanjing Ministry of Rites and those agencies loosely subordinate or attached to it[14] were generally responsible for holding sacrificial ceremonies and monitoring the Daoist and Buddhist communities in the Southern Capital and its surrounding area.[15] The Nanjing Ministry of Works was responsible for maintaining the Ancestral Temple, the Altar of Soil and Grain, the city walls, the civil, military, and eunuch offices in Nanjing, and the imperial tombs.[16] It was also concerned with repairing bridges and waterways in the Nanjing area and, in cooperation with the Nanjing Ministry of War, producing ships and other vessels for the Nanjing offices and guard units.[17]

Some Southern Capital departments, while assuming primary responsibilities for managing Nanjing and Nan Zhili area, had broader territorial jurisdiction and exercised their power in the south of the empire. Among them were the Nanjing Ministry of War, the Ministry of Justice, the Ministry of Personnel,

48   Ministers and Eunuchs

and the Court of the Imperial Stud. For example, the Nanjing Ministry of War, considered the most prominent ministry in the Southern Capital administration,[18] was charged with maintaining stability in south China. The suppression of popular uprisings and piracy in the southwestern provinces and the southeastern coastal area was largely its responsibility.[19] The Nanjing Court of the Imperial Stud (*taipusi*), an affiliate of the Nanjing Ministry of War, was charged with administering the horse pasturage around the northern and southern banks of the Yangzi River, whereas its counterpart in the Northern Capital administration managed those in Bei Zhili, Henan, and Shandong.[20]

The Nanjing National University was largely responsible for training students and provincial degree holders (*juren*) from the south, the so-called *Nantu zhi shi*, whereas its counterpart in the north, the Beijing National University, primarily admitted northerners (*Beishi*). For example, in the case of those *juren* who did not pass the metropolitan examination and who wanted to further their studies, the Nanjing National University primarily accepted those who were from the south.[21] The students dispatched by the governments of Japan, Ryukyu, and Siam were often enrolled in the Nanjing National University.[22] In 1482, the university received five Ryukyu students.[23] The north-south division between the Beijing and Nanjing National Universities is illustrated by the story of Yang Ding (fl. 1436). A *juren* from Shaanxi who was told that he "should enter the Beijing National University according to the precedents" (*lidang ru Beijian*), Yang instead requested to be enrolled in the Nanjing National University. His justification was that he wanted to study under Chen Jingzong (1377–1459), the president of the university and a nationally renowned scholar whom Yang admired. His request, deemed as sincere, was granted as an exception.[24]

In general, the Nanjing Ministry of Justice was in charge of judicial matters pertaining to the Nanjing offices, the dukes, marquises, earls, the Five Chief Military Commissions, and the guards in the Southern Capital region.[25] However, records in some Ming sources indicate that the ministry also handled judicial matters in the southern provinces of the realm. For example, in 1593 Wang Jiao (1521–99), the minister of the Nanjing Court of Judicial Review, asked to commute the sentence of nine criminals convicted by the Nanjing Ministry of Justice, one being a native of Min county, Fujian.[26] In 1594, one of two criminals who received capital sentences from the Nanjing Ministry of Justice was from Jingxian, Jiangxi.[27] In these two cases, the criminals were tried by the bureaus which bore the names of the provinces the criminals hailed from, the Fujian and Jiangxi bureaus of the ministry respectively.

In the Yongle era, the Nanjing Ministry of Justice could not issue an execution order without the consent of its Beijing counterpart. Criminals who received the death penalty from the Nanjing ministry were required to be brought to Beijing with their files. They were examined and a final decision was made as to their fate by the Ministry of Justice there. After the Xuande era, the Nanjing Ministry of Justice was allowed to mete out the capital punishment to criminals in its custody so long as they were reviewed by the Nanjing Court of Judicial Review and reported to the Ministry of Justice in Beijing later on.[28]

The main responsibility of the Nanjing Ministry of Personnel was to evaluate the middle and lower ranking officials in the Southern Capital administration once every six years.[29] Those officials with the rank of grade 4 and above were only required to submit self-evaluations (*zichen*) to the court, and those of grade 5 and below were reviewed by the Nanjing Ministry of Personnel.[30] The Beijing Ministry of Personnel held the final authority over promoting and demoting those middle- and lower-ranking Nanjing officials, but the decisions were based on the evaluation reports provided by its southern counterpart.[31] The usual practice was for the Nanjing Ministry of Personnel to evaluate the Nanjing officials and issue them a sealed evaluation report (*jiyou*) containing a brief biography and record of the official's activities, both positive and negative.[32] The official had to present this in person to the Bureau of Evaluation of the Beijing Ministry of Personnel within three month of the issuance. A delay in presenting the evaluation report would render the official subject to punishment. As a case in point, Fang Zhongchong, the instructor (*zhujiao*) at the Nanjing National University, was given his evaluation report in the tenth month of 1542. He reported to the Bureau of Evaluation in Beijing in the eighth month of the following year and was transferred to the Ministry of Justice to stand trial for his ten-month delay.[33]

Although the Nanjing Ministry of Personnel did not have the last word in the fate of Nanjing officials, it did possess the power to examine the evaluation reports of lesser functionaries from the provinces of Guangdong, Guangxi, Sichuan, Zhejiang, Jiangxi, Huguang, and Fujian and from Suzhou and Songjiang prefectures in Nan Zhili, all in south China. This authority was extended to the ministry only gradually. During the Yongle era, the ministry was charged with examining functionaries from Guangxi and Sichuan. In 1435, the power was extended to include examining clerks from prefectures in Jiangxi, Fujian, and Huguang provinces. In the following year the office gained jurisdiction over the assessment of the functionaries from a few more prefectures in Huguang and Fujian. In 1490 and 1497 these duties were further expanded, and in 1506, Zhejiang, Jiangxi, Huguang, Fujian, and Suzhou and Songjiang in Nan Zhili were also included.[34] Thus, by the middle of the dynasty, the Nanjing Ministry of Personnel was responsible for the evaluations of clerks from roughly half the country. As Wang Zhi (1379–1462), the author of Huang Fu's biography, remarked, "although the Nanjing [Ministry of Personnel] has no responsibility for selecting officials (i.e. has no power to promote and demote officials), it is busied with controlling the clerks."[35]

A few Southern Capital departments had certain national roles to play. For instance, in addition to collecting part of the grain taxes of Nan Zhili, Zhejiang, Jiangxi, and Huguang, the four most advanced and prosperous provinces in the Ming empire,[36] the Nanjing Ministry of Revenue had various less prominent national functions, including the collection of sundry miscellaneous taxes, issuing salt certificates (*yanyin*) nationwide,[37] and administering and storing the Yellow Registers (*huangce*) or local cadastral records of the whole empire.[38]

50   *Ministers and Eunuchs*

The power of the Nanjing Censorate and the Six Offices of Scrutiny was even less restricted. Officials from those offices, especially censors and speaking secretaries, scrutinized and impeached officials in both the capitals and the provinces. One of the motives behind this procedure was to attract the attention of the emperor and eventually to obtain promotion. Some achieved what they sought but many suffered demotion and other kinds of punishment as a result of their audacity. For example, the Nanjing censor Zeng Jun (*jinshi* 1532) successively impeached a variety of prominent Nanjing and Beijing officials, including Nanjing Minister of War Liu Long (1477–1553), and Censor-in-Chief and River Controller (*caojiang duyushi*) Cai Jin. But he failed to bring down Guo Xun, Duke of Yi, Yan Song (1480–1565), minister of rites in Beijing, or Jiang Gan, vice minister of works and the grand coordinator (*xunfu*) of the Yan'an-Suiyuan area. Zeng garnered considerable fame for his actions.[39] Li Xi was an example of a Nanjing censor who suffered both politically and physically for his impeachment. He was arrested and beaten for impeaching Liu Jin (1451–1510), a powerful eunuch chief and an unassailable target in the early Zhengde era.[40]

Although the Southern Capital administration largely took care of affairs in the south, especially those in Nanjing and the Southern administration, it does not mean that the Southern Capital mainly employed natives of the south and the Northern Capital chiefly recruited those from the north, due to mutual prejudice and a sense of slight between certain southern and northern residents.[41] Owing to economic prosperity and wealth, the south was more culturally developed than the north. Some southerners looked down on northerners, who in turn bore resentment against them. These feelings of slight and resentment among the residents of the south and the north was even shared by many Ming officials. The financial and cultural imbalance between the two regions also struck a Korean official, who was caught up in a storm and driven to China in the late fifteenth century. The visible differences recorded by the Korean covered the residences, customs, dress, literacy levels, temperaments, and manners of the people. On the contrary, as the recruitment of Ming officials was highly centralized, many southerners became powerful officials in Beijing, notably Yan Song of Jiangxi and Zhang Juzheng (1525–82) of Huguang, and numerous northerners were assigned to Nanjing, including Wang Shu (1416–1508) from Shaanxi.[42]

2. The military apparatuses

The structure of the military bureaucracy in the Southern Capital was also identical to that of the Northern Capital. In theory, the army in Nanjing was organized under two systems, the five Chief Military Commissions (*wujundu-dufu*) and the imperial guards (*qinjunwei* or *shangzhiwei*), which were theoretically under the direct control of the emperor.[43] However, in practice, owing to the absence of the emperor and court, the imperial guards in Nanjing were placed under the command of the head of the Chief Military Commission of the Center, who was concurrently the Nanjing grand commandant, a prominent member of the powerful military triumvirate in the Southern Capital.[44]

One of the more noteworthy military units in the Southern Capital was the Nanjing Embroidered-Uniform Guard (Nanjing Jinyiwei).[45] Students of Ming history are well aware that the Embroidered-Uniform Guard served as the first secret service and the most prestigious imperial bodyguard created by the Hongwu emperor, but few are aware that the guard continued in post-1421 Nanjing.[46] The extant and incomplete register of the Nanjing secret service guard, *Nanjing Jinyiwei xuanbu*, provides valuable information on its subordinate units: ten battalions of left, right, front, rear, center left, center right, farming, water force, and elephant training, as well as a prison management office (*zhenfusi*). Since there was no emperor to safeguard in the Southern Capital, the primary duties of the Nanjing Jinyiwei were probably intelligence gathering and population surveillance.[47]

As shown in Table 2.3, if we compare only the numbers of the guard units stationed within Beijing and Nanjing, the number of guards under the command of the five Nanjing Chief Military Commissions was impressive compared with the 81 units stationed in Beijing. However, the five Chief Military Commissions in Beijing also commanded the guard units across the empire, whereas the power of their Nanjing counterparts was restricted to leading the units garrisoned in Nanijng.

During the Ming, troop training was undertaken in all local garrison units, but special tactical training was the responsibility of the Three Great Training Divisions (*sandaying*): Shenji (firearms) Division, Sanqian (three thousand) Division, and Wujun (five armies) Division. The Three Great Divisions were just like other military offices in Beijing in having Nanjing counterparts.[48] The only difference was that the three Nanjing divisions bore different names: Dajiaochang (grand drill ground), Xiaojiaochang (small drill ground), and Shenji.[49] It seems that the three Nanjing divisions did not undergo a process of reorganization like their Beijing counterparts.[50] Troops from all over the empire were rotated to the training divisions in both Beijing and Nanjing, where they served as a reserve of combat-ready troops.

Table 2.3 The army stationed in the city of Beijing and city of Nanjing (units: Guard)

System	Beijing	Nanjing
Military Commission of the Left	6	10
Military Commission of the Right	3	5
Military Commission of the Center	4	5
Military Commission of the Front	3	7
Military Commission of the Rear	21	5
Imperial Guards	44	18
Total	81	50

Source: *MS,* 1860–5

52 Ministers and Eunuchs

The chief commanders of the guards and the training divisions in the Southern Capital were the grand commandant (*Nanjing shoubei*) and the vice grand commandant (*Nanjing xietong shoubei*). The post of grand commandant originated in 1421 when the Yongle emperor relocated his primary capital to Beijing. The commissioner-in-chief (*dudu*) of the Chief Military Commission of the Center in Nanijng was entrusted to "command" (*shoubei*) the Nanjing guard units. In 1424 the Hongxi emperor ordered the duke of Xiangcheng Li Long (d. 1447) to be the "Guard Defender" (*zhenshou*) of Nanjing, the title of which was changed to "Grand Commandant" (*shoubei*) in 1430.[51] The grand commandant was typically a duke (*gong*), marquis (*hou*), or earl (*bo*) who was concurrently head of the Nanjing Chief Military Commission of the Center. In his capacity as grand commandant and commander-in-chief of the Nanjing Chief Military Commission of the Center, he was the supreme commander of all the military forces in Nanjing. The troops under the other four Chief Military Commissions (the Right, Left, Front, and Rear) were also under his supervision.[52] The position of vice grand commandant was created in 1452.[53] It was also exclusively assumed by imperial nobles.[54] Presumably the vice grand commandant headed one of the other four Chief Military Commissions.

3. The eunuch establishment

Although there was no emperor or inner court in the post-1421 Southern Capital, the 24 palace eunuch departments (*ershisi yamen*) in Beijing still had their counterparts in Nanjing (see Table 2.4).[55]

Of them, the Twelve Directorates (*shi'er jian*) were the major units in which palace eunuchs were organized; each was supervised by a eunuch director (*taijian*) of grade 4a. Less notable agencies were the Four Offices (*si si*) which were headed by directors (*sizheng*) of grade 5a, and the Eight Services (*ba ju*) which were directed by commissioner-in-chief (*dashi*) of grade 5a.[56] The palace treasuries (*neifuku*) run by the eunuchs in Nanjing also numbered ten and bore the same names as those in Beijing: Neichengyun, Jiazi (number one), Yizi (number two), Bingzi (number three), Dingzi (number four), Wuzi (number five), Guangyin, Guanghui (treasury for the benevolent issuance of paper money), and Zangfa (depository for the confiscated property).[57]

As with its counterpart in Beijing, the Nanjing Directorate of Ceremonial was also the most prestigious and powerful of all 24 Nanjing eunuch agencies. Its director was concurrently the Nanjing eunuch grand commandant. The post was created in 1425, ten years before that of the grand adjutant, and 27 years prior to that of the vice grand commandant.[58] Although the eunuch grand commandant was an equal of the Nanjing grand commandant and the Nanjing minister of war, due to his close connection with the omnipotent eunuch chiefs in Beijing he was considered an "assignee" (*weicahi*) of the Directorate of Ceremonial in Beijing and was treated deferentially by his civil and military peers. Every month on the first and fifteenth day when the

Ministers and Eunuchs 53

Table 2.4 The 24 eunuch departments in both Beijing and Nanjing in the Ming

Directorate of Ceremonial (*silijian*)
Directorate for Imperial Accouterments (*yuyongjian*)
Directorate of Palace Eunuchs (*neiguanjian*)
Directorate of the Imperial Horses (*yumajian*)
Directorate for Imperial Regalia (*sishejian*)
Directorate of Palace Seals (*shangbaojian*)
Directorate for Imperial Temple (*shengongjian*)
Directorate of Imperial Delicacies (*shangshanjian*)
Directorate for Imperial Apparel (*shangyijian*)
Directorate for Credentials (*yinshoujian*)
Directorate for Palace Maintenance (*zhidianjian*)
Directorate for Intimate Attendance (*duzhijian*)
Firewood Office (*xixinsi*)
Paper Office (*baochaosi*)
Bells and Drums Office (*zhouggusi*)
Bathing Office (*huntangsi*)
Palace Armory Service (*bingzhangju*)
Caps and Kerchiefs Service (*jinmaoju*)
Sewing Service (*zhengongju*)
Palace Weaving and Dyeing Service (*neizhiranju*)
Condiments Service (*jiucumianju*)
Palace Laundry Service (*huanyiju*)
Garden Service (*siyuanju*) and Jewelry Service (*yinzuoju*)

Source: Liu, *Zhuozhong zhi*, 16.97; *Minggong shi*, 24; MS, 1818–20
Notes: After listing the names of the 24 eunuch agencies, Liu states that they also existed in Nanjing. At least six Nanjing eunuch directorates were mentioned by other Ming writers: the directorates of Ceremonial, Palace Eunuch, Imperial Horses, Credential, Imperial Delicacies, and Imperial Accoutrements. See Tan Qian, *Zaolin zazu*, 1 (zhiji), 22a–b; Shen Defu, *Wanli yehuobian*, 430–2; *DMHD*, 158.24b–30a.

eunuch grand commandant, the grand commandant, the Nanjing minister of war, and the heads of the other four Chief Military Commissions met in the office of the grant commandant, the eunuch grand commandant usually sat at the head of the table (*shouxi*).[59]

The Nanjing eunuch grand commandant was assisted by a number of deputies (*fu shoubei taijian*). The *Official History of the Ming Dynasty* relates that there was one eunuch grand commandant and one deputy eunuch grand commandant in Nanjing,[60] but it seems that this figure only reflects the reality of the early Ming. Starting from the Chenghua era, the number of grand commandants (including deputies) increased to three or four, and during the Zhengde reign rose to six or seven.[61]

The number of eunuchs employed in the Southern Capital varied over time as well. In the early Ming, the staff for each Nanjing eunuch agency was fixed at a low level, increased slightly during the Chenghua reign, and reduced in the Hongzhi era to the level of five to six men for each of the directorates (*jian*) and offices (*ju*) and three to four men for each of the palace storehouses (*kuchang*) and palace gates (*menguan*). Corresponding to the increase in

54 Ministers and Eunuchs

eunuch power and personnel during the domination of Liu Jin, the eunuch staffing level in the Southern Capital rose rapidly. The number of staff at each of the directorates and offices reached 10–12 and 17–18 at every palace gate.[62] In a memorial in the late 1510s, Nanjing Minister of War Chai Sheng (1456–1532) proposed that the number of Nanjing eunuchs be reduced to four for the Chengyun, Jiazi, Dingzi, and Guanghui treasuries and two for the remainder of the treasuries.[63] The large number of eunuchs was reflected to some extent by the volume of the tribute articles collected from the southern provinces and sent to the Northern Capital (see the enumeration below), and by the number of artisans employed and the storehouses run by these eunuch agencies. A Ming source records that prior to the Tianshun era, the Nanjing Directorate of Palace Eunuchs employed 3,900 artisans (both military and civilian), and the Hall of Sacrificial Silk (*shenbo tang*) of the Directorate of Ceremonial hired more than 400 households (1,140 households at its peak).[64] In 1442, a fire destroyed 60 rooms of the Nanjing Palace Treasury, including more than 700,000 wares, financial transaction records (*qianliang buji*), and armor.[65] In 1463, 660 storehouse rooms belonging to the Nanjing Directorate for Imperial Accoutrements were repaired.[66] This information reveals the scale of the eunuch household departments in Nanjing.

The huge eunuch presence in the Southern Capital reflects the omnipresent nature of the Ming eunuchs. From the Yongle reign onward, the eunuchs gradually became an institutionalized bureaucracy as indispensable in its own way as the regular bureaucracy. They were not only used to attend to the emperor, his family, palace compounds, and imperial mausoleums, but increasingly dispatched outside the palace, on a temporary basis, as special imperial agents to carry out diplomatic missions abroad, supervise military operations, command armies and navies, oversee tax collections, and handle various other matters.[67] On a permanent basis, in addition to those in the household departments in Beijing and Nanjing, eunuchs were also posted to the Flourishing Capital at Chengtian and Middle Capital at Fengyang to take care of the palace buildings in the two nominal capitals. The Maritime Trade Supervisorates (*shibo tijusi*) of the empire, established along the southeast and south seacoasts to collect customs duties and prevent the smuggling of contraband goods, were all under the control of the eunuchs.[68]

The primary responsibility of the eunuch agencies in the Southern Capital was to maintain the former imperial palace and tombs of the founding emperor and his eldest son Zhu Biao (1355–92), the so-called "*gongque lingqin*" (palaces and mausoleums).[69] Another major function of the Nanjing eunuch agencies was to exact local specialties from Nan Zhili and other southern provinces and to deliver them to the palace treasuries in Beijing.[70] Tan Qian's *Miscellaneous Notes from the Date Grove (Zaolin zazu)* enumerates the variety and annual amounts of local products collected and shipped by some of the Nanjing eunuch agencies. This reveals the scale of their working in Nanjing.

- The Directorate of Ceremonial: sacrificial silk (5 boats); writing brushes, ink sticks, inkslabs, and paper (3 boats);
- The Office of Eunuch Grand Commandant: fresh plums (8 boats), loquats (8 boats), red bayberries (8 boats), Chinese olives (6 boats), bamboo shoots (7 boats), osmanthus flowers (2 boats), pomegranates and persimmons (6 boats), tangerines and sugarcanes (1 boat);
- The Directorate of Delicacies: bamboo shoots (6 boats), crucian carps (14 boats), swans (3 boats), pickles (4 boats), candied cherries (4 boats), cake (8 boats), osmanthus flowers (4 boats), partridges and bustards (2 boats);
- The Garden Service: water chestnuts (4 boats), gingers and baby taros (5 boats), baby gingers (6 boats), lotus roots (5 boats), various fruits (6 boats);
- The Supply Storehouse of the Nanjing Palace Treasury: glutinous rice (6 boats), baby gingers (6 boats), various fruits (5 boats);
- The Directorate of the Imperial Horses: alfalfa (2 boats).[71]

4. The leadership of the Nanjing administration

Unlike the Northern Capital where the emperor resided, the Southern Capital did not have a paramount leader in Nanjing, and strictly speaking, there was no single person in Nanjing who supervised the three branches of civil, military, and eunuch officials.

All departments and officials in the Southern Capital were subject to the direction of the emperor in Beijing. They were responsible only to the emperor. The promotion, demotion, and appointment of Nanjing officials of grade 4 and above were decided by the emperor upon the recommendation of the grand secretaries. The Nanjing departments were the equals of the corresponding Beijing departments. In other words, they were not subordinate to their Beijing counterparts.

It appears that there were two informal collective leadership groups in the Southern Capital. The first, a civilian one, was formed by the chief officials (*tangshangguan*) of the civilian departments in the Nanjing administration, viz. those of the six ministries, the censorate, the office of transmission, the five courts, and other minor offices. Twice a month these dignitaries assembled to discuss routine matters, presumably of a civilian nature. Every year in the autumn, these chief officials gathered together with the heads of the Nanjing Court of Judicial Review to scrutinize and evaluate recommendations about judicial cases concerning serious criminals (*shenglu zhongqiu*).[72] Due to the lack of records from the available sources, it is uncertain who convened those regular meetings of senior officials.[73]

The second leadership group, a military one, was much smaller in size and was composed of the military leaders in the Southern Capital: the grand commandant, the heads of the other four Chief Military Commissions, the eunuch grand commandant, and the Nanjing minister of war. Like the civilian leaders, this group also convened fortnightly at the office of the grand

56 *Ministers and Eunuchs*

commandant, to discuss routine matters, probably military in nature.[74] Since one of the prominent roles of the Nanjing administration was to safeguard Nan Zhili and the south, it is reasonable to assume that the second leadership group enjoyed more power. The group was dominated by three individuals: the grand commandant, the eunuch grand commandant, and the Nanjing minister of war. The grand commandant, in his capacity as the commander-in-chief of the Nanjing Military Commission of the Center (*zhongjun dudufu*), and the head of all the five Nanjing Chief Military Commissions, was the leader of the Nanjing military forces. The eunuch grand commandant, in his capacity as the director of the Nanjing Directorate of Ceremonial, the most powerful eunuch agency in the Southern Capital, was the chief of all the eunuch departments in Nanjing. Although the Nanjing minister of war was by no means the head of the civil bureaucrats in Nanjing, his participation in the three-man informal leadership group was largely justified by the fact that his ministry was generally regarded as the most important one in the Nanjing civil bureaucracy and by his additional title as the grand adjutant (*canzan jiwu*).[75]

5. The reduction and restoration of the Nanjing offices

During the reigns of the emperors Zhengtong, Jiajing, Longqing, Wanli, and Chongzhen, numerous attempts were made by the Ming government to streamline its central and provincial governments. As part of the bureaucratic machine of the Ming state, the Southern Capital administration was no exception.

The first large-scale reduction of the Nanjing bureaucracy occurred in the second month of 1443, fifteen months after the final confirmation of the respective status of Beijing and Nanjing as the primary and auxiliary capitals of the empire.[76] At that time, two of the extremely powerful and highly competent Three Yangs, Yang Shiqi (1365–1444) and Yang Fu (1372–1446), still controlled the helm of the state.[77] The measure to reduce the size of the Nanjing administration was a continuation of the reforms initiated by the Three Yangs. In 1436, the first year of the Zhengtong era, 3,800 musicians from the Beijing Music Office were released from the palace and 17,000 laborers were freed from the construction of the imperial mausoleum.[78] Three years later, more office-holders were discharged from government service.[79] It is interesting to note that a bureau secretary at the Nanjing Ministry of Revenue memorialized the court that it was wasteful to maintain present staff levels. As a result, more than 100 middle- and low-level positions in the Southern Capital administration were eliminated. Chief among them were eight vice-directorships (from the Nanjing ministries of Personnel and Rites) and fourteen secretaries (from the Nanjing ministries of Revenue, War, and Justice). The other affected Nanjing offices included the Censorate and the courts of Judicial Review, Imperial Sacrifices, Imperial Entertainments, and State Ceremonial.[80]

During the Jiajing era, also as part of an overall effort to create a more effective and leaner Ming bureaucracy, the Nanjing administration was further downsized. In 1529, more than forty positions including twenty-one vice directorships from five Nanjing ministries were removed.[81] Of them, approximately a dozen positions were restored in the next two years.[82] At least another twenty-five middle and lower posts in the Nanjing administration were further abolished in 1558. Approximately a dozen offices were affected.[83]

The downsizing of the Southern Capital bureaucracy continued in the early Longqing era. In 1568, the vice minister's position in the Nanjing Court of the Imperial Stud was eliminated.[84] In the following year, the vice-directorship of the Guangxi Bureau and two secretariats (the bureaus of Guangxi and Guangdong respectively) at the Nanjing Ministry of Revenue were abolished.[85] In the third month of 1570, a dozen more positions in Nanjing were removed, which included a vice minister's post, a vice-directorship, bureau secretaryships, and other minor postings. The affected offices included the ministries of Personnel, Revenue, and Justice, the Censorate, the Office of Transmission, the Court of Imperial Entertainments, the Court of the Imperial Stud, and the National University.[86]

A fourth reduction in Nanjing officials occurred in the early Wanli era when the reform-minded chief grand secretary, Zhang Juzheng (1525–82), attempted to invigorate the bureaucracy.[87] Prior to the reduction of the Nanjing administration, more than 100 positions in the Beijing administration were abolished in the first month of 1581. These included 38 bureau secretaries, four directors, and one vice director.[88] In the same year, all the provincial bureaucracies across the country were also ordered to reduce their size.[89] In Nanjing, more than 30 positions were eliminated in 1581. Among them, the primary ones were vice-ministerships of the five ministries (except for the Nanjing Ministry of Revenue), the right assistant minister's position (*yousicheng*) in the Nanjing Court of Judicial Review and the Court of Imperial Sacrifices, and a number of vice-directorships and secretariats.[90] Fortunately for the bureaucrats in both the Southern and Northern capitals, most of the abolished positions were restored in 1583, one year after Zhang Juzheng's death and posthumous disgrace.[91]

The fifth and last large-scale curtailment of the Nanjing bureaucracy occurred during the Chongzhen reign. The last Ming monarch, inexperienced but conscientious, was anxious to take measures to arrest the decline of the Ming state.[92] In 1638 a total of 89 positions were eliminated from the Nanjing administration. These included two assistant minister's posts, two directorships, one vice-directorship, and a few secretaries.[93]

In addition to the reduction of official posts, sub-official functionaries in the Southern Capital were also targeted at least twice during the Ming. In 1527, slightly more than 100 clerical positions, from almost all of the Nanjing offices, were eliminated.[94] In 1581, approximately 200 clerical positions in the Southern Capital were further removed by central government under Zhang Juzheng; some of the eliminated clerkships were restored two years later.[95]

58 *Ministers and Eunuchs*

In conclusion, the organizational features of the Southern Capital administration can be summarized as follows: first, its civil, military, and eunuch apparatuses were almost completely identical to those of the primary Northern Capital. Only two institutions were absent from Nanjing: the emperor and the Grand Secretariat. Second, staffing levels in the Nanjing administration were lower than those of Beijing. After the numerous staff reductions in the middle and late Ming, the number of graded officials in Nanjing was approximately half that of Beijing, and the number of functionaries one-third. Generally, the left vice ministry and the vice-directorship were missing from most of the Nanjing ministries and their constituent bureaus. Third, the Nanjing departments and their leaders were the equals, not the subordinates, of the corresponding departments in Beijing. They reported directly to the emperor and his grand secretaries. The leadership in the Southern Capital was a collective one. There was no single dignitary who supervised every Nanjing department. The most prominent figures in Nanjing were the eunuch grand commandant, the grand commandant, and the Nanjing minister of war. Fourth, the territorial jurisdiction of the Nanjing administration was not completely restricted to the Southern Metropolitan Area and its surrounding region. Some Nanjing departments played a variety of prominent national roles in the governing of the Ming empire. This fact has been mentioned briefly in the preceding pages and will be further elaborated in the ensuing chapters.

Notes

1 See *DHMD*, 1701, 2837.
2 Tan Qian, *Guoque*, 3276.
3 The gazetteer is recorded in Wang Huanbiao's *Shoudu zhi*, 1364. The author and the date of publication are unknown. As a rule, the departmental gazetteer published by any Nanjing agency was compiled by the officials from that particular department. See Fang, "The *Gazetteer of the Nanjing Ministry of Revenue*," 77.
4 The vice-ministership of the six Nanjing ministries, created after the Hongxi era, was abolished in 1575 and reinstated in 1583. During the Tianqi reign, a vice-ministership of the left was added to each of the ministries, but it was soon abolished in the Chongzhen era. *MS*, 1832. Another source records that in 1662 only the Nanjing ministries of Revenue and of War were given vice-ministerships. See *NJLBZ*, 5.37b–41a.
5 Additional directorships were given to four bureaus (Shanxi, Shaanxi, Guizhou and Yunnan) of the Ministry of Revenue, two (Military Appointments, Operations) of the Ministry of War, and one (Irrigation and Transportation) of the Ministry of Works at certain periods. For details, see *MS*, 1734–59.
6 Two bureaus (Sichuan and Yunnan) of the Ministry of Revenue, three (Military Appointments, Provisions, and Operations) of the Ministry of War, and two (Construction, Forestry and Crafts) of the Ministry of Works were given more vice-directorships during the fifteenth and sixteenth centuries. Some were abolished later. For details, see *MS*, 1734–57.
7 Most of the bureaus were staffed with between one and three secretaries. From time to time, additional secretarial positions were added to the bureaus in the six ministries. For details, see *MS*, 1734–59.

8 For details of the distribution of the secretaryships among the bureaus of the six Nanjing ministries, see *MS*, 1832–3.

9 They were eight bureaus (Zhejiang, Jiangxi, Huguang, Fujian, Guangdong, Guangxi, Shanxi, and Shaanxi) of the Nanjing Ministry of Revenue, two bureaus (Operation, Equipment and Communications) of the Nanjing Ministry of War, five bureaus (Zhejiang, Jiangxi, Henan, Shaanxi and Guangdong) of the Nanjing Ministry of Justice, and two bureaus (Construction, Irrigation and Transportation) of the Nanjing Ministry of Works. Some of the directorships were repealed later in the Jiajing and Longqing reigns. For details, see *MS*, 1832–33.

10 They were: the registrar (*jingli*) in the Nanjing Court of the Imperial Clan, the chief minister (*qing*) in the Nanjing Seal Office, and the recorder (*zhubu*) in the Nanjing Offices of Princely Affairs. *MS*, 1832–35; *NJLBZ*, 5.45b-46a.

11 The two Hanlin officials in Nanjing were the junior compiler (*Hanlin bianxiu*) and the Hanlin clerk (*kongmu*). *MS*,1833; *NJLBZ*, 5.45a. For more on the Nanjing Hanlin Academy during the post-1421 period, see Tian Jifang, "Mingdai Nanjing Hanlinyuan de moluo zhuangtai jiqi yuanyin kaoshu," *Hubei xingzheng xueyuan xuebao*, No. 2 (2004), 64–8.

12 *MS*, 1832.

13 Zhang proposed to raise the rice-paper money payment ratio of the lower-ranking Nanjing officials to the level of their Beijing counterparts. See Huang Zuo, *Nanyong zhi*, 259–60.

14 They included the Nanjing Court of Imperial Sacrifices, the Court of Imperial Entertainment, the Court of State Ceremonial, the National University, the Imperial Academy of Medicine, the Central Daoist Registry, the Central Buddhist Registry, the Directorate of Astronomy (*qintianjian*), the Court of the Imperial Clan, and the Messenger Office.

15 *DMHD*, 1696–1703; Wang Huanbiao, *Ming Xiaoling zhi*, 59.

16 They included the imperial ancestral tombs in Sizhou, the tomb of the dynastic founder's father in Fengyang, and the tombs of the dynastic founder and his eldest son in Nanjing. *DMHD*, 2767–69; Chen Zilong et.al., *Ming jingshi wenbian*, 975.

17 *DMHD*, 2771–74. For more on the Nanjing shipyards operated by the Nanjing Ministries of War and Works, see Liu Yijie, "Mingdai Nanjing zaochuanchang tanwei," *Haijiaoshi yanjiu*, No. 1 (2010), 31–54.

18 *DMHD*, 2209; *MS*, 2183; Fan Jingwen, *Nanshu zhi*, 33.1b-2a.

19 For more on the military functions of the Southern Capital in general and the Nanjing Ministry of War in particular, see Jun Fang, "The military functions of the Southern Capital in Ming China," *Monumenta Serica*, Vol. 55, 133–55.

20 Lei Li, *Nanjing taipusi zhi*, 8.1a-2b.

21 Huang, *Nanyong zhi*, 693–95.

22 *DMHD*, 2935.

23 Tan, *Guoque*, 2459.

24 Huang, *Nanyong zhi*, 258. Exception can be also found in the case of Song Maocheng (*js* 1612), a native of Songjiang who was admitted to the National University in Beijing. After failing to pass in the metropolitan *jinshi* examination, he switched his registration to the Nanjing National University. The reasons for his first admittance to the Beijing National University and later transfer to Nanjing are not explained in the source. See *Songjiang fuzhi*, 42.30a.

25 *NJXBZ, juan* 2; *MS*, 1833. According to *DMHD* (2476), prior to the Hongzhi era the ministry was only allowed to handle judicial matter in the city of Nanjing.

26 Wang Qiao, *Fanglu ji*, 1.27a.

27 Wang Qiao, *Fanglu ji*, 1.46b-48a.

28 *DMHD*, 2476; *NJXBZ*, 3.14b.

29 He Liangjun, *Siyouzhai congshuo*, 86; *MS*, 1832. Previously the Nanjing officials were evaluated every ten years. It was changed to the six-year circle during the

60 Ministers and Eunuchs

Hongzhi reign under the suggestion of Lin Han, then the Nanjing minister of personnel. See Yu Jideng, *Diangu jiwen*, 292.

30 *NJLBZ*, 7.13a; *MS*, 4988.

31 *NJLBZ*, 7.14b; Xu Hong, *Ming mingchen wanyanlu*, 23.4b.

32 The contents of a *jiyou* are explained by David M. Farquhar, *The Government of China under Mongolian Rule*, 56.

33 Libu kaogong si, comp. *Libu kaogong tigao*, 637. The book is full of cases in which Nanjing officials came to Beijing later than they should and were consequently punished by the Ministry of Personnel in Beijing.

34 *DMHD*, 253.

35 Xu, *Ming mingchen wanyan lu*, 23.4b

36 *NJHBZ*, 18.19b.

37 *NJHBZ*, 14.14b-15a.

38 *NJHBZ*, 5.3a-14a.

39 *MS*, 5376-77.

40 Gu, *Kezuo zhuiyu*, 8.6. Liu Jin was accused in 1510 of plotting against the Zhengde emperor, who ordered his eunuch chief executed by *lingchi* or death by a thousand cuts. Liu was scheduled to be cut an unprecedented 3,357 times over a period of three days, but he expired in two days after suffering more than 300 cuts. See Timothy Brook et al., eds., *Death by a Thousand Cuts*, 272, note 48.

41 See John Meskill, trans., *Ch'oe Pu's Diary: A Record of Drifting Across the Sea*, 154-57.

42 For more on Yan Song and his time, see Cao Guoqing, *Yan Song pingzhuan*; Zhang Xianqing, *Yan Song zhuan*.

43 For more on the Ming military system, see Fan Zhongyi et al., *Mingdai junshi shi*, 35-60.

44 *DMHD*, 2996.

45 *MS*, 1865.

46 Apparently Charles Hucker is unaware of the existence of the Nanjing Embroidered-Uniform Guard, so is Shih-shan Tsai. See *A Dictionary of Official Titles in Imperial China*, 166; *The Eunuchs in the Ming Dynasty*, 88-9. Chinese authors of the Ming secret services, such as Ding Yi and Wei Qingyuan, are also unaware of the Nanjing Jinyiwei. See *Mingdai tewu zhengzhi*, 28-34; *Mingdai de Jinyiwei he Dong Xi chang*, 6-10.

47 *Nanjing Jinyiwei xuanbu*, 1-195; Zhou Song, "Mingdai Nanjing de Huihuiren wuguan," *Zhongguo shehui jingjishi yanjiu*, 3 (2010), 12.

48 *MS*, 2183.

49 Chen, *Ming jingshi wenbian*, 973.

50 The Three Great Divisions were established in 1424 as training units for troops rotated to one of the capitals from guard garrisons throughout the country. In 1450, they were developed into ten Integrated Divisions (*tuanying*) and again in 1467 further increased to 12 divisions. Each of the 12 divisions consisted of three subdivisions: Shenji, Sanqian, and Wujun. The latter two subdivisions were responsible for the training of cavalry and the former that of firerms. During the Zhengde era two Military Headquarters (*guanting*) were established in addition to the 12 Integrated Divisions. In 1550 the 12 Integrated Divisions and the two Military Headquarters were abolished and replaced by the original structure of Three Divisions, with the Sanqian renamed the Shenshu (inspired importance) Division. *MS*, 1856-58.

51 *DMHD*, 2995.

52 *DMHD*, 2996.

53 *DMHD*, 2995; *MS*, 2183.

54 *Gu, Kezuo zhuiyu*, 77; *DMHD*, 2996.

Ministers and Eunuchs   61

55 See Liu Ruoyu, *Zuozhong zhi*, 16.102; also see its abridged version, *Minggong shi*, 29.

56 *MS*, 1818–20.

57 Chen Zilong, *Ming jingshi wenbian*, 976. For a general description of the duties of each of these ten storehouses, see *MS*, 1820–21.

58 *MS*, 7767. The collators of the Zhonghua shuju edition of the *Mingshi*, as well as Lynn Struve, Charles Hucker, and Shih-shan Tsai, all mistake the grand command and eunuch grand commandant as one dignitary in Nanjing. See *MS*, 7796; F. W. Mote and Denis Twitchett, eds, *Cambridge History of China*, Vol. 7, part 1, 643; *A Dictionary of Official Titles in Imperial China*, 433; *The Eunuchs in the Ming Dynasty*, 70–1. For discussion of the different roles of the Nanjing grand commandant and Nanjing eunuch grand command, see Jun Fang, "The military triumvirate in the Southern Capital of the Ming dynasty," *Ming Studies*, No. 37 (Spring 1997), 7–21; Fang Jun, "Mingdai Nanjing de neiwai shoubei," *Zhongguo yanjiu*, No. 36 (July 1998), 42–4.

59 Wang Shizhen, *Fengzhou zabian*, 1.12–15; Zhou Hui, *Jinling suoshi*, 12–13; *DMHD*, 2996.

60 *MS*, 1822.

61 Chai Sheng, the Nanjing minister of war during the Zhengde era, suggested in his memorial that the number of the Nanjing grand commandants be reduced to two or three.

62 Chen, *Ming jingshi wenbian*, 975.

63 Chen, *Ming jingshi wenbian*, 976.

64 Tan Xisi, *Ming dazheng zhuanyao*, 45.7a; Wang Chunyu and Tu Wanyan, eds, *Mingdai huanguan yu jingji shiliao chutan*, 45.

65 *MSL: Yingzong*, 1803.

66 *Jiangsu sheng tongzhi gao*, 421.

67 The famous fleet admiral Zheng He (1371–1433), who commanded early Ming expeditionary voyages to Southeast Asia, South Asia, the Middle East, and East Africa in the first three decades of the fifteenth century, was one of the entrusted eunuch chiefs. For his life and the voyages, see Edward Dreyer, *Zheng He: China and the Oceans in the Early Ming Dynasty, 1405–1433*, Chapters 1, 2, 4 and 5; Louise Levathes, *When China Ruled the Seas: The Treasure Fleet of the Dragon Throne, 1405–1433*, 75–154; Ma Huan, *Ying-Yai Sheng-Lan: The Overall Survey of the Ocean's Shores*, 1–76.

68 For more on the eunuchs in the Ming and their political, economic, and military power, see Wang Chunyu and Tu Wanyan, *Mingchao huanguan*; Wen Gongyi, *Mingdai de huanguan he gongting*; *Mingdai huanguan*; Wei Jianli, *Mingdai huanguan zhengzhi*; Robert B. Crawford, "Eunuch power in the Ming dynasty," *T'oung Pao*, Vol. 49, No. 3, 115–48; and Shih-shan Tsai, *The Eunuchs in the Ming Dynasty*.

69 Liu, *Zuozhong zhi*, 16.102; *Minggong shi*, 29; *NJHBZ*, 1.5b.

70 Liu, *Zuozhong zhi*, 16.102; *Mingong shi*, 29.

71 Tan Qian, *Zaolin zazu*, 40–1. Shen Defu has a similar account of the goods and foodstuff delivered by the Nanjing eunuch agencies to Beijing, see Wang and Tu, *Mingdai huanguan yu jingji*, 54–5. On the shipment of tribute articles from the south to the north in late imperial times, see Li Denan, "Shilun Ming Qing Dayunhe de xingchuan cixu," *Shandong shifan daxue xuebao* (Renwen shehui kexue ban), Vol. 57, No. 3, 109–14.

72 *DMHD*, 2834.

73 The Nanjing minister of war, deemed the most powerful civilian official in the Nanjing administration, perhaps served as the convener of the meetings. Taking turn by the ministers to chair the meetings was another possibility.

74 *DMHD*, 2996.

62 Ministers and Eunuchs

75 The position was created in 1433 when Huang Fu (1363–1440), then the Nanjing minister of revenue, received this appointment. Huang was appointed by the court to assist Li Long (1393–1444), then the Nanjing grand commandant, to handle the military affairs in the Southern Capital. After Huang, the post of grand adjutant was held successively by the Nanjing vice minister of war (later, minister) Xu Qi, the Nanjing minister of personnel Cui Gong (1409–79), and the Nanjing censor-in-chief Wang Shu (1416–1508) until 1487 when it became a concurrent appointment of the Nanjing minister of war. *MSL: Yingzong*, 63.1b; *MS*, 1833; *MHY*, 541–43; Zheng Xiao, *Jinyan*, 50; *DMHD*, 158.1a.

76 The prefix "*xingzai*" was finally removed from the Beijing administration in the eleventh month of 1441. *MS*, 132.

77 For more on the Three Yangs and early Ming politics, see Luo Fenmei, *San Yang yu Mingchu zhi zhengzhi*.

78 *MS*, 127.

79 *MS*, 131. The record in *MS* is vague. It only states that in 1439 the government "dismissed superfluous officials from the service" (*tai rongguan*).

80 For details of the eliminated positions, see *MSL: Yingzong* 2033–4; Tan, *Guoque*, 1639; *MS*, 133; and Chen Zuolin, *Jinling tongji*, 415.

81 The other Nanjing offices affected were the Office of Transmission, the Court of the Imperial Stud, the Hanlin Academy, the Military School, the Censorate, the Court of Judicial Review, and the National University. Tan, *Guoque*, 3407.

82 Tan, *Guoque*, 3434, 3451. Tan's accounts on the eliminated positions and the restored ones do not match very well. For instance, according to him, only one secretaryship was abolished in 1529, whereas he records that among the positions restored in 1531, seven were secretarial.

83 They were the ministries of Revenue, Justice, and Works, the Crafts Institute (*wensiyuan*), the Nanjing Court of Imperial Sacrifices, the Directorate of the Altars of Heaven and Earth (*tianditan sijishu*), the Imperial Music Office (*shenyueguan*), the Office of Fine Wines (*liangyunshu*), the Winery (*zhangyunshu*), the Court of State Ceremonial, the National University, the Military School (*jingwei wuxue*), etc. *DMHD*, 83–92; *MS*, 1832–6.

84 *MSL: Muzong*, 6899; Tan, *Guoque*, 4097.

85 Tan, *Guoque*, 4116. *MSL* and *MS* do not contain any record of this reduction. Records in *DMHD* conflict with those of *Guoque*. According to the former, the eliminated positions included those of secretary of the Guangdong Bureau of the Nanjing Ministry of Revenue; commissioners-in-chief of the Armory for Weapons (*junchuchang*); commissioners (*fushi*) of the Dong'an, Xi'an, and Bei'an Gates granaries (one of each granary); vice director of the Zhejiang Bureau, secretary of the Guangdong Bureau, secretary of the Yunnan Bureau – all postings in the Nanjing Ministry of Justice; left case and right case reviewers of the Nanjing Court of Judicial Review (*dalisi*). See *DMHD, juan 3*.

86 Tan, *Guoque*, 4130.

87 For more on Zhang's reform, see Xiao Shaoqiu, *Zhang Juzheng gaige*; Nan Bing-wen et al., *Mingshi*, 425–39; Zhu Dongrun, *Zhang Juzheng dazhuang*, 185–215.

88 The affected Beijing departments included the ministries of Revenue, War, Rites, and Justice, the Censorate, the Office of Entertainments, the Banquets Office, the Seals Offices, the Directorate of Imperial Park, the Offices of Scrutiny, the Messenger Office, and the Household Department of the Heir Apparent. For details, see *MSL: Shenzong, 2076–77*.

89 *MS*, 267.

90 *MSL: Shenzong*, 2084; Tan, *Guoque*, 4381; *MS*, 266.

91 *MS*, 1832–35; Tan, *Guoque*, 4448.

92 For more on the Chongzhen emperor and his early reign, see Nan Bingwen et al., *Mingshi*, 895–914; Zhang Dexin and Tan Tianxing, *Chongzhen huangdi dazhuan*.

93 The reduction affected the Nanjing ministries of Personnel, Revenue, Works, the Censorate, the Office of Transmission, the Court of Judicial Review, the Household Department of the Heir Apparent, the Court of Imperial Entertainments, and the Court of the Imperial Clan. Tan, *Gouque*, 5798; *MS*, 325.

94 *DMHD*, 2228–29.

95 *DMHD*, 2229–30.

3 Patronage, Proving Ground, and Punishment

The political functions of the Southern Capital

1. Wang Shu and his posting to the Southern Capital

In 1448, one year before the disastrous Tumu Incident that ended the Zhengtong reign,[1] Wang Shu (1416–1508) passed the much coveted metropolitan examination at the age of 32. Like many *jinshi* (*js*) degree holders who were deemed to possess special literary promise, his first appointment was as the Hanlin Bachelor (*shujishi*), a low-ranking position in the Hanlin Academy in Beijing. A year later he was transferred to work in the Court of Judicial Review, first as left case reviewer and then as vice minister of the court. In 1454, the fifth year of the Jingtai reign, he was promoted to be prefect of Yangzhou, a prefecture in Nan Zhili noted for its commercial wealth and rich salt merchants. In the fourth year of the Tianshun era, his outstanding performance in local administration was recognized by an unusual promotion. He was raised from his present rank of grade 4a to become a grade 2b provincial commissioner in the province of Jiangxi.[2]

Wang had taken only 12 years to become a high-ranking official after he passed the *jinshi* examination, an enviable achievement for most Ming bureaucrats. For the next eight years he assumed different positions of essentially the same rank, first as the grand coordinator (*xunfu*) of northwestern Huguang with the concurrent title of right vice censor-in-chief. Finally in 1468, the fourth year of the Chenghua era, he was promoted to be Nanjing vice minister of justice. This was the first of Wang's four appointments during the Chenghua reign in Nanjing.[3]

Not long after assuming his post in Nanjing, Wang's father passed away and he left the office for a mandatory three-year period of mourning. In 1471, when the mourning period was over, he was made director-general of the Grand Canal (*zongdu hedao*) to take charge of conservancy of the Grand Canal while concurrently holding his former post of the Nanjing vice minister of justice.[4] In his new post, Wang supervised a variety of irrigation projects in the Nan Zhili area, such as the dredging of lakes and rivers and the repairing of locks.[5] In 1473 he was once again summoned back to the Southern Capital, where his second posting was as vice minister of revenue.[6]

Patronage, Proving Ground, and Punishment 65

Three years later, in 1476, Wang was transferred to assume the position of grand coordinator in Yunnan at the suggestion of Grand Secretary Shang Luo (1414–86). In the eyes of Shang and his close colleagues in the Grand Secretariat, the province was crucial to the effort to control the natives of the southwest and as a strategic link between Ming China and Annam. But to their dismay, the corrupt eunuch Qian Neng[7] was posted there as the eunuch grand defender (*zhenshou zhongguan*).[8] They therefore decided to send Wang, a courageous and well-respected official, to counterbalance the power of the eunuch chief.[9] Upon his arrival in Yunnan, Wang exposed Qian's bribe-taking and embezzlement and memorialized the Chenghua emperor repeatedly, demanding Qian's removal. A frightened Qian hastened to dispatch his agents to Beijing, where they pleaded with Wang Zhi (fl. 1477), the most powerful eunuch leader in the Chenghua court, to recall Wang to Beijing. By then, Shang Luo and Xiang Zhong (1421–1502), who had selected Wang Shu, had been forced out of office by Wang Zhi, leaving no one to speak for Wang Shu. As a result he was reappointed as Nanjing censor-in-chief and grand adjutant to take charge of the Nanjing Censorate.[10] This was Wang's third appointment to the Southern Capital administration, this time with a higher rank, as a censor-in-chief of grade 2a.

Wang's third Nanjing posting was a short one. Within a few months of his appointment he was transferred to become the Nanjing minister of war, generally regarded as the most important position in the Southern Capital civil bureaucracy, while concurrently holding the post of grand adjutant. A man of moral integrity, Wang refused to accept bribes from his subordinates, thus incurring their disfavor. Moreover, Qian Neng had returned to Beijing, where he repeatedly incriminated Wang before the Chenghua emperor. Already displeased with Wang's blunt memorials, the emperor relieved Wang of his ministerial duty and assigned him to inspect Nan Zhili and its surrounding areas in his capacity as vice censor-in-chief.[11] During his tenure as the grand coordinator of Nan Zhili from 1479 to 1484, Wang greatly reduced the level of grain taxes imposed on some prefectures in the area, and suspended a variety of extortionate eunuch projects.[12]

In 1484 Wang was recalled to the Southern Capital and given his previous post of Nanjing minister of war. Ironically, his old adversary Qian Neng was then serving in Nanjing as the eunuch grand commandant, chief of all the eunuch departments in Nanjing.[13] This time, however, there was not much conflict between the two. Wang's reputation, integrity and incorruptibility constrained Qian. In his seventies, Wang was well known for presenting memorials to the court expressing his opinion of state affairs, and these eventually became indispensable reading for the court. One story has it that, whenever an important issue was debated in the court and agreement could not be reached, the court officials would anxiously await Wang's memorial, which always arrived in time.[14] Unfortunately, Wang did not have the favor of the Chenghua emperor. In 1486, after Wang had criticized a new policy on the employment of eunuchs, the emperor took the opportunity to force him

66 *Patronage, Proving Ground, and Punishment*

into retirement. When the Hongzhi emperor assumed the throne a year later, he yielded to popular demand and recalled Wang to Beijing, where he became minister of personnel and was granted the honorific "Grand Guardian of the Heir Apparent" (*taizi taibao*). He worked for the court for another six years until he retired at the age of 77 in 1493.[15]

Wang's long life of 92 years and public service career of 45 years under four emperors and five reigns is certainly exceptional; however, the thing that I find most striking about his career is the frequency with which he was transferred to and from the Southern Capital. What can we learn from Wang's career about the secondary Southern Capital administration? What was the role of the Nanjing administration in the political life of the Ming dynasty? These are the questions that guide the following discussions.

2. A training ground for the junior officials

In his biography of Hai Rui (1514–87),[16] the Ming writer Huang Bingshi commented that Nanjing, where Hai once served as a censor-in-chief, was "a place for accumulating reputation and seniority (*yangwang di*)." What he meant was that the Southern Capital served, to a certain extent, as a training ground for the junior officials of the dynasty to enrich their bureaucratic experience and as a pool of experienced officials awaiting senior positions in the Northern Capital. In Huang's word, "soon after the officials accumulated some reputation (by serving in Nanjing), they were summoned back to the north (Beijing).[17]

The evidence indicates that this was indeed common practice in the Ming. Many Beijing officials were sent to Nanjing to assume higher positions and, after working in the Nanjing administration for a certain period of time and consequently gaining some relevant bureaucratic experience, were transferred back to Beijing to assume the same level of position there. This is especially true for vice ministers, who would assume a ministry in Nanjing, to be recalled to assume a minister's position in Beijing after several years. According to Ming specialist Huang Kaihua, of the 265 Beijing vice ministers who came to Nanjing to take up ministerships, roughly one-fourth (64) eventually went back to become ministers in the Beijing administration.[18] Equally common was the practice of transferring Nanjing ministers (not those who were originally vice ministers in Beijing) to Beijing to take up ministerships. In other words, Nanjing served as an official transfer station for higher positions.

This function of the Southern Capital is reflected in the following two tables. As indicated in Table 3.1, during the Jiajing era, slightly more than 40 percent (51 out of 123) of the ministers and censors-in-chief of the Nanjing administration were filled by vice ministers of the Beijing administration,[19] and close to one-third (39 out of 128, approximately 30 percent) of the Beijing ministerships were assumed by ministers from the various ministries and the censorate of the Nanjing administration.

In sharp contrast, Table 3.2 shows that during the Jiajing era, only one Nanjing vice minister was chosen to assume a ministership in Beijing. And in

Patronage, Proving Ground, and Punishment 67

Table 3.1 The composition of ministers of the Nanjing administration appointed during the 1522–66 period

Vice minister from Beijing ministries	51
Ministers from other Nanjing ministries	31
Vice ministers from other Nanjing ministries	14
Ministers from Beijing ministries	11
Others*	16
Total	123

Table 3.2 The composition of ministers of the Beijing administration appointed during the 1522–66 period

Ministers from other Beijing ministries	42
Ministers from Nanjing ministries	39
Vice ministers from Beijing ministries	32
Vice minister(s) from Nanjing ministries	1
Others*	14
Total	128

Source: Tan Qian, *Guoque*, 3250–4038
Notes: The ministers in tables 1 and 2 include the heads of the six ministries and the left and right censors-in-chief of the censorate. Vice ministers from these departments are not included. *The status of most of the officials in this category is not clearly identified in *Guoque*. Officials who came from government departments other than the six ministries and censorate are also included in this category.

the entire Ming era, only a very few, possibly less than ten, Nanjing vice ministers were appointed directly to be ministers in the Beijing administration.[20]

More importantly, it seems that most of these Nanjing vice ministers were promoted to ministerships in Beijing under special circumstances.[21] The only Nanjing vice minister in the Jiajing reign who was promoted to a Beijing ministership was Xi Shu (1461–1527), the Nanjing vice minister of war. Xi was appointed to the ministership of rites in Beijing by a special imperial edict (*tezhi*) of the Jiajing emperor for his support of the emperor in the Great Rites Controversy (*dali yi*)[22] in 1524 when the isolated emperor was desperately fighting with his court officials and had just dismissed his uncooperative minister of rites, Wang Jun (fl. 1522). Minister of Personnel Qiao Yu (1457–1524) recommended Jia Yong (1464–1547) and Wu Yipeng (1460–1542), respectively the left and right vice ministers of rites at the time, as possible candidates for the vacancy left by Wang, but the emperor chose Xi instead. Arguing that the choice was against the established precedents of the dynasty, Qiao asked the emperor to countermand this appointment, but he was ignored.[23]

The other four Nanjing vice ministers who received Beijing ministerships were all appointed in the late Ming, and their titles were honorary in nature: Ye Xianggao (1559–1627), the Nanijing vice minister of personnel, in 1607;[24] Shen Que (d. 1623), the Nanjing vice minister of personnel, in 1620 (during the

68 *Patronage, Proving Ground, and Punishment*

one-month Taichang reign);[25] Qian Longxi (1579–1645), the former Nanjing vice minister of personnel, in 1628;[26] and Qian Shisheng (1575–1652), the Nanjing vice minister of rites, in 1633.[27] It is noteworthy that the four received their minister of rites and grand secretary of the eastern hall (*dongge daxueshi*) appointments jointly with many other officials, and their new titles appear honorary in nature. For example, Ye Xianggao was promoted together with Yu Shenxing (1545–1608), the former minister of rites, and Li Tingji (*js* 1583), the vice minister of rites; Shen Que was elevated simultaneously with Shi Jixie, the minister of personnel. A few days after their appointments (in the eighth month of 1620), three Beijing vice ministers of rites were also promoted to be the ministers of rites and grand secretaries of the eastern hall. Qian was promoted together with Vice Minister of Rites Li Biao (*js* 1607), Minister of Rites Zhou Daodeng (*js* 1598), and Junior Supervisor of the Household of the Heir Apparent (*shaozhansh*) Liu Hongxun (1561–1639). Two months later, two vice ministers of rites in Beijing were promoted to be ministers of rites and grand secretaries of the eastern hall as well.[28]

Of the 11 Beijing ministers who were assigned to Nanjing ministerships during the Jiajing era, three can be viewed with certainty as having been shifted to new posts under normal circumstances,[29] one is represented by conflicting accounts,[30] and the other seven were disfavored by the emperor or grand secretaries, either for their dissenting stands or due to their poor health.

Of the latter seven, Zhou Lun (1463–1542) and Wu Yipeng were reassigned to Nanjing for opposing the Jiajing emperor and his supporters during the Great Rites Controversy. Wu, the minister of rites, was forced into the Nanjing Ministry of Personnel by Zhang Cong (1475–1539) and Gui E, who owned their promotion to grand secretaries to their endorsement of the emperor's controversial position.[31] Zhou, the minister of justice, was transferred to the Nanjing Ministry of Justice under the orders of the Jiajing emperor, who was irritated by Zhou's dissenting opinion.[32] Wang Xian (*js* 1490), the supreme commander of the Shaanxi area and the censor-in-chief, was also transferred to the Nanjing Ministry of War by Zhang and Gui, who wanted to give his post to Wang Qiong (1459–1532), an adversary of Grand Secretary Yang Tinghe (1459–1529) whom Zhang and Gui detested.[33] Sun Yingkui (*js* 1521), the minister of revenue, was assigned to the Nanjing Ministry of Works because the Jiajing emperor suspected him of graft and because he was accused by a supervising secretary of mishandling the finances of the empire.[34]

The remaining three officials were transferred to Nanjing because of their advanced age. Fang Liangyong (1461–1527), the director-general of supplies (*zongdu liangchu*)[35] and concurrently right censor-in-chief, died before his new appointment as Nanjing minister of justice reached him in 1527;[36] Tao Yan (1447–1531), the minister of works, was transferred to the Nanjing Ministry of War in 1522 when he turned 75;[37] Qin Jin (1467–1544), the minister of works and junior guardian of the heir apparent, was shifted to be Nanjing minister of war because the Jiajing emperor considered him to be enfeebled.[38]

Patronage, Proving Ground, and Punishment   69

In summary, the common practice in the Ming was that Beijing vice ministers were dispatched to Nanjing to assume ministership and Nanjing ministers were chosen to take up minister position in Beijing. Very few Nanjing vice ministers were appointed directly to be ministers in Beijing, and it was just as rare for Beijing ministers to be assigned to Nanjing.

The primary reason for this bureaucratic practice was that the Southern Capital administration was not as highly regarded as the Northern Capital administration. Owing to the absence of the emperor, Nanjing officials had fewer opportunities to attract the emperor's attention and receive special promotion to prominent positions. For example, of the hundreds of grand secretaries (*daxueshi*)[39] in the Ming, only a few came from the Southern Capital, namely Yang Tinghe, Liang Chu (*js* 1478), Zhang Zhi (1488–1550), and the four already mentioned – Ye Xianggao, Shen Que, Qian Longxi, and Qian Shisheng.[40] The responsibilities of the Nanjing administration were also not as comprehensive as those of the Beijing administration. In the words of the biographer of Zhang Shenyan (*js* 1610), the Nanjing minister of personnel in the early Chongzhen era: "the officials in the Southern Capital had official titles, yet were without much real power."[41] Although in reality the Nanjing bureaucrats possessed less administrative authority, in theory they enjoyed the same official ranks and emoluments as their counterparts in Beijing. Accordingly, it was acceptable and beneficial for junior Beijing officials to take higher positions in the less powerful administration and enrich their bureaucratic records.

Also, thanks to heavier administrative workloads and extensive responsibilities, it made sense to assign Beijing ministerships to those Nanjing ministers who had prior experience of running the ministries. When a Beijing ministership became unoccupied, preference was normally given to those who had been ministers. The disagreement between the Jiajing emperor and his top officials over who should succeed a retired minister in the early 1550s is illustrative. Minister of Personnel Xia Bangmo (1484–1564) left his position in 1551. To fill the vacancy, the ministry recommended three candidates to the emperor for consideration: Tu Qiao (1480–1555), the censor-in-chief, Tu Kai (*js* 1523), the Nanjing minister of personnel, and Li Mo (d. 1556), the vice minister of personnel. To the surprise of his officials, the emperor picked Li. Many top officials disapproved of this choice, arguing that an important position like the ministership of personnel had always been assumed by a senior minister or an official with equivalent status (*zhengqing*). According to these critics, there was no precedent for a vice minister to be elevated to the ministership of personnel directly.[42] The episode helps us understand why many Beijing officials, especially vice ministers, were sent to Nanjing to take positions of higher rank and why many Nanjing ministers received appointments in Beijing after service in Nanjing.

A careful reading of the ministerial appointments between the Nanjing and Beijing administrations confirms that there was a clear pattern in the promotion and transfer of Beijing and Nanjing officials. More than half of the Beijing vice ministers were promoted to head Nanjing ministries which were

70 *Patronage, Proving Ground, and Punishment*

less prestigious than the ones they had occupied in Beijing, and a majority of the Nanjing ministers were transferred to take ministerships in ministries which were considered less esteemed than the ones they had held in Nanjing. This is demonstrated in tables 3 and 4.

Table 3.3 shows that 56 percent of the Beijing vice ministers promoted to be ministers in Nanjing went on to less prestigious departments (e.g. a Beijing vice minister of revenue was made the Nanjing minister of works), whereas less than 30 percent were transferred to head their counterpart ministry in Nanjing (e.g. a Beijing vice minister of revenue was appointed to be Nanjing minister of revenue), and only slightly more than 15 percent were elevated to ministries which were more prestigious than the departments where they had formerly held office in Beijing (e.g. a Beijing vice minister of revenue promoted to be the Nanjing minister of personnel).

As for the Nanjing ministers assigned to Beijing, Table 3.4 indicates that close to 60 percent of these (Nanjing) ministers were transferred to ministries which were less esteemed than the ones they headed in Nanjing, slightly more than 23 percent were switched to their counterpart ministries, and less than 18 percent were put in charge of ministries more important than the ones they led in Nanjing.

It appears that there was also a pattern in the transfer of ministers from one ministry to another in the Nanjing administration, and this pattern reflects the status of the departments. As stated in the previous chapter, the Nanjing ministry of war was considered more prestigious than the Nanjing ministry of

Table 3.3 Promotion patterns of Beijing vice ministers appointed to be Nanjing ministers during the 1522–66 period

To less prestigious ministries	30
To the same ministries	12
To more prestigious ministries	9

Source: Tan,*Guoque*, 3250–4038
Notes: This table includes the Censorate. The status of the Nanjing departments was, in descending order: Ministry of War, Personnel, Revenue, Rites, Justice, Works, and the Censorate.

Table 3.4 Transfer patterns of Nanjing ministers appointed to be Beijing ministers during the 1522–66 period

To less prestigious ministries	22
To the same ministries	11
To more prestigious ministries	6

Source: Tan, *Guoque*, 3250–4038
Notes: The numbers are derived from Tan's material. This table includes the censorate. The status of the government departments in the Beijing administration during the Jiajing era was, in descending order: Ministry of Rites, Personnel, Revenue, War, Justice, Works, and the Censorate. It should be noted that only during the Jiajing reign, owing to the emperor's obsession with rites issues, did the Ministry of Rites become the most influential department in the Beijing administration. See *Guoque*, 3739.

personnel, whose counterpart in Beijing was the most prominent department in the Ming civil bureaucracy except during the Jiajing reign (as in the other dynasties of imperial China).[43] When the Nanjing ministership of war became vacant, it was more often filled by a Nanjing minister of personnel than by a minister from any other department. A total of 96 Nanjing ministers of war serving during the 1424–1644 period can be identified from the currently available Ming sources. Of them, 56 were heads of the other five Nanjing ministries and censorate prior to their assignment to the war ministry, and among the 56, 19 or approximately one-third were ministers of personnel.[44] The official appointments Zhan Ruoshui (1466–1560) received in the later years of his lengthy political career are a case in point. The president of the Nanjing National University was appointed as the Nanjing right vice minister of personnel in 1528, and transferred to Beijing to become left vice minister of rites in the following year. In 1533 he was promoted to be the Nanjing minister of rites. Three years later he was shifted to head the Nanjing ministry of personnel, and in 1539 he moved on to become the Nanjing minister of war, a post he held concurrently with the title of grand adjutant.[45]

3. A source of specially appointed taskforce central officials

Although the Southern Capital was not as prestigious as the Northern Capital, it was nevertheless a central administration and its incumbents enjoyed the status of capital officials (*jingguan*). As such, the Nanjing bureaucrats were occasionally dispatched to the provinces and military regions to inspect the performance of officials and functionaries there and supervise relief operations when natural disasters occurred. More frequently they were delegated by the court to the provinces and other strategic areas to serve as grand coordinators (*xunfu*) and supreme commanders (*zongdu*) – in other words, as task-force agents sent out to expedite work locally.

The *xunfu* (literally, touring pacifier) system originated in the Hongwu era when the dynasty founder sent his heir apparent, the Prince of Yiwen, to inspect the Shaanxi area. Subsequently, other court dignitaries were occasionally dispatched on tours of inspection to the provinces and strategic regions. In 1430, this temporary measure became a permanent practice. These touring pacifiers gradually became resident coordinators in the provinces and special frontier zones, with the special charge of supervising and controlling the triad of regular provincial agencies. However, they always remained nominal officials of the central government, usually vice ministers, on special territorial assignment. After 1453, all grand coordinators were routinely given nominal concurrent appointments as vice or assistant censor-in-chief. This conferred on them broad impeachment powers and increased their prestige. Because there was often a special need for cross-provincial coordination of military affairs, the office of *zongdu* (literally, the person generally in charge) gradually evolved out of the grand coordinated system. Like the grand coordinators, the supreme commander was an official of the central government

72 *Patronage, Proving Ground, and Punishment*

delegated to territorial service, originally and normally on a temporary basis to deal with a particular – especially military – crisis. The first such appointment was made in 1430 and appointments increased in the second half of the fifteenth century. Often the supreme commander was the grand coordinator of one of the provinces or other strategic areas in his broad jurisdiction. His military authority might extend over as many as five provinces. Sometimes supreme commanders were assigned non-military responsibilities. For example, overseeing the collection and transport of rice revenue from the Nanjing area to Beijing (i.e. as director-general of tax grain transport and director-general of supplies).[46]

Although, as appointees to grand coordinatorships and supreme commandery, the Nanjing bureaucrats were dispatched to almost every part of the empire, it is equally true that most Nanjing officials were assigned to posts in the south. Tables 3.5 and 3.6 below clearly indicate this tendency. It should be pointed out that, during the Ming, most of the grand coordinators and supreme commanders were from the Beijing administration, even in the southern part of the country where the Nanjing officials were posted.

As can be seen from Table 3.5, Nanjing officials were mainly employed as supreme commanders whose territorial jurisdictions were in the southern area. The ten appointed as supreme commanders of the Liangguang area (Guangdong and Guangxi), were concurrently the grand coordinators of Guangdong and were charged with supervising and controlling the grand coordinators of Guangxi.[47] Ten served as directors-general of grain transport, their chief responsibility being to supervise the transport of tax grain from the Yangzi delta to the Beijing area along the Grand Canal.[48] Five served as directors-general of (tax grain) supplies (*zongli liangchu*), their main duties being to supervise the reception and storage of tax grain at Nanjing.[49] Conversely, none of the Nanjing officials were appointed supreme commander of Jiliao,[50] Xuanda[51] or Shaanxi sanbian,[52] which were considered crucial strategic areas in the north. In the case of Wang Shu, mentioned at the beginning of this chapter, three of his four grand coordinatorships were taken in the south (Huguang, Yunnan, and Nan Zhili). The one he assumed in the north, the grand coordinatorship of Henan, was assigned to him prior to his first appointment to the Southern Capital.

Table 3.5 Nanjing officials appointed to supreme commandership in the Ming

Region/Province	Number appointed
Liangguang	10
Zongli caoyun and Fengyang	10
Zongli liangchu and Yingtian	5
Zongli hedao	4
Jiliao	0
Xuanda	0
Shaanxi sanbian	0

Source: Wu Tingxie, *Ming dufu niaobiao*

Patronage, Proving Ground, and Punishment   73

Table 3.6 Nanjing officials appointed to grand coordinatorship in the Ming

Region/Province	Number appointed
Nan'gan	7
Jiangxi	6
Shandong	6
Zhejiang	3
Huguang	3
Guizhou	3
Gansu	3
Baoding	3
Henan	3
Sichuan	2
Yunnan	2
Fujian	2
Shuntian	2
Yansui	2
Ningxia	1
Liaodong	1
Yunyang	1
Xuanfu	1
Shanxi	1
Guangxi	0
Datong	0

Source: Wu, *Ming dufu nianbiao*

Similarly, as Table 3.6 indicates, very few Nanjing officials were assigned grand coordinatorships in the northern part of the empire.[53] Places like Ningxia, Liaodong, Xuanfu, and Shanxi had only one Nanjing official serving as grand coordinator, with none appointed to Datong. On the contrary, most of the grand coordinators from the Nanjing administration assumed their posts in the south or in areas not far from Nan Zhili. Places such as Nan'gan, Jiangxi, and Shandong had six or more grand coordinators from Nanjing.[54] The north-south division in the assignment of grand coordinators and supreme commanders apparently related to the division of labor between the Northern and Southern capitals. Although it was never clearly regulated, an unofficial division of labor between the two capitals did seem to exist, with the Nanjing administration being primarily south-oriented.

Another fact worthy of mention is that 60 percent of the Nanjing officials who received an appointment as grand coordinator were ministers of the five courts (*si*): the Nanjing Courts of Judicial Review, the State Ceremonial, Entertainment, Sacrifices, and the Imperial Stud,[55] while most of the Beijing officials who received the post of grand coordinator were vice ministers of the six ministries.[56] The career backgrounds of the Beijing officials who received supreme commanderships were more diverse, while the Nanjing officials appointed to supreme commanderships were primarily ministers and vice ministers of the six ministries and heads of the censorate. The possible

74 *Patronage, Proving Ground, and Punishment*

explanation is that there were fewer ministry officials in the Nanjing administration available for such appointments. As noted in the first section of the preceding chapter on the Nanjing administration, the number of Nanjing officials was approximately half that of the Beijing officials, and administrative duties in the departments other than the six Nanjing ministries were comparatively less demanding.[57]

4. A place of exile for disfavored officials

Another bureaucratic role played by the Southern Capital was as a retreat for those officials who had lost favor with the emperor and his chief assistants (the grand secretaries or eunuch chiefs) and for those who suffered demotions of a sort not serious enough for them to be deprived of official rank or receive a sentence. The origin of this practice is unclear. What is known is that the earliest case occurred in the Zhengtong reign when the designation of Beijing and Nanjing as the primary and secondary capitals of the empire was finalized.[58] Gradually, reassigning a Beijing official to Nanjing to take up a position of identical rank became a punitive action frequently used by the Ming court.

As a castigating measure, the assigning of officials to serve in Nanjing can be classified into three types on the basis of the degree of demotion involved. The first and most common applied to those who had offended the emperor, grand secretaries, or eunuch chiefs by their blunt criticism or "improper" court behavior; or simply to those whom power holders regarded as outsiders, namely those who held different views on policy issues and those who did not belong to the authoritative faction. The victims were typically consigned to positions equivalent to those they had held previously.

Many officials received such a punishment by incurring the emperor's disfavor. For instance, Minister of Rites Xiao Xuan (1396–1461), a man considered earnest and taciturn, was not adept at answering imperial inquiries. Dissatisfied with his oral performance, the Tianshun emperor had Xiao transferred to the Nanjing ministry of rites in 1460.[59] He Mengchun (1474–1536), the vice minister of personnel at the beginning of the Great Rites Controversy, along with a group of officials he led, strongly opposed the Jiajing emperor. He was consequently driven to Nanjing to assume the left vice ministership of works. The usual practice in the Ming was that a Nanjing ministry was staffed by only one vice minister of the right. At the time when He was transferred to the Nanjing Ministry of Works, the position of vice minister of the right had already been filled. The appointment of He Mengchun as Nanjing vice minister of the left was purely Jiajing's arrangement to get rid of a disfavored official.[60] As noted, Wang Shu's numerous appointments to Nanjing were largely due to his falling out of favor with the Chenghua emperor.

Most of the officials sidelined to Nanjing were either factional outsiders or had in some way offended the powerful grand secretaries or eunuch chiefs. For example, Yang Tinghe, grand secretary in the early Jiajing reign, had in the previous Zhengde era been forced out to Nanjing by the domineering eunuch director Liu Jin. In the Great Rites Controversy, Yang used the same method to handle those who disagreed with him. Zhang Cong, who was later catapulted to become minister of rites and chief grand secretary due to his staunch support of the Jiajing emperor, was sent out to become a secretary at the Nanjing Ministry of Justice in 1521. Yang told Zhang bluntly that he should stay quietly in the Southern Capital and not make trouble.[61] In another example, when Senior Grand Secretary Zhang Juzheng's (1525–82) father died in 1577, Zhang, unwilling to relinquish his absolute power, managed to be exempted from the obligatory three-year mourning period. He Weibo (1511–87), minister of personnel in Beijing, disapproved of Zhang's behavior and demanded his removal. In response, Zhang had He transferred to the Nanjing Ministry of Rites.[62]

The list of similar cases is extensive. To just name a few: Yao Kui (1414–73), Zhang Lun (1413–83), and Xu Bin (d. 1467), vice ministers of rites during the Tianshun reign, were for various reasons all pushed out to the Nanjing Ministry of Rites by Shi Heng (d. 1460), who dominated the court after the Tianshun restoration in 1457;[63] Sun Jiao (1453–1532), vice minister of personnel in the early Zhengde reign, was squeezed out to Nanjing by Zhang Cai (fl. 1515), his superior, the minister of personnel, for admonishing him not to be too close to Liu Jin;[64] He Qiaoxin (1427–1502), an outspoken vice censor-in-chief, was resented by the grand secretaries Wan An (d.1489) and Liu Ji (1427–93) and reassigned to the Nanjing Ministry of Justice;[65] Zhang Sheng (*js* 1469), a mentor (*shuzi*) at the Secretariat of the Heir Apparent, was pushed aside to Nanjing by Liu Ji to become a vice director at the Nanjing Ministry of Works;[66] Chen Shou (*js* 1472), assistant minister of the Court of Judicial Review, was forced out by Liu Jin to become the vice minister of the Nanjing Court of Imperial Entertainment;[67] Wu Yipeng, minister of rites, and Wang Xuekui, director of the Bureau of Appointments at the Ministry of Personnel, were pushed aside by grand secretaries Zhang Cong and Gui E (1478–1531) to be the Nanjing minister of personnel and vice minister of the Nanjing Court of the Imperial Stud respectively;[68] Zou Yuanbiao (1551–1624), the supervising secretary for personnel, was assigned to be the record keeper (*zhaomo*) at the Nanjing Ministry of Justice by Senior Grand Secretary Shen Shixing (1535–1614) for impeaching and bringing down Xu Xuemo (1522–93), Shen's relative by marriage and minister of rites.[69]

It seems that Liu Jin was the person who most frequently used Nanjing as a place to send officials whom he resented and wished to see punished. In the early Zhengde reign when the status of Liu and his seven associates[70] was not stable, many court officials called for their banishment. Their rivals in the eunuch departments, the heads of the Directorate of Ceremonial, Chen Kuan, Li Rong and Wang Yue, suggested they be exiled to Nanjing. However, Liu and his clique managed to change the Zhengde emperor's mind. Instead of displacing Liu Jin and his henchmen to Nanjing, the monarch appointed Liu as head of the Directorate of Ceremonial, Ma Yongcheng as head of the Eastern Depot (*dongchang*)[71] and Gu Dayong as the head of the Western

76 *Patronage, Proving Ground, and Punishment*

Depot (*xichang*).[72] Wang Yue and two other eunuchs were ordered to serve in the Xiaoling Eunuch Troop (*Xiaoling jingjun*)[73] in Nanjing. Wang Yue and one eunuch were murdered en route to Nanjing, while the third was severely beaten and his arms broken.[74]

Liu Jin's unchallengeable status in the Zhengde court was established thereafter. Assigning officials who offended him or whom he despised to Nanjing became one of the punitive methods Liu repeatedly employed. In the summer of 1508, an anonymous letter denouncing Liu Jin was circulated. Determined to find the culprit, Liu forced all civil officials to kneel in front of Fengtian Gate to the point that several died of sunstroke. When eunuch Huang Wei complained on their behalf, he was expelled to Nanjing.[75]

In 1509, when the *Veritable Records of the Hongzhi Emperor* (*Xiaozong shilu*) were completed and presented to the court, the secretariat suggested a promotion for the Hanlin officials involved in the project. Liu Jin resented these academicians, with whom he was on bad terms. Instead of elevating them, he proposed to the Zhengde emperor that they be transferred to Nanjing. Expositor-in-waiting (*shijiang*) Wu Yipeng, Reader-in-waiting (*shidu*) Xu Mu, Compiler (*bianxiu*) Gu Qing, all of whom had the rank of grade 5a, were to be assigned to the Nanjing ministries of Justice, Rites, and Works respectively as bureau vice directors; compilers Cui Xian and Lu Shen, officials with the rank of grade 6a, were to be transferred to the Nanjing ministries of Personnel and Revenue respectively to take up secretaryship.[76]

Others who were forced by Liu to take positions in Nanjing included: Wu Wendu (1441–1510), the Nanjing censor-in-chief of the right, for ignoring Liu's request for a bribe;[77] Ma Zhongxi (1446–1512), vice minister of war, for dismissing the exaggerated military exploits of Liu's cohort, Zhu Ying;[78] Zhang Nai (*js* 1547), vice censor-in-chief, for opposing Liu's intention to pardon a county magistrate who had bribed Liu;[79] Feng Xi (*js* 1499), the right advisor (*youyude*) at the Secretariat of the Heir Apparent, for refusing to flatter Liu.[80]

The second and less frequently employed means by which Nanjing was used as a light punishment for those found guilty of a misdemeanor was to reassign officials to positions slightly lower than those they had previously held. For example, Han Bangqi (1479–1555), the right mentor (*youshuzi*) of grade 5a at the Secretariat of the Heir Apparent (*chunfang*) in the early Jiajing reign, was accused of mishandling the recruitment procedure when supervising the Yingtian provincial examination in 1528. As a result he was demoted to become assistant minister of the Nanjing Court of the Imperial Stud (rank 6a).[81] Zhang Wei (*js* 1619), the vice minister of the Court of the Imperial Stud (rank 4a) in the early Chongzhen reign, was transferred to become assistant minister of the Nanjing Judicial Review (rank 5a), for unspecified misconduct.[82]

The third reason for sending officials to Nanjing was to impose a more severe penalty. Officials punished in this context were usually relegated to a much lower position. This penalty was usually imposed on the eunuch chiefs

Patronage, Proving Ground, and Punishment 77

who were deprived of their power and banished to Nanjing.[83] There are 27 principal eunuchs recorded in the biography section on eunuchs in the *Official History of the Ming Dynasty* (*Mingshi*).[84] Among them, eight ended their once-celebrated careers with death,[85] seven escaped punishment,[86] three ended their services in the Ming palace in the midst of the late Ming rebellion and Qing conquest,[87] one was deprived of his eunuch rank,[88] and eight were punished by being expelled to Nanjing.[89] Of the eight, only Wang Zhi, chief of the Directorate of the Imperial Horses and director of the Western Depot in the Chenghua reign, was reassigned an equivalent post, the directorship of the Nanjing Directorate of the Imperial Horses.[90] The other seven were relegated to considerably lower positions. Gu Dayong (fl. 1516), director of the Western Depot in the Zhengde years, and Feng Bao (fl. 1580), the once-domineering head of the Directorate of Ceremonial and director of the Eastern Depot in the late Longqing and early Wanli reigns, were relegated to be chief stewards in Nanjing.[91] Zhang Yong (1465–1526), one of the notorious "Eight Tigers" of the Zhengde reign, was assigned to become the Xiaoling incense handler (*sixiang*).[92] Liang Fang (fl. 1470), the favorite eunuch in the Chenghua reign, was later exiled to Nanjing and soon after imprisoned there.[93] The other three, Jiang Zong (fl. 1490), the eunuch grand commandant in the Hongzhi reign, Li Fang (fl. 1567), head of the Directorate of the Palace Eunuchs in the Longqing reign, and Cui Wensheng (fl.1620), director of the Directorate of Ceremonial in the short-lived Taichang reign, were all later forced to serve in the Xiaoling Eunuch Army.[94]

Three points should be made clear here. First, Nanjing was not the only or even the major place in the Ming to receive unpopular or demoted officials. Less fortunate bureaucrats were often assigned to regional posts, and some were relegated to remote provinces such as Yunnan, Guizhou, and Guangxi. For example, Zhang Mao (1437–1522), Huang Zhongzhao (1435–1508), and Zhuang Yong, all *jinshi* of 1466 and Hanlin academicians in the Chenghua era, memorialized against the extravagant display of lanterns in the court for the Lantern Festival. Consequently, Zhang was given the magistracy of Lingwu country, Huang the magistracy of Xiangtan county, and Zhuang the judgeship of Guiyang subprefecture.[95] Wang Yangming (1472–1528) is another case in point. In 1506, Liu Jin ordered the arrest of Nanjing Supervising Secretary Dai Xian (*js* 1496) and some twenty other officials who had censured him in a joint memorial. Wang, then a secretary in the Ministry of War, petitioned for their pardon. He was consequently relegated to northwestern Guizhou as head of the Longchang Postal Station.[96]

The second point is that sending out Beijing officials to Nanjing or the provinces was certainly not the main means of punishing officials in the Ming. Many were deprived of their titles and ranks, beaten savagely at court, thrown into prison, or even executed. Wang Yangming, Zhang Mao, Huang Zhongzhao, and Zhuang Yong, were all flogged at court before being exiled to isolated areas.[97] The point here is that sending officials to Nanjing, a relatively mild punitive measure, became one of the many options available to the

78 *Patronage, Proving Ground, and Punishment*

Ming ruler and his chief administrative assistants for dealing with subordinate bureaucrats during the post-Xuande period.

The last point to be made is that being moved to Nanjing did not spell the end of an official's political career. As a matter of fact, most of the punished officials were later rehabilitated and summoned back to Beijing after the downfall of the powerful figures who had assigned them. Their fate followed closely the vicissitudes of the political situation in Beijing. Ming sources are full of examples of this, for instance the case of Ma Wensheng (1426–1510), formerly minister of war in Beijing, who was transferred to Nanjing after being slandered by eunuch Li Zisheng (fl. 1485). When the Hongzhi emperor ascended to the throne and had Li executed, Ma returned to Beijing to assume the post of censor-in-chief of the left.[98]

A number of factors contributed to the adoption of the practice of dispatching disfavored officials to Nanjing as a punitive measure. First, the Nanjng administration, being of secondary importance, was less attractive to politically ambitious officials. For most Nanjing officials, the absence of the emperor and the court meant no direct access to the process of policy-making and fewer chances to perform in front of the emperor and thus capture his attention. The dissatisfaction of Huo Tao (1481–1540) over his new appointment in Nanjing illustrated this reality vividly. The vice minister of personnel was made the Nanjing minister of rites. Even with this promotion of one grade in official rank, he was still downcast. In revenge, he repeatedly memorialized the emperor, accusing other officials in the Ministry of Personnel, whom he thought were responsible for his new posting, of accepting bribes.[99]

Second, it appears that the practice matched the general trend in the middle and late Ming of making the penalties imposed on officials less severe than they had been in the Hongwu and Yongle eras. To send officials to Nanjing was a much lighter punishment than the traditional Five Punishments (*wuxing*)[100] and deprivation of official status.

A popular perception of the Ming is that the dynasty was "an age of terror" and that its government was exceedingly cruel and harsh to its officials.[101] The primary sources of this understanding are: first, the torture and execution of a large number of court officials and their relatives in the reign of the founding emperor, Hongwu, and the merciless purges of a good many Jianwen loyalists in the Yongle reign.[102] Second, the vicious treatment of civil officials by a few disreputable eunuch chiefs, notably Wang Zhen (d. 1449) in the Zhengtong reign, Wang Zhi in the Chenghua reign, Liu Jin in the early Zhengde era, and Wei Zhongxian (1568–1627) in the Tianqi era. Third, we have the reputation of the secret service agencies, chiefly the Embroidered-Uniform Guard (*jinyiwei*),[103] the Eastern Depot, and Western Depot, which ran amuck in the reigns of Hongwu, Yongle Chenghua, Zhengde, and Tianqi, especially during the periods when Wang Zhen, Wang Zhi, Liu Jin, and Wei Zhongxian were in power. Fourth, the Ming reputation is tainted by the notorious beatings of officials at court (*tingzhang*) by the government throughout the dynasty;[104] and finally the harshness of the Ming Code.[105]

My analysis of the above-mentioned historical facts, however, leads to a slightly different conclusion. In the post-Yongle era there were neither massive executions of officials, as in the purges of Hu Weiyong (d. 1380) and Lan Yu (d. 1393), nor large-scale purges of Jianwen loyalists. The four most discredited eunuch chiefs only dominated the Ming court for approximately a quarter century of the 220-year post-Yongle period.[106] And with the exception of high-profile incidents in 1479, 1506, 1519, and 1524,[107] the method of physically humiliating officials in public was seldom used in the middle and late period of the dynasty. The legal practice, or the implementation of the legal provisions, in the post-Yongle period was much less severe.

According to the *Official History of the Ming Dynasty*, all the excesses in the Hongwu and Yongle reigns (1368–1424) were adjusted in the following Hongxi and Xuande eras. The short-lived Hongxi reign is considered benevolent. One of the 55 items contained in the Imperial Instructions (*dixun*) written by the Xuande emperor was the leniency of penalty. The abusive punishment of officials was prohibited in the early Zhengtong reign when the famed three Yangs, Yang Rong (1371–1440), Yang Pu (1372–1446), and Yang Shiqi (1365–1444), held political sway. Legal practice in the Hongzhi era also exhibited a tendency towards leniency. The ministers of justice who served in the Hongzhi reign, He Qiaoxin (1427–1502), Peng Shao (1430–95), Bai Ang (1435–1503), and Wen Gui were all praised as men of integrity. The abuse of judicial power rarely occurred. The Jiajing reign was marked by an erratic use of punishments. Many of the officials who opposed the emperor in the Great Rites Controversy were either deprived of official rank or beaten at court. However, the emperor, who indulged in Daoist pursuits for longevity, granted amnesty to the punished whenever there was an autumn Daoist ceremony (*qiujiao*) from 1530 onwards. In the early Wanli years, under the leadership of Zhang Juzheng, the operation of government by and large followed set legal procedures. When the Wanli emperor began to rule the realm after the death of Zhang, he mistreated those censors and supervising secretaries who admonished and criticized him. However, the monarch, uninterested in and unwilling to deal with state affairs, rarely meted out harsh penalties to other court officials. The last emperor, Chongzhen, for the purpose of correcting the laxity of the previous reigns, disciplined officials harshly.[108] In short, the penalties imposed on the officials in the post-Yongle Ming were generally not harsh except in the Zhengde, Tianqi and Chongzhen reigns, as well as the Zhengtong years under Wang Zhen and the Chenghua years under Wang Zhi. The eras of Hongxi, Xuande, early Zhengtong, and Hongzhi were dominated by leniency. Punishment in the Jiajing and Wanli reigns was precarious and erratic, marked by the alternation of harshness and leniency. Punishing officials by relocating them to Nanjing coincided with the general trend of lenient punishment in the post-Yongle period, and this phenomenon might be viewed as an indicator of that tendency.

Third, this practice indicates, to a certain extent, that the power of those who dominated the political scene was not boundless: even extremely

80 *Patronage, Proving Ground, and Punishment*

powerful figures, such as eunuch chiefs Liu Jin and Wei Zhongxian and senior grand secretaries Yan Song and Zhang Juzheng, could not routinely mistreat or punish all those they disfavored. To drive out officials they regarded with distaste was already an inappropriate exercise of power, but to further punish the disfavored would incur a backlash. The Hanlin academician and reader-in-waiting (*shidu xueshi*) Liu Zhong (1452–1523) is a good example. Using his opportunity to present a daily lecture (*rijiang*) to the Zhengde emperor, Liu admonished the young monarch not to indulge in wine and women excessively and denounced those eunuchs who induced the emperor to seek pleasure. Irritated, Liu Jin prompted the minister of personnel Xu Jin (1437–1510) to assign the Hanlin official to Nanjing. At the time the Nanjing Ministry of Rites already had one vice minister of the right. Xu created the post of left vice minister of rites especially for Liu Zhong.[109] The appointment was criticized by numerous court officials, and under this pressure Xu recommended that Liu be promoted to Nanjing minister of rites after two months and then to Nanjing minister of personnel in the following winter.[110] As for the emperor, although in theory he had the power to punish his officials at will, in practice he could not act without restraint. Most of the Ming emperors seemed to understand that harshness towards their bureaucrats alienated them and that terror and intimidation did not work in the long run. One way of enhancing the centripetal force of his bureaucrats and boosting their morale was to treat them decently.

5. A sinecure for superannuated officials

Another regulating function of the Southern Capital was to act as a retreat for aged or physically infirm officials. Assuming office in Nanjing enabled those officials to maintain their previous official status and emoluments while bearing lighter administrative responsibilities. This practice was related to the Ming's improved treatment of officials as of the early fifteenth century and to the prevailing perception among Ming contemporaries that official duties in Nanjing were less arduous. Most Ming officials seemed to understand that the workload in Nanjing was not challenging, and the Ming sources are full of episodes and comments reflecting this perception. For instance, when a certain *jinshi* was appointed secretary in the Bureau of Reception at the Nanjing Ministry of Rites, his father, a senior official in Beijing, admonished him: "the official duties in the Southern Capital are simple, but you should not take a laissez-faire attitude; in order to achieve great accomplishments, you should pursue studies diligently."[111] A comment made by the Chongzhen emperor also testifies to this notion. Having been deprived of all of his official titles (for having submitted an "offensive" memorial to Chongzhen), Shi Bangyao (1585–1644) was reappointed as the commissioner of the Nanjing Office of Transmission. Before departing for the Southern Capital, Shi attended an audience with the emperor, where he made a number of frank suggestions regarding state affairs that greatly impressed the emperor. Three days after Shi's departure,

Chongzhen ordered the eunuchs to summon him back, saying, "there is not much to do in Nanjing, so [let him] stay here to serve me."[112]

The biography of Sun Jiao (1453–1532) in the *Official History of the Ming Dynasty* also reveals the degree of leisure enjoyed by Nanjing officials. While praising Sun for his determination in pursuing scholarship, it is noted that during Sun's stint in Nanjing most of his colleagues, having too much leisure time, amused themselves by chatting, bantering, drinking and playing.[113] Similarly, a paragraph in the preface to the *Gazetteer of the Nanjing Hanlin Academy* (*Jiujing cilin zhi*) vividly reveals the moderate workload of the Nanjing Hanlin Academy:

> Hanlin officials are close to the emperor. They are highly respected by the common folk who think they are (leading the lives of) supernatural beings (*shenxian*). To come to the Nanjing Academy, [the officials] bore no responsibility of serving the emperor and of participating in political affairs. In the meantime, [they] enjoy the pleasure of writing, drinking, and loitering on the hills and rivers, which really makes their life that of a supernatural being.[114]

The practice of dispatching physically feeble officials to Nanjing, like that of consigning disliked or demoted officials there, probably began with the Zhengtong era and may have peaked during the Jiajing reign. Of the following six cases, five took place during the Jiajing era and three were handled by the emperor himself.

Wei Ji (1374–1471) was appointed vice minister of personnel in 1438. Soon after becoming minister of rites in 1443, he requested retirement on the grounds of advanced age. Wang Zhi (1379–1462), the minister of personnel, replied that Wei was not yet senile but, to show consideration, he should be relieved of laborious administrative duties and assigned an undemanding position. As a result, Wei was transferred to the Nanjing Ministry of Personnel.[115] Another case is found in Xu Xuemo's *Records on the Events in the Jiajing Era* (*Shimiao shiyulu*). Wang Yongbin, a senior Beijing minister, was confined to bed for months due to an affliction of the hip. After recovering from the ailment, he went to the Yinghe Gate in the imperial palace to express his gratitude to the emperor. Too weak to rise to his feet after prostrating, he had to stand up with the assistance of two clerks. When this occurrence was reported to the emperor, Wang was reassigned to the Nanjing Ministry of Personnel.[116]

Qin Jin (1467–1544) was appointed minister of works and junior guardian (*shaobao*) in 1532 after serving at the Nanjing Ministry of Revenue for a certain period of time. One day the Jiajing emperor summoned grand secretaries Zhang Cong and Li Shi (1471–1538) to the palace to deliberate the merits and demerits of his senior ministers. They concluded that Qin was meritorious but senile. Consequently, he was granted the title of grand guardian (*taibao*) and transferred back to Nanjing.[117] Ru Nan (*js* 1532), vice minister

82 *Patronage, Proving Ground, and Punishment*

of war in the Jiajing reign, had a similar fate to that of Qin. When he and a group of senior officials accompanied the Jiajing emperor on an inspection tour to the Western Palace (*Xigong*), he attracted the attention of the emperor, who considered him decrepit in appearance. Ru was therefore assigned to be vice minister of the Nanjing Ministry of Works.[118]

Preferential treatment was also extended to officials with slight physical disabilities. Yang Ning (d. 1548), minister of rites in the Jiajing reign, had a foot ailment. When the pain became too severe to walk, he was reassigned to become Nanjing minister of justice.[119]

Zheng Bengong (*js* 1514), after serving in Beijing as assistant commissioner (*tongzheng canyi*) at the office of transmission for nine years and receiving no promotion,[120] pleaded for transfer to Nanjing on the pretence of illness. As a result, he was reappointed assistant minister of the Nanjing Court of Judicial Review.[121] It is noteworthy that in this case, Zhang himself made the request, indicating that the practice of moving the superannuated to Nanjing was well understood by Ming officials. Having lost interest in climbing the official ladder, Zheng sought a less prestigious yet more secure political life.

Another favor granted by the Ming government to its officials was to allow some southerners to serve in Nanjing in order to be closer to their aged parents.[122] For instance, when Zhang Bangqi (1481–1528), a native of Yin country (present-day Ningbo, Zhejiang) and minister of rites, asked the Jiajing emperor's permission to be relocated to Nanjing to attend to his aged mother, he was granted the ministership of personnel in Nanjing.[123] Fang Peng (b. 1470) and Fang Feng, two filial brothers who passed the *jinshi* examination together in 1508 and were officials at, respectively, the Ministry of Rites and the Messenger Office, both requested to be transferred to Nanjing in order to be able to care for their mother. Their plea was accorded and one was appointed as director of the Fujian Bureau at the Nanjing Ministry of Justice and the other as censor at the Zhejiang Circuit of the Nanjing Censorate.[124]

This practice, which allowed some officials to work in Nanjing in order to attend to their elderly parents, may not have been common, although, together with the arrangement of moving superannuated and physically infirm officials to Nanjing, it does reflect the favorable treatment by the Ming government of its officials in the middle and late Ming. The benefit to the Ming was that it strengthened the allegiance of Ming bureaucrats to the imperial court.

Although there is no way of knowing the exact percentage of the officials in the Southern Capital who were disfavored, relegated or superannuated, it should be pointed out that the majority of Nanjing officials could not be classified into any of these categories. It is clear that most Nanjing officials assumed their posts in a normal bureaucratic fashion. Most of them, as shown in the second section of this chapter, were posted to Nanjing to enrich their bureaucratic service record. In fact powerful figures in Beijing often placed their own cronies in Nanjing for various reasons. Chief among them was to use those associates as informers and spies. For example, one of Zhang Juzheng's well-known agents was Fu Zuozhou, Zhang's fellow townsman

Patronage, Proving Ground, and Punishment   83

(*tongyi*) and supervising secretary in Nanjing. In the general evaluation of capital officials in 1581, Fu helped Zhang drive Tao Chengxue (1518–98), the Nanjing minister of rites, out of officialdom. Tao, who had passed the *jinshi* examination with Zhang in the same year, had ignored Fu's association with Zhang and refused to seek favor with this junior bureaucrat as many others did. He had also incurred Zhang's hatred by expressing his disapproval of Zhang's intention to stay in office after the death of his father in 1577. When the "great reckoning" (*daji*) of officials came in 1581, Fu took the opportunity to avenge himself and cater to Zhang Juzheng. Fu presented evidence showing Tao's "guilt" to Beijing, which Zhang used to prompt censors in Beijing to impeach Tao, who was eventually forced to retire.[125]

Grand Secretary Yan Song (1480–1565) also had his henchmen assume office in the Southern Capital. When he fell into disgrace in 1562, a number of high officials closely associated with him were dismissed from office. Among them, four were from Nanjing: He Jian, the Nanjing vice minister of justice; Hu Rulin, vice commissioner of the Nanjing Office of the Transmission; Bai Qichang, vice minister of the Nanjing Court of State Ceremonial; and Wang Cai (1508–84), vice minister of the Nanjing Court of Imperial Entertainment who concurrently took charge of the Nanjing National University. When serving as a provincial grand coordinator, He bribed Yan and his son, Yan Shifan (d. 1565), in order to obtain a speedy promotion. Bai was accused of involving himself in sensual indulgence with Yan Shifan, and Wang was accused of fawning on the Yans and frequently offering bribes.

Influential eunuch chiefs also had followers posted to Nanjing to consolidate their power. Ying Qiu, one of the ten close agents contemptuously dubbed the "Ten Dogs" by Ming contemporaries, was given the position of Nanjing vice minister of justice by Wei Zhongxian in 1624.[126] When Wei was finally forced to commit suicide in the early Chongzhen era, many high-ranking officials were implicated in his case and dismissed from officialdom. Among these were two Nanjing ministers, Fan Jishi and Zhang Pu, and the Nanjing censor Li Shixin.[127]

Two primary considerations led powerful figures in the Northern Capital to post their confederates in Nanjing. First, they needed their own men to keep watch on the other officials in Nanjing. Although Nanjing was a political center of secondary importance, it was nevertheless a national capital staffed with many ranking officials. Since many of these officials were sent there as a kind of punishment or were treated less favorably, the possibility of them forming an anti-Beijing faction was real. To prevent this from happening, the leaders in Beijing needed to have informants in Nanjing. This practice was perhaps one of the factors contributing to the absence of anti-Beijing factions or groups in the Southern Capital throughout the Ming. Second, Nanjing was after all a great cosmopolitan city where one could enjoy a rich cultural and intellectual life. The posts in Nanjing, though not political plums, did offer the office holders some measure of enjoyment of comfortable city life.[128] To go to Nanjing was better than to assume office in remote areas for a position of identical rank.

84 *Patronage, Proving Ground, and Punishment*

6. Concluding remarks

In summary, the role of the Nanjing administration in the political life of the Ming dynasty was largely determined by the nature of the administration. As a central capital government theoretically equal to the Beijing government but in reality enjoying less prestige, it served as a training ground for senior positions. The Southern Capital administration also furnished a number of grand coordinators and supreme commanders, special-purpose central officials dispatched to inspect and facilitate work in the provinces and strategic areas. By providing a retreat for disgraced Beijing officials, Nanjing helped to reduce tension among officials and regulate the operation of the Ming bureaucratic machine. The secondary capital, on account of its less demanding workload, became a place to accommodate physically feeble or aged officials. In fact, serving in Nanjing for many was by no means a miserable fate; junior officials used Nanjing to enrich their bureaucratic experience, and the superannuated stayed there to maintain their status. Nanjing could represent a setback in the political career of a disfavored or demoted official, but on the other hand, it could be used as a political haven, allowing them to be rehabilitated and recalled to Beijing to assume a position of identical rank after the downfall of their political opponents. The official career of Wang Shu mentioned in the first section of this chapter is rather illustrative. His first two appointments to Nanjing were normal promotion, while the third and fourth were typical Ming bureaucratic arrangements for getting rid of disfavored officials. Although Wang's administrative ability, bureaucratic experience, and moral integrity were widely recognized, he was always posted outside Beijing by the Chenghua emperor. It was only with the enthronement of the Hongzhi emperor that Wang was given a prominent position in the Northern Capital.

Before closing the chapter, it may be useful to add two notes regarding the personnel management of the Ming dynasty. First, although there were many cases of officials being relentlessly purged and punished, Ming bureaucrats in general were treated decently. That superannuated officials were often reassigned to Nanjing to take undemanding positions while maintaining their previous status is evidence of this lenient attitude. It is also attested by the fact that even when Beijing officials were punished by being sent down to Nanjing, they were, in most cases, given identical positions. Second, although irregularities occurred from time to time, it appears that the promotion and demotion of officials in the Ming essentially followed some established rules. Ming officials were regularly appraised by their superiors and subsequently reassigned. In addition to the regular rating (*kao*), by which officials were rated every three years until they received a total of three ratings and reassigned to new posts in accordance with their performance, there was a complement evaluation (*cha*): outer evaluation (*waicha*) for local officials.[129] The fate of the officials was in effect determined by their administrative performance. When a position was vacant prior to the conducting of the regular rating and evaluation, the normal procedure was that the vacancy would be

Patronage, Proving Ground, and Punishment   85

filled by one of the few collectively recommended. Depending on the rank of the vacant position, the recommendation could be made by the Ministry of Personnel, or the heads of the six ministries, the Censorate, the Court of Judicial Review, and the Office of Transmission, as well as officials from the six Offices of Scrutiny.[130] This process largely guaranteed a fair selection of suitable candidates, although the final decision rested with the emperor. Ming adherence to established bureaucratic norms is reflected by the pattern seen in the transfer of officials from Beijing to Nanjing and vice versa. In short, drastic promotion or demotion of officials was the exception rather than the rule in Ming officialdom.

Notes

1 For details of the Tumu Incident, see F. W. Mote, "The T'u-Mu Incident of 1449," in Frank Kierman and John K. Fairbank, eds, *Chinese Ways in Warfare*, 243–72.
2 He Qiaoyuan, *Mingshan cang*, 3989–91; Jiao Hong, *Guochao xianzheng lu*, 995. In writing this section, I have referred to the entry on Wang Shu in L. C. Goodrich and Chaoying Fang, eds, *Dictionary of Ming Biography*, 1416–20. I have adopted some of the dates given by the author Chaoying Fang, but the sources I cite are different from his.
3 Jiao, *Guochao xianzheng lu*, 994; He, *Mingshan cang*, 1945.
4 *MS*, 4831; He, *Mingshan cang*, 1945; Jiao, *Guochao xianzheng lu*, 995.
5 *MS*, 4831.
6 He, *Mingshan cang*, 1945; Jiao, *Guochao xianzheng lu*, 995.
7 For more on Qian Neng and his abusive stint in Yunnan, see Yang Sanshou, "Ming Xianzong shiqi de Yuannan zhenshou taijian Qian Neng," *Yunnan shifan daxue xuebao*, Vol. 34, No. 3 (May 2002), 53–5; Qi Chang, "Mingdai huanguan yu shidaifu guanxi de lingyimian," *Shixue jikan*, No. 4 (2008), 107–12.
8 The grand defender (*zhenshou*) was a special delegate from the central government to a large area such as a province (*sheng*) or a defender command (*zhen*) on the northern frontier. He was the tactical commander of military forces there. Sometimes a eunuch was employed to serve in such a capacity. Charles Hucker, *A Dictionary of Officials Titles in Imperial China*, 122.
9 He Liangjun, *Siyouzhai congshuo*, 65; Jiao, *Guochao xianzheng lu*, 995.
10 *MS*, 4832. The post of grand adjutant became a concurrent appointment of the Nanjing minister of war after 1487.
11 He, *Mingshan cang*, 1946.
12 Jiao, *Guochao xianzheng lu*, 996–7.
13 For more information on the eunuch grand commandant in the Ming Southern Capital, see Jun Fang, "The military triumvirate in the Southern Capital in the Ming dynasty," 10–11; Jun Fang, "Mingdai Nanjing de neiwai shoubei," 42–4.
14 He, *Mingshan cang*, 1948; Jiao, *Guochao xainzheng lu*, 997.
15 He, *Mingshan cang*, 1950; Jiao, *Guochao xianxheng lu*, 997.
16 For more on the political career of Hai Rui, see Ray Huang, "Hai Jui, the eccentric model official," in 1587, *A Year of No Significance*, 130–55; Li Jinquan, *Hai Rui pingzhuan*.
17 The Chinese are "shao ji wang suiyue, que qian bei yi". Hai Rui, *Hai Rui Ji*, 572.
18 Huang Kaihua, "Ming zhengzhi shang bingshe Nanjing buyuan zhi tese," *Mingshi lunji*, 29–35.
19 The Jiajing era was not an exception, but an epitome of the dynasty. Throughout the Ming, more than a half of the Nanjing ministers (256 out of the total of 497,

86 *Patronage, Proving Ground, and Punishment*

approximately 53 percent) were filled by the Beijing vice ministers. See Huang, "Ming zhengzhi shang bingshe Nanjing buyuan zhi tese," 29.

20 Huang Kaihua concludes incorrectly that in the Ming only one Nanjing vice minister received the appointment of ministership in the Beijing administration. See "Ming zhengzhi shang bingshe Nanjing buyuan zhi tese," 37. I have found at least five other vice ministers from the Nanjing administration who were elevated directly to ministerships in Beijing.

21 Xuan Ni (fl. 1460), the Nanjing vice censor-in-chief, was elevated to minister of justice in 1457, the first year of the Tianshun reign. He was the very person whom Huang Kaihua thinks was the only Nanjing vice minister promoted to a ministership in Beijing during the Ming. For his official career, see He, *Mingshan cang*, 3735–8; *MS*, 4324.

22 The Jiajing emperor succeeded his cousin, the Zhengde emperor, on condition that he accepted his predecessor's parents as his own parents. However, when he ascended the throne, he wanted to change this arrangement. He proposed recognizing his birth parents as his real parents and consequently granted them the necessary imperial titles. The young emperor's intention met with strong opposition from his court officials. The dispute, which lasted for more than a decade, is termed by historians as the "Great Rites Controversy." For details of this controversy, see Gu Yingtai, *Mingshi jishi benmo*, 508–31; Carney T. Fisher, *The Chosen One: Succession and Adoption in the Court of Ming Shizong*, 46–176.

23 Tan Qian, *Guoque*, 3298.

24 *MS*, 286.

25 *MS*, 294.

26 *MS*, 309.

27 *MS*, 316.

28 *MS*, 286, 294, 309.

29 Gao Youji (1461–1546) was the director of grain transport (*zongdu caoyun*) and censor-in-chief before being appointed Nanjing minister of works in 1527; Liu Tianhe (1479–1545), censor-in-chief and supreme commander (*zongdu*) of the Shaanxi area, was assigned to the post of Nanjing minister of revenue in 1540; Jia Yingchun (1485–1565) was also censor-in-chief and supreme commander of the Shannxi area before being appointed Nanjing minister of revenue. Tan, *Guoque*, 3357, 3603, 3890; Jiao, *Guochao xianzheng lu*,1863, 1601, 1228.

30 *Guoque* records that Wan Tang (*js* 1505) was minister of justice before being transferred to be the Nanjing minister of rites in 1551. The account in the *MS* says that Wan was transferred to become Nanjing minister of justice from his former post as the vice minister of war. Tan, *Guoque*, 3409; *MS*, 5340.

31 *MS*, 5062; Tan, *Guoque*, 3361.

32 He, *Mingshan cang*, 4410.

33 *MS*, 3232–33.

34 *MS*, 5335.

35 The post of director-general of supplies shuttled between the Beijing censor-in-chief and the Nanjing vice minister of revenue several times during the Ming. In the early Ming period the post was held by the Beijing censor-in-chief, then in 1447 the Nanjing vice minister of revenue was ordered to assume the position. During the Jiajing reign, the post was assigned back to the Beijing censor-in-chief. In 1547 the Nanjing vice minister of revenue was again assigned to the post. In 1560 the Ming government, for the third time, gave the post to the Beijing censor-in-chief, and ten years later, in 1570, the Nanjing vice minister of revenue was ordered once again to take charge of the transportation of tax grain.

36 Tan, *Guoque*, 3367; Jiao, *Guochao xianzheng lu*, 2037.

37 *MS*, 5306; Tan, *Guoque*, 3270.

38 *MS*, 5145.

Patronage, Proving Ground, and Punishment   87

39 Grand secretaries were officials of great power in the Ming central government, comparable to the prime ministers of early dynasties. Originating in 1382 as a new category of post in the Hanlin Academy, rank 5a, with the specific duties of tutoring the heir apparent and assisting the emperor with his paperwork, in the early 1400s their influence increased, and from 1424 they were regularly given concurrent nominal appointment as vice minister or minister in the six ministries, which raised their rank to the level of 3a or 2a. In addition, they came to be given even more prestigious status in the officialdom with top-echelon but non-functioning posts among the three dukes (*sangong*) or three solitaries (*sangu*), with 1a or 1b rank. Their numbers varied from three to six and their working procedures gradually stabilized under a senior grand secretary (*shoufu*) as recognized leader and decision-maker in the group. Their principal function came to be recommending imperial action on memorials and preparing edicts after an imperial decision was made. Charles Hucker, *Official Titles in Imperial China*, 466–7.
40 Understandably, Gu Qiyuan, who died in 1628, listed in his book only Yang, Liang, Zhang, and Ye as the grand secretaries who were from Nanjing. See *Kezuo zhuiyu*, 73.
41 Xu Zi, *Xiaotian jizhuan*, 12.179. Huang Bingshi also had a similar comment. See *Hai Rui ji*, 572.
42 Zheng Xiao (1499–1566), who later became minister of justice in the late Jiajing reign, was asked to comment on the appointment. He supported the emperor's choice by citing precedents which indicated that there were instances in previous reigns when vice ministers of personnel became ministers (of personnel) directly. See *Jinyan*, 158.
43 Zhu Guozhen, who served as senior grand secretary during the Tianqi era, had noticed that this pattern, He complained that was against the set rule. See *Yongzhuang xiaopin*, 169.
44 See Fan Jingwen, *Nanshu zhi*, 95.14a–95.24a, 143.1a–145.63b; Wang Shizhen, *Yanshantang biejie*, *juan* 50, 939–43.
45 Tan, *Guoque*, 3485, 3528, 3579; Li Yeming, *Zhan Ruoshui nianpu*, 142, 162, 219, 248.
46 For more on the genesis and evolution of the system of grand coordinator and supreme commander, see *MS*, 1773–88; Gu, *Kezuo zhuiyu*, 3.5b; Hucker, *The Censorial System of Ming China*, 51–2; *Official Titles in Imperial China*, 75–6; Chu and Saywell, *Career Patterns in the Ch'ing Dynasty: The Office of Governorgeneral*, 1–2.
47 *MS*, 1774; Wu, *Ming dufu nianbiao*, 1982, 647–8.
48 The director-general of grain transport was concurrently the grand coordinator of Fengyang. *MS*, 1773; Wu, *Ming dufu niaobiao*, 322.
49 *MS*, 1775; *Ming dufu nianbiao*, 346.
50 Jiliao is an abbreviation of Jizhou and Liaodong, two of the nine permanent border defense commands (Jiubian) set up by the Ming along the Great Wall line from Manchuria to Gansu to counter Mongol raids. The supreme commander of Jiliao supervised the grand coordinator of Shuntian, Baoding, and Liaodong. *MS*, 1773; Wu, *Ming dufu niaobiao*, 1.
51 Xuanda is an abbreviation of Xuanfu and Datong, another two of the nine border defense commands. The grand coordinators of Xuanfu, Datong, and Shanxi were under the control of the supreme commander of Xuanda. *MS*, 1773–4; Wu, *Ming dufu niaobiao*, 103.
52 Shaanxi sanbian denotes the three border defense commanders at Shanxi, Yansui, and Guyuan. The supreme commander of Shaanxi sanbian was charged with supervising and controlling the grand coordinators of Shaanxi, Yansui, Ningxia, and Gansu. *MS*, 1774; Wu, *Ming dufu naiobian*, 199–200.

88 Patronage, Proving Ground, and Punishment

53 One exception might be Gansu, where three Nanjing officials were appointed as grand coordinators.

54 One reason why Guangxi had no grand coordinator from the Nanjing administration might be that the grand coordinator of Guangxi was under the supervision of the Liangguang supreme commander.

55 The others were: two ministers, seven vice ministers, one censor-in-chief, one vice censor-in-chief, nine assistant censor-in-chief, one minister of the Seals Office.

56 There were, of course, ministers from the five courts in Beijing who were appointed as grand coordinators.

57 Jun Fang, "The military triumvirate in the Southern Capital of the Ming dynasty," 9; Jun Fang, "Mingdai Nanjing guanshuzhi gaishuo," 141.

58 For the evolution of Beijing and Nanjing as the primary and secondary capitals of the Ming dynasty, see Edward L. Farmer, *Early Ming Government: The Evolution of Dual Capitals*.

59 *Ming Shilu: Yingzong*, 67551–2.

60 Jiao, *Guochao xianzheng lu*, 1087; *Mingshi*, 5065–70.

61 Gu, *Mingshi jishi benmo*, 513.

62 *MS*, 5552. For more on Zhang Juzheng and his political domination in the early Wanli years, see Ray Huang, *1587, A Year of No Significance*, 75–103; Henry Miller, *State versus Gentry in Late Ming Dynasty China* 55–74; Zhu Dongrun, *Zhang Juzheng dazhuan*; Liu Zhiqin, *Zhang Juzheng pingzhuan*.

63 Yao was hated by Shi; Zhang offended Shi because he declined his invitation to drink together (he also offended Yang Shan, the minister of personnel, for expressing different views); Xu used to be a close friend of both Shi and Xu Youzhen (fl. 1560), another domineering figure in the Tianshun era. After Shi broke ties with Xu Youzhen, Xu Bin was implicated and squeezed out. See Xu Hong, *Ming minchen wanyan xulu*, 12.6b; *MS*, 4412, 4714.

64 He, *Mingshan cang*, 4487–8; Tan, *Guoque*, 3479.

65 *MS*, 4853.

66 *MS*, 4883.

67 Chen was promoted to the position by Wang Shu, the minister of personnel. Resenting Wang and hoping to implicate him through Chen, Liu Ji instigated his henchmen to accuse Chen of being ignorant of judicial matters. *MS*, 4933.

68 *MS*, 4888, 5058, 5061–3.

69 Huang Zongxi, *Mingru xue'an*, 533.

70 They were dubbed the "Eight Tigers" (*bahu*) by civil officials. The other seven were Ma Yongcheng, Gao Feng, Luo Xiang, Wei Bin, Qiu Ju, Gu Dayong, and Zhang Yong. *MS*, 7768.

71 The eunuch agency was created in 1420 to investigate treasonable offenses of any kind. It gradually became an imperial secret service not subject to the control of any regular governmental organization. The depot was originally headed by the powerful eunuch director of the Directorate of Ceremonial, who used the personnel of the Imperial Bodyguard (*jinyiwei*) as the depot's policemen. See Liu Ruoyu, *Minggong shi*, 30–2; Hucker, *Official Titles in Imperial China*, 551.

72 Another eunuch secret service agency established in 1477 on the pattern of the Eastern Depot. Gu, *Mingshi jishi benmo*, 385–90; Hucker, *Official Titles in Imperial China*, 226.

73 Xiaoling jingjun was an imperial eunuch army responsible for protecting the mausoleums of the Ming founder and his eldest son. *Minggong shi*, 29; Shi Li, "Jingjun kao," 49.

74 *MS*, 7786–87.

75 *MS*, 7789.

76 *MS*, 7789; Long Wenbin, *Ming huiyao*, 636.

Patronage, Proving Ground, and Punishment 89

77 Wu was recommended by the Secretariat as a candidate for the vacant ministership of works when its minister, Li Sui, retired. Liu managed to assign Wu to be the Nanjing minister of revenue. *MS*, 4941.

78 Ma was transferred to the Nanjing Ministry of Works. *MS*, 4951.

79 Zhang was assigned to become the vice censor-in-chief of the Nanjing Censorate. Jiao, *Guochao xianzheng lu*, 2781.

80 Feng was assigned to the Nanjing Hanlin Academy. Jiao, *Guochao xianzheng lu*, 808.

81 Tan, *Guoque*, 3384; Jiao, *Guochao xianzheng lu*, 1757.

82 *MS*, 6569. Zhang was recorded in the source as *zuoshi*, an ambiguous term for committing a misconduct.

83 Another place to send punished eunuchs off to was the nominal Middle Capital, Fengyang, where the imperial tombs of the Ming founder's ancestors were located. The eunuch agency there was the Office of the (Fengyang Eunuch) Grand Commandant. See Liu, *Minggong shi*, 29.

84 In some cases the biography of a eunuch also includes those of his associates, whom I have excluded from this count.

85 Seven (Wang Zhen, Cao Jixiang, He Ding, Liu Jin, Chen Zeng, Wang An, and Wei Zhongxian) lost their lives, either decapitated or murdered, and one (Li Guang) committed suicide fearing severe punishment. Liu and Wei were exiled to Fengyang and murdered en route. Wang An was also exiled to the Nanjing Eunuch Army and later murdered. *MS*, 7766–7831.

86 They were Zheng He, Jin Ying, Huai En, Zhang Jing, Chen Ju, Zhang Yixian. *MS*, 7766–7831.

87 One (Gao Qiqian) surrendered to the Qing, one (Wang Cheng'en) committed suicide after Chongzhen emperor hanged himself, the third (Fang Zhenghua) was slain by the rebels, *MS*, 7829–31.

88 *MS*, 7825.

89 They were Wang Zhi, Liang Fang, Jiang Zong, Zhang Yong, Gu Dayong, Li Fang, Feng Bao, and Cui Wensheng. *MS*, 7766–7831.

90 He was soon relegated to be a chief steward. *MS*, 7781. In the eunuch hierarchy regulated in 1359, its officials in descending order were director (*taijian*, 4a), vice director (*shaojian*, 4b), assistant director (*jianchen*, 5a), archivist (*dianbu*, 6a), member of the regular entourage (*changsui*, 6a), chief steward (*fengyu*, 6a). *MS*, 1825.

91 Wang Qiao, *Fanglu ji*, 15.74b-75a; *MS*, 7794, 7800–803.

92 Incense handler was a low-ranking position in the eunuch hierarchy, with a rank from 7a to 8a. *MS*, 1824. Recommended by Grand Secretary Yang Yiqing, Zhang was reappointed as director of the Directorate for Imperial Accouterments in 1529. *MS*, 7793.

93 *MS*, 7782.

94 *MS*, 7785–86, 7800, 7827.

95 *MS*, 4751–54. Due to the plea of Supervising Secretary Mao Hong, Zhang was reappointed to the Nanjing Court of Judicial Review to be a case reviewer.

96 Jiao, *Guochao xianzheng lu*, 314; Huang, *Mingru xue'an*, 180.

97 *MS*, 4751–54; Jiao, *Guochao xianzheng lu*, 314; Huang, *Mingru xue'an*, 180.

98 Jiao, *Guochao xianzheng lu*, 1011.

99 Xu Xuemo, *Shimiao shiyu lu*, 242–3.

100 They were: blows of light bamboo (*chi*), blows of heavy bamboo (*zhang*), exile (*tu*), military exile (*liu*), and death (*si*).

101 For example, F. W. Mote, in his famous critique of Wittfogel's theory of Oriental Despotism, twice characterizes the Ming as "an age of terror." See his "The growth of Chinese despotism," *Oriens Extremus*, Vol. 8, No. 1 (1961), 22, 26.

102 The best-known examples are the executions surrounding the Hu Weiyong case in 1380 and the Lan Yu case 13 years later. The number put to death in the former is

90 Patronage, Proving Ground, and Punishment

said to have exceeded 30,000, and in the latter, more than 15,000. For the cruel treatment of court officials in the Hongwu era, see Mote, "The growth of Chinese despotism," 26–9.

103 The most prestigious and influential of the Imperial Guards (*qinjunwei*), *Jinyiwei* functioned as the personal bodyguard of the emperor as well as a secret police organization of great scope in act and size. A forerunner of this unit was founded in 1367, a year before the dynasty was founded. It was reorganized in 1369 and fully developed under the name of *Jinyiwei* in 1382. See Mote,"The growth of Chinese despotism," 28.

104 For a recent study of the court beatings in the Ming, see Xu Chunyan, "Mingdai tingzhang tanxi," 93–100.

105 The compilers of *MS* states that the Ming code was simpler than the Tang code in terms of number of statutes, and harsher than the Song code in terms of punishment. *MS*, 2285. For the contents of the *Da Ming lü*, see Jiang Yonglin, transl., *The Great Ming Code*; for detailed studies of the code, see Jiang Yonglin, *The Mandate of Heaven and* The Great Ming Code, and Edward Farmer, *Zhu Yuanzhang and Early Ming Legislation*.

106 Wang Zhen was in power from 1442–9, Wang Zhi from 1476–81, Liu Jin from 1506–10, Wei Zhongxian from 1621–7.

107 In the fourth month of 1479, 56 court officials were ordered by Wang Zhi to be thrashed. In the second month of 1506, Liu Jin had 21 officials beaten. In the first month of 1519, 107 officials were flogged in public for opposing the Zhengde emperor's pleasure-seeking southern trip (*nanxun*); 11 died of the beatings. In the seventh month of that year, 134 high officials were clubbed at court for opposing the Jiajing emperor in the Great Rites Controversy; 16 died of the torture. *MS*, 175, 201, 211, 219.

108 *MS*, 2321–26.

109 Shen Zhaoyang, *Huang Ming Jia Long liangchao wenjian lu*, 101; Xia Xie, *Ming tongjian*, 1572–3.

110 He, *Mingshan cang*, 4232; Jiao, *Guochao xianzheng lu*, 505–6.

111 He Qiaoxin, *Jiaoqiu wenji*, 20.4a.

112 *MS*, 6851.

113 *MS*, 5134–35.

114 Preface to Zhou Yingbin, *Jiujing cilin zhi*.

115 *MS*, 4319.

116 Xu, *Shimiao shiyu lu*, 772.

117 *MS*, 5144–5.

118 *MS*, 7369–70.

119 Xu Hong, *Ming mingchen wanyan xulu*, 4.16a–b; *Ming shilu: Yingzong*, 6323.

120 In the Ming, the maximum tenure for an official in a post was normally nine years. Every three years, each official was rated (*kao*) by his superiors. When "rating were completed" (*kaoman*), namely, after an official had spent nine years in one post and received three ratings, he reported to the Ministry of Personnel in Beijing for reconsideration of his status which might result in being promoted, retained, or demoted. Those who were considered "competent" received promotion; those rated "normal" retained their present position; those rated "incompetent" received demotion. See Bai Gang, ed., *Zhongguo zhengzhi zhidu shi*, 839–40; Hucker, *Official Titles in Imperial China*, 82.

121 *MS*, 5099.

122 Those officials might be natives of south China, or simply those who preferred the warmer climate in the south.

123 Jiao, *Guochao xianzheng lu*, 1755.

124 Shao Bao, *Rongchuntang houji*, 4.28b–9a. A similar case was that of Chen Chen (1477–1545). After obtaining his *jinshi* degree in 1517 and receiving an

appointment as secretary at the Ministry of Justice in Beijing, he asked to be transferred to the Southern Capital in order to attend to his aged parents. He was therefore reappointed to the Nanjing Ministry of Revenue. Huang Zongxi, *Ming wenhai*, 399.6b.

125 Shen Defu, *Wanli Yehuo bian*, 788.

126 *MS*, 7862.

127 *MS*, 6660, 7852.

128 For the vibrant urban life in Ming Nanjing, see Mote, "The transformation of Nanjing, 1350–1400," 147–50; Si-yen Fei, *Negotiating Urban Space: Urbanization and Late Ming Nanjing*, 149–85; Nanjingshi difangzhi bianzuan weiyuanhui bangongshi, ed., *Nanjing tongshi: Mingdai juan*, 484–529; Duan Zhijun, *Gudu Nanjing*, 279–303.

129 The usual practice of the outer evaluation was that magistrates of counties and subprefectures submitted to their prefects monthly reports (*yueji*), in which they took note of personnel considered misfits or incompetents. Prefects presented consolidated annual reports (*suiji*) of such special evaluations to the provincial authorities. Then every third year the provincial authorities submitted consolidated evaluation reports to the central government, triggering a large-scale outer evaluation. The capital evaluation was held once every six years. Officials of grade 4 and above were only required to submit self-evaluations (*zichen*), confessing their faults. Hucker, *Official Titles in Imperial China*, 82.

130 Bai, *Zhongguo zhengzhi zhidu shi*, 837.

4 Center of Wealth

The financial functions of the Southern Capital

The economic center of the post-1421 Ming dynasty, like those of its predecessors, the Sui, Tang, Song, and Yuan, was distinct from the dynastic locus of political power.[1] Since the nation's primary capital was relocated to the north, Beijing became the political and military center of the empire, while the center of population and tax revenue of the dynasty was in the region south of the Yangzi River. To ensure a stable financial income and therefore a lasting regime, the Ming court made every effort to maintain its grip over the south. The Southern Capital administration was in this regard an indispensable auxiliary institution which helped stabilize the south and generate more tax revenue. This chapter focuses on the economic functions of the Nanjing administration, especially those of its fiscal branch, the Nanjing Ministry of Revenue.

1. Regional roles

Like its counterpart in the Beijing administration, the Nanjing Ministry of Revenue was the largest department in the Nanjing administration, with a staff of some 50 officials and more than 100 lesser functionaries. Under the minister and vice minister were 13 functional bureaus which bore the names of the empire's 13 provinces. The bureau was normally administered by a director, a vice director,[2] and one to two secretaries. They were assisted by double the number of lesser functionaries. Some 50 students from the Nanjing National University were assigned to work in the ministry as apprentices, four for each bureau (except for the Guizhou Bureau, which had fewer students).[3]

There were a number of other agencies under the direct supervision of the Nanjing Ministry of Revenue: a supervisorate of paper money (*baochao tijusi*), nine treasuries (*ku*, i.e. Baochao, Guanghui, Zangfa, Chengyun, Jiazi, Yizi, Bingzi, Dingzi, and Wuzi),[4] five granaries (*cang*),[5] a silver vault (*yinku*), a salt control station (Longjiang *yancang piyansuo*), a storehouse for the salt certificates (*yanyinku*), and two archives (*jiageku*).[6]

Like other departments in the Nanjing administration, which were independent of their counterparts in Beijing, the Nanjing Ministry of Revenue was not a branch office of the Beijing Ministry of Revenue. Subordinate only to the throne, the Nanjing minister of revenue reported directly to the emperor. However, the ministry's role in the management of national financial matters, especially in the decision-making process regarding the empire's fiscal policies, were modest. Under the Ming system there was no central authority administering the empire's finances other than the emperor himself.[7] The premiership was abolished in 1380 and never revived. The grand secretaries limited their functions to rescript-drafting. Although they were consulted by the emperor and did participate in decision-making, they were never officially accorded any power. The minister of revenue supervised routine fiscal matters, yet he could never act without prior imperial approval.[8] The emperor received memorials from a large number of censors, supervising secretaries, and ministerial officials, and made his own decisions based on their suggestions and proposals. The Ministry of Revenue, officially charged with "managing the population, land, grain, and revenue of the empire," had never been intended to shape policy. Most of the time, the minister of revenue acted as fiscal adviser to the crown. Under normal circumstances his ministerial duties involved only limited planning. The Ministry of Revenue under the Ming was therefore much less an executive agency than a massive accounting office.[9] In terms of the decision-making process, the major form of participation for the Nanjing Ministry of Revenue officials was to present memorials to the court expressing their views. In fact, in the Ming, suggestions and criticisms on fiscal matters could be initiated by practically any official, regardless of his area of specialization and current assignment.[10] One body of evidence that demonstrates the involvement of Nanjing officials in the discussion of national fiscal matters is the *Memorials from the Nanjing Ministry of Revenue* (*Liuji shucao*), a collection of memorials submitted by Bi Ziyan (1569–1638), the Nanjing minister of revenue in the late 1620s.[11]

This evidence shows that the bulk of routine work of the Nanjing Ministry of Revenue was regional. The ministry controlled the salaries of the civil bureaucrats, military personnel, and eunuch staff in the Southern Capital administration, as well as the nobles residing in Nanjing and its surrounding areas. The management of the annual military subsidy (*nianli*),[12] "traveling grain" (*xingliang*) for the transportation soldiers, and horse fodder of the Nanjing guard units was also under the Nanjing Ministry of Revenue. The amount of the salary grain for all the personnel in the Nanjing administration was budgeted two years in advance, deducted from the tax grain of the year immediately before the actual year of issuance. For instance, salary grain for staff in the Nanjing administration for the year 1551 would be budgeted in 1549, deducted from the tax grain collected by the Nanjing Ministry of Revenue in 1550, and then distributed in 1551.[13]

The duties of managing the salary grain, the military subsidy, the traveling grain, and the fodder, was shared by the 13 bureaus of the ministry. For example, the Bureau of Shaanxi was charged with managing the salary grain of the staff of the Nanjing Chief Military Commission of the Right, the Nanjing Court of Judicial Review, the Nanjing Court of State Ceremonial,

94 *Center of Wealth*

the Nanjing Hanlin Academy, and the military subsidy for officers and soldiers of three Nanjing guard units (Yulinyou, Liushouyou, and Henghai) and their granaries. The Bureau of Henan was responsible for the salary grain of the staff of the Nanjing Ministry of Rites, the Nanjing Court of Sacrifice, as well as the subsidy for three guard units (Jinyi, Yingwu, Guangwu) and one battalion.[14]

However, it would be a mistake to conclude that the fiscal functions of the Nanjing administration, especially its fiscal branch, the Nanjing Ministry of Revenue, were entirely regional. In fact, the ministry had a plethora of roles to play in the administration of the empire's finance. This will be shown in the ensuing sections.

2. Collection of tax grain

Like many of its imperial predecessors, the Ming relied primarily on revenue from land. Because most taxes were assessed in grain,[15] which fluctuated in value, it is impossible to determine revenue in exact monetary terms. However, it is possible to make a rough estimate based on the commutation rate of grain and silver, which varied from a low of 0.5–0.7 tael per picul (*shi* or *dan*) in south China to a high of 0.8–1 tael per picul in north China. According to Ray Huang's estimate, the total annual revenue from agricultural land in the late sixteenth century approximated 25 million taels.[16] During the 1575–1600 period, the annual revenue of salt, the second largest source of income in the Ming, was estimated at 2,000,000 taels, and the annual income from all the other various miscellaneous taxes during the 1570–90 period was estimated to be 3,780,000 taels.[17] Thus, the grain taxes constituted approximately 80 percent of the national tax revenue.

One of the roles of the Nanjing administration in the management of national fiscal matters was involvement in the collection of tax grain. The duty was shared by the Ministry of Revenue and the Nanjing Ministry of Revenue. The former was responsible for ten provinces and one metropolitan area: Shaanxi, Shanxi, Henan, Fujian, Sichuan, Guangdong, Guangxi, Yunnan, Guizhou, and Bei Zhili. The latter, three provinces and one metropolitan area: Zhejiang, Jiangxi, Huguang, and Nan Zhili.[18]

It should be noted that not all the tax grains went to Beijing or Nanjing. In fact, only a small portion of them were delivered to the two capitals. Most of the grains were retained at various local administrations (counties, prefectures, and provinces) as salaries of officials, stipends of government students, payments to princes and imperial clansmen, as well as subsidies to local army units. This is shown in the following table (4.1).

Autumn grain (*qiuliangmi*) and summer tax (*xiashuimai*) were two major land taxes in kind during the Ming period. The former, the bulk of which was rice, was to be submitted before the second month of the subsequent year. The latter, primarily wheat, had to be submitted before the eighth month after the winter wheat harvest.[19] As Table 4.1 shows, the total amount of the tax grain in *c.* 1578 was 26,600,000 piculs. Approximately 44 percent of this tax

Center of Wealth 95

Table 4.1 Estimated land tax collection and distribution in piculs of grain, *c.* 1578

Collection	Distribution	
Summer tax	(4,600,000)	
	Retained funds and supplies	11,700,000
Autumn grain	(22,000,000)	
	Delivered to frontier posts	3,300,000
	Delivered to Nanjing	1,500,000
	Delivered to Beijing	9,534,000
	As tribute grain	(4,000,000)
	As 'white grain'	(214,000)[20]
	In cotton cloth and other supplies	(900,000)
	In Gold Floral Silver	(4,050,000)[21]
	Otherwise permanently commuted	(370,000)
	Miscellaneous and unaccounted for	566,000
Total 26,600,000	26,600,000	

Source: Haung, *Taxation in Ming China*, 177
Note: The figures are derived from summarizing the data given in *juan* 25–28 and 42 of *DMHD*.

was retained as funds and supplies at various local taxpaying administrations, 12 percent was delivered directly to frontier posts,[22] and 2 percent was miscellaneous and unaccounted for. The amounts that were collected and stored by the Nanjing Ministry of Revenue and its counterpart in Beijing, 1.5 million and 9.5 million respectively, constituted 6 and 36 percent of the national total.

The four groups of figures available in the Ming sources indicate that the basic quota of the tax grains (autumn grain and summer tax) changed very little over time. The tax grains of 1393, 1502, 1542, and 1578 were 28,442,350; 26,792,619; 29,190,606; and 26,638,412 piculs respectively.[23] The disbursement of the tax grains did not change much either, as indicated by a report of the Ministry of Revenue in 1501.[24] This means that the workload of the Nanjing Ministry of Revenue and its Beijing counterpart remained largely unchanged from one century to the next. It is also necessary to point out that although the amount of tax grain delivered directly to the Nanjing administration by the four provinces (Nan Zhili, Zhejiang, Jiangxi, and Huguan) was minimal, the total amount was much higher, because most of it was directly delivered to the army stations in the northern frontier by taxpayers and the military transport.

Ever since the Tang, and especially since the Southern Song, south China (the region south of the Yangzi river) had surpassed the northwest and central plain in terms of population density, production and consumption levels, agricultural technology, per unit yield, irrigation systems, and commercial activity. Consequently, the south became heavily taxed. It was said that in the Tang, nine-tenths of the dynasty's financial revenue came from the south.[25]

96 *Center of Wealth*

The succeeding Song and Yuan dynasties also relied heavily on southern tax revenues to sustain the operation of the bureaucratic machine and pay the salaries of their officials.[26] The Ming dynasty was no exception. The four southern provinces, which delivered part of their tax grain directly to Nanjing, were the most advanced and prosperous as well as the most heavily taxed in the empire. Of the four, Nan Zhili shouldered the heaviest tax burden, as two of its fourteen prefectures, Suzhou and Songjiang, furnished approximately 13 to 15 percent of the total autumn grain. In 1393, the two prefectures paid 15 percent of the empire's autumn grain, and in 1502 and 1578, they paid slightly more than 13 percent.[27]

According to Ming sources, the tax grain submitted by Nan Zhili,[28] Zhejiang, Jiangxi, and Huguang in the years 1393, 1502, 1542, and 1598, counted for more than half the national total. Summer tax submitted by the four provinces approximated one-third of the national amount. In terms of percentage, the autumn grain supplied by Nan Zhili, Zhejiang, Jiangxi, and Huguang in the four different eras ranged from a low of 53 percent (1502) to a high of 60 percent (1393);[29] while the summer tax ranged from a low of 28 percent (1393) to a high of 35 percent (1542).[30] Among the four, Nan Zhili shared roughly one-fourth of the empire's autumn grain, paying 29 percent in 1393, 22 percent in 1502, 25 percent in 1542, and 23 percent in 1578. Its share in the nation's summer tax was approximately one-fifth, submitting 22 percent in 1393, 20 percent in 1502, 27 percent in 1542, and 20 percent in 1578.[31] Given that most of the Ming provincial figures on the land were random estimates and that it was standard practice to under-report population, the official figures on land and population have little intrinsic value.[32] Nevertheless, they accord with the fundamental reality of the empire and do reflect the basic financial situation in the Ming realm.

In the Ming, under the bureaus of the Ministry of Revenue and Nanjing Ministry of Revenue were five subdivisions: the statistics section (*minke*), general accounts section (*zhike*, or *duzhike*), special accounts section (*jinke*), granaries section (*cangke*), and auditing section (*suanke*). The statistics section was mainly responsible for the storage of household registers; the general accounts section was concerned with awards, monthly rations of the soldiers (*yueliang*), and the salaries of officials and nobles; the special accounts section was charged with the management of silk, currency, and various material supplies; granaries section took charged of the collection and storage of the tax grain as well as the colony produce (*tunliang*) and fodder. The auditing section was established later than the other four to check the expenditure of the guard units.[33] The tax grains of Nan Zhili, Zhejiang, Jiangxi, and Huguang were handled by the granaries sections of the 11 bureaus (except for Shangdong and Guizhou bureaus) in the Nanjing Ministry of Revenue. Those from Zhejiang, Jiangxi, and Huguang provinces were administered by the granaries sections in the Zhejiang Bureau, Jiangxi Bureau, and Huguang Bureau respectively. The collection of the tax grains of Nan Zhili were shared by all the other eight bureaus at the ministry. This is shown in Table 4.2.

Table 4.2 The bureaus which administered the tax grain

Bureau	Provinces and prefectures
Zhejiang	Zhejiang
Jiangxi	Jiangxi
Huguang	Huguang, Guangdezhou
Shaanxi	Ningguo, Chuzhou
Guangdong	Taiping, Zhenjiang, Hezhou
Fujian	Anqing, Luzhou
Henan	Songjiang, Fengyang
Shanxi	Suzhou
Sichuan	Cizhou
Guangxi	Huizhou, Huai'an
Yunnan	Changzhou

Source: *NJHBZ*, 4.9a–4.19b

The tax grain delivered to the Southern Capital was stored in the granaries of the Nanjing Ministry of Revenue. Approximately two-thirds of the grain was used as the salaries of the civil, military, and eunuch officials in the Nanjing administration, as well as the wages and supplies of the soldiers and horses in the Nanjing guard units. The guard soldiers consumed as much as 90 percent or more of the salary/wage grain. For example, in the year 1551, the expenditure of the Nanjing administration was budgeted at 1.1 million piculs of grain. Of this, 1.01 million, or approximately 93 percent, were allocated to the guard soldiers and only 7 percent were used as salaries for officials at various offices.[34] The remaining one-third of the tax grain stored in the granaries of the Nanjing Ministry of Revenue was reserved for urgent needs such as famine relief. In 1466, when the city of Nanjing and surrounding counties were struck by devastating crop failure, 40,000 piculs of grain were released from the Nanjing granaries for sale at a reduced price to famine victims. In 1544 when the Nanjing area was once again hit by debilitating drought, 20,000 piculs of grain were sold to refugees at a reduced price.[35]

In the Ming, the central official responsible for supervising the collection and storage of the tax grain delivered to the Southern Capital was the Nanjing director-general of supplies (*zongdu Nanjing liangchu*), also known as *Nanjing liangchu*, or *zongli liangchu*. For approximately half the post-1421 Ming period, the post was assumed by the Nanjing vice minister of revenue, and the other half, by the chiefs of the Beijing Censorate.[36] In the early years of the dynasty the position was held by the censors-in-chief or vice censors-in-chief from the Beijing Censorate. In 1447, six years after Beijing was finally declared the dynasty's primary capital, the post was assigned to the vice minister of the Nanjing Ministry of Revenue.[37] In 1451, the second year of the Jingtai reign, the assignment was returned to the Beijing vice censor-in-chief.[38] Until 1547, the directorship-general of grain supplies was primarily controlled by top officials in the Beijing Censorate. Only one Nanjing vice

98 Center of Wealth

minister of revenue (Pan Rong, d. 1496) is found to have been given this appointment in the mid-Chenghua reign.[39] In 1547 the position was again assigned to the Nanjing vice minister of revenue.[40] In the fourth month of 1560, two months after the riot of the Prowess-Inspiring Division (*zhenwuying*) and following the request of many censorial officials, the post of director-general of supplies was once again shifted to the head of the Beijing Censorate.[41] In 1570, the post of director-general of supplies was, for the third time, assigned to the Nanjing vice minister.[42]

It cannot presently be determined why the Ming government assigned the Nanjing Ministry of Revenue to collect the tax grain of Nan Zhlli, Zhenjiang, Jiangxi, and Huguang, or why it was not allocated more provinces – or fewer. Nor are we certain about precisely why the directorship-general of supplies fluctuated between Beijing and Nanjing officials. What is certain is that the Ming court wanted the Nanjing administration to share some of the responsibility of managing the fiscal affairs of the realm. When the directorship-general of supplies was first entrusted to the Nanjing Ministry of Revenue, the main consideration of the court was that the duties of the Nanjing Ministry of Revenue were relatively undemanding and thus it should be charged with more responsibilities.[43] This was also perhaps one of the reasons for reassigning the post to the Nanjing vice minister of revenue in 1547 and 1570. On the other hand, the court in Beijing wanted to retain some measure of control over the tax grain delivered to the Southern Capital. It is plausible that the court felt more comfortable in assigning the duty to officials directly from Beijing, as suggested by an imperial edict of 1478. In that year it was decreed that officials who were natives of Zhejiang, Jiangxi, Suzhou and Songjiang could not be given the duty of inspecting granaries (*xuncang*) in the Nanjing area.[44] This edict clearly indicates that the central government feared such officials might be sympathetic to the people from the most heavily taxed areas, thus impeding tax collection and storage.[45]

3. Transport of tribute grain

In addition to its major responsibility of collecting and storing part of the tax grains from Nan Zhili, Zhejiang, Jiangxi, and Huguang, the Nanjing administration also played a role in the transport of the tribute grain (*caoliang*) from the south to the north.

The tribute grain transport (*caoyun*) was the system of moving tax grain and other goods by water from the provinces to the capital, and sometimes from the capital to other regions. Control of the system had been essential to the political power of successive Chinese dynasties since the Han, and the practice continued in the Ming. In the early years of the dynasty, when the primary capital was still in Nanjing, provisions were shipped northwards to supply the armies battling the Northern Mongols. When the court was relocated to Beijing in 1421, the transport of grain from the south to the north became virtually indispensable for the Ming government.

The Ming tribute grain consisted of the volume of the autumn grain that remained after deducting the amount for local administrative use, granary reserves, and the palace treasuries in the Southern Capital. It was supplied by Nan Zhili, Zhejiang, Jiangxi, and Huguang in the south and Shandong and Henan in the north and was destined for granaries and treasuries in Beijing.[46] Another four million piculs of grain from Nan Zhili, Zhejiang, Jiangxi, Huguang, Fujian, Guangdong, and Guangxi were delivered to Beijing in the form of Gold Floral Silver, a type of high-grade silver collected in lieu of tax grain.

The annual amount of the tribute grain to be shipped to the north varied in the early years[47] but was fixed at 4,000,000 piculs per annum from 1472.[48] Of the aggregate, 3,244,000 piculs came from Nan Zhili, Zhejiang, Jiangxi and Huguang (termed southern grain, *Nanliang*), 755,600 piculs were from Shandong and Henan (called northern grain, *Beiliang*).[49] In other words, more than three-fourths (81 percent) of the tribute grain was contributed by the southern provinces and less than one-fourth (19 percent) by the northern provinces. Of the 4,000,000 piculs of tribute grain, 3,300,000 were transported to the north by the *duiyun* method (see Table 4.3), a system which allowed the commoners from Nan Zlili, Jiangxi, Zhejiang, and Huguang to deliver their rice to local waterside granaries (*shuici*) where government troops could deduct a certain amount of "wastage rice" (*haomi*) and travel expenses ("easy delivery silver," *qingjiyin*), before transporting the grain to the north.[50] The remaining 700,000 piculs were shipped by the *gaidui* method (see Table 4.4), whereby soldiers stationed at Huai'an and Guazhou were ordered to cross the Yangzi to fetch some of the rice which had previously been delivered by

Table 4.3 The tribute grain delivered via the *duiyun* system (unit: picul)

Administrative unit	Amount
Suzhou	655,000
Zhejiang	600,000
Jiangxi	400,000
Shandong	280,000
Huguang	250,000
Songjiang	203,000
Changzhou	175,000
Zhenjiang	80,000
Anqing	60,000
Yangzhou	60,000
Xuzhou	30,000
Ningguo	30,000
Fengyang	30,000
Huai'an	25,000
Cizhou	25,000
Taiping	17,000
Luzhou	10,000
Total	3,300,000

Source: *NJHBZ*, 10.3b-4a

100   *Center of Wealth*

Table 4.4 The tribute grain delivered via the *gaidui* system (unit: picul)

Administrative unit	Amount
Jiangxi	170,000
Henan	110,000
Shandong	95,600
Huan'an	79,150
Suzhou	42,000
Yangzhou	37,000
Zhejiang	30,000
Fengyang	30,300
Songjiang	29,950
Yingtian	28,000
Zhenjiang	22,000
Xuzhou	18,000
Guangdezhou	8,000
Total	700,000

Source: *NJHBZ*, 10.4a–b.

civilians. The soldiers were to be paid porterage rice (*jiaomi*) as well as wastage and travel expenses.[51]

In the post-1450 Ming, the transport of the tribute grain was supervised by a triumvirate:[52] the director-general of grain transport (*caoyun zongdu*, or *zongdu caoyun*), concurrently the grand coordinator of Fengyang and its neighboring prefectures and subprefectures, who had general supervisory responsibility for the transport of tax grains from the Yangzi delta to the Beijing area along the Grand Canal;[53] the grain transport commander (*caoyun zongbingguan*), who as a noble or eminent military officer cooperated with the director-general of grain transport;[54] and the assistant commander of the grain transport (*caoyun canjiang*). The civil service director-general of grain transport was superior to the other two. He had a much wider territorial jurisdiction than the grain transport commander or assistant commander. The commander's duties were more specific. He was in direct charge of the transport army, while the director-general's role was more to provide general support. The two normally came to Beijing in the eighth month to consult about the next year's transport. The assistant commander's post was essentially similar to that of the commander, but more oriented toward practical matters and possessing markedly reduced authority. His civil powers were limited to maintaining order in Huai'an and he had no disciplinary power over transport army officers. Prior to 1571, when the assistant commandership of grain transport was abolished, the director-general of grain transport resided at Huai'an, the commander at Xuzhou, and the assistant commander at Guazhou or Yizhen. Thereafter, the director-general assumed the overall responsibility for the southern half of the Grand Canal, while the commander controlled the northern half.[55] Under these dignitaries were 12 brigades (*zong*) and 120,000 soldiers.[56]

Center of Wealth 101

Since the tribute grain was a tax, its transport was also supervised by the Ministry of Revenue and, at times, jointly overseen by the Nanjing Ministry of Revenue. In 1475 it was decreed that one secretary from the Ministry of Revenue be dispatched to Shandong and Henan and four from the Nanjing Ministry of Revenue to Nan Zhili, Zhejiang, Jiangxi, and Huguang respectively, where they were to inspect the handling of the tribute grain. Cooperating with the transport control censor (*xuncao yushi*), they inspected the delivery and transport of the tribute grain along the Grand Canal. A half century later in 1520, the four secretaries from the Nanjing Ministry of Revenue were ordered to be replaced by their counterparts from the Beijing Ministry of Revenue.[57] The reason for this change is unknown, but it seems possible that the court wished to ensure the smooth transportation of tribute grain by referring it to the Ministry of Revenue in Beijing.

Unlike the post of the director-general of supplies, which alternated between the Nanjing vice ministers and the censors-in-chief or vice censors-in-chief of the Beijing Censorate during the post-1421 Ming, most of the directors-general of grain transport were from the Beijing administration, although the influential position was occasionally awarded to top-ranking Nanjing officials. They included: Zhang Peng (*js* 1541), the Nanjing assistant censor-in-chief in 1471;[58] Zhang Fuhua (1439–1508), the Nanjing vice minister of war in 1499;[59] Chen Dao (1436–1504), the Nanjing minister of justice who replaced Zhang Fuhua in 1501;[60] Qu Zhi (*js* 1484), the minister of the Nanjing Court of Judicial Review in 1509;[61] Zhang Jin, the Nanjing minister of revenue in 1511;[62] Gao Youji (1461–1546), the Nanjing vice minister of justice in 1525;[63] Zheng Yi, the Nanjing censor-in-chief in 1527;[64] Fang Lian (1513–82), the minister of the Nanjing Court of Judicial Review, and Hong Chaoxuan (1516–82), the Nanjing vice minister of revenue, who were appointed to the position in the same eighth month of 1567;[65] Yang Yikui (*js* 1565), the Nanjing vice minister of revenue, concurrently the assistant censor-in-chief in 1586; Shu Yinglong (*js* 1562), the Nanjing vice minister of works who replaced Yang in 1588;[66] and Li Yi, the Nanjing censor-in-chief in 1601.[67]

The role of the Southern Capital administration in the transport of the tribute grain was indirect and less prominent compared to its role in the collection and storage of the tax grains, which was primarily the responsibility of the Ministry of Revenue in Beijing.[68] One of the reasons was that the Ministry of Revenue in general was more powerful and assumed more responsibilities than the Nanjing Ministry of Revenue. The other reason, as already suggested, was that the court may have been more trustful of its fiscal branch in Beijing, especially as far as the transfer of tribute grain from the south to north was concerned.

4. Role in the state salt monopoly

As an indispensable household necessity, salt had been an important source of revenue for imperial Chinese government for more than a millennium. In the

102 Center of Wealth

late sixteenth and early seventeenth centuries, the annual salt revenue, the second largest source of income after land taxes, was estimated at two million taels of silver, approximately 6.5 percent of the national revenue of the Ming.[69] For this reason, the production and circulation of salt was placed under strict government control. The Nanjing administration, playing a part as it did in many other financial aspects of the empire, participated in the state salt monopoly. One of the most essential trading licenses of the dynasty, the salt certificate (*yanyin*), was printed by the Nanjing Office of Scrutiny for Revenue and issued by the Nanjing Ministry of Revenue.[70]

The division of labor amongst the various major financial agencies of the Ming empire was as follows: the Ministry of Revenue in Beijing formulated policy and proposed regulations on the production and distribution of salt (*yanfa*), the Nanjing Ministry of Revenue issued the *yin* certificates circulated empire-wide,[71] and the salt distribution commissions (*du zhuanyun yanshisi*) and supervisorates (*yanke tijusi*) supervised and directed the actual purchasing and selling of salt across the country.[72]

Due to the perennial threat from the Mongols and other nomadic peoples and the difficulty in providing adequate provisions to its troop stationed on the northern frontiers, salt and salt certificates were closely tied to the practice of *kaizhong*, a barter system by which salt merchants transported grain and other strategic materials to the northern frontier in exchange for the right to purchase and sell salt. In order to conduct the salt business legally in the empire, all salt merchants were required to obtain the *yin* certificate. Merchants who sold salt without the certificate were subject to severe punishment, and those found to have forged the certificates were decapitated.[73]

Every year the Ministry of Revenue in Beijing determined the frontier location to which salt merchants were to transport the grain or other materials,[74] as well as the location of the participating salt distribution commission where the merchants encashed salt after the completion of their delivery. Orders were then given to the Nanjing Office of Scrutiny for Revenue to print the stub-books (*kanhe*), which were official documents to be used in the *kaizhong* barter trade. The stub-books most commonly consisted of numbered sheets, each divided into a detachable coupon and a stub, which together bore the vermilion seal of the Nanjing Ministry of Revenue. The coupon would be retained by the deliverer (salt merchant), and the book of stubs sent to the receiving agency (salt distribution commission or supervisorate) which would piece the coupon and the stub together to verify the order upon delivery.[75] Afterwards, the printed stub-books were brought back to the Nanjing Ministry of Revenue to be stamped with the ministry seal, and delivered to the governor's office of the frontier where the *kaizhong* business was conducted.[76]

When the salt merchants transported the grain to the designated granaries of the local guards and battalions, they were given in return granary receipts (*cangchao*), the detachable coupons of the stub-books, which specified the number of *yin* to which the merchants were entitled. The merchants then presented the receipts to the salt distribution commission or supervisorate for payment in salt. The latter checked the receipts against the stubs it received from the frontier, and then proceeded to prepare the certificates.[77]

At this stage the distribution commission dispatched an agent to Nanjing to present the granary receipts and the stubs to the Nanjing Ministry of Revenue officials so that the exact number of *yin* certificates could be printed. No commission was allowed to keep certificates in reserve for future use.[78] Once the certificates had been obtained from Nanjing, the distribution commission filled in the holders' names on the blanks and directed them to one of its subordinate salt fields (*yanchang*) to encash them for salt. The salt field released salt on the presentation of the *yin*.[79]

The *yin* was also a unit of weight. In other words, a certificate of one *yin* authorized the bearer to transport one *yin* of salt. In the Ming, the standard *yin* was 400 catties, and the weight of *yin* differed from one region to another and at different times.[80] The exchange rate between the grain and the *yin* varied as well. The factors involved included the place of the *kaizhong* (where the grain to be delivered), the quality of salt,[81] and the location of the salt fields (where the merchants encashed salt). For example, in 1402, when the delivery of grain to Beiping (Beijing) was called, every 0.3 picul of rice delivered entitled the merchants one *yin* of salt from Lianghuai and Liangzhe, every 0.2 picul of rice transported entitled one *yin* of salt from Hedong, every 0.15 picul of rice for one *yin* of salt from Sichuan. And in 1414, when the *kaizhong* was conducted in Xuanfu, the grain-salt rate was 0.4 picul of rice per *yin*.[82]

Once salt was procured, the merchants had to transport their stock to the salt control office (*yanyin piyansuo*) to be weighed and inspected. They then headed to the designated subprefecture or county to sell their goods. Upon arrival at the place, the merchant was required to report to the office of the magistrate and have the certificates and salt checked again. Only after all these procedures had been completed could he legally sell his stock.[83] When the sale was complete, the merchant was required to return the used *yin* certificates to the offices of the subprefecture or county where salt had been sold. Those who failed to comply with this rule were liable to 60 blows with heavy sticks.[84] The office subsequently transferred the collected used certificates to the respective salt distribution commission. The latter then delivered them to the Ministry of Revenue in Beijing on a quarterly basis for cancellation.[85]

According to the *Gazetteer of the Nanjing Ministry of Revenue* published in 1550, there were 78 artisans in the Nanjing administration responsible for making and printing the salt certificates. Half of them worked for the Nanjing Office of Scrutiny for Revenue, the other half for the Nanjing Ministry of Revenue.[86] In the year of 1549, more than 1 million certificates were printed and issued, as reflected in Table 4. 5.

Although it is uncertain why the court decided to allow the Nanjing administration to produce and issue salt certificates but not anything else, the city of Nanjing's geographical proximity to most of the salt distribution commissions and supervisorates might be one of the considerations, as it is clear that the court was conscious about the division of labor between the two capital

104   *Center of Wealth*

Table 4.5 Salt certificates issued by the Nanjing Ministry of Revenue in 1549

Salt Distribution Commission	Number of certificates
Lianghuai	696,030
Liangzhe	444,769
Changlu	135,775
Shandong	65,348
Total	1,341,922

Source: *NJHBZ*, 14.26b–27a
Note: The number of the *yin* certificates of the Fujian and Hedong salt distribution commissions is not recorded.

administrations, especially their fiscal branches. The fact that the salt certificates were issued in Nanjing and canceled in Beijing testifies to the intention of the court. The following episode may help to explain the division of labor. When the Ming court was officially moved to Beijing in 1421, all artisans involved in the production of the salt certificates, official seals, and metal plates were ordered to transfer to Beijing to start the production there. Six years later in 1427, all the salt certificate artisans and their equipment were brought back to Nanjing, and the duty of issuing the salt certificates was reassigned to the Nanjing Ministry of Revenue.[87] It is noteworthy that the decision was made during the reign of the Xuande emperor, who had reversed the Hongxi emperor's decree to move the court back to Nanjing. This event further affirms that the court intended for the two administrations to share the management of the empire's fiscal matters, although the bulk of the responsibilities were granted to the Beijing Ministry of Revenue.

5. Collection of miscellaneous taxes

State revenues other than land taxes and salt revenue in the Ming totaled approximately 3,780,000 taels of silver annually. Classified by Ray Huang as miscellaneous incomes and covering as many as 26 items, they represented roughly 13.5 percent of the national revenue. Most of these miscellaneous taxes were collected by the Ministry of Revenue or by local administrations on behalf of the ministry, a few were jointly handled by the ministry and the Nanjing Ministry of Revenue, and one was exclusively collected by the latter. Those involving the participation of the Nanjing Ministry of Revenue are discussed in this section.

(a) Tea revenue (*chake*). As in the previous dynasties, tea was a source of income as well as an essential means for the Ming government to obtain horses from the frontier peoples. The involvement of the Nanjing Ministry of Revenue in the government monopoly of tea trade is reflected by the fact that most, if not all, of the tea certificates (*chayin*) used in the empire were printed by the ministry.[88] Tea produced in the western part of Sichuan (Luzhou, Yazhou, and Songpan) and Shaanxi, which totaled 1 million and 26,000

Center of Wealth 105

catties each year respectively,[89] were controlled directly by the government and traded for horses with the nomadic peoples on the western and northern frontiers.[90] Tea from other areas – notably Changzhou, Luzhou, Cizhou, Huizhou of Nan Zhili; Huzhou, Quzhou, Yanzhou, Shaoxin of Zhejiang; Nanchang, Raozhou, Nankan, Jiujiang, Jie'an of Jiangxi; Wuchang, Xingzhou, Changsha, Baoqing of Huguang; Chengdu, Chongqing, Jiading, Kuizhou, Luzhou of eastern Sichuan – was circulated for domestic consumption.[91] As a means of monopoly, the trading of tea for domestic consumption required a tea certificate, an official license for legally purchasing and circulating tea in the empire. Each year the provincial governments dispatched their agents to the Nanjing Ministry of Revenue to purchase the certificates at a cost of 500 cash (*wen*) of paper currency per certificate; they then sold them to the tea merchants for 1,000 per certificate,[92] which entitled the merchants to buy 100 catties of tea.[93]

The Ming regulations regarding the production and distribution of tea (*chafa*) were identical to those for *yanfa*. To legitimate his business, the tea merchant had first to go to the local administration to purchase the tea certificates and then take them to the tea plantation to purchase the specific amount of tea allowed by the certificates he bought.[94] When selling his tea, the merchant had to carry the tea certificates with him at all times, and the amount of tea he possessed was required to tally with that prescribed in the certificates. Anyone who sold tea without the *yin* was subject to stern penalties, and anyone who forged the tea certificates was subject to capital punishment and the confiscation of his property.[95]

After purchasing tea from the tea production area, the tea merchant was required to proceed to the tea control station (*chayin piyansuo*) to have his certificates verified.[96] When all tea transactions were completed, the merchant submitted his tea certificates to the government offices in the place of his residence or the place he sold his tea. The latter then delivered the used certificates to the Nanjing Ministry of Revenue for further verification and cancellation.[97]

Of the tea certificates issued by the Nanjing Ministry of Revenue, those for use in Yunnan province were furnished by the Yunnan Bureau of the ministry via the Zhangzhu Tea Control Station; those for circulation in Chengdu, Chongqing, Jiading, Kuizhou, and Luzhou in Sichuan were administered by the ministry's Sichuan Bureau; those to be used in Nan Zhili, Zhejiang, Jiangxi, and Huguang were handled by the Jiangxi Bureau of the ministry via the Yingtian Tea Control Station.[98]

The monopoly on tea was, however, much less effective than that on salt because its production was too scattered to enable the government to effectively exercise direct control. The revenue generated from this monopoly was of limited value. It was reported that in 1578 Sichuan province collected altogether less than 20,000 taels of silver in tea revenue. Of that amount, 14,367 taels went to the Nanjing Ministry of Revenue as the purchasing fees for the tea certificates and between 1,500 and 2,000 taels were delivered to Shaanxi province for the tea-horse trade. The rest of the funds were retained in the province to subsidize local administration.[99] Other provinces assessed

106 *Center of Wealth*

Table 4.6 The transit duties and local business tax collected from the seven major customs houses (early Ming)

Customs house	Revenue		
	Paper currency	*Copper*	*Silver*
Hexiwu	1,190,000	–	22,900
Linqing	12,600,000	25,200,000	83,800
Hushu	5,860,000	11,730,000	39,900
Jiujiang	2,930,000	6,890,000	15,000
Hangzhou	1,900,000	3,800,000	36,800
Huai'an	3,000,000	6,000,000	22,700
Yangzhou	1,690,000	3,300,000	12,900

Source: *DMHD*, 35.1b-2ab
Notes: (1) The unit for the paper currency is string (*guan*), for copper coin (*wen*), and for silver, tael (*liang*). (2) The amount of transit duties and local tax collected from these customs houses was not fixed; it varied from year to year. (3) Revenues from the customs houses at Linqing and Hangzhou include both transit duties and local business tax. (4) *NJHBZ* (12.24a–27b) only lists income from the customs houses at Huai'an, Yangzhou, and Hangzhou in 1548.

and collected these taxes in paper currency, and when these were converted into silver at the sixteenth-century rate, the total collection was negligible: 17 taels in Yunnan, for example, and about 6 taels in Zhejiang.[100] One contemporary writer summarized the situation as follows: "Tea growers in the interior have no idea of the government regulations on tea trade. Even some fiscal officials are unaware of the existence of such laws."[101]

(b) Transit duties (*chuanliao*) and (c) local business tax (*shangshui*). In the Ming there were a number of customs houses (*chaoguan*) established along the Grand Canal and the Yangzi River[102] to collect transit duties and local business tax. The former was levied on the carrier and paid by the shipowner; the latter, levied on all merchandise transported by land or water, was paid by the merchant.[103] Originally the customs houses were established to collect only the transit duties on shipping, but they gradually started to collect the local business tax at the ports as well. This occurred first at Hangzhou (Beixin) in 1511, then at Linqing shortly thereafter. But up to 1530 the customs houses at all the other places still handled only transit duties. The takeover of the administration of local business tax was only complete in 1579.[104]

The first seven were established in 1429 at Shangxinhe,[105] Yangzhou, Huai'an, Xuzhou, Jining, Linqing, and Guoxian (which was replaced by Hexiwu in 1446).[106] Later on, customs houses were also set up at Suzhou, Hushu, Hangzhou, Jinshazhou, Jiujiang,[107] and some other places.[108] Of the customs houses, seven, namely Huai'an, Yangzhou, Hangzhou, Hushu, Jiujiang, Linqing, and Hexiwu, were of national importance. Starting in 1493, it was decreed that customs houses at Huai'an, Yangzhou, and Hangzhou, where the revenue collected was deemed relatively low, should be managed by the Nanjing Ministry of Revenue. Those at Suzhou,[109] Jiujiang, Linqing, and

Hexiwu, where the incomes were considered higher, were to be administered by the Ministry of Revenue.[110] At one point, the Shangxinhe Custom House was also supervised by the Nanjing Ministry of Revenue.[111]

The transit duties and local business tax from Huai'an, Yangzhou, and Hangzhou were collected by the Nanjing Ministry of Revenue[112] and delivered on a quarterly basis. The transit duties were taken to the palace treasury via the Ministry of Revenue in Beijing and the local business duties to the provincial government where the customs house was located; only an unspecific remnant of these taxes, classified as *maichao yuyin* and *shangshui fuyuyin*, was kept in the silver vault of the Nanjing Ministry of Revenue.[113]

Three customs houses, at Longjiang, Shihuishan, and Dasheng, seemingly of local nature, were directly controlled by the Nanjing Ministry of Revenue. The revenue from these three customs houses was considerably lower. Transit duties from the customs houses were gathered on a quarterly basis and delivered directly to the silver vault of the Nanjing Ministry of Revenue.[114] Table 4.6 below lists the revenue collected from the customs houses at Hexiwu, Lingqing, Hushu, Jiujiang, Hangzhou, Huai'an, and Yangzhou, which indicates that, in the early Ming period, more than 30 percent of the transit duties were collected by the Nanjing Ministry of Revenue.

(d) Fish duty (*yuke*) was a tax imposed on fishermen. In areas where fishing was of considerable importance, fish-duty stations (*hebosuo*) were established under the jurisdiction of the prefectural and county government. In theory, fishermen were only allowed to conduct their business in designated areas and had to pay the duty to the fish-duty station. All fish duty had to be delivered to Beijing, except for that from the prefectures of Yingtian and Changzhou in Nan Zhili, which was sent to the Nanjing Ministry of Revenue.[115]

The major responsibility of the Nanjing administration was to issue the stub-books used in the collection of fish duty (*yuke kanhe*). Each year the Nanjing Office of Scrutiny for Revenue printed a total of some 700 stub-books. They were stamped by the Nanjing Ministry of Revenue and then sent to the local administrations. At the end of the year it was required that all stubs be channeled to Beijing, where they were checked by Ministry of Revenue officials to make sure that the amount of the fish duty corresponded to the stubs.[116] However, the exact workings of the stub-books are not explained either by primary sources such as the *Statutes of the Ming Dynasty* and the *Gazetteer of the Nanjing Ministry of Revenue* or by modern scholars.[117] It is possible that, after receiving the stub-books, the local administration issued the coupon (half of the stamped sheet in the stub-book) to fishermen, who in turn paid the fish duty. The coupon was used as a fishing license. At the end of the year the local authorities may have submitted the collected fish duty, along with both used and unused stub-books, to the Ministry of Revenue for examination.

In practice, it is doubtful that the stub-book system was effective. The high mobility of fishermen made it difficult for local authorities to supervise them. The diminished numbers of the fish-duty stations in the realm probably

108   Center of Wealth

reflects the impracticability of the system. In 1382, when the system was first introduced, 252 stations were established. By 1578 there were only 139 left. The total revenue from the fish duty was around 58,000 taels per annum.[118]

(e) The payments for the rationed salt (*yanchao*) was a levy collected by the Ming government when it distributed salt to the general population for daily consumption.[119] It appears that there was no unified regulation in the empire as to how much salt be distributed to each individual and how much to levy.[120] For example, each adult in Guangdong province during the Hongwu era was required to purchase three catties of salt every year, and in return, each had to pay 0.08 picul of rice.[121] In 1403 it was determined that each adult be given one catty of salt per month and charged one *guan*[122] of paper currency, while juveniles were given half the adult amount.[123] A modern estimate is that the per capita annual consumption of salt in the Ming was ten catties and each consumer paid the government 0.024 taels for their annual salt supply.[124]

After the Zhengtong reign, possibly due to the increase in the amount of the salt provided by the salt merchants,[125] the government ceased to distribute salt to the general population, but it continued to collect the *yanchao*[126] until the levy was combined with land taxes in the Single Whip Reform of the mid- and late sixteenth century.[127] In 1479 it was decreed that six provinces (Shaanxi, Shanxi, Sichuan, Yunnan, Guangdong, Guangxi, and Guizhou) and two prefectures of Bei Zhili (Longqing and Bao'an), which were considered financially straitened, could retain the *yanchao*. The other six provinces (Zhejiang, Jiangxi, Fujian, Henan, Shandong, Huguang), Nan Zhili, and four prefectures of Bei Zhili, which were relatively affluent, were ordered to deliver half of the *yanchao* to the treasuries in the two capitals, while retaining the other half. Of the delivered payments, those from Jiangxi, Huguang, and Fujian, which approximated 32,000 taels of silver a year, were required to be consigned to the treasuries in Nanjing.[128]

(f) The forest product levy (*zhumu choufen*) was a tax levied on shipbuilding materials. The levy and its collecting stations arose from the Hongwu emperor's attempts to make the Ministry of Works self-sufficient in the matter of supplies. The most essential items, timber and bamboo, were therefore kept separate from ordinary taxation. There were at least 16 stations set up to collect this levy across the country.[129] Of them, 14 were directed by the Ministry of Works or by local government on behalf of the ministry, and two, the Longjiang and Waxiaoba stations, by the Nanjing Ministry of Works. Wuhu, Shashi, Hangzhou, Huai'an, and Longjiang were the most important of these since they were located on major water routes with a large volume of commercial traffic. In general, the levy rate was 20 percent of the timber in transit when the payment was made in kind and approximately five to ten percent in silver.[130]

Information on the income obtained from this source is scattered and fragmentary. In 1484 Hangzhou had an annual income of 23,000 taels, and in 1525 the Wuhu station produced a revenue of more than 20,000 taels. The revenue at Huai'an in 1608 is estimated to have been approximately 11,500 taels. There is no source providing exact information on the revenue from the Longjiang and Waxiaoba stations, but the annual income of the former is estimated at roughly 20,000 taels or more.[131] The levy income from the Longjiang and Waxiaoba stations, both in kind and in silver, were primarily utilized by the Nanjing Ministry of Works for its construction projects.[132]

(g) The reeds tax (*luke*) was gathered on reed-growing land along the Yangzi river in Huguang, Jiangxi, and Nan Zhili, and administered by the Nanjing Ministry of Works. In the fifteenth century the collection was made in kind, the reeds being used as fuel. In the sixteenth century the payments were commuted to silver. The annual income from this source was approximately 26,350 taels.[133]

(h) Store franchise fees (*mentanshui*) were levied on street stalls and permanent shops. They were collected by the county and subprefecture and then submitted to the prefecture. The prefecture delivered them to the province, which in turn submitted them to the Ministry of Revenue.[134] Only the collection from the shopkeepers in the prefectures of Yingtian and Changzhou were delivered to the Nanjing Ministry of Revenue. That annual amount was slightly more than 2,000 taels of silver.[135]

In sum, the Nanjing administration was directly and indirectly involved in the collection of around one-third of the empire's miscellaneous taxes. In most of the cases, the collected tax revenue was delivered to Beijing and only a small amount retained in Nanjing.

How much of the national revenue, which combined the land taxes and salt revenue as well as all the miscellaneous incomes, eventually went to the treasuries of the Nanjing administration? It appears that the amount was fairly low. In 1644 Grand Secretary Gao Hongtu (1583–1645) reported to the Hongguang government of the Southern Ming, the loyalist regime that continued in southern China following the collapse of the Ming government in Beijing in 1644, that the Nanjing Ministry of Revenue controlled a sum of slightly more than 1,170,000 piculs of grain and 230,000 taels of silver per annum.[136] That amount was perhaps more or less the average revenue managed by the Nanjing Ministry of Revenue. As shown in Section Two above, in the last quarter of the sixteenth century the grain delivered to the Southern Capital was 1,500,000 piculs annually, and roughly one million of that was used for the salaries of all the officials in the Nanjing administration, as well as the wages and supplies of the soldiers in the Nanjing guards. The revenue of the Nanjing administration reached its peak during the Zhang Juzheng decade, when it was reported that reserves in the Nanjing vaults accumulated during the 1573–84 period exceeded 2.5 million taels.[137] This ample amount of revenue in Nanjing coincided with the national abundance of wealth during the same period. The granaries in Beijing were recorded to have enough grain in stock to meet the needs of the next nine years. The deposits in the vaults of the Taicang Treasury rose to over six million taels of silver,[138] and the Court of the Imperial Stud held another four million taels.[139] The period

110 *Center of Wealth*

of Zhang's administration was, however, an exceptional phase in Ming financial history. In general, the revenue directly controlled by the Nanjing administration was approximately one-tenth of that held by the Beijing administration.

6. The storage and verification of the Yellow Registers

Another significant function assumed by the Nanjing Ministry of Revenue was the storage and verification of the empire's population records, the Yellow Registers (*huangce*).

The Yellow Register system was one of the most fundamental institutions of the Ming dynasty. Together with the empire's land records, the Fish-Scale Registers (*yulingce*),[140] they formed the basis for the Ming government's collection of taxes from and levying of labor services on its people. At least in the early period of the dynasty, the Yellow Register system enhanced the state's control over the general population and effectively reduced the concealment of households and evasion of the grain tax and corvee service.[141]

From their inception in 1381 until the last census conducted in 1642, the Yellow Registers were compiled once every ten years – a total of 27 compilations. The registers were made in four sets, to be deposited at the offices of the county, prefecture, province, and Ministry of Revenue (after 1420, the Nanjing Ministry of Revenue) respectively.[142] The first three were given blue covers and therefore referred as blue registers (*qingce*).[143] The fourth set, to be deposited at the archives on the islets of the Back Lake (Houhu, modern Xuanwu Lake) in Nanjing, was covered with yellow sheet, from which the term "Yellow Register" was derived.[144]

The statistics section of the 13 functional bureaus under the Nanjing Ministry of Revenue were responsible for the administration of the Yellow Registers. The registers from each province were administered by the statistics section of the bureau which bore the name of that particular province. For example, the statistics section of the Zhejiang Bureau was responsible for the Yellow Yegisters from Zhejiang. The administration of the registers from the two metropolitan areas was shared by the 13 bureaus.[145]

The regular staff working for the archives included officials from the Nanjing Ministry of Revenue (normally four secretaries)[146] and the Nanjing Offices of Scrutiny who took charge of the archives, functionaries, archive artisans, students from the Nanjing National University, sailors (who poled the boats to across the lake), medical doctors, and cooks. The total number exceeded 200. In the year when the "great verification" of the Yellow Registers (*dacha huangce*) was conducted, the number of staff could exceed 1,400.[147]

The managing and storing of the registers was by no means a simple task, since around 60,000 copies were added to the Back Lake archives every decade.[148] According to the *Gazetteer of the Back Lake [Archives]* (*Houhu zhi*), in 1436 there were more than 400,000 copies in the Back Lake archives.

Center of Wealth 111

In 1490 the number jumped to 772,900, further increasing to 1,531,458 in 1592.[149] By the end of the dynasty, the number was in the neighborhood of two million.[150] Consequently, every ten years, on the eve of the national census, approximately 30 rooms had to be built in order to accommodate incoming registers, and between 1391 and 1592 the archive rooms at the Back Lake increased from 34 to 900.[151]

After the arrival of the registers at the Back Lake archives, the staff there began to classify and calculate them, in order to gather information concerning: the number of registers compiled in that year, the number of households (*hu*), and the population (*kou*), and the breakdown of this information in the two metropolitan areas (Bei Zhili and Nan Zhili) and 13 provinces; the cultivated land of the empire and its distribution in the two Zhilis and provinces; and the national and provincial quota of the summer tax and autumn grain. All these figures were essential for the central government to formulate its policy and manage the finances of the state.[152]

The Yellow Registers were stored on the three tiny islets in the Back Lake according to the date of their compilation. For example, Yellow Registers compiled in the years of 1381, 1391, 1403, 1423, 1432, 1441, 1452, 1462, 1472, 1482, and 1492 were stored on Jiuzhou Islet, those produced in 1502, 1512, and 1522 were kept on Zhongzhou Islet, those compiled in 1532, 1542, 1552, and 1562 were placed on Xinzhou Islet. They were then arranged according to area, with the two metropolitan areas first, followed by the 13 provinces. Each of the areas was further followed by prefectures and counties.[153]

To prevent the Yellow Registers from being mildewed or moth-eaten, the clerks, Nanjing National University students, and artisans at the archives regularly dried the registers between the fourth and tenth months of the year. The remainder of the year was considered to be either too windy or too damp.[154]

It was regulated that all the Yellow Registers must be delivered to Nanjing before the end of the year when the population census and the compilation of registers were undertaken. The time limit for delivering them ranged from 20 days (for Zhejiang province) to 180 days (for Yunnan province).[155]

To avoid deceit and various abuses relating to household registration, payment of taxes, and provisioning of labor service, the Nanjing Ministry of Revenue was ordered to verify the Yellow Registers submitted by the local administrations. The verification process, referred to as "*dacha huangce*," also "*dacha*" or "*chahuang*," began almost immediately after the arrival of the registers from the provinces. The ministry, with the assistance of the Nanjing Censorate, the Nanjing Offices of Scrutiny, and the Nanjing National University,[156] employed a large number of temporary members of staff,[157] together with regular staff, to check the Yellow Registers against those compiled in the previous decades, household by household, page by page, item by item. Items such as the household category of the family,[158] the *lijia* (hundred-and-tithing system) that it belonged to, birth and death dates of family members,

112   *Center of Wealth*

yields, land and other property transactions, tax level,[159] etc. Once a deception – such as hiding the actual amount of the land in one's possession or placing one's land in the name of someone who did not own much land – was exposed, the register would be stamped as invalidated (*feice*) and had to be returned to the relevant administrative unit for correction. A large number of the Yellow Registers were rejected as the result of the verification. For instance, in 1513, approximately 140,000 household registers from Nan Zhili were found to contain errors and sent back.[160] The number of households in Nan Zhili in 1503 was 2,015,646 (the 1513 number is not available),[161] but if we accept this 1503 number as being close to the 1513 number, then it means that close to 7 percent of the registers from Nan Zhili were rejected. The corrected register had to be redelivered to the Back Lake archives within six months, excluding the time spent en route, otherwise the officials and clerks who were involved in the compilation would be stripped of their salaries for a certain period of time.[162]

The verification process was lengthy and the workload enormous. In the early Ming, as many as 1,400 students from the National University were hired to do the work. To inspect more than ten million households in the empire,[163] each student had to go through approximately 10,000 households. With the number of the participating National University students decreasing, the checking process took one to two years, sometimes even three to five years, to complete.[164]

The actual effectiveness of the Yellow Register system was limited. The usual Ming practice was to spot the mathematical errors in the population reports and, when the breakdown figures did not correspond to the aggregates, the register was rejected. In order to avoid the rejection and fine, some counties and prefectures merely resubmitted their earlier returns as current reports, sometimes with slight modifications in the last two or three digits. For example, during the 1522–52 period when four compilations of the Yellow Registers were conducted, Fenghua county in Zhejiang persistently reported neither an increase nor decrease in its 18,865 households. Xiaoshan county in the same province even recorded its population as consistently comprising 17,812 persons throughout the three decades.[165] In the 1582 registers of Xinghua county in Nan Zhili there were as many as 3,700 households to have family members a 100 years old or older. In 1656 the minister of revenue in the early Qing reported that many late Ming records still retained the personal names and property-holdings of the Hongwu era.[166]

There were a number of reasons for the Ming court's decision to retain all the Yellow Registers in the Back Lake archives. One was to avoid the trouble of transporting the enormous number of documents. Another, suggested by the Right Commissioner of the Nanjing Office of Transmission Yang Lian (1452–1525) in 1513, was the excellent storage condition in Nanjing. The Back Lake had a circumference of 40 *li*, with a few islets high in the water at a distance of some 300 meters from the bank. The Yellow Registers stored there were thus conveniently protected and their safety ensured.[167] Another consideration had to do with the planned division of labor between the two capital administrations. The storage of the Yellow Registers and the verification of these documents were two of the responsibilities assigned to the Nanjing administration.

There was evidently an intentional division of labor between the Beijing and Nanjing administrations by the Ming court. The transfer of the printing of salt licenses to Beijing under Yongle and the moving back to Nanjing in the early Xuande reign provides evidence. The issuance of the salt certificates in Nanjing and their final cancellation in Beijing further testifies to tasks being split between the two centers. The storage of the Yellow Registers and the verification of these state population records in Nanjing furnish another example. However, this was not an equal division of labor. Compared to that of the Beijing administration, the role of the Nanjing administration in the management of the empire's financial affairs was modest. Its fiscal branch, the Nanjing Ministry of Revenue, was responsible for a variety of regional tasks. Its chief officials did not directly participate in the decision-making process with regard to imperial fiscal policy matters, although they frequently presented their memorials to express their opinion. The revenue at the disposal of the Nanjing Ministry of Revenue were also fairly low – only approximately 1,500,000 piculs of grain and 200,000–300,000 taels of silver per annum, or in other words, about one-tenth of that held by the Beijing administration. Nevertheless, the fiscal functions of the Nanjing administration were by no means entirely regional and negligible. In fact, they contributed considerably to the Ming state treasury. The Nanjing Ministry of Revenue assisted its Beijing counterpart in many ways to generate more revenue, both in silver and in kind. It collected part of the tax grains from the four most advanced provinces and played a part in the transport of tribute grain from the south to the north. It also participated in the salt monopoly and the collection of many other miscellaneous taxes by either issuing and inspecting the trade licenses or sharing the imposition duties. Most of the tax revenue that it collected was delivered to Beijing and only a small amount was retained in Nanjing. In summary, the Nanjing administration played an essential auxiliary role in assisting the Beijing administration in managing the state finances of the Ming.

Notes

1 From the Han period onwards, the economic center of gravity of the Chinese empire shifted gradually from the northwest to the Yangzi basin, and the Sui-Tang period saw the completion of this process. See, for example, D. C. Twitchett, *Financial Administration under the T'ang Dynasty*, 84. According to Robert Hartwell, the Chinese demographic landscape was also dramatically altered between 750 and 1550. In the mid-Tang, less than half the population lived in south China, but by 1550, close to 70 percent of Chinese households were located in the south. See "Demographic, Political, and Social Transformation of China, 750–1550," *Harvard Journal of Asiatic Studies*, Vol. 42, No. 2 (Dec. 1982), 363–4.

114 Center of Wealth

2 After the staff reduction of 1529, the bureaus of Henan, Shandong, Sichuan, and Guizhou in the Nanjing Ministry of Revenue no longer had vice directors. *NJHBZ*, 2.3a.

3 *NJHBZ*, 2.8a-b.

4 I.e. the Baochao, Guanghui, Zangfa, Hengyun, Jiazi, Yizi, Bingzi, Dingzi, and Wuzi Treasuries. They bore the same names as those run by the enunchs, which were normally prefixed with the word "*nei*" (inner or palace).

5 I.e. Junchu, Chang'anmen, Dong'anmen, Xi'anmen, Bei'anmen Granaries.

6 *NJHBZ*, 2.10a.

7 This was a policy conceived by Zhu Yuanzhang for the purpose of maximizing control over the state. For more on the Ming founder's consolidation of imperial power, see Edward Farmer, *Zhu Yuanzhang and Early Ming Legislation*, 33–58; F. W. Mote, *Imperial China*, 549–82.

8 On the origin, evolution, and features of the grant secretariat of the Ming, see Wang Qiju, *Mingdai neige zhidu shi*, 1–353.

9 For more on the Ministry of Revenue, see Ray Huang, *Taxation and Governmental Finance in Sixteenth-Century Ming China*, 11–17.

10 Huang, *Taxation and Governmental Finance in Sixteenth-Century Ming China*, 4.

11 It is a three-volume collection of Bi's memorials in 1626. The Fu Ssu-nien Library of the Academia Sinica in Taiwan holds a copy of the late Ming original edition. Zhang Weiren, *Zhongguo fazhishi shumu*, 857.

12 Under the scheme devised by the Hongwu emperor, the hereditary soldiers of the guard-battalion (*weisuo*) system were supposed to support themselves by part-time farming on state-allocated lands. Probably from the first Ming reign, and certainly not later than the 1450s, the *weisuo* units could neither maintain an adequate national defense nor supply themselves with enough food. The central government had to subsidize them, and the annual subsidy to the military was called *nianli*. Hucker, *Dictionary of Official Titles in Imperial China*, 355, entry 4309.

13 *NJHBZ*, 6.1b-2a.

14 *NJHBZ*, 6b-8a.

15 The Ming system represented a step backwards. Under the Song dynasty, copper cash was established as the universal fiscal standard and even in the early years of the Yuan, land taxes were at first assessed in copper coins. When taxes in kind were needed, the required commodities were computed on the basis of the cash assessments. Huang, *Taxation in Ming China*, 155.

16 Huang, *Taxation in Ming China*, 175.

17 Huang, *Taxation in Ming China*, 216, 263.

18 *NJHBZ*, 18.31a.

19 *MS*, 1893.

20 The so-called *bailiang* was highly polished ordinary and glutinous rice destined for palace consumption. It was submitted by the prefectures in Nan Zhili.

21 Since 1436, a total of 4.05 million piculs of tax grain from six southern provinces (Zhejiang, Jiangxi, Huguang, Fujian, Guangdong, and Guangxi) and Nan Zhili was allowed to be commuted at the flat rate of 0.25 tael per picul. The slightly more than one million taels of silver, called Gold Floral Silver, was to be stored in the palace Chenyun Treasury in Beijing. *MS*, 1896.

22 For more discussion of the transportation of the tax grains, see Huang Renyu, *Mingdai de caoyun*, 64–98.

23 The figures are respectively derived from *DMHD*, 24.4a-13b, 24.14a-41b, *NJHBZ*, 5.20a-21a, and *DMHD*, 25.1a–29a. Obviously Huang's figure for the year 1578 does not include the odd numbers (*weishu*).

24 *MLS: Xiaozong*, 3548–55.

25 A comment of Han Yu (786–824), quoted by Qiu Jun (1421–95) to support his argument against heavy taxation imposed on the Jiangnan area. See Qiu Jun, *Daxue yanyi bu*, 24.20a.

Center of Wealth 115

26 Wei Qingyuan, "Mingchu Jiangnan diqu jingji zhengce de ruogan wenti," *Ming Qing shi bianxi*, 35–36.

27 *DMHD*, 24.4b–9a, 16a, 33b; 25.3a, 20b, 21a. Suzhou and Songjiang were perhaps the most frequently quoted examples of unfairly treated taxpayers by scholars in the Ming and Qing. The traditional explanation for the heavy tax burden imposed on the two prefectures is that it was due to the wrath felt by Zhu Yuanzhang for the residents of Suzhou and Songjiang, who supported his archrival Zhang Shicheng (1321–67) in the late Yuan. Zhu decided to punish the residents in the two areas by sharply increasing their tax burden. *MS*, 1896; *Songjiang fuzhi*, 21.10a–b; Gu Yanwu, *Tianxia junguo libing shu*, 6.63a. For explanations by some contemporary scholars, see Wu Jihua, "Lun Mingdai shuiliang zhongxin zhi diyu jiqi zhongshui youlai," in *Zhongyang yanjiuyuan lishi yuyan yanjiusuo jikan*, 38 (Jan. 1968), 351–74; Wei, "Mingchu 'Jiangnan fushui qizhong' yuanyin bianxi," *Ming Qing shi bianxi*, 1–33.

28 It was Zhili prior to the relocation of the primary capital to Beijing in 1421.

29 The other two years, 1542 and 1578, the four paid 54 percent of the whole empire's autumn grain respectively.

30 The other two years, 1502 and 1578, the four supplied 31 percent and 29 percent of the national total respectively.

31 Figures on the years 1393, 1502, and 1578 are recorded in the *juan* 24 and 25 of *DMHD*. The 1542 figure is from *juan* 5 of *NJHBZ*. The calculation of the percentage is mine.

32 For more on the problems of the official data in late imperial China, see Ping-ti Ho, *Studies on the Population of China*, 1–23; Huang, *Taxation in Ming China*, 60–63.

33 See *NJHBZ*, 4.19b–20a. Translation of *minke*, *zhike*, *jinke*, and *cangke* are from Hucker, *Official Titles in Imperial China*. The rendering of *suanke* is my own.

34 *NJHBZ*, 6.2b–3b.

35 *NJHBZ* 21.22.

36 Hucker holds that the post of director-general of supplies was a duty assignment for the vice minister of the Nanjing Ministry of Revenue, who was concurrently a censor-in-chief. This is not correct. See *Official Titles in Imperial China*, 534, entry 7160.

37 *NJHBZ*, 2.2a. According to *MS*, Zhang Feng (d. 1461), formerly the Beijing vice minister of revenue, was transferred to be the Nanjing vice minister of revenue in 1447, and was de facto head of department when its ministership was vacant. *MS*, 4296–97. When citing this piece from *MS*, Long Wenbin mistook Zhang as the vice minister of the Beijing Ministry of Revenue. See *MHY*, 526.

38 *NJHBZ*, 21.9b.

39 *MSL: Hongzhi*, 118.5a. The record in *MS* has it that the post of *Nanjing liangchu* was assumed by all Beijing censors-in-chief from the Chenghua era onwards. *MS*, 5664.

40 *NJHBZ*, 2.2a, 21.11a. *MS* (5664) incorrectly records that the post was assigned to the vice minister of revenue in that year. For in 1570, when the post was reassigned to the Nanjing vice minister of revenue, the imperial edict prepared by Grand Secretary Gao Gong (1514–78) states that, "in accordance with the imperially sanctioned precedents of the early Zhengtong era and the 26th year of the Jiajing era (1547), [it is decided that] the director-general of grain supplies (*Nanjing liangchu*) should still be assumed by the Nanjing vice minister of revenue." *Zhangquan tigao*, 14.7a.

41 The post was given to Zhang Huan, vice censor-in-chief of the Beijing Censorate. Wang Ting, who assumed the post just one month earlier, was shifted to the Nanjing Ministry of Justice. *MS*, 5664; Tan Qian, *Guoque*, 3940.

42 Tan, *Guoque*, 4130; Gao Gong, *Zhangquan tigao*, 14.7a.

43 *NJHBZ*, 2.2a.

44 *NJHBZ*, 21.10a.

116   Center of Wealth

45 For more on the heavy tax burden of the Jiangnan farmers in the Ming, see Tang Wenji, *Mingdai fushui zhidu shi*, 80–93.

46 *DMHD*, 27.2a.

47 For example, during the Yongle years, the grains transported to the north fluctuated between two million and five million piculs. *MS*, 4207.

48 *DMHD*, 27.24b; *MS*, 1918.

49 *DMHD*, 27.24b-26b; *MS*, 1918.

50 Due to the ambiguity in the records of the primary sources (e.g. *MS*, 1916–19; *DMHD*, 27.24a), the exact working of the *duiyun* system is not logically clear. For better understanding of the system, see Ayao Hoshi, trans. Mark Elvin, *The Ming Tribute Grain System*, 6–9.

51 *MS*, 1917; *DMHD*, 27.246; Hoshi, *The Ming Tribute Grain System*, 16.

52 *MS*, 1922.

53 The post was created in 1450. For the evolution of the position, see Wu Tingxie, *Ming dufu nianbiao*, 322.

54 Created in 1404, the grain transport commander was originally ordered to organize the coastal transport of tax grain from the south to the Beijing area in support of military operations in the north and in preparation for the transfer of the dynastic capital from Nanjing to Beijing in 1421, then from 1411 concurrently to reconstruct the Grand Canal and direct the shipment of tax grain to Beijing. Hoshi, *The Ming Tribute Grain System*, 23–24.

55 Hoshi, *The Ming Tribute Grain System*, 20–24.

56 *MS*, 1922.

57 *NJHBZ*, 10.3a.

58 *MSL: Chenghua*, 1715. Much of the following information about the Nanjing officials who assumed the directorship-general of grain transport is from Wu, *Ming dufu nianbiao*, 322–46.

59 Tan, *Guoque*, 2740. Two years, later in the twelth month of 1501, Zhang was back as censor-in-chief of the Nanjing Censorate. Tan, *Guoque*, 2779.

60 Tan, *Guoque*, 2779.

61 Tan, *Guoque*, 2961.

62 *MSL: Zhengde*, 1711. The name of the official in question recorded in *Guoque* (3007) was Zhang Jun.

63 Tan, *Guoque*, 3316.

64 Tan, *Guoque*, 3357.

65 The record in *Guoque* has it that Hong was appointed to be *"tidu chaoyun"* (superintendent of grain transport) and Fang was made *"zongli chaoyun, jian tidu junwu, xunfu Fengyang"* (supervisor of grain transport, and concurrent superintendent of military affairs as well as grand coordinator of Fengyang). Tan, *Guoque*, 4065.

66 *MSL: Wanli*, 3635; Tan, *Guoque*, 4569.

67 *MSL: Wanli*, 6859–60.

68 *NJHBZ*, 10.1a.

69 As shown in Section Two, the land taxes and other combined miscellaneous taxes constituted roughly 80 and 13.5 percent respectively of national revenue.

70 *NJHBZ*, 14.1a, 14.7b; Zhu Tingli, *Yanzheng zhi*, 7.49; Huang, *Taxation in Ming China*, 194. According to *Zhusi zhizhang*, in the early years when the primary capital was still in Nanjing, the salt certificates were printed by the Palace Treasury (*neifu*) and issued by the Ministry of Revenue. He Weining therefore maintains that throughout the Ming, the yin certificates were printed and issued by the Palace Treasury. See his *Zhongguo yanzheng shi*, 216.

71 *NJHBZ*, 14.1a.

72 A commission controlled a major productive center and a supervisorate a minor one. There were six commissions (Lianghuai, Liangzhe, Changlu, Shandong,

Center of Wealth 117

Fujian, and Hedong) and seven supervisorates (Guangdong, Hebei, Sichuan, Heiyanjin, Baiyanjin, Anningyanjin, and Wujin) in the Ming. *MS*, 1931–33.

73 *NJHBZ*, 14.29a. For more on the *kaizhong* practice, see Liu Miao, *Mingdai yanye jingji yanjiu*, 221–76; Wing-Kin Puk, "The Ming salt certificate: a public debt system in sixteenth-century China?" *Ming Studies*, No. 61 (April 2010), 1–12.

74 Horses, iron, fodder could be also used in exchange for salt in the *kaizhong* trade. During the Hongzhi reign, salt merchants were requested to pay for salt in silver. *MS*, 1939; *DMHD*, 14.12b.

75 The working of the stub-book is explained in Huang, *Taxation in Ming China*, 14.

76 *NJHBZ*, 14.7b; *DMHD*, 42.63b.

77 Huang, *Taxation in Ming China*, 193; Li Longqian, "Mingdai yan de kaizhong zhidu yu yanshang ziben de fazhan," in *Ming Qing ziben zhuyi mengya yanjiu lunwenji*, 498–9.

78 Zhu Tingli, *Yenzheng zhi*, 7.49; Huang, *Taxation in Ming China*, 194.

79 Huang, *Taxation in Ming China*, 194.

80 For example, for a greater part of the sixteenth century in the Lianghuai region, the *yin* was 550 catties, but it was reduced to 430 catties in 1616. In the Liangzhe region, the *yin* varied from 350 to 300 catties. Huang, *Taxation in Ming China*, 193.

81 In the Ming, salt produced in Lianghuai and Liangzhe areas were considered to be of high quality.

82 *NJHBZ*, 14.9a.

83 Dong Sizhang, *Wuxing beizhi*, 16.12a; Li Longqian, "Mingdai yan de kaizhong zhidu," 499; Huang, *Taxation in Ming China*, 194–95.

84 *NJHBZ*, 14.29a.

85 *NJHBZ*, 14.29a.

86 *NJHBZ*, 14.7b. The number of the salt certificate artisans in the Nanjing Ministry of Revenue recorded in *DMHD* is 29. *DHMD*, 42.63b.

87 *NJHBZ*, 14.36a.

88 Although there is no specific account in any particular Ming source stating this, evidence from various sources indicates that this is the case.

89 *MS*, 1947.

90 Morris Rossabi, "Tea and horse trade with inner Asia during the Ming dynasty," *Journal of Asian History*, No. 4 (1970), 142–43.

91 *MS*, 1954–55. Information on the tea production in Shandong, Henan, Bei Zhili, Guangdong, and Guangxi is not readily available in *MS*, *DMHD*, or *NJHBZ*. Some of the tea produced in Fujian was shipped to Beijing as a tribute article. *MS*, 1955.

92 *DMHD*, 37.9b (687); *NJBHZ*, 12.36b, 40b.

93 There was another, less standard, certificate, *chayou*, which cost 600 copper coins and entitled the purchaser to buy 60 catties of tea. *NJHBZ*, 12.36b.

94 *NJHBZ*, 12.38b.

95 *NJHBZ*, 12.36b, 39a.

93 *NJHBZ*, 12.39a.

97 *NJHBZ*, 12.37b.

98 *MS*, 1955; *NJHBZ*, 12.39b–40a. The records in *MS* and *NJHBZ* are ambiguous, and subject to interpretation. It is not clear whether the tea certificates of Fujian, also a tea-producing province, were issued by the Nanjing Ministry of Revenue. The ambiguity extends to the other five provinces in the empire: Shandong, Henan, Bei Zhili, Guangdong, and Guangxi.

99 *DMHD*, 37.2,9; *MS*, 1953.

100 *DMHD*, 37.3; Huang, *Taxation in Ming China*, 261.

101 Sun Chengze, *Chunming mengyulu*, 35.64.

102 According to Hucker, the number was 12. See *Official Titles in Imperial China*, 119, entry 329.

118 *Center of Wealth*

103 Huang holds that the transit duties were collected by the Ministry of Revenue and local business tax by provincial officials. See *Taxation in Ming China*, 226. According to the record in *NJHBZ*, it seems that the management and collection of these taxes was not unified in the Ming, and most of the time it was central officials (from the ministries of revenue of both Beijing and Nanjing) and provincial officials who jointly administered the customs houses. *NJHBZ*, 12.15a–17a.

104 *DMHD*, 35.6a. The date in Huang's work was 1569. See, *Taxation in Ming China*, 226.

105 The Shangxinhe Customs House was abolished in 1527. *DMHD*, 35.46.

106 *NJHBZ*, 112.15a–b; *DMHD*, 35.2b. On the Grand Canal and its role in the emergence of Jining as an economic and cultural center from the early fifteenth century, see Sun Jinghao, "A Jiangnan identity in North China: the making of Jining urban culture in the late imperial period," *Late Imperial China*, Vol. 32, No. 2 (Dec. 2011), 34–73.

107 In 1468, customs houses at Suzhou, Hushu, Jinshazhou, and Jiujiang were abolished. They were reopened in 1470 and 1471. *NJHBZ*, 12.16a.

108 Customs houses at Jinshazhou and Jiujiang were established in 1450. *NJHBZ*, 12.16a. But it is not clear when the rest of the customs houses were opened.

109 It is not certain why, later on, the Suzhou customs house was replaced by the Hushu customs house.

110 *NJHBZ*, 12.17a; *DMHD*, 3b–4a. Both Ray Huang and Charles Hucker hold that all the customs houses were controlled by the Ministry of Revenue in Beijing. See Huang, *Taxation in Ming China*, 226; C. Hucker, *Official Titles in Imperial China*, 119, entry 329.

111 For example, in 1455 it was ordered that a secretary from the Nanjing Ministry of Revenue be dispatched there to collect the transit duties. *NJHBZ*, 12.16.

112 *NJHBZ*, 4.18a; 12.22b.

113 *NJHBZ*, 12.27b.

114 *NJHBZ*, 12.30b.

115 *NJHBZ*, 10.30b.

116 *NJHBZ*, 10.30b–31a.

117 Accounts in *DMHD* and *NJHBZ* are incomprehensible. See *DMHD*, 36.1a (669), *NJHBZ*, 10.30b–31a. Ray Huang does not mention the fish duty stub-books at all, while Wu Zhihe simply copies the original source in *DMHD* verbatim. See, "Mingdai yuhu yu yangzhi shiye," in *Mingshi yanjiu zhuankan*, 116.

118 *DHMD*, 31.1a–26b; Huang, *Taxation in Ming China*, 244–45.

119 Tian Yiheng, *Liuqin rizha*, 275.

120 For more detail, see Li Longqian, "Mingdai huko shiyanchao zhidu," in Chan Ran et al., eds, *Zhongguo yanyeshi lungcong*, 252–58.

121 Gu Yanwu, *Tianxia junguo libing shu, juan* 98, Guangdong 2.

122 In the early Ming, one *guan* of paper currency was equal to 1,000 copper coins. It devalued considerably in later years.

123 *MS*, 1963; *MHY*, 1049.

124 Yadong Xueshe, *Zhongguo lidai renkou wenti lunji*, 299.

125 Wang Leimin, *Lidai shihuozhi zhushi*, 191. Li Longqian maintains that the reason was that the government did not have enough salt under its control to supply the general population. See his "Mingdai hukou shiyanchao zhidu," 256–7.

126 Wang Qi, *Xu wenxian tongkao*, 10.5b; Wang Leimin, *Lidai shihuozhi zhushi*, 171; Li Longqian, "Mingdai hukou shiyanchao zhidu," 258.

127 *MS*, 1946.

128 *NJHBZ*, 14.53b–55b. The accounts of the Taicang Treasury in Beijing for 1580 indicate that in that year it received 46,897 taels of silver from the payments for the rationed salt. Sun, *Chunming mengyulu*, 35.10b.

129 *MS* lists 13, Huang has added two. See *Taxation in Ming China*, 237. I have found one more, namely the Waxiaoba station near the city of Nanjing. *DMHD*, 208.15b.

130 *DHMD*, 204.1, 7; Huang, *Taxation in Ming China*, 238.

131 *MSL: Xianzong*, 4319; *MSL: Shizong*, 1232; Huang, *Taxation in Ming China*, 240.

132 *DMHD*, 208.3a.

133 *DMHD*, 208.18a–19b. The amount was recorded at roughly 20,000 taels per annum in Chen Zilong et al., *Ming jingshi wenbian*, 975.

134 *NJHBZ*, 12.1b.

135 *NJHBZ*, 12.10b–13b. According to Shen Bang, the Shuntian prefecture in 1579 yielded 10,641 taels of silver from the store franchise fees. *Wanshu zaji*, 92–3.

136 Tan, *Guoque*, 6102. Based on Gao's report, Lynn Struve writes that in the late Ming years the Nanjing Ministry of Revenue "had handled annually only about 1,400,000 taels in silver and payments in kind ... " See *The Southern Ming*, 43. Apparently Struve assumes that 1 picul of grain equaled 1 tael of silver in the late Ming, which was not necessarily the case, especially in South China where 1 picul of grain was worth roughly 0.5–0.7 tael of silver.

137 *MLS: Shenzong*, 5312.

138 *MLS: Shenzong*, 3318.

139 *MLS: Shenzong*, 1503.

140 For a detailed study of the Fish-Scale Register system, see Liang Fangzhong, "Mingdai yulin tuce kao," in *Liang Fangzhong jingjishi lunwenji*, 1–9.

141 For the origin, evolution, essential elements, and decay of the Yellow Register system of the Ming, see Liang Fangzhong, "Mingdai hunagce kao," in *Liang Fangzhong jingji lunwenji*, 264–300; Wei Qingyuan, *Mingdai hunagce zhidu*, 7–245; Luan Chengxian, *Mingdai huangce yanjiu*, 254–354.

142 *MS*, 1878.

143 Wei, *Mingdai huangce*, 110, note 1.

144 *MS*, 1878.

145 *NJHBZ*, 4.8b–9b.

146 They were called "secretaries charging with the yellow registers" (*guan hunagce zushi*). *NJHBZ*, 5.11b.

147 Zhao Guan et al., *Houhu zhi*, 55; Liang, "Mingdai hunagce kao," 289; Wei, *Mingdai huangce*, 92.

148 For example, in a certain year in the Hongwu era, the number of the yellow registers was 53,393 copies, in 1502 it was 67,468 copies, and in 1542, 65,859 copies. *NJHBZ*, 5.15b–16a; Wei, *Mingdai huangce*, 92–3.

149 Wei, *Mingdai huangce*, 93.

150 Zhao, *Houhu zhi*, 147; Luan, *Mingdai huangce yanjiu*, 1.

151 Liang, "Mingdai hunagce kao," 288; Wei, *Mingdai huangce*, 92.

152 Wei, *Mingdai huangce*, 100.

153 Zhao, *Houhu zhi*, 19–20; Wei, *Mingdai huangce*, 97–8.

154 Liang, "Mingdai hunagce kao," 287; Wei, *Mingdai huangce*, 98–9.

155 *NJHBZ*, 5.24.

156 Starting from 1493, two Nanjing censors and one supervising secretary were ordered to assist the Nanjing Ministry of Revenue in the verification work. *NJHBZ*, 5.11a–b.

157 In 1391, when the second compilation of the yellow registers was complete, it was decreed that 1,200 national university students, led by two investigating censors, one supervising secretary for revenue, four secretaries of the ministry of revenue, to check the new record against the previous ones. In 1442, the number of national university students was reduced to 800. Since 1493 the number of the national university students involved was fixed at 350. *NJHBZ*, 5.10b-11b.

120 *Center of Wealth*

158 In the Ming, most of the households under registration were classified into one of the four categories, namely the civilian households (*minhu*), military households (*junhu*), artisan households (*jianghu*) and saltern households (*zaohu*). *MS* (1878) classifies the Ming population into three categories (civilian, military, and artisan), Ray Huang adds one (saltern household) according to the records in *DMHD*. Each of these four categories can be further divided into some subcategories, for example, the artisan household included masons, carpenters, weavers, and printers. The vocational classification, applicable to households, instead of individuals, implied that a family trade was to be inherited in perpetuity. *MS*, 1906.

159 The Ming households were divided into three levels (upper, middle, and lower) in accordance with the property (both movable and immovable) of the households. In theory, the tax levels corresponded to the household levels.

160 *Houhu zhi*, 83.

161 *NJHBZ*, 5.17b.

162 *NJHBZ*, 10a–b; 12a.

163 In the early Hongwu era, the official estimated population was 10,652,789. *NJHBZ*, 5.17a.

164 Wei, *Mingdai huangce*, 158.

165 Ho, *Studies on the Population of China*, 18.

166 Wei, *Mingdai huangce*, 224.

167 Huang Xun, *Huang Ming mingchen jingji lu*, 554.

5 Southern Stronghold

The military functions of the Southern Capital administration

> The practice by which the Nanjing minister of war concurrently held the post of grand adjutant started in the year of 1487. Consequently he was placed ahead of the Nanjing minister of personnel and the Nanjing Ministership of War was regularly assumed by the officials who had previously served as the Nanjing minister of personnel. [...] The [descending] order of the ministries of Personnel, Revenue, Rites, War, Justice, and Works [in the official hierarchy] had been an accepted rule since the time of the Duke of Zhou, and it was perfectly created by nature (*tianzhao dishe*). Why should we allow this deviant practice [of giving prominence to the Nanjing Ministry of War] to continue?[1]
>
> Zhu Guozhen (1557–1632)

Here Zhu Guozhen, the senior grand secretary in the Tianqi era, was a critic of the special Southern Capital bureaucratic practice under which the Nanjing Ministry of War ranked first in the ministerial hierarchy, in which Personnel had traditionally been ranked ahead of Revenue, Rites, War, Justice, and Works in a descending order of prestige. The prominence of the Nanjing Ministry of War in the Southern Capital obviously relates to the heightened military responsibilities and functions of the Nanjing administration, especially its military branch.

1. Military forces under the command of the Southern Capital administration

The basic element of the military system during the high Ming period consisted of 493 guard units (*wei*).[2] These units were placed under the control of two different commands. The imperial guards (*shangzhiwei* or *qinjunwei*), numbering 62 in total (44 in Beijing and 18 in Nanjing),[3] were charged with protecting the imperial palace and in theory were directly commanded by the emperor. The others were supervised by the five Chief Military Commissions in Beijing and their counterparts in Nanjing. Of the 493 guard units, 81 (44 imperial and 37 ordinary guards) were garrisoned in Beijing, 50 (18 imperial and 32 ordinary guards) were deployed in Nanjing,[4] and the remaining 365 ordinary guards were scattered across the empire. Since there was no emperor

122   *Southern Stronghold*

in the Southern Capital, all the guard units in Nanjing, including the imperial guards, were in practice commanded by the five Nanjing Chief Military Commissions. Except for the 44 imperial guards in Beijing and the Nanjing guards, all units were under the direction of the five Chief Military Commissions in Beijing. Of them, the 362 guard units which were stationed in the 13 provinces and two metropolitan areas were directly commanded by 16 Regional Military Commissions (*du zhihuishi si*) and five Branch Regional Military Commissions (*xing du zhihuishi si*) as well as two Regencies (*liushou si*).[5] In other words, the guard force in Nanjing constituted slightly more than 10 percent of the empire's total contigent.[6]

There were a number of training divisions (*ying*) stationed in and around the city of Nanjing which provided training for the guard soldiers from Nanjing and its surrounding areas. The most prestigious of these were the Nanjing counterparts of the "Three Great Divisions" (*sandaying*) in Beijing, the Dajiaochang, Xiaojiaochang, and Shenji divisions.[7] In addition, there were divisions which only existed for a certain time in the Southern Capital, notably the Zhenwu (strength-inspiring) Division, Cihe Division, Lubing (land force) Division, Shuibing (naval force) Division, and Biao (spear) Division. The Zhenwu and Cihe divisions were created to train soldiers to combat the pirates in the Jiajing era when the empire was beset with rampant piracy along the southeast coast. The Zhenwu Division operated out of Nanjing proper between 1545 and 1567.[8] The Cihe Division, for which exact dates of operation are not clear, was garrisoned on the north bank of the Yangzi River.[9] The Land Force Division and Naval Force Division were created in 1592 after Toyotomi Hedeyoshi (1536–98) launched his invasion of Korea, and the Spear Division was founded after the Liu Tianxu Incident of 1606.[10] All of the 50 guards and the above-mentioned five divisions were under the control of a military triumvirate in Nanjing which, as discussed in Chapter Two, was composed of the grand commandant, the eunuch grand commandant, and the Nanjing minister of war, who was concurrently the grand adjutant.

Due to the geographic location of Nanjing, special divisions, the Xinjiangkou Division, Pukou Division, and Naval Force Division, were set up successively to provide naval combat training for soldiers from the Nanjing guards and those along the lower reaches of the Yangzi River.[11] The Xinjiangkou Division was created in the early Yongle era to train the Nanjing guards and later began to receive soldiers from the Zhenjiang, Xin'an and Jianyang guard units along the Yangzi River.[12] The Naval Force Division was set up immediately after the 1592 Korea Incident.[13] The date of the creation of the Pukou Division is unknown.

These three naval training divisions and the guards stationed along the lower reaches of the Yangzi River and its tributaries, namely those stationed in the area from Jiujiang, Jiangxi down to Tuanshan and Sanjianghuikou in Nan Zhili, were under the jurisdiction of the river controllers (*tidu chaojiang* or *chaojiang*) from the Nanjing administration.[14] Also under their supervision were a dozen of regional divisions along the lower reaches of the Yangzi.

Southern Stronghold 123

Most of these regional divisions were created during the Jiajing reign for the training of naval forces, presumably for the defense of the area from assault by pirates. They were the Nanhu Division (Jiujiang), Anqing Division, Taiping Division, Diegang Division (Cizhou), Yizhen divisions (both naval and ground), Guazhou divisions (both naval and ground) (Yangzhou), Tuanshan Division (Zhenjiang), Sanjiang Division, and Youbing Division (Changzhou).[15]

There were two river controllers in the Southern Capital administration. One was a civilian, normally the vice censor-in-chief or assistant censor-in-chief of the Nanjing Censorate.[16] The other, a military dignitary, was typically a noble (marquis or earl) and head of one of the five Nanjing Chief Military Commissions[17] The division of labor between the civilian and military river controllers is not very clear. It is plausible that the former was a supervisor and the latter a commander and coordinator of the forces along the lower reaches of the Yangzi. During the late years of the Chongzhen reign, the emperor attempted to eliminate the civilian post of the river controller,[18] possibly due to the ambiguous division of labor between the two.

The other officials in the Nanjing bureaucracy who wielded considerable military power over the local divisions and guards in Nan Zhili area were the river-patrol censors (*xunjiang yushi*). Normally investigating censors from the Nanjing Censorate, the river-patrol censors were charged with maintaining surveillance over the lower reaches of the Yangzi, including the area extending from Jiujiang down to Suzhou and Songjiang. The official who was stationed at Anqing was mainly responsible for the security of the area from Jiujiang to Longjiangguan. The other, headquartered at Zhenjiang, was chiefly responsible for the area from Longjiangguan to Suzhou and Songjiang.[19] Under the jurisdiction of the river controllers and river-patrol censors were the circuits of Suzhou, Songjiang, Changzhou, Zhenjiang, Huai'an, Xuzhou, and Yangzhou, as well as the vice regional commanders (*fu zongbing guan*) at Wusong and Langshan, the two commanders-in-chief responsible for the defense of, respectively, the areas north and south of the Yangzi. Also under the control of the river-patrol censor were the military leaders[20] of the 27 regional divisions in the four Jiangnan prefectures of Suzhou, Songjiang, Changzhou, and Zhenjiang, and those of the 20 local divisions of the two Jiangbei prefectures of Huai'an and Yangzhou.[21] In addition, 11 guard units and 15 battalions along the lower reaches of the Yangzi, on both the south and north banks of the river, were also placed under the control of the river-patrol censor.[22]

Although there is no account specifying the division of duties between the river controllers and river-patrol censors, it is plausible that one was supervisor to the other. River controllers were usually vice or assistant censors-in-chief whose official rank was, respectively, grade 3a or grade 4a, and the river-patrol censors were normally investigating censors whose rank was grade 7a. In fact, in many cases the civilian river controller was concurrently the river-patrol censor: for example, Xu Bida (*js* 1592), assistant censor-in-chief of the Nanjing Censorate in the 1610s and author of the *Gazetteer of the Nanjing Censorate*, assumed the two positions at the same time.[23]

124   *Southern Stronghold*

How strong was the military force under the control of the Southern Capital administration? At full strength a Ming guard unit had 5,600 soldiers and so in theory the Nanjing guards may have had as many as 280,000 soldiers. In practice, however, from the Yongle era and especially from the Zhengtong reign onward, many of the soldiers began to desert their guard units,[24] so the military force in Nanjing during the post-1421 period probably never reached its full potential. Table 5.1 below details the composition of 48 Nanjing guard units in the late Ming period, showing that the units were uniformly undermanned.

As we can see from the table, the guard units in Nanjing in the 1610s were far from their nominal strength of 5,600. Only two exceeded 4,000 troops, 26 units had just more than 1,000, and many others numbered only in the hundreds, with the result that the total size of the Nanjing force was no more than 60,000. This accorded with the situation across the whole country, where regional guards filled only five-eighths of their prescribed enlistments by the end of the Hongwu reign, and less than half by mid-Ming.[25]

The number of troops who received training in Nanjing varied from division to division. The Zhenwu and Cihe divisions each had 3,000 soldiers,[26] the Shenji Division slightly more than 3,000,[27] and the Pukou Division around 2,000.[28] The Land Force Division, Naval Force Division and the Spear Division had strengths of 1,800, 1,700, and 1,300 respectively.[29] The Dajiaochang, Xiaojiaochang, and Xinjiangkou divisions accommodated more than 10,000 respectively.[30] Like the guard units, the number of soldiers in the divisions also fluctuated over time. For example, at its full strength, the Xinjiangkou Division trained approximately 15,000 soldiers, with 400 ships provided for the water drill.[31] In the ninth month of 1575, there were only 5,200 soldiers left in the division and 40 vessels available for training.[32] In the 1610s the men at the Dajiaochang and Xiaojiaochang divisions numbered 6,000 and 9,100 respectively.[33] On the whole, at its peak, the soldiers dispatched to the Nanjing divisions exceeded 120,000.[34] In 1519 the number of troops in the various Nanjing divisions was slightly in excess of 36,900,[35] and in 1583 the soldiers enrolled in the Nanjing divisions numbered only 20,000.[36] There is some redundancy in these figures, since soldiers from the Nanjing guard units were also rotated to the Nanjing divisions to receive specialized training. In fact, the short-lived Cihe Division only trained soldiers from the guards of Feixiong (flying bear), Yingwu (prowess), and Guangying (extensive bravery) in Nanjing.[37] Even taking these factors into account, the forces controlled by the Nanjing administration officials, as well as the regional guard units and divisions under the command of the river controllers and river-patrol censors, were formidable.[38]

2. Maintaining stability at the second political center

A number of factors explain why the Ming government deployed so many troops in the Southern Capital and its surrounding area. In the first place, the

Southern Stronghold 125

Table 5.1 The number of officers and soldiers in 48 Nanjing Guard units (*c.* 1615)

Guard unit	Guard Com.	Bat. Com.	Comp. Com.	Soldier
Jinyi	18	37	79	2,400
Qishou	9	35	24	710
Fujun	8	27	30	789
Fujunzuo	12	44	17	1,281
Fujunyou	11	35	53	990
Fujunhou	11	30	42	1,245
Hubenzuo	12	38	51	990
Yulingzuo	23	40	35	1,698
Yulingyou	20	32	40	1,136
Yulingqian	24	45	32	457
Jichuan	19	25	–	3,798
Jinwuzuo	44	66	32	485
Jinwuyou	34	56	40	491
Jinwuqian	11	40	35	1,835
Jinwuhou	9	29	26	1,077
Jianghai	11	22	2	4,239
Xiaoling	12	14	40	4,094
Liushouzuo	7	22	29	1,750
Liushouyou	7	19	46	1,900
Liushouzhong	10	29	40	1,332
Liushouqian	9	21	27	1,551
Liushouhou	39	136	80	2,374
Longhu	9	15	34	999
Longhuzuo	13	17	35	1,225
Jiangyin	11	21	34	1,396
Hubenyou	9	27	36	902
Zhennan	6	20	38	662
Shenyangzuo	1	12	18	804
Yingtian	14	21	57	793
Shuijunzuo	7	30	35	1,467
Shuijunyou	12	18	31	1,141
Wude	11	12	25	710
Guangwu	4	23	21	1,190
Longjiangzuo	14	27	54	1,502
Longjiangyou	13	28	39	2,022
Baotao	6	13	22	677
Baotaozuo	15	19	30	948
Xiaoqiyou	7	25	19	689
Tianche	9	10	17	586
Heyang	11	18	34	115
Longxiang	13	26	26	301
Xinwu	41	123	105	1,341
Guangyang	12	18	47	1,364
Yingyang	72	108	102	1,330
Henghai	11	17	62	925
Yingwu	8	10	8	733
Feixiong	2	9	4	1,044
Shenyangyou	8	11	11	131
Total	699	1,520	1,708	60,728

Source: *NJDCYZ*, 12.3a–10a

126 *Southern Stronghold*

Southern Capital had been regarded as a place of fundamental significance throughout the Ming[39] and was the second most important political center of the dynasty. Serving as a substitute capital, it provided a place of retreat for the central government in Beijing should the need arise. One of the main considerations of early Chinese rulers in choosing a seat of government, as pointed out in Chapter One, was its defensibility. When the Yongle emperor decided to move the primary capital to Beijing, he aimed at strengthening defenses along the northern frontier, and the auxiliary capital in Nanjing was retained in the hope that it would help defend and stabilize the southern part of the country. By maintaining it as a stable, orderly, and peaceful location of government, Nanjing provided the Ming rulers with a viable alternative.

During the period from 1421 to 1644, when the Ming dynasty was overthrown, officials twice suggested that the court be moved to Nanjing, although the suggestion was never taken up. The first such proposal was put forward after the disastrous Tumu Incident of 1449 when roughly half a million Ming troops were annihilated and the reigning Yingzong emperor was taken captive by the Mongol troops led by Esen (d. 1455).[40] According to Xu Youzhen (1407–72), the Hanlin expositor-in-waiting, his astrological "observation" indicated that the mandate of heaven given to the Northern Capital had disappeared, and to avoid further disaster, the transfer of the main capital to Nanjing was necessary. Due to the vehement opposition of Vice Minister of War Yu Qian (1398–1457),[41] Minister of Rites Hu Ying, and the court eunuch Jin Ying, the motion was dismissed.[42] The second and final proposal was made at the end of the Ming. In the second month of 1644 when Shanxi was captured by the rebel forces of Li Zhicheng (1606–45), which were advancing towards Beijing, Li Banghua (d. 1644), the right censor-in-chief who served as the Nanjing minister of war in 1439 and Li Mingrui, the right mentor (*youshuzi*), pleaded with the Chongzhen emperor to move the court to Nanjing and send the heir apparent to supervise state affairs, in preparation for the worst. The following month, Grand Secretary Li Jiantai made a similar request, but all such pleas were eventually turned down by the obstinate emperor.[43]

The rapid formation of the Hongguang regime after the fall of Beijing to the peasant rebels and the death of the Chongzhen emperor in the spring of 1644 bore testimony to the substitute role of the Southern Capital in a time of exigency. The Chongzhen emperor committed suicide by hanging himself in the third month of 1644, shortly before the rebel forces of Li Zicheng entered the imperial palace compounds.[44] Three weeks later, when the shocking news reached the Southern Capital,[45] senior officials became enmeshed in a fierce month-long debate over the choice of a new ruler for the fallen Ming.[46] Lynn Struve maintains that the "reconversion of Nanjing into the hub of Ming government" was "wrenchingly fast":[47]

> The Hung-kuang [Hongguang] regimes's first month witnessed an impressively rapid transformation of the auxiliary capital, with its skeleton administration consisting largely of sinecures, into the nerve center of

the country, as it had been in the first century of the dynasty. The new regime had to recreate almost the entire Pei-ching (Beijing) governmental structure, including the capital guard system, redirect the flow of tax revenues and transport services, rearrange administrative circuits, and rebuild or renovate the halls, temples, and living quarters which had fallen into disuse within the old imperial palace compound. All this was done with admirable dispatch, considering the confusion of the time.[48]

As a matter of fact, the transformation of the Southern Capital into the center of Ming government was by no means "impressively rapid," for the new Hongguang government was merely a slightly reshuffled version of the pre-existing Nanjing administration. The new regime did not need to recreate "the entire Beijing governmental structure," because, as has been shown in Chapter Two of this book, all the Beijing governmental departments (civil, military, and eunuch) had their counterparts in Nanjing. The only institutions missing from the Southern Capital were the emperor and the grand secretariat. During the one-month period from the suicide of Chongzhen to the formation of the Hongguang regime, Nanjing officials spent most of the time arguing over the succession to the Ming throne. When a consensus was finally reached and the chosen one (prince of Fu) was welcomed at Longjiangguan on the 30th of the fourth month (June 4) and began to assume the title of regent (*jianguo*) on the fifth of the fifth month (June 9), the core of the Hongguang government was formed in less than ten days. The leading officials of the new government came almost entirely from the previous Nanjing administration. Shi Kefa, the Nanjing minister of war, was promoted to the secretariat while retaining his position as minister of war; Gao Hongtu (1583–1645), the former Nanjing minister of revenue, was made grand secretary and minister of rites; Zhou Ken, former Nanjing vice minister of works, became minister of revenue; Zhang Shenyan (1578–1646), former Nanjing censor-in-chief, was made minister of personnel; Lü Daqi (1586–1649), former Nanjing vice minister of war, was reassigned as vice minister of personnel; Liu Zongzhou (1578–1645), former left censor-in-chief dismissed by the Chongzhen emperor in the early 1640s, was reinstated to his former position.[49] The only top official named from outside the previous Nanjing administration was Ma Shiying (d. 1646), the supreme commander of the Fengyang region. He was elevated to the grand secretariat, with concurrent appointments as minister of war and right censor-in-chief, as well as supreme commander of the Fengyang region.[50]

The Hongguang regime was short-lived, as were the other Southern Ming governments of the prince of Tang and prince of Gui. Had the Chongzhen emperor listened to the pleading of some of his courtiers and retreated to the Southern Capital instead of hanging himself on Jingshan Hill in the spring of 1644, it is conceivable that an arrangement similar to that of the Eastern Jin and Southern Song might have allowed the Ming to rule China south of the Yangzi River or even regain the lost northern territories. However, Chongzhen's guilty conscience led him to follow the example of General Xiang Yu

(232–202 BC), who refused to cross the Wu River and committed suicide by slitting his throat after suffering a crushing defeat by the rival force, rather than retreating to the south and attempting to strike back. The precious political and military resources in Nanjing were wasted.

The status of the Southern Capital was also enhanced by the fact that the tombs of the dynastic founder and his empress and their eldest son, Zhu Biao, as well as many imposing buildings – such as the former imperial palace and ancestral temple – all existed in Nanjing. Starting from the early Jianwen years, all the civil officials, military officers, and eunuch chiefs in Nanjing had to pay homage to Xiaoling, the mausoleum of the Hongwu emperor and Empress Ma, at the Qingming and Zhongyuan festivals, as well as on the winter solstice. They were also required to do the same nine times a year at Yiwenling, the tomb of Hongwu's eldest son and father of Emperor Jianwen, on the first and last days of the year, the first day of each of the four seasons, and the anniversary of Prince Yiwen's passing, as well as at the festivals of Qingming and Zhongyuan, and the winter solstice. This ritual practice was strictly observed until the end of the dynasty.[51] In a sense, Nanjing was regarded as the ancestral place (*zuzong zhidi*) of the Ming imperial family. And because of this, Nanjing always received special attention from the Ming court.[52]

Thanks to the presence of large military forces in and around Nanjing and a considerable number of local divisions and guards along the lower reaches of the Yangzi, which were commanded and supervised by the Nanjing administration officials and deployed with the primary purpose of safeguarding the Southern Capital, Nanjing never fell into the hands of hostile forces during the 1420–1645 period, although it twice faced a grave crisis. The first was presented by the rebels of Zhu Chenhao (d. 1520), prince of Ning, at Nanchang, Jiangxi, when he revolted against the Ming court in 1519. His troops seized Jiujiang and Nankang, and were about to attack Anqing and Nanjing. Qiao Yu (1457–1524), the Nanjing minister of war at that time, organized an effective defense around the city and executed 300 agents who were accused of collaborating with the rebels.[53] Zhu Chenhao's rebel forces were eventually deterred and routed by troops led by Wang Yangming (1472–1528) before they had the chance to raid Nanjing.[54] The second threat to the Southern Capital was posed by a group of pirates that inflicted heavy casualties on the Nanjing troops in 1555. Although the intruders were ultimately repelled, the performance of the Nanjing troops in this incident was vehemently criticized by many, who cited it as an indication of the weakness and inefficiency of the Nanjing military. It was recorded that the 70-odd marauders killed hundreds of Nanjing soldiers and two squad leaders (*bazong*) before they were forced to retreat.[55]

3. Suppression of piracy along the southeast coast

In addition to defending the Southern Capital administration itself and thus securing a safe rear base for the imperial court in Beijing, the Nanjing government was also vital in maintaining the stability of the southern provinces. Although there was no specific regulation on the division of power and labor between the Beijing and Nanjing administrations, it was the general perception that the Southern Capital government held some responsibility for the defense and safety of the south. This role of stabilizing the southern part of the empire was reflected in its participation in suppressing the piracy along the southeast coast during the middle of the Ming[56] and quelling rebellions by the aborigines in the southwest provinces.

The first group of senior officials who were empowered to command the combined forces of the southern provinces to combat pirates in the early period of the 1550s, the peak decade for piracy and anti-piracy in the Ming period, came from the Nanjing Ministry of War. However, due to the obstruction of certain Beijing officials, especially Yan Song (1480–1565), Zhao Wenhua (d. 1557), and Hu Zongxian (1511–65), their power was considerably restricted, and the latter two overshadowed their command of the southern troops.

Zhang Jing (d. 1555), the Nanjing minister of war, was the first Nanjing official to be entrusted to lead the inter-provincial troops to combat the pirates. In the fifth month of 1554 he was commissioned to supervise the troops from Nan Zhili, Zhejiang, Shandong, Fujian, and Huguang.[57] Unfortunately, Zhang's mission was impaired by Zhao Wenhua, the vice minister of works who was sent to assess the military situation on the southeast coast. By the time Zhang was given the discretionary powers to suppress the piracy, the raiders had established a fortified base at Zhelin, Huating, with a combined force of 20,000. To ensure the success of the military operation, Zhang set out to conscript aboriginal troops from Guangdong and Guangxi to supplement the imperial forces already in Zhejiang. In the fifth month of 1555, Zhang's combined forces surrounded a large group of raiding pirates at Wangjiangjing, north of Jiaxing, and took 2,000 heads. This was the first time that an imperial army had been able to defeat such a large force of marauders.[58]

However, what awaited Zhang was discharge and execution rather than reward. Shortly after his arrival, Zhao pressed Zhang to launch an attack without delay. Zhang, who was superior to Zhao in rank, slighted him and declined to discuss strategy with him. Harboring resentment for Zhang, Zhao secretly reported to the Jiajing emperor calumniating Zhang of misappropriating funds and failing to defend the region. After overpowering Grand Secretary Yan Song endorsed Zhao's slanderous memorial, the emperor ordered Zhang's arrest. The time was the fifth month of 1555, exactly one year after Zhang assumed his commandership.[59] Even after hearing of the victory at Wangjiangjing, the emperor still accepted the accusations and ordered that Zhang Jing be brought to Beijing. In the tenth month of 1555, Zhang was beheaded, together with Li Tianchong, the grand coordinator of Zhejiang, also framed by Zhao and Yan. Meanwhile Yan credited the victory to Zhao and recommended Hu Zongxian to fill the vacancy left by Li Tianchong.[60]

130   *Southern Stronghold*

Zhang was replaced by Zhou Chong, the recently appointed Nanjing vice minister of war, as the general commander of the combined forces of the southern provinces.[61] Zhou was dismissed after having occupied this position for only 34 days. He was also a victim of the accusations of Zhao Wenhua, who wanted to bequeath this position to his close associate, Hu Zongxian. Zhou was relegated to commoner and deprived of all his official titles. However, instead of going to Hu Zongxian, the vacant post was given to Yang Yi (*js* 1523), another newly appointed Nanjing vice minister of war.[62]

Unlike his two predecessors, Yang Yi pandered to Zhao, although the latter was not higher in terms of official rank. Zhao's close association with powerful Yan Song and the miserable ending of Zhang Jing and Li Tianchong intimidated Yang. Moreover, Yang's commanding ability was far inferior to that of Zhang Jing. Arguing that the "wolf soldiers "(*langbing*)[63] recruited by Zhang were uncontrollable, Yang requested permission to enlist volunteers and transport soldiers from Nan Zhili, Zhejiang, Shandong, Fujian, and Huguang, as well as troops from Henan and Sichuan. Unfortunately, he could not keep the armies from these various provinces under control and trouble broke out between the soldiers from Sichuan and Shandong. When Zhao Wenhua was recalled to Beijing by the emperor for consultation in the first month of 1556, he took the opportunity to request Yang's dismissal and recommended Hu as his replacement. The emperor, happening to receive a memorial from Censor Shao Weizhong impeaching Yang at that moment, had Yang stripped of official ranks in the second month of 1556. He was in power for a mere half-year and had never freely exercised his power as general commander of the various provincial forces.[64] Soon after Yang's dismissal, another Nanjing official, Wang Gao (1498–1557), the Nanjing vice minister of revenue, was made the Nanjing vice minister of war and concurrently assistant censor-in-chief, and put in charge of the military affairs of Nan Zhili, Zhejiang, and Fujian.[65] It appears that Wang never really had the necessary military authority and was completely overshadowed by Zhao and Hu. After his initial appointment in the second month of 1556, he virtually disappeared from the historical records. From then until the end of the decade, when piracy was fundamentally suppressed, the leadership of the anti-piracy campaign was taken over by Zhao Wenhua and Hu Zongxian, officials from Beijing.

The successive enlistment of Nanjing officials in the suppression of piracy in the early part of the 1550s clearly indicates the roles the administration played in stabilizing the southern part of the empire. Events also show the competition for power, favor, and dominant position between the officials of the two administrations that existed. The struggle between Beijing officials Zhao Wenhua and Hu Zongxian and Nanjing bureaucrats Zhang Jing, Zhou Chong, Yang Yi, and Wang Gao is the telling example. Since Beijing officials were in a certain sense closer to the emperor and the grand secretaries, it was relatively easier for them to obtain the decisive support (although they ran more risk of annoying them as well): that is, they were generally in a more advantageous position in the competition with officials from Nanjing.

Southern Stronghold 131

4. The suppression of aboriginal rebellions in the south

The Nanjing administration also bore some of the responsibility of quelling the uprisings of peasants and aborigines in the south, where popular revolts were widespread.[66] The most famous cases recorded in Ming sources include the suppression of the Milu rebellion in the Hongzhi era, the quelling of the rising of the Yao tribes in the early Jiajing reign, and the defeat of the insurrection led by the Bozhou Pacification Commissioner Yang Yinglong in the mid-Wanli era. Top Nanjing officials were commissioned to direct the operation to suppress each of these revolts.

The rebellion of Milu, a female chieftain in Pu'an, Guizhou, broke out in the seventh month of 1499, when troops under the command of the regional officials were soundly routed, Regional Commander Wu Yuan captured and Pu'an almost taken by the rebels. In the seventh month of 1500, exactly one year after the uprising, Nanjing Minister of Revenue Wang Shi (1439–1506) was given a concurrent appointment as vice censor-in-chief to command the military forces of Guizhou.[67] Prior to Wang's arrival at Guizhou in late 1501, a number of top provincial officials had been slain in the encounters with the rebels, including a provincial administration commissioner, a provincial judicial commissioner, and a few provincial military commanders.[68] Upon arrival, Wang Shi used his discretionary power to mobilize some 120,000 soldiers from the regular and tribal troops of Guangxi, Huguang, Yunnan, and Sichuan, as well as the regional troops of Guizhou. He divided the troops into four columns, and after five months of operation ending in early 1502, the troops under his command took over 1,000 rebel forts, beheaded close to 5,000 rebels, and took another 1,300 prisoner. For this, Wang was lavishly rewarded and granted the title of grand guardian of the heir apparent, and before long was appointed the Nanjing minister of war and grand adjutant.[69]

In 1526, Cen Meng, an aboriginal official and vice magistrate of the Tianzhou subprefecture in Guangxi, was impeached for disrespect towards his superiors and accused of plotting insurrection. He was consequently killed in a military operation launched against him.[70] His subordinates, Lu Su and Wang Shou, revolted at Tianzhou in early 1527. After taking neighboring Si'en, they overwhelmed the army led by the supreme commander of Guangxi. In the fifth month of 1526, former Nanjing Minister of War Wang Yangming, who had stayed away from active politics since the early Jiajing reign, was reappointed as the Nanjing minister of war and concurrently made left censor-in-chief, with orders to command the troops of Guangxi, Guangdong, Jiangxi, and Huguang to quell the 70,000 tribal rebels.[71] Attributing the root cause of the Tianzhou uprising to the rash implementation of the policy of "replacing the aboriginal officials [in the tribal areas] with regular civil officials (*gaitu guiliu*)," Wang Yangming decided to resolve the crisis by appeasing the rebels. He discharged the troops and invited the rebel leaders Lu Su and Wang Shou to his temporary headquarters for negotiation. To show his intention of resolving the crisis peacefully, he went to the rebel

132   *Southern Stronghold*

camps in person to demand their surrender, and the revolt ended without further bloodshed.[72]

After suppressing the Tianzhou rebellion, Wang Yangming turned his attention to the Yao tribal revolt of Datengxia (Big Rattan Gorge), also in the province of Guangxi. By then the tribal unrest had been going on for a number of decades, and the areas controlled by the rebel Yao tribesmen stretched for 300 *li*. Previously the Ming government had sent as many as 200,000 soldiers to quell the rebels, but to no avail. It was said that, after the initial failure, the discussion and proposal regarding the issues were rarely raised.[73] To the surprise of many, with the cooperation of Provincial Administrative Commissioner Lin Fu and the military support rendered by recently appeased Lu Su and Wang Shou, Wang Yangming was able to crush the Yao rebellion within a very short time.[74] According to Wang, as many as 15,000 rebels were slaughtered in this military operation.[75]

The campaign against Yang Yinglong, the pacification commissioner of Bozhou, Sichuan, in the 1590s was another case participated in by high-ranking officials from the Southern Capital administration. Bozhou, a mountainous region bordering the three provincial administrations of Huguang, Sichuan, and Guizhou, had been controlled by the Yang family since the ninth century.[76] In 1591, the Grand Coordinator of Guizhou Ye Mengxiong proposed that the five aboriginal offices (*tusi*) under the Bozhou Pacification Commission be converted to regular offices (*liuguan*), subject to the direct control of the provincial government in Chongqing. On hearing of this proposed change, all five aboriginal offices revolted.[77] The campaign against Yang and his followers was led by a Nanjing official in the early stage. Xing Jie (1540–1615), the Nanjing vice minister of war, was ordered to direct the military operation in Guizhou in the tenth month of 1594.[78] Using both deception and military strength, Xing initially achieved success, but due to the pressing situation in Korea, further military operations were halted,[79] and before long Xing was transferred to command Chinese troops against Hideyoshi in Korea.[80]

However, not all the military operations against anti-government rebels in south China were commanded by officials from the Nanjing administration. In fact, most of the suppression campaigns were directed by bureaucrats from Beijing or by provincial officials. For example, the Ye Zongliu rebellion in 1445–47 in Zhejiang was crushed by armies led by Censor-in-chief Zhang Kai; the Deng Maoqi rebels in Fujian in 1448 was suppressed by the combined forces commanded by the Marquise of Ningyang Chen Mao, Earl of Baoding Liang Yao, Earl of Pingjiang Chen Yu, and Minister of Justice Jin Lian; the Huang Xiaoyang peasant uprising in 1448 in Guangdong was quelled by the armies of Guangdong and Guangxi led by Right Assistant Censor-in-chief Yang Xinmin; in the 1470s a rebellion of displaced and unregistered people in the Xingxiang area of Huguang was put down by the forces of Henan and Huang led by Minister of Works Bai Gui, Censor-in-chief Xiang Zhong, and the commander-in-chief of Huguang, Li Zhen. Prior to the successful suppression of the Datengxia revolt by the Nanjing minister of war, Wang Yangming, a number of Beijing officials were commissioned to lead the military campaigns. In 1465, Right Assistant Censor-in-chief Hang Yong was ordered to lead a troop of 160,000 men to Guangxi to put down the insurrection, and in 1516, the supreme commander of Guangdong and Guangxi, Chen Xi, was given the power to command 130,000 soldiers to attack the Datengxia rebels.[81]

5. Non-combat functions

In addition to professional training, battlefield operation, and military farming,[82] the troops from the Southern Capital also assumed some non-combat roles. The most prominent of these involved the transport of tribute grain to the north. Thirty-four out of the 49 Nanjing guard units,[83] with more than 20,000 officers and soldiers and close to 2,000 ships, transported more than 600,000 piculs of tribute grain.[84] Put another way, approximately 25 percent of the guard units and 16 percent of the vessels involved in the transportation of the empire's tribute grain came from the Nanjing troops,[85] which transported 16 percent of the tribute grain.

Starting in the early fifteenth century, an unofficial line marking the division of labor between the armies in the south and those in the north was drawn. In 1430, Zhu Yong, the duke of Cheng, suggested to the Xuande emperor that, given the different situations facing the armies in the south and north, it was sensible to entrust the armies in the south with the transport of tribute grain, leaving the northern armies to defend the northern frontiers. His proposal was readily accepted by the emperor and from that time one of the main responsibilities assigned to the southern armies was to transport tribute grain along the Grand Canal to the north.[86]

The evolution of the tribute grain transportation system reflects the increased responsibility of the southern armies and the decreased role of the civilian taxpayers. Three different systems were used at different times during the Ming to transport the tribute grain by the Grand Canal. They were introduced in the following order: the relay transport (*zhiyun*) system, the transfer transport (*duiyun*) system, and the reformed transfer transport (*gaidui*) system. The three systems coexisted and overlapped to a certain extent.[87] The general trend of the evolution was that the transport distance of taxpayers became shorter and shorter and that of the army soldiers grew longer and longer. In other words, the role of taxpayers in the transport of tribute grain was gradually reduced, while the role of the army became increasingly prominent.

The relay transport system was first introduced in 1415. It required taxpayers to handle the first stage of the transport and the soldiers the second stage. Residents in the areas south of the Yangzi (e.g. Zhejiang, Suzhou, and Songjiang) had to deliver their tax grain to the Huai'an granary in Nan Zhili and the soldiers then shipped the grain to the Jining granary in Shandong; whereas people in Huai'an, Fengyang, Xuzhou, Yangzhou, and Yanzhou in

134 *Southern Stronghold*

Shandong delivered their tribute grain to the Jining granary, to be transported by soldiers northwards to the Tongzhou granary.[88] In 1432, a new system was put into effect. Under the transfer transport system, taxpayers delivered tax grain to the nearest major granary in their prefectures, subprefectures, and counties. For example, peasants who formerly delivered their grain to the Huai'an granary could now ship it to the Guazhou granary near Zhenjiang, and those who used to deliver their tribute grain to the Jining granary were allowed to transfer it to the Huai'an granary.[89] In return taxpayers paid a certain amount of porterage money rice (*jiaojia*) and easy delivery money (*qingjiyin*) to the transport soldiers.[90] The third method, the reformed transfer transport system, was started in 1481. Under this system, soldiers were ordered to go to the local waterside granaries, which were even closer to the prefectures and counties of the taxpayers, and then bring the grain to the major granaries, thus further shortening the taxpayer's delivery distance. In addition to the porterage rice and easy delivery money, the taxpayers paid the soldiers "Yangzi crossing money" (*guojiangfei*).[91]

Throughout the Ming, the majority of the transport soldiers came from guard units in the southern provinces. These transport soldiers were organized into brigades (*zong*). Each brigade was composed of a number of guards, which averaged around ten. Since more than 80 percent of the tribute grain came from the southern provinces of Nan Zhili, Zhejiang, Jiangxi, and Huguang, the armies in those southern provinces were chiefly employed in the transport of tribute grain. Of the empire's 12 grain transportation brigades, ten were formed by guard units from these four southern provinces. Of them, seven were from Nan Zhili, which included two Nanjing brigades, Middle Capital (*zhongdu*) Brigade, Upper Reaches (*shangjiang*) Brigade, Lower Reaches (*xiajiang*) Brigade, and two Northern Yangzi (*Jiangbei*) brigades. The remaining two, the Shandong and Dual-Purpose Ship (*zheyang*) brigades, were charged with shipping the grain from Shandong and Henan provinces.[92]

In addition to this role with tribute grain, the Southern Capital was also a major collector and transporter of local products gathered to meet the needs of the imperial family and the state coffer. As indicated in Chapter Two, one of the chief responsibilities of the 24 eunuch departments in Nanjing was to extract special products for the court in Beijing. The delivery duty rested on the Nanjing Ministry of War. More than 300 ships, including the Horse Ships (*machuan*), Fast Ships (*kuaichuan*), and Yellow Ships (*huangchuan*), were used to transport these tribute articles.[93] They were at the disposal of the ministry's Bureau of Equipment and Communications.[94]

The Yellow Ships, consisting of four classes, were mainly designed to transport the items required by the imperial house. The most luxurious and the largest class, *yubei dahuangchuan*, was reserved for use during imperial inspection tours. Originally under the office of the grand commandant, Yellow Ships were placed at the disposal of the Nanjing Ministry of War after 1587, and they were operated by a score of Nanjing guard units.[95] The Horse Ships derived their names from the early Ming, when the primary capital was still in Nanjing. They were initially used to transport horses (obtained in the markets in Sichuan and Yunnan or sent by the chieftains in these two provinces as tributes to the emperor) along the Yangzi River down to Nanjing. The Fast Ships were used to deliver military equipment in the early Ming. Later on, when the primary capital was relocated to Beijing, both types of ship were used to deliver tribute articles. The difference between Yellow, Horse, and Fast Ships disappeared. The Horse and Fast Ships were basically owned by the Jianghuai and Jichuan Guards in Nanjing; their number totaled 650.[96]

Most of the tribute articles delivered by the Bureau of Equipment and Communications were collected by the eunuch departments in Nanjing. Others were submitted by the civilian agencies, chiefly the Nanjing Ministry of Rites, the Nanjing Ministry of Works, and the Nanjing Court of Imperial Sacrifices. The following is a partial list of the tribute articles delivered by the Nanjing Ministry of War per annum around the 1610s, which provides us with some idea of the scale of the transportation of these articles from Nanjing:

- Office of the Nanjing Grand Commandant: Lotus roots, water chestnuts, tea, green plums, loquats, persimmons, pomegranates, Chinese parasol, 9 ships;
- The Nanjing Directorate of Palace Delicacies: Eggs, crucian carps, rapeseeds, fresh bamboo shoots, hilsa herrings (*shiyu*), dried herrings, candied cherries, candied plums, examination papers (*jinbangzhi*), purple perilla cakes, osmanthus jams, plum jams, peach jams, 52 ships;
- The Nanjing Garden Service: Water chestnuts, sword beans, baby gingers, gingers, taros, fresh lotus roots, oranges and *shiyangguo* fruit, 12 ships;
- The Nanjing Directorate of the Xiaoling Temple: Ginger, garlic, chestnuts, ginkgoes, Chinese yams, bricks and tiles, 6 ships;
- The Nanjing Directorate of Ceremonial: Silks (*zhibo*), plates and laths, 24 ships;
- The Nanjing Weaving and Dyeing Service: Silks, satins, damask silks, gauzes, 22 ships;
- The Nanjing Directorate for Credentials: Rollers for imperial decrees, 3 ships;
- The Nanjing Caps and Kerchiefs Service: Deer skins, ramie clothes, 3 ships;
- The Nanjing Directorate for Palace Eunuchs: Winnowing fans, dustpans, dining tables, copper wares, red bayberry, timber (of fir, elm, and sandalwood), coir matting, 101 ships;
- The Nanjing Directorate for Palace Accoutrements: Planks of fir and cedar, 42 ships;
- The Nanjing Sewing Service: Cupboards, cabinets, 11 ships;
- The Nanjing Ministry of Works: Rice buckets, pinewood plates, bamboo, red sandalwood, 31 ships;
- The Nanjing Court of Imperial Sacrifices: Geese, bamboo shoots, green plums, pears, water chestnuts, oranges, tangerines, sugarcane, 13 ships.[97]

As can be seen from the list, 14 Nanjing departments, mainly eunuch agencies, were involved in sending various tribute articles to Beijing, and

136   *Southern Stronghold*

more than 300 vessels were enlisted by the Bureau of the Equipment and Communications to deliver these produces on an annual basis. In addition, there were also many goods transported by land. For example, the various articles of clothing submitted by the Nanjing Loom Mill (*gongying jifang*),[98] the silver submitted by the Nanjing Ministry of Revenue, and the musical instruments submitted by the Nanjing Ministry of Rites were all delivered to Beijing by land.[99] Although the volume of the tribute articles and the shipping vehicles and vessels involved in the transportation during the period from the reign of Jiajing to the Wanli reign varied and the volume and variety listed above are only an approximation, they are nevertheless representative.

Another administrative role of the Nanjing government, closely associated with the northward transportation of tribute goods, was the construction of shipping vehicles and vessels. Throughout the Ming, Nanjing was a major, perhaps the largest, ship-building center in the empire, with at least five shipyards co-existing: the Longjiang, Treasure Ship (baochuan), Fast Ship, Horse Ship, and Yellow Ship yards, together manufacturing practically all ship types plying watercourses inside and outside the country, including the famous treasure ships used by Zheng He, the Zheyang (ocean-going) yellow ships, and Wusong battle ships, flat ships, horse ships, speedy ships, and tribute grain ships. Of the five Nanjing shipyards, three, viz., Horse Ship, Fast Ship, and Treasure Ship, were managed by the Bureau of Equipment and Communications under the Nanjing Ministry of War. The Longjiang shipyard, whose mandate was to build tribute grain ships for sailing along the Grand Canal, was administered by the Bureau of Construction of the Nanjing Ministry of Works, while the last, the Yellow Ship dockyard, was jointly supervised by the two Nanjing ministries.[100] Although information on the scale of these shipyards is not readily available, the fact that Jianghuai and Jichuan, the two Nanjing guard units responsible for operating the horse ships, possessed more than 800 such vessels reveals to some extent the production capacity of the Horse Ship dockyard.[101]

It is clear that the Southern Capital administration was instrumental in maintaining the stability of Nanjing, its surrounding area, and to some extent South China. The concentration of large numbers of guard units in and around Nanjing ensured the safety of the empire's second political center and thus provided a place of retreat for the government in Beijing at times of crisis. The deliberate deployment of these military forces also protected the ancestral tombs of the Ming imperial family and other imperial buildings from being threatened by hostile forces. As for its role in stabilizing the southern part of the empire, the auxiliary capital administration played a part in suppressing piracy on the southeast coast and in quelling the uprisings of the aborigines in the southwest provinces. The administration and the army under its control were also pivotal in transporting tribute grain and other tribute articles to the north. However, the military functions of the Nanjing administration should not be overemphasized. The Nanjing administration had neither much say in the decision-making process concerning Ming

Southern Stronghold   137

military policies nor any direct role in the defence of the northern frontier, which was undoubtly the primary military concern of the empire. Even in the suppression of piracy and the rebellions of the non-Han Chinese peoples, the role of the Nanjing administration was secondary. In short, although the Nanjing Ministry of War was regarded as the most prominent in the Southern Capital, its importance was relative to the other ministries in the administration. The role of the Nanjing administration in the military sphere was much less important than that of the Beijing administration. Nevertheless, its secondary roles were indispensable.

Notes

1 Zhu Guozhen, *Yongzhuang xiaopin*, 169.
2 *MS*, 2204.
3 The number of imperial guards recorded in the *baiguanzhi* and *bingzhi* sections of *MS* do not match each other. According to the *baiguanzhi*, there were 41 and 17 imperial guards in Beijing and Nanjing respectively; whereas the number recorded in the *bingzhi* is 44 and 18 respectively. *MS*, 1860–65, 2204–22.
4 The number of the Nanjing guards recorded in *NJDCYZ* (12.3a–10b) is 48.
5 *MS*, 2204–20. The Regional Military Commissions existed in every province and also in three vital defense zones along the northern frontier: Liaodong, Daning, and Wanquan. The five Branch Regional Military Commissions were located in Shanxi, Shaanxi, Sichuan, Fujian, and Huguang. The two regencies were at two nominal capitals: the Middle Capital Fengyang and the Flourishing Capital Anlu, Huguang.
6 According to Mote, a special command structure also existed for the Nine Defense Areas (*jiubian*) of the northern frontier, and actual troop strength under its control in the Chenghua-Hongzhi eras was about 300,000. See F. W. Mote and Denis Twitchett, eds, *Cambridge History of China, Ming Dynasty*, part 1, 373.
7 The Three Great Divisions in Beijing were the Wujun, Sanqian, and Shenji divisions.
8 *MS*, 2183–4; Tan Qian, *Guoque*, 3762, 3865. Liu Tianxu, a self-claimed master of Non-Action Teaching who attracted a substantial followings, planned to rebel against the Ming government in 1606. The plot was revealed to the Nanjing authorities and he and his followers were suppressed by a force led by the Nanjing Ministry of War. For more on Liu and his plot, see Shen Defu, *Wanli yehuo bian*, 755–6; Zhou Zhibin, "Wan Ming Nanjing bingbian erti," *Xuehai*, No. 3 (2006), 76–7; Hubert Seiwert, *Popular Religious Movements and Heterodox Sects in Chinese History*, 291–3; Xiaoxiang Luo, "Soldiers and the city: urban experience of guard households in late Ming Nanjing," *Frontiers of History in China*, Vol. 5, No.1 (March 2010), 43.
9 The two divisions were troublemakers for the Ming government. Both were disobedient and their soldiers mutinied against their authorities. *MS*, 2183–4. For the mutiny of the Zhenwu Division during the mid-Jiajing era, see Xu Xuemo, *Shimiao shiyu lu*, 591–3; Zhou Zhibin, "Wan Ming Nanjing bingbian erti," 76–80; Xiaoxiang Luo, "Soldiers and the city," 42–3.
10 Gu Qiyuan, *Kezuo zhuiyu*, 2.10; *NJDCYZ*, 12.2b.
11 Pukouzi Division was initially a land force division, and was later converted to be the naval force training division. *Jiangsu sheng tongzhi gao*, 497.
12 *NJDCYZ*, 10.45a–b, 31.54b.
13 Gu, *Kezuo zhuiyu*, 46.
14 *NJDCYZ*, 12.1a, 31.11a. The Pukou Division was supervised by the Nanjing Ministry of War prior to 1544. In the ninth month of 1544, Wan Yukai, the supervising

138   *Southern Stronghold*

secretary for war, suggested in his memorial that the Pukouzi Division should be put under the supervision of the river controllers, and his proposal was accepted. *Jiangsu sheng tongzhi gao*, 490.

15 *NJDCYZ*, 10.45a–55b.

16 *NJDCYZ*, 3.1a.

17 He could be commissioner-in-chief, vice commissioner-in-chief, or assistant commissioner-in-chief. *MHY*, 566.

18 *MS*, 6504; *MHY*, 567.

19 *DMHD*, 211.23b–24a.

20 For example, the assistant regional commanders (*canjiang*), brigade commanders (*youji*), and squad leaders (*bazong*).

21 *NJDCYZ*, 14.3b–5a.

22 The 11 guard units were the Suzhou, Taicang, Zhehai, Jinshan, Zhenjiang, Huai'an, Dahe, Pizhou, Yangzhou, Yizhen, and Gaoyou Guards. *NJDCYZ*, 14.5a.

23 See Xu's preface to *NJDCYZ*.

24 Li Guangming, *Jiajing yuwo Jiang Zhe zhukejun kao*, 2.

25 Edward Dreyer, *Early Ming China*, 187–8; Mote and Twitchett, *Cambridge History of China, the Ming Dynasty*, part 1, 373; Liu Jinxiang, "queyuan de yuanyin tanxi," *Beifang luntan*, No. 5 (2003), 73.

26 *MS*, 2183; *Jiangsu sheng tongzhi gao*, 514.

27 In 1583, the soldiers trained in the Shenji Division numbered 3,600 who shared only 500 muskets (*shenqiang*). *Jiangsu sheng tonzhi gao*, 558.

28 Gu, *Kezuo zhuiyu*, 46.

29 Gu, *Kezuo zhuiyu*, 46.

30 Zhang Chunxiu, *Shi Kefa ji*, 13–14; *Kezuo zhuiyu*, 46.

31 *NJDCYZ*, 10.45a, 31.61a, 32:38a; *Jiangsu sheng tongzhi gao*, 533–4.

32 *Jiangsu sheng tongzhi gao*, 533–4.

33 Gu, *Kezuo zuiyu*, 46.

34 In his memorial in 1583, Pan Jixun (1521–95), the Nanjing minister of war, lamented that at the time when he wrote his report the number of the soldiers who received combat training in Nanjing dwindled to a mere 20,000. *MS*, 2184.

35 *Jiangsu sheng tongzhi gao*, 464.

36 *MS*, 2184.

37 *Jiangsu sheng tongzhi gao*, 514.

38 The actual fighting ability of the Ming force is a question beyond the scope of this study. For an analysis of the cause and state of the low quality of the regular Ming troops, see Kwan-wai So, *Japanese Piracy in Ming China during the Sixteenth Century*, 135–40.

39 *Genben zhongdi* (lit. place of fundamental importance) was the phrase Ming contemporaries frequently used to describe the Southern Capital.

40 For a detailed account of the Tumu Incident, see F. W. Mote, "The T'u-mu Incident of 1449," 243–72.

41 Kuang Ye (1385–1449), the minister of war who accompanied the Zhengtong emperor in his campaign against the Mongol forces in 1449, lost his life in the Tumu debacle. Yu Qian, then vice minister of war, led an effective defense of the capital when it was besieged by the invading Mongol forces. For more on his role in the defense of Beijing, see *MS*, 4543–50; Lai Jiadu and Li Guangbi, *Yu Qian he Beijing*, 72–80.

42 *MS*, 4545; 4561; Fu Weiling, *Mingshu*, 120:2448–49. For some unknown reason, *Cambridge History of China* identifies Han Yong as the minister of rites. See Mote and Twitchett, *The Cambridge History of China, The Ming Dynasty, 1368–1644*, part 1, 326.

43 *MS*, 334, 6846; Tan, *Guoque*, 6034.

44 *MS*, 335; Shi Jianzhi, *Shi Kefa xiansheng nianpu*, 158–9. On the final days of the Chongzhen emperor, see Kenneth Swope, *The Military Collapse of China's Ming Dynasty, 1618–44*, 190–203.

45 Xu Zi, *Xiaotian jinian*, 1.1.

46 Officials such as Shi Kefa (1601–45), minister of war, Zhang Shenyan, censor-in-chief, Lü Daqi, vice minister of war, and Jiang Yueguang, supervisor of the Household of the Heir Apparent, preferred Zhu Changfang, the prince of Lu. The others in the Southern Capital, led by Ma Shiying, grand commander of the Fengyang area, Xu Hongji, the duke of Wei and grand commandant, Liu Kongzhao, earl of Chengyi and river controller, favored Zhu Yousong, the prince of Fu. After an intense competition, a consensus was eventually reached to choose the prince of Fu as the successor to the throne. On the 30th of the fourth month (4 June), the prince of Fu was welcomed to Nanjing. First assuming the title of regent on the 2nd of the fifth month (6 June), on the 15th of the same month (19 June) he ascended to the throne. And in the early days of the fifth month, the new government was formed. For more information on the competition among senior Nanjing officials over the choice of new ruler, see Xu, *Xiaotian jizhuan*, 1.1–5; Li Qing, *Nandu lu*, 1.1–2; Lynn Struve, *The Southern Ming*, 15–19.

47 Lynn Struve, ed. and trans., *Voices from the Ming-Qing Cataclysm: China in Tigers' Jaws*, 55.

48 Struve, *The Southern Ming*, 37.

49 Xu, *Xiaotian jinian*, 1.3; Li, *Nandu lu*, 1.4–5.

50 Xu, *Xiaotian jinian*, 1.3. Accounts in *Nandu lu* state that Ma was given the position of vice censor-in-chief. Li, *Nandu lu*, 1.5. Minister of War Shi Kefa was elbowed out to defend Yangzhou against the invading Manchu troops. For a detailed study of the Southern Ming, see Xie Guozhen, *Nan Ming shilüe*; Struve, *The Southern Ming, 1644–1662*.

51 Gu Qiyuan, *Kuzuo zhuiyu*, 70; Wang Huanbiao, *Ming Xiaoling zhi*, 37–63. It was a puzzle even to Ming officials that the amount of homage paid to Prince Yiwen was three times that to his father, the Ming founder. *Kezuo zhuiyu*, 70.

52 For a detailed discussion of the symbolic values of Nanjing in the Ming politics, see Luo Xiaoxiang, "'Jinling genben zhongdi': Mingmo zhengzhi yujing zhong de fengshuiguan," *Zhongguo lishi dili luncong*, Vol. 23, No. 3 (July 2008), 22–9.

53 *MS*, 5132.

54 For detail of the Zhu Chenhao rebellion and Wang Yangming's successful suppression campaign, see Gu Yingtai, *Mingshi jishi benmo, juan* 47; Mote and Twitchett, *The Cambridge History of China, The Ming Dynasty*, part 1, 423–30; Guan Minyi, "Cong ping Ningfan zhiyi kan Wang Shouren de junshi sixiang," *Ningbo daxue xuebao* (Renwen kexue ban), Vol. 11, No. 2 (June 1998), 1–7.

55 Zhou Hui, *Jinling suoshi*, 133–4. Cai Jiude's account has it that the intruders slew more than 10,000 soldiers before they fled to Wuxi and Suzhou. Cai Jiude, *Wobian shilüe*, 3.60. It appears that Zhou's account is more believable.

56 For a detailed study of piracy in the sixteenth century Ming, see So, *Japanese Piracy in Ming China*.

57 *MS*, 5407; Tan, *Guoque*, 3833.

58 *MS*, 5407; Gu, *Mingshi jishi benmo*, 48–9.

59 *MLS: Shizong*, 7321–2; *MS*, 5407.

60 *MS*, 5407–8. For more on Zhang Jing's pirate-suppressing strategies, his frame-up, and his tragic ending, see Hou Fuzhong, "Jiao Wo fangzhen yu Zhang Jing zhisi," *Nei Menggu daxue xuebao* (Renwen shehui kexue ban), Vol. 40, No. 1 (Jan. 2008), 59–63; "Cong Zhang Jing zhisi kan Jiajing zhengju," *Hainan daxue xuebao* (Renwen shehui kexue ban), Vol. 26, No. 4 (Aug. 2008), 473–7.

61 Records in *MS* state that Zhou was promoted to be vice minister of war from his previous post of grand coordinator of the Suzhou and Songjiang area. Zhou's new

140   *Southern Stronghold*

position was in fact the Nanjing vice minister of war, because when relating the career of his successor Yang Yi, *MS* states that Yang was ordered to fill the office left vacant by Zhou, and in the second month of 1556 when Yang was removed, his position recorded in *MSL* was "the Nanjing vice minister of war, concurrently the commander-in-chief of the armies of Nan Zhili, Zhejiang, and Fujian." *MS*, 5408–9; *MSL: Shizong*, 7452; Zheng Liangsheng, *Mingdai woko shiliao*, 291.

62 *MS*, 5408–9.

63 On Langren (wolf people) and langbing (wolf soldiers) in the Ming Qing period, see Wang Shuanghuai and Fang Jun, "Zhongguo Xinan Langren kao," *Beijing shifan daxue xuebao* (Shehui kexue ban), No. 4 (2013), 77–86; Luo Xianglin, "Langbing Langtian kao," *Bei Yue yuanliu yu wenhua*, 281–2; Tang Xiaotao, "Mingdai zhongqi Guangxi Langbing Langren de lishi kaocha," *Minzu yanjiu*, No. 3 (2012), 81–92; Li Jiyuan, "Mingdai Zhuangzu Langbing kang Wo wuyi kaoshu," *Tiyu xuekan*, Vol. 19, No. 1 (Jan. 2012), 114–19; Wei Tianfu, "Lun Guangxi Langbing zai Mingdai yanhai kang Wo zhanzheng zhong de diwei he zuoyong," *Guangxi defang zhi*, No. 5 (2010), 43–6.

64 *MS*, 5409; *MSL: Shizong*, 7452; *Mingdai wokou shiliao*, 291–92.

65 *MSL: Shizong*, 7454.

66 In his study of collective violence in the Ming, James Tong finds that south China had much more rebellion and banditry than the north. See his *Disorder under Heaven: Collective Violence in the Ming Dynasty*, 49–52. David Robinson argues that banditry was a serious problem even in the Beijing region in the Ming. See "Banditry and the subversion of state authority in China: the capital region during the middle Ming period (1450–1525)," *Journal of Social History*, Vol. 33, No. 3 (Spring 2000), 527–63.

67 Jiao Hong, *Guochao xianzheng lu*, 1734.

68 *MS*, 4603.

69 Jiao, *Guochao xianzheng lu*, 1734.

70 Gu, *Mingshi jishi benmo*, 559.

71 *MS*, 221, 5166.

72 *MS*, 5166. The compilers of *Mingshi* regard Wang Yangming as the most successful civilian official in leading military campaigns during the Ming period. *MS*, 5170. For more on his military strategies and commanding skills, see Larry Israel, "To accommodate or subjugate: Wang Yangming's settlement of conflict in Guangxi in light of Ming political and strategic culture," *Ming Studies*, No. 60 (Nov. 2009), 4–44; Guan Minyi, "Cong ping Ningfan zhiyi kan Wang Shouren de junshi sixiang."

73 Wang Yangming, *Wang Wencheng gong quanji*, 450; *MS*, 5167.

74 *MS*, 5167.

75 Wang, *Wang Wencheng gong quanji*, 445–48.

76 *MS*, 8039.

77 *MS*, 8045.

78 *MS*, 276. Records in the later part of *MS* (8046) specifies Xing Jie as the vice minister of war. Kenneth Swope identifies Xing Jie as "the minister of war of the right in Nanjing" prior to his appointment in 1594 as commander of Sichuan and Guizhou in charge of suppressing the Yang Yinglong rebellion. See *A Dragon's Head and a Serpent's Tail: Ming China and the First Great East Asian War, 1592–1598*, 206. For details of the Yang Yinglong rebellion, see Gu, *Mingshi jishi benmo*, *juan* 64; *MS*, 8046; Mote and Twitchett, *Cambridge History of China, The Ming Dynasty*, part 1, 564–7; Zhang Guihuai and Lei Changjiao, "Pozhou Yangshi xingwang yu ping Bo zhiyi," *Guizhou wenshi congkan*, No. 2 (2001), 20–5.

79 Gu, *Mingshi jishi benmo*, 64.66.

80 *MSL: Shenzong*, 9282. Shortly after the Korean war had ended, the court in Beijing appointed Censor-in-chief and Vice Minister of War Li Hualong supreme

commander and commissioned him to suppress Yang Yinglong. The bulk of the 200,000-man troops were drawn from provincial auxiliaries and other aboriginal tribesmen. Some veterans from the Korean campaign were enlisted. The actual fighting lasted less than four months. Li reported that 22,687 rebels were killed and 1,124 captured. Yang committed suicide and his body was delivered to Beijing for desecration. For more, see Li Hualong, *Ping Bo quanshu*; Gu, *Mingshi jishi benmo*, 691–8; Mote and Twitchett, *Cambridge History of China, The Ming Dynasty*, part 1, 565.

81 For more on these rebellions and the military campaigns against them, see Nan Bingwen and Tang Gang, *Mingshi, shang*, 329–59; Mote and Twitchett, *Cambridge of History, The Ming Dynasty*, part 1, 312–14, 377–89. On the prominent role of civil officials in the military affairs and its impact during the Ming, see Kai Filipiak, "The effects of civil officials handling military affairs in Ming times," *Ming Studies*, No. 66, 1–15; Jun Fang, "Literati statecraft and military resistance during the Ming-Qing transition," *The Chinese Historical Review*, Vol. 19, No. 2 (Dec. 2012), 98–104.

82 Soldiers in the Ming were required to become self-sufficient by part-time farming. For a detailed study of the military farming system in the Ming, see Wang Yuquan, *Mingdai de juntun*, 1–230.

83 *NJHBZ*, 10.10b. The number according to Gu Qiyuan is 32. Gu, *Kezuo zhuiyu*, 46.

84 The 1549 figures which were cited in *NJHBZ* as exemplary, are: 20,608 soldiers, 1,897 ships, and they shipped a total of 629,152 piculs of grain to the north. *NJHBZ*, 10:10b. The figures varied year by year, but basically speaking, they are close to the recorded 1549 figures.

85 The total of the guards and ships involved in the transport, according to Gu Qiyuan, were 123 and 12,143 respectively. Gu, *Kezuo zhuiyu*, 184–5.

86 *MSL: Yingzong*, 181.2a.

87 *MS*, 1916–19; *NJHBZ*, 10.2a-3b; Hoshi Ayao, *The Ming Tribute Grain System*, 10.

88 *NJHBZ*, 10.2a; *MS*, 1916–17.

89 This paragraph is based on my reading of the account in *NJHBZ* which relates that "people from the prefectures, subprefectures, and counties in Jiangnan delivered the [tribute] grain to the Guazhou and Huai'an Granaries." *NJHBZ*, 10.2b. Gu, *Kezuo zhuiyu*, 2.

90 Gu, *Kezuo zhuiyu*, 2; *MS*, 1917.

91 *NJHBZ*, 10.2b; Gu, *Kezuo zhuiyu*, 2; *MS*, 1918–19.

92 *NJHBZ*, 10.6a.

93 The number is the result of my calculation of the ships involved in the transportation recorded in Qi Erguang, *Ming Nanjing chejiasi zhizhang*. The number in *NJDCYZ* (25.2b) is 162.

94 Shen, *Wanli yehuo bian*, 430–2; Wang Chunyu and Tu Wanyan, eds, *Mingdai huanguan yu jingji shiliao chutan*, 54.

95 *NJDCYZ*, 25.11a–b. On the four classes of Yellow Ships, see Shen Qi, *Nan chuan ji, juan* 1; Liu Yijie, "Mingdai Nanjing zaochuanchang tanwei," *Haijiaoshi yanjiu*, No. 1 (2010), 40.

96 *NJDCYZ*, 25.10; Tan Xisi, *Ming dazheng zuanyao*, 49.9a; Wang and Tu, *Mingdai huanguan yu jingji shiliao chutan*, 46.

97 Qi, *Ming Nanjing chejiasi zhizhang*, 12–29. The number of ships sent by the bureau of equipment and communications to ship the various tribute articles recorded in *NJDCYZ* (25:1) is 162.

98 Which agency had jurisdiction over this mill is not clear; presumably it was one of the Nanjing eunuch directorates.

99 Qi, *Ming Nanjing chejiasi zhizhang*, 26.

100 Liu, "Mingdai Nanjing zaochuanchang tanwei," *Haijiaoshi yanjiu*, 36–7; Li Longqian, "Mingdai Nanjing Ma Kuai chuan kaoshi," *Jinan shixue*, No. 3 (2004), 204–8.

101 *DMHD*, 158.16b.

Conclusion

1. The Southern Capital: an auxiliary implement of state control in Ming China

> Alas, this [comment] fails to display awareness of the dynasty's profound calculation and far-ranging considerations! For there are palaces and imperial tombs located here. There are the affairs of the armies and the defense garrisons. This is the place where there are treasuries and the nation's land registers are stored. This is the hub of all the wealth and resources of the southeast. Though there have been established here the six ministries to carry on their separate management of all these affairs, yet one might fear that still would not be adequate. How can one slightingly refer to them as superfluous offices?
>
> Ably stated indeed are the views of the late Qiu [Jun], who observed: "[T]he wealth of the realm is all provided in the southeast and Nanjing is its center; garrisoning and military affairs assume great proportions in the northwest and Beijing is its key. Establishing two capitals is to dwell amidst [each] and provide for good order; food is thereby sufficient and soldiers are consequently adequate; it is based on the strategic features of the situation and it accomplishes mastery on all sides."[1]

More than 460 year ago, Xie Bin, a bureau director at the Nanjing Ministry of Revenue in the 1550s and author of the ministry's gazetteer, vigorously refuted the charge that the Nanjing administration was of limited function and hence superfluous in nature.[2] As an official who was serving in the Southern Capital, Xie may be suspected of exaggerating the significance of his administration. However, my findings in the previous chapters indicate that most of Xie Bin's arguments are based on fact: Nanjing was the center of the wealth and resources of the rich Jiangnan region, the storehouse of the nation's land registers, the locus of palaces and imperial tombs, and the base for a large armed force.

Except for the emperor and the Grand Secretariat, the Nanjing administration duplicated the Northern Capital in almost all elements of its bureaucratic setup, though on a less grand scale. Its staffing levels of ranked officials and lesser functionaries were approximately half and one-third respectively of those in the Beijing administration. The official ranks and emoluments of the

Conclusion 143

Nanjing bureaucrats were identical to those of their counterparts in Beijing. All the Nanjing departments reported directly to the emperor. They were the equals, not the subordinates, of the corresponding departments in Beijing.

As for the leadership in the Southern Capital, no one individual supervised all the civil, military, and eunuch departments. The leadership in the Southern Capital was more or less collective. Twice a month, the eunuch grand commandant and the chief commanders of the five Military Commissions, as well as the heads of the six ministries, the censorate, and the five imperial courts, met in the office of the grand commandant to discuss the important matters facing the Nanjing administration. There were, however, three dignitaries who were considered the most prominent figures in Nanjing: the Nanjing grand commandant, the eunuch grand commandant, and the Nanjing minister of war. The grand commandant commanded the military forces in Nanjing in his capacity as head of the Nanjing Military Commission of the Center. The eunuch grand commandant supervised all 24 eunuch departments in Nanjing in his capacity as the Nanjing director of ceremonial. The Nanjing minister of war was part of the tripartite leadership because his ministry was generally considered preeminent among the civil offices in Nanjing.

Although the Ming was a highly centralized state, its vast territorial expanse and inadequate communications presented difficulties for the central government. To centralize all power in Beijing's hands was administratively impractical, if not impossible, considering that it took a minimum of seven days to travel the 3,000 *li* between the two capitals.[3] Under these circumstances, it was extremely difficult for the central government in Beijing to address a crisis promptly if it occurred in the far-away south. The establishment of a secondary capital government in the south to a certain extent alleviated the problem. When an emergency arose, the Nanjing administration could make decisions and act without having to wait two weeks or more for directions from Beijing.

In terms of the functioning of the bureaucracy, the Nanjing Ministry of Personnel examined the evaluation of lesser functionaries of the southern provinces and decided their promotion, retention, and demotion. The Southern Capital itself also served as a training ground for junior officials to familiarize themselves with the state system and thus enrich their bureaucratic service experience. It also regulated and adjusted the Ming bureaucratic machine by providing an acceptable retreat for those officials who had lost the favor of their superiors and those who were elderly and physically infirm.

In terms of state finances, although the Southern Capital played a secondary role in the decision-making process regarding the fiscal policies of the empire and the revenue under its direct control was approximately one-tenth of that possessed by Beijing, its contribution to the management of state finances was nevertheless indispensable. The major fiscal function of the administration was to assist the Beijing administration to generate more revenues and deliver them to treasuries in Beijing. This is reflected in its involvement in the collection of tax grain and transportation of tribute grain, as well as its participation in the salt and tea monopoly and collection of miscellaneous taxes.

144   *Conclusion*

Militarily, the Southern Capital assisted the Beijing administration in securing the stability of the south. It was active in suppressing piracy in the southeast area, especially during the mid-sixteenth century when piracy was rampant along the southeast coast. It also contributed to the pacification of the southwest, where Nanjing bureaucrats were occasionally dispatched to lead military operations to quell aboriginal revolts. But the most important contribution of the Southern Capital administration was to protect the imperial tombs and palaces in Nanjing and ensure the city's safety. By so doing, it provided the Ming rulers with peace of mind and a safe retreat for the court in case of emergency.

In summary, the immense geographical expanse of the Ming empire and the challenges of communication necessitated the establishment of an additional capital administration for effective control of the realm. The existence of the Southern Capital administration was largely justified by its ability to assist the primary Northern Capital better control the southern part of the imperial realm.

But why did the central government prefer an auxiliary capital administration to other forms of administration? For example, why not raise the staff level in the Beijing Ministry of Personnel to make it possible for the ministry to examine the evaluation of the lesser functionaries in the southern provinces? Why not enlarge the Beijing Ministry of Revenue to let it take over the responsibilities of the Nanjing Ministry of Revenue?

It seems plausible that a central government was in a better position to handle inter-provincial matters than one having only provincial status. Since the Nanjing administration was a secondary central government and its bureaucrats were capital officials, it was relatively easy for Nanjing officials to assume a coordinating role when dealing with crises of an inter-provincial nature. Unlike the provincial officials who lacked authority over their equivalents in the other provinces, officials in Nanjing were in a position to coordinate the activities of a number of provinces. The military operations in the southeast coastal area and southwest regions, which were commanded by the Nanjing officials and involved more than one province, provide a case in point.

As for granting more power to the departments in the Beijing administration and increasing staff, this expedient would probably not have offered any advantages over the creation and retention of a secondary capital administration. If the additional staff stayed in Beijing, the communication problem would not be solved; if a large number of personnel were assigned to a station in the south, they would be functionally recreating the secondary capital administration.

Not all questions concerning the Southern Capital, however, can be answered convincingly at present. For example, why did the Ming government maintain an auxiliary capital administration whose bureaucratic apparatuses were exactly identical to those in Beijing? Why did it not retain some relevant and essential agencies in Nanjing instead of creating an almost complete duplicate of the Beijing administration? This bureaucratic arrangement may have had something to do with the reluctance of the later Ming emperors to alter the practice established by their predecessors, who had kept the offices intact ever since the Xuande reign. Making Nanjing a real capital comparable to Beijing in order to lend it more authority was another possible reason.

2. The relationship between Beijing and Nanjing

Although there were no official regulations outlining the division of labor between the Northern and Southern capitals, it did exist to a certain extent. As a rule, the Northern Capital, where the emperor resided and the Grand Secretariat exercised its rescript-drafting advisory power, was the nerve center of the empire. Its power extended in theory to every corner of the empire. In practice, a considerable amount of administrative responsibility concerning south China was delegated to and taken over by the Southern Capital administration. Generally speaking, the role of the Nanjing administration was to assist the Beijing administration in managing the affairs in the south, although it is difficult to specify the precise extent of the division of labor between the two administrations.

It is incorrect, however, to assume that the Nanjing administration had no interest in state affairs north of the Yangzi River. As a matter of fact, Nanjing bureaucrats often consciously involved themselves in the discussion of national affairs by regularly submitting memorials to the court in Beijing. That is why Zhang Cong and Gui E (*js* 1511), two minor officials in the Southern Capital, caught the attention of the Jiajing emperor and received meteoric promotion for their staunch support of the emperor during the Grand Ritual Controversy in the early Jiajing years. Thrilled by their memorials condemning dissenting officials, Jiajing ordered the two to be transferred to Beijing and granted them special appointments as Hanlin academicians. Two years later, Gui E was promoted to be minister of rites, followed by Zhang Cong, who was said to enjoy more of the Jiajing emperor's favor than Yang Yiqing, as chief grand secretary.[4] The censors in Nanjing were even less restricted by the unofficial south-north boundary line. For example, Liu Hongxun (1565–1634), the Nanjing supervising secretary for personnel during the late Wanli era, condemned Chief Grand Secretary Zhang Juzheng after his death. He was subsequently punished by Zhang's remnant associates in the court and transferred to a remote area.[5] Li Xikong (*js* 1610), a Nanjing censor, impeached the Beijing supervising secretary Yao Zhongwen for his attempt to oust General Xiong Tingbi (1573–1625).[6] Such cases are abundant in the Ming sources.

Was there competition for power and influence between officials at the two capitals? Did the Nanjing administration ever pose a threat to the Beijing government? There was undoubtedly competition between the bureaucrats of the two capitals, as suggested by the rivalry between the Nanjing minister of war Zhang Jing and the Beijing vice minister of work Zhao Wenhua, the two central officials empowered to direct the anti-piracy campaign in the mid-Jiajing reign. But it appears that since Nanjing officials could not reasonably hope to compete for power and prestige with their better-placed Beijing

146   *Conclusion*

counterparts, most Nanjing officials were more concerned with gaining attention and equal status. One of their strategies for outdoing their Beijing counterparts and attracting the attention of the emperor and his chief assistants was expressing views and offering suggestions frequently.

There is no clear evidence indicating that the Nanjing administration ever posed a real threat to the central government in Beijing. There are two possible reasons for this. First, the Southern Capital was an integral part of the Ming bureaucratic machine; the promotion, retention, and demotion of its officials was decided by Beijing. Senior Nanjing officials were chosen by the emperor and the grand secretaries, and the junior ones by the Ministry of Personnel. An incident of 1533 vividly reveals how crucial this process was to the Ming rulers. In that year, the Nanjing minister of personnel, Liu Long (1477–1553), was deprived of four months' salary just for requesting that Nanjing officials of grade 5 and below be exempted from reporting directly to the Beijing Ministry of Personnel, which implied that his ministry would assume the power of deciding the fate of middle-and lower-ranking Nanjing officials.[7] The firm retention of decision-making power by the Beijing administration to a certain extent reflects its apprehension of losing some of its vital powers to the Nanjing administration. Nanjing officials, like all other civil and military officials in the empire, were regularly evaluated and transferred. The regular transfer of officials prevented, to a large extent, the formation of cliques among office holders. Second, as has been shown in Chapter Three, many Nanjing officials were neither disliked nor shunned by the emperor and his chief assistants. Among them there were junior Beijing officials, who were sent to familiarize themselves with the operation of the bureaucratic system and enrich their bureaucratic service record, as well as henchmen of powerful figures in Beijing, who were dispatched to keep a watchful eye on the rest of the Nanjing officials. The presence of those political underlings made the formation of anti-Beijing cliques out of the question.

Notes

1 *NJHBZ*, 1.5b. This translation is based on F. W. Mote, "The Transformation of Nanking, 1350–1400," 130, with slight alternations by the author. The original was quoted in *Kezuo zhuiyu* by Gu Qiyuan from Xie Bin's *Nanjing hubu zhi*. Mote translated the paragraphs from *Kezuo zhuiyu*.
2 For the contemporary derision of the Nanjing administration, see the Introduction of this book.
3 When the Hongxi emperor died in Beijing in 1425, Kuang Zhong, then a director at the Ministry of Rites, was dispatched to Nanjing to greet and accompany the crown prince, the future Xuande emperor, to Beijing to succeed the throne. Kuang, who was commended for his dedication and physical durability, galloped non-stop along the journey and reached the destination in seven days. See Yin Shouheng, *Mingshi qie*, 78.7b. Ten days were more normal for most of the travels between Nanjing and Beijing. The two capitals were connected by a total of 47 land and water stations. See *Huanyu tongqu*, in Yang Zhengtai, ed., *Mingdai yizhan kao*, 161.
4 See the biographies of the two in *MS*, 5173–80, 5181–85; Yu Jideng, *Diangu jiwen*, 302.

5 *MS*, 6481.
6 *MS*, 6383. On Xiong and his military strategies in defending Liaodong, see Li Guangtao, *Xiong Tingbi yu Liaodong*; Yu Rongrong, *Xiong Tingbi yu Liaodong jinglüe*.
7 Tan, *Guoque*, 3484.

Bibliography

Works cited by alphabetical abbreviations

DMHD   Li Dongyang 李東陽 (1447–1516), et al. *Da Ming huidian* 大明會典 (Collected administrative statutes of the Ming dynasty). 1587. Photographic reprint. Taibei: Zhongwen shuju, 1963.

MS   Zhang Tingyu 張廷玉 (1672–1755), et al. *Mingshi* 明史 (Official history of the Ming dynasty). 1736. Punctuated and collated reprint. Beijing: Zhonghua shuju, 1974.

MHY   Long Wenbin 龍文彬 (1821–93). *Ming huiyao* 明會要 (A collection of essential material on the Ming dynasty). 1887. Punctuated reprint. Taibei: Shijie shuju, 1963.

MSL   *Ming shilu* 明實錄 (Veritable records of the Ming dynasty). Photographic reproduction of National Beijing Library copy. Taibei: Zhongyang yanjiuyuan lishi yuyan yanjiusuo, 1962–67. The annals of individual emperors are identified by the temple names, e.g. Taizu, Yingzong, Wuzong, Shizong, Muzong, Shenzong, etc.

NJDCYZ   Xu Bida 徐必達 (1562–1631). *Nanjing duchayuan zhi* 南京都察院志 (Gazetteer of the Nanjing Censorate). 1623.

NJHBZ   Xie Bin 謝彬. *Nanjing hubu zhi* 南京戶部志 (Gazetteer of the Nanjing Ministry of Revenue). 1550.

NJLBZ   Wang Fengnian 汪逢年. *Nanjing hubu zhi* 南京吏部志 (Gazetteer of the Nanjing Ministry of Personnel). 1622.

NJXBZ   Pang Song 龐嵩. *Nanjing hubu zhi* 南京邢部志 (Gazetteer of the Nanjing Ministry of Justice). 1555.

Traditional Chinese sources

Ban Gu 班固 (32–92). *Hanshu* 漢書 (History of the Former Han dynasty). First century. Reprint. Beijing: Zhonghua shuju, 1970.

Bi Yuan 畢沅 (1730–97). *Xu Zizhi tongjian* 續資治通鑒 (Supplement to the *Comprehensive Mirror for Aid in Government*). 1879. Reprint. Taibei: Shijie shuju, 1964.

Bibliography 149

Bi Ziyan 畢自嚴 (1569–1638). *Liuji shucao* 留計疏草 (Memorials from the Nanjing Ministry of Revenue). Tianqi era.

Cai Jiude 采九德. *Wobian shilue* 倭變事略 (A brief account of the Japanese piracy). After 1560. Reprint. Shanghai: Shangwu yinshuguan, 1936.

Chen Shou 陳壽 (233–97). *Sanguo zhi* 三國志 (History of the Three Kingdoms). C. fourth century. Reprint. Beijing: Zhonghua shuju, 1971.

Chen Yi 陳沂 (*js* 1517). *Jinling shiji* 金陵世紀 (Record of things about Nanjing). 1569. Reprint. Nanjing: Nanjing chubanshe, 2009.

Chen Zilong 陳子龍 (1608–47) et al. *Ming jingshi wenbian* 明經世文編 (Collected writings on statecraft of the Ming dynasty). 1638. Reprint. Beijing: Zhonghua shuju, 1962.

Chen Zuolin 陳作霖 (1837–1920). *Jinling tongji* 金陵通紀 (General record of Nanjing). 1903. Reprint. Taibei: Chengwen chuban gongsi, 1970.

Chen Zuolin and Chen Daifu 陳詒紱 (1873–1937). *Jinling suozhi jiuzhong* 金陵瑣志九種. (Nine miscellaneous records of Nanjing). Nanjing: Nanjing chubanshe, 2008.

Da Qing huidian 大清會典 (Collected administrative statutes of the Qing dynasty). 1899.

Dong Sizhang 董斯張 (1586–1628). *Wuxing beizhi* 吳興備志 (Gazetteer of Huzhou). 1624. Reprint. Shanghai: Shanghai guji chubanshe, 1987.

Fan Jingwen 范景文 (1587–1644). *Nanshu zhi* 南樞志 (Gazetteer of the Southern Metropolitan Area). Reprint. Taibei: Chengwen chubanshe, 1983.

Feng Yingjing 馮應京 (1555–1606). *Huang Ming jingshi shiyong bian* 皇明經世實用編 (Collection of statecraft writings of the Ming). Wanli era. Reprint. Taibei: Chengwen chuban gongsi, 1967.

Fu Weiling 傅維鱗 (1608–67). *Mingshu* 明書 (History of the Ming dynasty). Early Kangxi era (1661–1722). Reprint. Shanghai: Shangwu yinshuguan, 1936.

Gao Gong 高拱 (1513–78). *Zhjangquan tigao* 掌銓題稿 (Memorials and rescripts of Gao Gong). 1572.

Ge Yinliang 葛寅亮 (1570–1646). *Jinling xuanguan zhi* 金陵玄觀志 (Record of Daoist monasteries in Nanjing). Wanli era. Reprint. Nanjing: Nanjing chubanshe, 2011.

Gu Qiyuan 顧起元 (1565–1628). *Kezuo zhuiyu* 客座贅語 (Idle talks with guests). 1617. Reprint. Beijing: Zhonghua shuju, 1987.

Gu Yanwu 顧炎武 (1613–82). *Lidai zhaijing ji* 歷代宅京記 (Imperial capitals of previous dynasties). 1888. Reprint. Beijing: Zhonghua shuju, 1984.

——. *Tianxia junguo libing shu* 天下郡國利病書 (A treatise on the relative merits of the provinces of the empire). 1662. Reprint. Sibu congkan sanbian edition.

Gu Yingtai 谷應泰 (1620–90). *Mingshi jishi benmo* 明史記事本末 (History of the Ming dynasty devided into single subjects). 1658. Reprint. Taibei: Sanmin shuju, 1963.

Gui Youguang 歸有光 (1506–71). *Gui Zhenchuan ji* 歸震川集 (Colelcted works of Gui Youguang). 1673. Reprint. Taibei: Shijie shuju, 1963.

Hai Rui 海瑞 (1515–87). *Hai Rui ji* 海瑞集 (Collected writings of Hai Rui). Beijing: Zhonghua shuju, 1962.

He Liangjun 何良俊 (1506–73). *Siyouzhai congshuo* 四友齋叢說 (Compendium of interpretations from the Studio of the Four Friends). 1569. Reprint. Beijing: Zhonghua shuju, 1959.

He Qiaoxin 何喬新 (1427–1503). *Jiaoqiu wenji* 椒丘文集 (Collected works of He Qiaoxin). 1522. Reprint. Taibei: Wenhai chubanshe, 1970.

He Qiaoyuan 何喬遠 (1558–1631). *Mingshan zang* 名山藏 (Private history of the Ming, 1368–1572). 1640. Reprint. Fuzhou: Fujian renmin chubanshe, 2010.

150 *Bibliography*

Huang Jin 黃溍 (1277–1357). *Jinhua Huang xiansheng wenji* 金華黃先生文集 (Collected works of Huang Jin). Yuan dynasty (1279–1368). Reprint. Sibu congkan chuji edition.

Huang Xun 黃訓 (1481–1514). *Huang Ming mingchen jingji lu* 皇明名臣經濟錄 (Collection of statecraft writings by prominent Ming officials). Jiajing era. Reprint. Taibei: Xuehai chubanshe, 1984.

Huang Zongxi 黃宗羲 (1610–95). *Mingru xue'an* 明儒學案 (Record of Ming scholars). 1676. Reprint. Beijing: Zhonghua shuju, 1985.

——. *Ming wenhai* 明文海 (Collection of literary works from the Ming dynasty). 1693. Reprint. Taibei: Shangwu yinshuguan, 1977.

Huang Zuo 黃佐 (1490–1566). *Nanyong zhi* 南雍志 (Gazetteer of the Nanjing National University). Early Wanli era. Reprint. Taibei: Weiwen tushu chuban gongsi, 1976.

Jiao Hong 焦竑 (1541–1620). *Guochao xianzheng lu* 國朝獻徵錄 (Biographies of eminent Ming officials). 1594–1616. Reprint. Taibei: Xuesheng shuju, 1965.

Jin Ao 金鰲 (Qing dynasty). *Jinling daizheng lu* 金陵待征錄 (Corrective record of Nanjing). 1844. Reprint. Nanjing: Nanjing chubanshe, 2009.

Lei Li 雷禮 (1505–81). *Nanjing taipusi zhi* 南京太僕寺志 (The Gazetteer of the Nanjing Court of the Imperial Stud). Jiajing era. Reprint. Yangzhou: Jiangsu guangling keshuchu, 1987.

Li Hualong 李化龍 (1554–1611). *Ping Bo quanshu* 平播全書 (Complete record of the suppression of the Bozhou rebellion). 1601. Reprint. Shanghai: Shangwu yinshuguan, 1937.

Li Qing 李清. *Nandu lu* 南渡錄 (Record of the early Southern Ming). Nineteenth century. Reprint. Hangzhou: Zhejiang guji chubanshe, 1989.

Li Xian 李賢 (1408–67). *Da Ming yitong zhi* 大明一統志 (National gazetteer of the Ming dynasty). 1461. Reprint. Taibei: Shangwu yinshuguan, 1977.

Li Xu 李詡 (1506–92). *Jiean laoren manbi* 戒安老人漫筆 (Literary notes of Li Xu). Late Wanli era. Reprint. Beijing: Zhonghua shuju, 1982.

Libu kaogong si 吏部考功司, comp. *Libu kaogong tigao* 吏部考功題稿 (Memorials from the Bureau of Evaluation [of the Ministry of Personnel]). 1512. Reprint. Taibei: Weiwen tushu gongsi, 1977.

Lin Shidui 林時對 (1615–1705). *Hezha congtan* 荷牐叢談 (Miscellaneous record from Hezha). Early Qing. Reprint. Taibei: Taiwan xinghang jingji yanjiushi, 1962.

Liu Jinzao 劉錦藻 (1862–1934). *Qingchao xu wenxian tongkao* 清朝續文獻通考 (General history of institutions and critical examination of documents of the Qing dynasty from 1785 to 1911). 1921. Reprint. Shitong edition.

Liu Ruoyu 劉若愚 (b. 1584). *Zhuozhong zhi* 酌中志 (A history of the inner court of the Ming dyansty). *C.* 1638. Reprint. Congshu jicheng chubian edition.

——. 明宮史 (A history of the Ming court). Abridged edition of *Zhuozhong zhi*. Reprint. Beijing: Beijing guji chubanshe, 1983.

Liu Xu 劉煦 (887–944). *Jiu Tangshu* 舊唐書 (Old Tang history). 945. Reprint. Beijing: Zhonghua shuju, 1976.

Lu Shen 陸深 (1436–94). *Shuyuan zaji* 菽園雜記 (Miscellaneous notes from the Pea Garden). Ming dynasty. Reprint. Beijing: Zhonghua shuju, 1985.

Luan Chengxian 欒成顯. *Mingdai huangce yanjiu* 明代黃冊研究 (A study of the Yellow Registers of the Ming dynasty). Beijing: Zhongguo shehui kexue chubanshe, 1998.

Nanjing Jinyiwei xuanbu 南京錦衣衛選簿 (The register of the Nanjing Embroidered-Uniform Guard). In *Zhongguo Mingchao dang'an zonghui* 中國明朝檔案總匯 (Complete collections of the Ming archives), Vol. 73. Guilin: Guangxi shifan daxue chubanshe, 1999.

Bibliography 151

Ouyang Xiu 歐陽修 (1007–73). *Xin Tangshu* 新唐書 (New Tang history). 1060. Reprint. Beijing: Zhonghua shuju, 1975.

Qi Erguang 祁爾光 (1563–1628). *Ming Nanjing chejiasi zhizhang* 明南京車駕司職掌 (Administrative responsibilities of the Bureau of Equipment and Communications [of the Nanjing Ministry of War]). 1620. Reprint. Shanghai: Shangwu yinshuguan, 1934.

Qingchao wenxian tongkao 清朝文獻通考 (General history of institutions and critical examination of documents of the Qing dynasty from 1644–1785). 1767. Reprint. Shitong edition.

Qiu Jun 丘濬 (1421–95). *Daxue yanyi bu* 大學衍義補 (A supplement to the *Extended Meaning of the Great Learning*). 1487. Reprint. Taibei: Shangwu yinshuguan, 1974.

Shao Bao 邵寶 (1460–1527). *Rongchuntang houji* 容春堂後集 (Supplement to the collected works from the Rongchun Hall). 1518. Reprint. Taibei: Shangwu yinshuguan, 1974.

Shen Bang 沈榜 (1540–97). *Wanshu zaji* 宛署雜記 (Miscellaneous notes from Wanping county office). 1593. Reprint. Beijing: Guji chubanshe, 1980.

Shen Defu 沈德符 (1578–1642). *Wanli yehuo bian* 萬曆野獲編 (Private gleanings in the Wanli reign). 1619. Reprint. Beijing: Zhonghua shuju, 1959.

Shen Li 沈鯉 (1531–1615). *Yiyutang gao* 亦玉堂稿 (Collected works from the Yiyu Hall). Siku quanshu ed. Reprint. Shanghai: Shanghai guji chubanshe, 1987.

Shen Qi 沈棨 (1491–1568). *Nan chuan ji* 南船紀 (Record of the southern ships). 1541. Reprint. Shanghai: Shanghai guji chubanshe, 1995.

Shen Zhaoyang 沈朝陽. *Huang Ming Jia Long liangchao wenjian lu* 皇明嘉隆兩朝聞見錄 (Record of things I have heard and seen during the Jiajing and Longqing eras). 1599. Reprint. Taibei: Xuesheng shuju, 1969.

Shi Kefa 史可法 (1601–45). *Shi Zhongchenggong ji* 史忠丞公集 (Collected works of Shi Kefa). 1868. Reprint. Shanghai: Shangwu yinshuguan, 1936.

Sima Guang 司馬光 (1019–86). *Zizhi tongjian* 資治通鑒 (Comprehensive mirror for aid in government). Eleventh century. Reprint. Beijing: Guji chubanshe, 1956.

Song huiyao jigao 宋會要輯稿 (Draft of documents pertaining to matters of state in the Song dynasty). Early nineteenth century. Reprint. Taibei: Shijie shuju, 1964.

Song Lian 宋濂 (1310–81), et al. *Yuanshi* 元史 (Official history of the Yuan dynasty). 1370. Reprint. Beijing: Zhonghua shuju, 1976.

Songjiang fuzhi 松江府志 (Gazetteer of the Songjiang prefecture). 1818. Reprint. Taibei: Chengwen chuban gongsi, 1970.

Sun Chengze 孫承澤 (1593–1676). *Chunming mengyu lu* 春明夢餘錄 (Miscellaneous notes about the capital city of Beijing and the central administration in the Ming dynasty). Early Qing. Reprint. Taibei: Shangwu yinshuguan, 1976.

Sun Wenlong 孫文龍 (*jinshi* 1589). *Chengtian fuzhi* 承天府志 (Prefectural gazetteer of Chengtian). 1602. Reprint. Beijing: Shumu wenxian chubanshe, 1990.

Sun Yingyue 孫應嶽 (*jueren* 1609). *Jinling xuansheng* 金陵選勝 (Wonders of Nanjing). 1622. Reprint. Nanjing: Nanjing chubanshe, 2009.

Tan Qian 談遷 (1594–1658). *Guoque* 國榷 (Discourse on state affairs). *C.* 1653. Reprint. Beijing: Guji chubanshe, 1958.

——. *Zaolin zazu* 棗林雜俎 (Miscellaneous notes from the date grove). Mid-seventeenth century. Reprint. Beijing: Zhonghua shuju, 2005.

Tan Xisi 覃希思. *Ming dazheng zuanyao* 明大政纂要 (Brief record of the important political affairs of the Ming dyansty). 1619. Reprint. Taibei: Wenhai chubanshe, 1988.

152   *Bibliography*

Tian Yiheng 田藝衡. *Liuqing rizha* 留青日紮 (Miscellaneous notes of Tian Yiheng). 1573. Reprint. Shanghai: Shanghai guji chubanshe, 1992.

Tuo Tuo 脫脫 (Toghto, 1314–65). *Jinshi* 金史 (History of the Jin dynasty). 1344. Reprint. Beijing: Zhonghua shuju, 1975.

——. *Liaoshi* 遼史 (History of the Liao dynasty). 1344. Reprint. Beijing: Zhonghua shuju, 1974.

——. *Songshi* 宋史 (History of the Song dynasty). 1344. Reprint. Beijing: Zhonghua shuju, 1976.

Wang Fu 王敷. *Tang huiyao* 唐會要 (A collection of essential material on the Tang dynasty). 961. Reprint. Taibei: Shijie shuju, 1963.

Wang Qi 王圻 (*js* 1565). *Xu Wenxian tongkao* 續文獻通考 (Supplement to the *Comprehensive Examination of Literature*). 1603. Reprint. Beijing: Xiandai chubanshe, 1986.

Wang Qiao 王樵 (*js* 1548). *Fanglu ji* 方麓集 (Collected works of Fang Qiao). Late Wanli era. Reprint. Taibei: Shangwu yinshuguan, 1972.

Wang Shidian 王士點 and Shang Qiweng 商企翁. *Mishujian zhi* 秘書監志 (Gazetteer of the palace library of the Yuan dynasty). Fourteenth century. Reprint. Hangzhou: Zhejiang guji chubanshe, 1992.

Wang Shixing 王士性 (1547–98). *Wuyue youcao* 五嶽遊草 (Travalogue of the whole country). Kangxi era. Reprint. Beijing: Zhinghua shuju, 2006.

——. *Guangzhi yi* 廣志繹 (Geographical conditions of the empire). 1644. Reprint. Beijing: Zhionghua shuju, 1981.

Wang Shizhen 王世貞 (1526–90). *Fengzhou zabian* 鳳洲雜編 (Miscellaneous notes of Wang Shizhen). Second half of sixteenth century. Reprint. Shanghai: Shangwu yinshuguan, 1937.

——. *Yanshantang bieji* 弇山堂別集 (Collected historical works of Wang Shizhen). 1590. Reprint. Beijing: Zhonghua shuju, 1985.

Wang Yangming 王陽明 (1472–1529). *Wang wencheng gong quanji* 王文成公全集 (Complete works of Wang Yangming). Longqing era. Reprint. Sibu congkan chubian edition.

Wang Yun 王惲 (1228–1304). *Qiujian xiansheng daquanji* 秋澗先生大全集 (Complete works of Wang Yun). 1498. Reprint. Shanghai: Shangwu yinshuguan, 1939.

Wei Shou 魏收 (506–72). *Weishu* 魏書 (History of the Northern Wei dynasty). 554. Reprint. Beijing: Zhonghua shuju, 1974.

Wei Zheng 魏徵 (580–643). *Suishu* 隋書 (History of the Sui dynasty). 636. Reprint. Beijing: Zhonghua shuju, 1973.

Wenren Quan 聞人銓. *Nanji zhi* 南畿志 (Gazetteer of the Southern Capital). Jiajing era.

Wu Jingzi 吳敬梓 (1701–54). *Rulin waishi* 儒林外史 (The scholars). *C.* 1750. Reprint. Beijing: Renmin wenxue chubanshe, 1985.

——. Yang Hsien-yi (1915–2009) and Gladys Yang (1919–99), trans. *The Scholars.* New York: Columbia University Press, 1992.

Wu Yingji 吳應箕 (1594–1645). *Liudu jianwen lu* 留都見聞錄 (Record of the auxiliary capital Nanjing). 1680. Reprint. Nanjing: Nanjing chubanshe, 2009.

Wu Tingxie 吳廷燮 (1865–1947). *Ming dufu nianbiao* 明督撫年表 (A chronology of the grand coordinators and supreme commanders of the Ming dynasty). *C.* 1930. Reprint. Beijing: Zhonghua shuju, 1982.

Wu Wenhua 吳文華 (1521–98). *Liudu shugao* 留都疏稿 (Memorials from Nanjing). *Siku quanshu cunmu congshu, jibu* 131. Jinan: Qilu shushe, 1997.

Bibliography 153

Xia Xie 夏燮 (1800–875). *Ming tongjian* 明通鑒 (An annalistic account of the Ming dynasty). *C.* 1870. Reprint. Beijing: Zhonghua shuju, 1980.

Xie Jin 解縉 (1369–1415). *Nanjing* 南京. Early Yongle era. Reprint. Nanjing: Nanjing chubanshe, 2012.

Xiao Tong 蕭統 (501–31). *Wenxuan*文選 (Selections of literary works). Sixth century. Reprint. Hong Kong: Shangwu yinshuguan, 1960.

Xiong mengxiang 熊夢祥 (fl. 1360). *Xijin zhi jiyi* 析津志輯佚 (Collection of surviving sections of *the Gazetteer of Xijin*). Beijing: Beijing guji chubanshe, 1983.

Xu Hong 徐紘 (*js* 1490). *Ming mingchen wanyan lu* 明名臣琬琰錄 (Record of the meritorious needs of prominent officials from the Hongwu to Hongzhi eras). 1505. Reprint. Taibei: Shangwu yinshuguan, 1976.

Xu Shouqing 徐壽卿. *Jinling zazhi* 金陵雜誌 (Miscellaneous record of Nanjing) and *Jinlingzazhi xuji* 續集 (Supplement to *Miscellaneous record of Nanjing*). 1910 and 1922. Reprint. Nanjing: Nanjing chubanshe, 2013.

Xu Tianlin 徐天麟. *Dong Han huiyao* 東漢會要 (Collection of documents of the Later Han dynasty). 1226. Reprint. Shanghai: Shanghai guji chubanshe, 1976.

Xu Xuemo 徐學謨 (1521–93). *Shimiao shiyu lu* 世廟拾餘錄 (A record of my observations during the Jiajing reign). 1608. Reprint. Taibei: Guofeng chubanshe, 1965.

Xu Zi 徐鼒 (1810–62). *Xiaotian jinian* 小腆紀年 (Chronological record of Southern Ming officials). 1887. Reprint. Taibei: Taiwan yinhang jingji yanjiushi, 1963.

Xue Juzheng 薛居正 (912–81) et al. *Jiu wudai shi* 舊五代史 (Old history of the Five Dynasties). 974. Reprint. Beijing: Zhonghua shuju, 1976.

Ye Sheng 葉盛 (1420–74). *Shuidong riji* 水東日記 (Diaries from the east bank of the Song River). Hongzhi era. Reprint. Beijing: Zhonghua shuju, 1980.

Yin Shouheng 尹守衡 (1420–74). *Mingshi qie* 明史竊 (Unofficial history of the Ming dynasty). Chongzhen era. Reprint. Taibei: Huashi chubanshe, 1978.

Yu Huai 余懷 (b. 1616). *Banqiao zaji* 板橋雜記 (Miscellaneous record of Banqiao). Early Qing. Reprint. Nanjing: Nanjing chubanshe, 2006.

Yu Jideng 余繼登 (1544–1600). *Diangu jiwen* 典故紀聞 (Hearsay notes on statutory precedents). 1606. Reprint. Beijing: Zhonghua shuju, 1981.

Zhang Chunxiu 張純修. *Shi Kefa ji* 史可法集 (Collected works of Shi Kefa). Shanghai: Shanghai guji chubanshe, 1984.

Zhang Heng 張衡 (78–139). *Dongdu fu* 東都賦 (Rhapsody of the eastern capital of the Later Han), *Xijing fu* 西京賦 (Rhapsody of the western capital of the Later Han), *Nandu fu* 南都賦 (Rhapsody of the southern capital of the Later Han). In *Wenxuan*, 25–81.

Zhang Yanghao 張養浩 (1269–1309). *Guitian leigao* 歸田類稿 (Classified writings from Guitian). Fourteenth century. Reprint. Taibei: Shangwu yinshuguan, 1972.

Zhao Guan 趙官 (*js* 1511), et al. *Houhu zhi* 後湖志 (Gazetteer of the Back Lake). 1549. Reprint. Nanjing: Nanjing chubanshe, 2011.

Zheng Xiao 鄭曉 (1499–1566). *Jinyan* 今言 (Current comments). 1566. Beijing: Zhonghua shuju, 1984.

Zhou Boqi 周伯琦 (1298–1369). *Jinguang ji* 近光集 (Collected works of Zhou Boqi). 1345. Reprint. Taibei: Shangwu yinshuguan, 1971.

Zhou Cheng 周城. *Song Dongjing kao* 宋東京考 (Notes on the eastern capital of the Northern Song). 1762. Reprint. Beijing: Zhonghua shuju, 1988.

Zhou Hui 周暉 (b. 1546). *Jinling suoshi* 金陵瑣事 (Nanjing trifles); *Xu Jinling suoshi* 續 (Supplement to *Nanjing Trifles*); *Erxu Jinling suoshi* 二續 (Second supplement to *Nanjing Trifles*). 1610. Reprint. Nanjing: Nanjing chubanshe, 2007.

154   *Bibliography*

Zhou Yingbin 周應賓 (d. 1626). *Jiujing cilin zhi* 舊京詞林志 (Gazetteer of the Nanjing Hanlin Academy). 1597. Reprint. Xuanlantang congshu edition.

Zhu Guozhen 朱國禎 (1558–1632). *Yongzhuang xiaopin* 湧幢小品 (Miscellaneous notes from the Yongzhuang Pavilion). 1621. Reprint. Beijing: Zhonghua shuju, 1959.

Zhu Tingli 朱廷立 (*js* 1523). *Yanzheng zhi* 鹽政志 (Record of salt administration). 1529. Reprint. Shanghai: Shanghai guji chubanshe, 1995.

Zhu Wubi 朱吾弼 (*js* 1589). *Huang Ming liutai zouyi* 皇明留台奏議 (Memorials from the auxiliary capital censorate of the imperial Ming). 1605. Reprint. Shanghai: Shanghai guji chubanshe, 1995.

Modern Chinese and English works

Bai Gang 白鋼, ed. *Zhongguo zhengzhi zhidu shi* 中國政治制度史 (History of the political systems in China). Tianjin: Tianjin renmin chubanshe, 1991.

Balazs, Etienne (1905–63). *Chinese Civilization and Bureaucracy.* New Haven, CT and London: Yale University Press, 1964.

Bodde, Derk (1909–2003). *China's Cultural Tradition: What and Wither?* New York: Holt, Rinehart and Winston, 1966.

Brook, Timothy. *The Troubled Empire: China in the Yuan and Ming Dynasties.* Cambridge, MA: Belknap Press of Harvard University Press, 2010.

——. *The Chinese State in Ming Dynasty.* London and New York: RoutledgeCurzon, 2005.

——. *The Confusions of Pleasure: Commerce and Culture in Ming China.* Berkeley: University of California Press, 1998.

——. *Geographical Sources of Ming-Qing History.* Ann Arbor: Center for Chinese Studies, University of Michigan, 1988.

——. "The Spatial structure of Ming legal administration." *Late Imperial China,* Vol. 6, No.1 (June 1985), 1–55.

Brook, Timothy, Jerome Bourgon, and Gregory Blue. *Death by a Thousand Cuts.* Cambridge and London: Harvard University Press, 2008.

Cao Erqin 曹爾琴. "Luoyang cong Han Wei dao Sui Tang de bianqian" 洛陽從漢魏至隋唐的變遷 (The evolution of Luoyang from the Han-Wei period to the Sui-Tang period). In Zhongguo gudu xuehui, ed., *Zhongguo gudu yanjiu* 中國古都研究. Vol. 3. Hanzhou: Zhejiang renmin chubanshe, 1987.

Cao Guoqing 曹國慶 et al. *Yan Song pingzhuan* 嚴嵩評傳 (A critical biography of Yan Song). Shanghai: Shanghai shehui kexue chubanshe, 1989.

Chan, Hok-lam (Chen Xuelin, 1938–2011). *Legitimation in Imperial China: Discussions under the Jurchen-Chin Dynasty (1115–1234).* Seattle: University of Washington Press, 1984.

——. *Legends of the Building of Old Beijing.* Hong Kong: The Chinese University Press, 2008.

Chen Gaohua 陳高華. "Yuan Zhongdu de xingfei" 元中都的興廢 (The establishment and abandonment of the Middle Capital of the Yuan dynasty). *Wenwu chunqiu* 文物春秋, No. 3 (1998), 17–20.

Chen Gaohua and Shi Weimin 史卫民. *Yuan Shangdu* 元上都 (The Upper Capital of the Yuan dynasty). Changchun: Jilin jiaoyu chubanshe, 1988.

——. *Yuandai Dadu Shangdu yanjiu* 元代大都上都研究 (Studies on the Grand Capital and Upper Capital of the Yuan dynasty). Beijing: Zhongguo renmin daxue chubanshe, 2010.

Bibliography   155

Chen Ran 陳然. *Zhongguo yanye shi luncong* 中國鹽業史論叢 (Studies on the history of salt industry in China). Beijing: Zhongguo shehui kexue chubanshe, 1987.

Cheng Caiping 程彩萍. "Mingdai Wucheng bingmasi zhian yu sifa zhineng zhi yanbian" 明代五城兵馬司治安與司法職能之演變 (The evolution of the roles of the Wardens' Offices of the Five Wards in the Ming period). *Xueshu pinglun* 學術評論, No. 2 (2012), 48–52.

Chu, Raymond and William Saywell. *Career Pattern in the Ch'ing Dynasty: The Office of Governor-General*. Ann Arbor: Center for Chinese Studies, University of Michigan, 1984.

Crawford, Robert. "Eunuch power in the Ming dynasty." *T'oung Pao*, Vol. 49, No. 3 (1961), 115–48.

Dardess, John. *Governing China, 150–1850*. Indianapolis: Hackett Publishing Company, 2010.

——. *Blood and History in China: The Donglin Faction and Its Repression, 1620–1627*. Honolulu: University of Hawaii Press, 2002.

——. *A Ming Society: T'ai-ho County, Kiangsi, in the Fourteenth to Seventeenth Centuries*. Berkeley and London: University of California Press, 1996.

Deng Guangming 鄧廣銘 (1907–98), ed. *Zhongguo lishi dacidian: Songshi* 中國歷史大辭典: 宋史 (Encyclopedia of Chinese history: The Song dyansty). Shanghai: Shanghai cishu chubanshe, 1984.

Ding Haibin 丁海斌. *Zhongguo gudai peidu shi* 中國古代陪都史 (History of auxiliary capitals in pre-modern China). Beijing: Zhongguo shehui kexue chubanshe, 2012.

Ding Haibin and Shi Yi 時義. *Qingdai peidu Shengjing yanjiu* 清代陪都盛京研究 (Studies on the auxiliary capital of the Qing dynasty Shengjing). Beijing: Zhongguo shehui kexue chubanshe, 2007.

Ding Yi 丁易 (1913–54). *Mingdai tewu zhengzhi* 明代特務政治 (The secret services in the Ming period). Beijing: Qunzhong chubanshe, 1983.

Dong Xiangying 董向英. "Yuan Zhongdu gaishu" 元中都概述 (An introduction to the Middle Capital of the Yuan dynasty). *Wenwu chunqiu*, No. 3 (1998), 70–3.

Dongya xueshe 東亞學社. *Zhongguo lidai renkou wenti lunji* 中國歷代人口問題論集 (Studies on the population of China). Hong Kong: Dongya xueshe, 1965.

Dreyer, Edward (1940–2007). *Zheng He: China and the Oceans in the Early Ming Dynasty, 1405–1433*. New York: Pearson Longman, 2006.

——. *Early Ming China: A Political History 1355–1435*. Stanford, CA: Stanford University Press, 1982.

Duan Zhijun 段智鈞. *Gudu Nanjing* 古都南京 (Ancient capital Nanjing). Beijing: Qinghua daxue chubanshe, 2012.

Endicott-West, Elizabeth. *Mongolian Rule in China: Local Administration in the Yuan Dynasty*. Cambridge, MA: Council on East Asian Studies, Harvard University, 1989.

Fan Jinmin 范金民. "Mingdai Nanjing de lishi diwei he shehui fazhan" 明代南京的歷史地位和社會發展 (The historical place and social development of Ming Nanjing). *Nanjing shehui kexue* 南京社會科學, No. 11 (2012), 143–51.

——. *Guoji minsheng: Ming Qing shehui jingji yanjiu* 國計民生: 明清社會經濟研究 (National economy and people's livelihood: Studies on the society and economy of Ming-Qing China). Fuzhou: Fujian renmin chubanshe, 2008.

Fan Zhongyi 范中義. *Mingdai junshi shi* 明代軍事史 (Military history of the Ming dynasty). Beijing: Junshi kexue chubanshe, 1998.

156　*Bibliography*

Fang, Jun 方駿. "Literati statecraft and military resistance during the Ming-Qing transition: the case of the Possibility Society (Jishe)." *The Chinese Historical Review*, Vol. 19, No. 2 (December 2012), 87–106.

——. "The military functions of the Southern Capital in Ming China." *Monumenta Serica*, Vol. 55 (2007), 133–56.

——. "The political functions of the Southern Capital in Ming China." *Ming Studies*, No. 54 (Fall 2006), 71–106.

——. "Mingdai Nanjing guanshuzhi gaishu" 明代南京官署志概述 (The departmental gazetteers of the Southern Capital of Ming China), *Nanjing shida xuebao* 南京師大學報, No. 4 (2000), 138–44.

——. "Xiancun Mingchao Nanjing guanshuzhi shuyao" 現存明朝南京官署志述要 (The extant departmental gazetteers of the Southern Capital of the Ming Dynasty), *Shaanxi shida jixu jiaoyu xuebao* 陝西師大繼續教育學報, Vol. 17, No. 1 (2000), 79–82.

——. "Song Yuan shiqi de guanshuzhi" 宋元時期的官署志 (Departmental gazetteers of the Song-Yuan period). *Yuanshi luncong* 元史論叢, Vol. 7 (1999), 54–62.

——. "Mingdai Nanjing de neiwai shoubei" 明代南京的內外守備 (The Grand Commandants at the Southern Capital of Ming China), *Zhongguo yanjiu* 中國研究, No. 36 (1998), 42–4.

——. "The military triumvirate in the Southern Capital of the Ming dynasty: A research note." *Ming Studies*, No. 37 (1997), 7–21.

——. "The *Gazetteer of the Nanjing Ministry of Revenue*: The record of an auxiliary capital department in the Ming dynasty." *East Asian Library Journal*, Vol. 7, No. 1 (Spring 1994), 73–97.

Farmer, Edward. *Early Ming Government: The Evolution of Dual Capitals.* Cambridge, MA: East Asian Research Council, Harvard University, 1976.

——, ed. *Zhu Yuanzhang and Early Ming Legislation.* Leiden and New York: E. J. Brill, 1995.

Farquhar, David M. *The Government of China under Mongolian Rule: A Reference Guide.* Stuttgart: Steiner, 1990.

Fei, Si-yen. *Negotiating Urban Space: Urbanization and Late Ming Nanjing.* Cambridge, MA: Harvard University Asia Center, 2010.

Filipiak, Kai. "The Effects of Civil Officials Handling Military Affairs in Ming Times." *Ming Studies*, No. 66 (September 2012), 1–15.

Fisher, T. Carney. *The Chosen One: Succession and Adoption in the Court of Ming Shizong.* Sydney: Allen and Unwin, 1990.

Fontana, Michela. *Matteo Ricci: A Jesuit in the Ming Court.* Lanham, MD: Rowman & Littlefield Publishers, 2011.

Forte, Antonio. *Mingtang and Buddhist Utopia in the History of Astronomical Clock: The Tower, Statue, and Armillary Sphere Constructed by Empress Wu.* Roma: Instituto Italiano Per il Medio ed Estremo Oriente, 1998.

Gallagher, Louis J., trans. *China in the Sixteenth Century: The Journals of Matthew Ricci: 1583–1610.* New York: Random House, 1953.

Gao Shouxian 高壽仙. "Mingdai Beijing chengshi renkou shue yanjiu" 明代北京城市人口數額研究 (A study of the population numbers of Beijing city in the Ming). *Haidian zoudu daxue xuebao* 海淀走讀大學學報, No. 4 (2003), 32–6 and 94.

——. "Mingdai renkou shue de zairenshi" 明代人口數額再認識 (A re-appraisal of the population number of the Ming dyansty). *Mingshi yanjiu*, No. 7 (2001), 58–76.

Bibliography 157

Goodrich, Carrington (1894–1986) and Chaoying Fang (1908–85), eds. *Dictionary of Ming Biography 1368–1644*. New York and London: Columbia University Press, 1976.

Gu Cheng 顧城 (1934–2003). *Yinni de jiangtu: Weisuo zhidu yu Ming diguo* 隱匿的疆土: 衛所制度與明帝國 (Hidden territory: The Guard-Battallion system and the Ming empire). Beijing: Guangming ribao chubanshe, 2012.

Guan Minyi 管敏義. "Cong ping Ningfan zhiyi kan Wang Shouren de junshi sixiang" 從平宸藩之役看王守仁的軍事思想 (Wang Shouren's military thinking as seen in the campaign against the Ning prince). *Ningbo daxue xuebao* (Renwen kexue ban), Vol. 11, No. 2 (June 1998), 1–7.

Guisso, R. W. L. *Wu Tse-t'ien and the Politics of Legitimation in T'ang China*. Bellingham, WA: Program in East Asian Studies, Western Washington University, 1978.

Han Dacheng 韓大成. *Mingdai chengshi yanjiu* 明代城市研究 (Studies on cities in the Ming). Beijing: Zhonghua shuju, 2009.

Han Guopan 韓國磐 (1919–2003). *Sui Yangdi* 隋煬帝 (Emperor Yangdi of the Sui dynasty). Wuhan: Hubei renmin chubanshe, 1957.

Hartwell, Robert. "Demographic, political, and social transformation of China, 750–1550." *Harvard Journal of Asiatic Studies*, Vol. 42, No. 2 (Dec. 1982), 365–442.

Hay, Jonathan. "Ming palace and tomb in early Qing Jiangning: dynastic memory and the openness of history." *Late Imperial China*, Vol. 20, No. 1 (June 1999), 1–48.

He Weining 何維凝. *Zhongguo yanzheng shi* 中國鹽政史 (History of salt administration in China). Taibei: Da Zhongguo tushu youxian gongsi, 1966.

Hsia, R. Po-chia. *A Jesuit in the Forbidden City*. Oxford: Oxford University Press, 2010.

Ho, Ping-ti (1917–2012). *Studies on the Population of China, 1368–1953*. Cambridge, MA: Harvard University Press, 1959.

——. *The Ladder of Success in Imperial China: Aspects of Social Mobility, 1368–1911*. New York: Columbia University Press, 1962.

Hou Fuzhong 侯馥中. "Cong Zhang Jing zhisi kan Jiajing zhengju" 從張經之死看嘉靖政局 (The death of Zhang Jing and the politics of the Jiajing reign). *Hainan daxue xuebao* 海南大學學報 (Renwen shehui kexue ban). Vol. 26, No. 4 (Aug. 2008), 473–7.

——. "Jiao Wo fangzhen yu Zhang Jing zhisi" 剿倭方針與張經之死 (The Ming pirate-supressing strategies and the death of Zhang Jing). *Nei Menggu daxue xuebao* 內蒙古大學學報, Vol. 40, No. 1 (Jan. 2008), 59–63.

Hoshi, Ayao (1912–89). Trans. Mark Elvin. *The Ming Tribute Grain System*. Ann Arbor: Center for Chinese Studies, University of Michigan, 1969.

Hsu, Cho-yun and Katheryn Linduff. *Western Chou Civilization*. New Haven and London: Yale University Press, 1988.

Hu Mengfei 胡夢飛. "Mingdai Nanjing liushou jigou jingji zhineng chutan" 明代南京留守機構經濟職能初探 (A preliminary study of the economic functions of the auxiliary agencies of Ming Nanjing). *Hexi xueyuan xuebao* 河西學院學報, Vol. 29, No. 1 (2013), 72–76.

Huang Kaihua 黃開華. "Ming zhengzhi shang bingshe Nanjing buyuan zhi tese" 明政制上並設南京部院之特色 (On the administrative characteristics of the Nanjing government in the Ming). In *Mingshi lunji* 明史論集 (Studies on Ming history). Hong Kong: Chengming chubanshe, 1972.

Huang, Ray (1918–2000). *1587, A Year of No Significance: The Ming Dynasty in Decline*. New Haven: Yale University Press, 1981.

158   *Bibliography*

——. *Taxation and Governmental Finance in Sixteenth-Century Ming China*. Cambridge: Cambridge University Press, 1974.

Huang Renyu 黃仁宇 (Ray Huang). *Mingdai de caoyun* 明代的漕運 (Tribute grain transport in the Ming period). Beijing: Xinxing chubanshe, 2005.

Huang Zhangjian 黃彰健 (1919–2009). "Ming Hongwu Yongle chao de bangwen junling" 明洪武永樂朝的榜文峻令 (On the legal regulations of the Hongwu and Yongle reigns). In *Ming Qing shi yanjiu conggao* 明清史研究叢稿 (Studies on Ming-Qing history). Taibei: Shangwu yinshuguan, 1977.

Hucker, Charles O. (1919–94). *The Censorial System of Ming China*. Stanford, CA: Stanford University Press, 1966.

——. "Governmental Organization of the Ming Dynasty." In John Bishop, ed., *Studies of the Governmental Institutions in Chinese History*. Cambridge, MA: Harvard University Press, 1968.

——, ed. *Chinese Government in Ming Times: Seven Studies*. New York: Columbia University Press, 1969.

——. *Ming Dynasty: Its Origins and Evolving Institutions*. Ann Arbor: Center for Chinese Studies, University of Michigan, 1978.

——. *A Dictionary of Official Titles in Imperial China*. Stanford, CA: Stanford University Press, 1985.

Israel, Larry. "To accommodate or subjugate: Wang Yangming's settlement of conflict in Guangxi in Llght of Ming political and strategic culture." *Ming Studies*, No. 60 (November 2009), 4–44.

Jia Zheng 賈征. *Pan Jixun pingzhuan* 潘季馴評傳 (A critical biography of Pan Jixun). Nanjing: Nanjing daxue chubanshe, 1996.

Jiang Shunxing 蔣順興 and Sun Zhaiwei 孫宅魏. *Minguo daqiandu* 民國大遷都 (Capital relocations during the Republican period). Nanjing: Jiangsu renmin chubanshe, 1997.

Jiang, Yonglin. *The Great Ming Code*. Seattle and London: University of Washington Press, 2005.

——. *The Mandate of Heaven and* The Great Ming Code. Seattle and London: University of Washington Press, 2011.

Jiang Zanchu 蔣贊初. *Nanjing shihua* 南京史話 (A brief history of Nanjing). Nanjing: Jiangsu renmin chubanshe, 1980.

Jiangsu sheng difangzhi bianzhuan weiyuanhui 江蘇省地方誌編撰委員會. *Jiangsu tongzhi gao* 江蘇通志稿 (Comprehensive gazetteer of Jiangsu province). Nanjing: Jiangsu guji chubanshe, 1991.

Jin Yufu 金毓黻 (1887–1962). *Fengtian tongzhi* 奉天通志 (Gazetteer of Fengtian). 1935–6. Reprint. Shenyang: Liaohai chubanshe, 2003.

Joe, Wanne J. *Traditional Korea: A Cultural History*. Seoul: Chun'ang University Press, 1972.

Kierman, Frank A. and John King Fairbank (1907–91), eds. *Chinese Ways in Warfare*. Cambridge, MA: Harvard University Press, 1974.

Kubota Kazuo 久保田和男. *Songdai Kaifeng yanjiu* 宋代開封研究 (Studies on Song Kaifeng). Shanghai: Shanghai guji chubanshe, 2010.

Kurt, Johannes L. *China's Southern Tang Dynasty, 937–976*. London and New York: Routledge, 2011.

Lai Jiadu 賴家度 and Li Guangbi 李光壁. *Yu Qian he Beijing* 于謙和北京 (Yu Qian and Beijing). Beijing: Beijing chubanshe, 1961.

Leng Dong 冷東. *Ye Xianggao yu Mingmo zhengtan* 葉向高與明末政壇 (Ye Xianggao and the late Ming politics). Shantou: Shantou daxue chubanshe, 1996.

Levathes, Louise. *When China Ruled the Seas: The Treasure Fleet of the Dragon Throne, 1405–1433*. New York: Oxford University Press, 1996.

Li Denan 李德楠. "Shilun Ming Qing Dayunhe shang de xingchuan cixu"試論明清大運河上的行船次序 (On the sailing orders along the Grand Canal during the Ming-Qing period). *Shandong shifan daxue xuebao* 山東師範大學學報 (Renwen shehui kexue), Vol. 57, No. 3 (May 2012), 109–14.

Li Guangming 黎光民 (1900–46). *Jiajing yuwo Jiangzhe zhukejun kao* 嘉靖禦倭江浙主客軍考 (A study of the provincial and extra-provincial anti-pirate armies in the Jiangnan region during the Jiajing reign). Beijing: Yenching (Yanjing) University, 1933.

Li Guangtao 李光濤 (1902–84). *Xiong Tingbi yu Liaodong* 熊廷弼與遼東 (Xiong Tingbi and Liaodong). Taibei: Zhongyang yanjiuyuan lishi yuyan yanjiusuo, 1976.

Li Jianren 李健人 *Luoyang gujin tan* 洛陽古今考 (Luoyang, past and present). Luoyang: Shixue yanjiushe, 1936.

Li Jinquan 李錦全. *Hai Rui pingzhuan* 海瑞評傳 (A critical biography of Hai Rui). Nanjing: Nanjing daxue chubanshe, 1994.

Li Jiuchang 李久昌. *Guojia kongjian yu shehui: Gudai Luoyang ducheng kongjian yanbian yanjiu* 國家空間與社會: 古代洛陽都城空間演變研究 (State, space, and society: Studies on the spatial evolution of Luoyang in pre-modern times). Xi'an: San Qin chubanshe, 2007.

Li Longqian 李龍潛. "Mingdai Nanjing Makuaichuan kaoshi" 明代南京馬快船考釋 (A study of the Horse Ships and Fast Ships in Ming Nanjing). *Jinan shixue* 暨南史學, No. 3 (2004), 202–25.

——. "Mingdai hukou shiyanchao zhidu" 明代戶口食鹽鈔制度 (The household salt tax in the Ming). In Chen Ran 陳然 et al., eds, *Zhongguo yanyeshi luncong* 中國鹽業史論叢 (Beijing: Zhongguo shehui kexue chubanshe, 1987), 252–8.

——. "Mingdai yan de kaizhong zhidu yu yanshang ziben de fazhan" 明代鹽的開中制度與鹽商資本的發展 (The salt *kaizhong* system and the development of salt merchant capital in the Ming). Nanjing daxue lishixi Ming Qing shi yanjiushi, ed., *Ming Qing ziben zhuyi mengya yanjiu lunwenji* 明清資本主義萌芽研究論文集 (Shanghai: Shanghai renmin chubanshe, 1981), 498–537.

Li Xueqin. Trans. K. C. Chang (1931–2001). *Eastern Zhou and Qin Civilization*. New Haven and London: Yale University Press, 1985.

Li Jiyuan 李吉遠. "Mingdai Zhuangzu Langbing kang Wo wuyi kaoshu" 明代壯族狼兵抗倭武藝考述 (A study of the military feat of the "Wolf Soldiers" of the Zhuang nationality in the Ming). *Tiyu xuekan* 體育學刊, Vol. 19, No. 1 (Jan. 2012), 114–19.

Li Yeming 黎業明. *Zhan Ruoshui nianpu* 湛若水年譜 (Chronological biography of Zhan Ruoshui). Shanghai: Shanghai guji chubanshe, 2009.

Liang Fangzhong 梁方仲 (1908–70). *Liang Fangzhong jingjishi lunwenji* 梁方仲經濟史論文集 (Collected works of Liang Fangzhong on Chinese economic history). Beijing: Zhonghua shuju, 1989.

Liu, Cary Y. "The Yuan dynasty capital, Ta-Tu: imperial building program and bureaucracy." *T'oung Pao*, LXXVIII (1992), 264–301.

Liu Jinxiang 劉金祥. "Mingdai weisuo quewu de yuanyin tanxi" 明代衛所缺伍的原因探析 (The causes of the manpower shortage of the Ming guards). *Beifang luncong* 北方論叢, No. 5 (2008) 71–4.

160   *Bibliography*

Liu Miao 劉淼. *Mingdai yanye jingji yanjiu* 明代鹽業經濟研究 (Studies on the salt economy in the Ming). Shantou: Shantou daxue chubanshe, 1996.

Liu Yijie 劉義傑. "Mingdai Nanjing zaochuanchang tanwei" 明代南京造船廠探微 (A preliminary study of the shipyards in Ming Nanjing). *Haijiaoshi yanjiu* 海交史研究, No. 1 (2010), 31–54.

Liu Zhiqin 劉志琴. *Zhang Juzheng pingzhuan* 張居正評傳 (A critical biography of Zhang Juzheng). Nanjing: Nanjing daxue chubanshe, 2006.

Liu Zhongping 劉中平. "Mingdai liangjing zhidu xia de Nanjing" 明代兩京制度下的南京 (Nanjing under the Ming dual-capital system). *Shehui kexue jikan* 社會科學輯刊, No. 3 (2005), 127–29.

Luo Fenmei 駱芬美. "San Yang yu Mingchu zhi zhengzhi" 三楊與明初之政治 (The Three Yangs and early Ming politics). Taibei: Zhongguo wenhua daxue shixue yanjiusuo, 1982.

Luo Xianglin 羅香林 (1906–78). "Langbing Langtian kao" (A study of the "Wolf Soldiers" and their farming fields). In *Bai Yue yuanliu yu wenhua* 百越源流與文化 (The origin and culture of the Viet people). Taibei: Zhonghua congshu weiyuanhui, 1955.

Luo, Xiaoxiang. "Soldiers and the city: urban experience of guard households in late Ming Nanjing." *Frontiers of History in China*, Vol. 5, No. 1 (March 2010), 30–51.

—— 羅曉翔. "'Jinling genben zhongdi:' Mingmo zhengzhi yujing zhong de fengshuiguan" 金陵根本之地: 明末政治語境中的風水觀 (Jinling is a fundamentally important place: the Geomanic viewpoint within the late Ming political context). *Zhongguo lishi dili luncong* 中國歷史地理論叢, Vol. 23, No. 3 (July 2008), 22–9 and 74.

Ma Huan 馬歡 (fl. 1413–33). J. V. G. Mills, trans. *Ying-Yai Sheng-Lan: The Overall Survey of the Ocean's Shores.* Cambridge: The Hakluyt Society, 1970.

Meskill, John, trans. *Ch'oe Pu's Diary: A Record of Drifting Across the Sea.* Tucson: University of Arizona Press, 1965.

Miyazaki Ichisada (1901–95), trans Conrad Schirokauer. *China's Examination Hell: The Civil Service Exmination of Imperial China.* New Haven, CT and London: Yale University Press, 1981.

Mote, F. W. (1922–2005). *Imperial China, 900–1800.* Cambridge, MA: Harvard University Press, 1999.

——. "The transformation of Nanking, 1350–1400." In William Skinner (1925–2008), ed., *The City in Late Imperial China.* Stanford, CA: Stanford University Press, 1977.

——. "The T'u-mu Incident of 1449." In Frank Kierman and John Fairbank (1907–1991), ed., *Chinese Ways in Warfare.* Cambridge, MA: Harvard University Press, 1974.

——. "The growth of Chinese despotism: a critique of Wittfogel's theory of oriental despotism as applied to China." *Oriens Extremus*, No. 8 (August 1961), 1–41.

Mote, F. W. and Denis Twitchett, eds. *Cambridge History of China, Volume 7: The Ming Dynasty, 1368–1644, part 1.* Cambridge: Cambridge University Press, 1988.

Nan Bingwen 南炳文 and Tang Gang 湯綱. *Mingshi* 明史 (History of the Ming dynasty). Shanghai: Shanghai renmin chubanshe, 1991. 2 vols.

Nanjing daxue lishixi Ming Qing shi yanjiushi 南京大學歷史系明清史研究室 ed. *Ming Qing ziben zhuyi mengya yanjiu lunwenji* 明清資本主義萌芽研究論文集 (Collected essays on the issue of capitalist sprouts during the Ming-Qing period). Shanghai: Shanghai renmin chubanshe, 1981.

Nanjingshi difangzhi bianzuan weiyuanhui bangongshi 南京市地方誌編纂委員會辦公室, ed. *Nanjing tongshi: Mingdai juan* 南京通史: 明代卷 (A comprehensive history of Nanjing: the Ming dynasty). Nanjing: Nanjing chubanshe, 2012.

Nanjingshi difangzhi bianzuan weiyuanhui, ed. *Nanjing jianzhi zhi* 南京建置志 (An institutional history of Nanjing). Shenzhen: Haitian chubanshe, 1994.

Nimick, Thomas G. *Local Administration in Ming China: The Changing Roles of Magistrates, Prefects, and Provincial Officials.* Minneapolis: Society for Ming Studies, 2008.

Pan Mingjuan 潘明娟. "Cong Zhengzhou Shangcheng he Yanshi Shangcheng de guanxi kan zao Shang de zhudu he peidu"從鄭州商城和偃師商城的關係看早商的主都和陪都 (The primary and auxiliary capitals as reflected in the relationship between Shang cities of Zhengzhou and Yanshi). *Kaogu* 考古, No. 2 (2008), 55–62.

Pan Xinghui 潘星輝. *Mingdaiwenguan quanxuan zhidu yanjiu*明代文官銓選制度研究 (Studies on the appointment system of civil officials in the Ming period). Beijing: Beijing daxue chubanshe, 2005.

Puk, Wing-kin 卜永堅 (Bu Yongjian). "The Ming Salt Certificate: A Public Debt System in Sixteenth-Century China?" *Ming Studies*, No. 61 (April 2010), 1–12.

Qiao Xunxiang 喬迅翔. "Mingdai Nanjing yushi zhuzhai yu chongtangshi xingzhi" 明代南京禦史住宅與"重堂式"形制 (The residence of the Nanjing censors and its multi-hall style in the Ming dynasty). *Zhongguo wenwu kexue yanjiu* 中國文物科學研究, No. 2 (2012), 54–61.

Ren Shuang 任爽. *Nan Tang shi* 南唐史 (A history of the Southern Tang dynasty). Changchun: Dongbei shifan daxue chubanshe, 1995.

Robinson, David M. *Culture, Courtiers, and Competition in the Ming Court (1368–1644).* Cambridge, MA: Harvard University Asia Center, 2008.

——. *Bandits, Eunuchs, and Son of Heaven: Rebellion and Economy of Violence in Mid-Ming China.* Honolulu: University of Hawaii Press, 2001.

——. "Banditary and the subversion of state authority in China: the capital region during the middle Ming period (1450–1525)." *Journal of Social History*, Vol. 33, No. 3 (Spring 2000), 527–63.

Rossabi, Morris. "Tea and horse trade with Inner Asia during the Ming dynasty." *Journal of Asian History*, No. 4 (1970), 136–68.

Schneewind, Sarah. *Long Live the Emperor: Use of the Ming Founder across Six Centuries of East Asian History.* Minneapolis, MN: Society for Ming Studies, 2008.

Sechin, Jagchid. *Essays in Mongolian Studies.* Provo: David M. Kennedy Center for International Studies, Brigham Young University, 1988.

——(Zhaqi Siqin 札奇斯欽). "Yuandai Zhongdu kao" 元代中都考 (A note on the Middle Capital of the Yuan dynasty). *(Taiwan daxue) Bianzheng yanjiusuo nianbao* (臺灣大學) 邊政研究所年報, No. 18 (1987), 31–41.

Seiwert, Hubert. *Popular Religious Movements and Heterodox Sects in Chinese History.* Leiden: Brill, 2003.

Shen Guofeng 沈國峰. Nanjing xingbu zhi *zhong de mingdai bangwen* 南京刑部志中的明代榜文 (The Ming proclamations contained in the *Gazetteer of the Nanjing Ministry of Justice*). *Zhongguo falü nianjian* 中國法律年鑒, No. 1 (1993), 913.

Shi Jianzhi 史鑒之. *Shi Kefa xiansheng nianpu* 史可法先生年譜 (Biographical chronology of Shi Kefa). Taibei: Huaxin wenhua shiye zhongxin, 1979.

Shi Li 師里. "Jingjun kao" 淨軍考 (A note on eunuch armies in the Ming). *Dongbei shifan daxue xuebao* 東北師範大學學報, No. 3 (1991), 49.

Shi Weimin. "Yuandai ducheng zhidu de yanjiu yu Zhongdu de lishi diwei"元代都城制度的研究與中都的歷史地位 (The study of the Yuan capital system and the historical place of the Middle Capital). *Wenwu chunqiu*, No. 3 (1998), 12–16 and 20.

So, Kwan-wai. *Japanese Piracy in Ming China during the Sixteenth Century.* East Lansing: Michigan State University Press, 1975.

162 Bibliography

Sohn Pow-key et al. *The History of Korea*. Seoul: National Commission for UNESCO, 1970.

Song Yubin 宋玉彬 and Qu Yili 曲軼莉. "Bohai guo de wujing zhidu yu ducheng" 渤海國的五京制度與都城 (The five-capital system of the Bohai Kingdom). *Dongbei shidi* 東北史地, No. 6 (2008), 2–6.

Spence, Jonathan. *The Memory Palace of Matteo Ricci*. New York: Viking Penguin, 1984.

Su Tongbing 蘇同炳. *Mingdai yidi zhidu* 明代驛遞制度 (The postal relay system in the Ming). Taibei: Zhonghua congshu biansheng weiyuanhui, 1969.

Sun Jinghao. "A Jiangnan identity in North China: the making of Jining urban culture in the late imperial period." *Late Imperial China*, Vol. 32, No. 2 (Dec. 2011), 34–73.

Steinhardt, Nancy Shatzman. *Chinese Imperial City Planning*. Honolulu: University of Hawaii Press, 1990.

Struve, Lynn. *The Southern Ming, 1644–1662*. New Haven and London: Yale University Press, 1984.

——, ed. and trans. *Voice from the Ming-Qing Cataclysm: China in Tigers' Jaws*. New Haven and London: Yale University Press, 1993.

Su Bai 宿白. "Sui Tang Chang'an cheng yu Luoyang cheng" 隋唐長安城與洛陽城 (The cities of Chang'an and Luoyang during the Sui-Tang period). *Kaogu*, No. 6 (1987), 423.

Su Shuangbi 蘇雙碧, ed. *Wu Han xuanji* 吳晗選集 (Selected works of Wu Han). Tianjin: Tianjin renmin chubanshe, 1988.

Su Shuangbi and Wang Hongzhi 王宏志. *Wu Han zhuan* 吳晗傳 (A biography of Wu Han). Beijing: Beijing chubanshe, 1984.

Swope, Kenneth, ed. *Warfare in China since 1600*. Burlington, VT: Ashgate Publishing Company, 2005.

——. *A Dragon's Head and a Serpent's Tail: Ming China and the First Great East Asian War, 1592–1598*. Norman: University of Oklahoma Press, 2012.

——. *The Military Collapse of China's Ming Dynasty, 1618–44*. London and New York: Routledge, 2014.

Tang Xiaotao 唐曉濤. "Mingdai zhongqi Guangxi Langbing Langren de lishi kaocha" 明代中期廣西狼兵狼人的歷史考察 (A historical investigation of "Wolf Soldiers" and "Wolf People" in mid-Ming Guangxi). *Minzu yanjiu* 民族研究, No. 3 (2012), 81–92.

Tang Wenji 唐文基. *Mingdai fuyi zhidu shi* 明代賦役制度史 (A history of taxation and corvee service in the Ming period). Beijing: Zhongguo shehui kexue chubanshe, 1991.

Tian Jifang 田吉方. "Mingdai Nanjing Hanlinyuan de moluo zhuangtai jiqi yuanyin kaoshu" 明代南京翰林院的沒落狀態及其原因考述 (A study on the decline of the Nanjing Hanlin Academy in the Ming and its contributing factors). *Hubei xingzheng xueyuan xuebao* 湖北行政學院學報, No. 2 (2004), 64–8.

Tong, James W. *Disorder under Heaven: Collective Violence in the Ming*. Stanford, CA: Stanford University Press, 1991.

Toriyama Kiichi. *Bokkai shijo no shomondai* (Issues on the history of Bohai State). Tokyo: Kazama Shobo, 1969.

Toynbee, Arnold J. (1889–1975). *A Study of History*. London: Oxford University Press, 1954.

Bibliography 163

Tsai, Shih-shan Henry. *Perpetual Happiness: The Yongle Emperor*. Seattle: University of Washington Press, 2002.

——. *The Eunuchs in the Ming Dynasty*. Albany: State University of New York Press, 1996.

Twitchett, Denis Crispin (1925–2006). *Financial Administration under the Tang Dynasty*. Cambridge: Cambridge University Press, 1963.

Wakeman, Frederic, Jr. (1937–2006). *The Great Enterprise: The Manchu Restoration of Imperial Order in Seventeenth-Century China*. 2 vols. Berkeley: University of California Press, 1985.

Wan Ming 萬明. "Mingdai liangjing zhidu de xingcheng jiqi queli" 明代兩京制度的形成及其確立 (The formation and establishment of the dual-capital system of the Ming dyansty). *Zhongguoshi yanjiu* 中國史研究, No. 1 (1993), 123–32.

Wan Yi 萬依. "Lun Zhu Di yingjian Beijing gongdian qiandu de zhuyao dongji ji houguo" 論朱棣營建北京宮殿、遷都的主要動機及後果 (The motives and consequences of Zhu Di's moving of capital and building of Beijing palace). *Gugong bowuyuan yuankan* 故宮博物院院刊, No. 3 (1990), 31–6.

Wang Chunyu 王春瑜 and Du Wanyan 杜婉言, eds. *Mingdai huanguan yu jingji shiliao chutan* 明代宦官與經濟史料初探 (A preliminary study of the sources on the eunuch and economy in the Ming dynasty). Beijing: Zhongguo shehui kexue chubanshe, 1986.

Wang Chunyu. *Mingchao huanguan* 明朝宦官 (Eunuchs in the Ming dynasty). Beijing: Zijincheng chubanshe, 1989.

Wang Huanbiao 王煥鑣 (1900–82). *Ming Xiaolinhg zhi* 明孝陵志 (Gazetteer of the Hongwu emperor's Mausoleum). Nanjing: Nanjing chubanshe, 2006.

——. *Shoudu zhi* 首都志 (Gazetteer of the Capital [Nanjing]). Taibei: Zhengzhong shuju, 1966.

Wang Jianying 王劍英 (1921–96). *Ming Zhongdu yanjiu* 明中都研究 (Studies on the Middle Capital of the Ming dynasty). Beijing: Zhongguo qinnian chubanshe, 2005.

——. *Ming Zhongdu* 明中都 (The Middle Capital of the Ming). Beijing: Zhonghua shuju, 1992.

Wang Leiming 王雷鳴. *Lidai shihuozhi zhushi* 歷代食貨志注釋 (Annotations to the "Monographs on economy and commerce" of the official dynastic histories). Beijing: Nongye chubanshe, 1991.

Wang Mingsun 王明蓀. *Song Liao Jin Yuan shi* 宋遼金元史 (A history of the Song, Liao, Jin, and Yuan dynasties). Taibei: Changqiao chubanshe, 1979.

Wang Peihuan 王佩環. *Guanwai sandu* 關外三都 (Three capitals outside the Shanhai Pass). Shenyang: Shenyang chubanshe, 2004.

——. *Qingdi dongxun* 清帝東巡 (The Qing imperial tours to Shengjing). Shenyang: Liaoning daxue chubanshe, 1991.

Wang Qiju 王其榘 (1922–2001), *Mingdai neige zhidu shi* 明代內閣制度史 (History of the Grand Secretariat in the Ming period). Beijing: Zhonghua shuju, 1989.

Wang Rui 王瑞. "Mingchao Wucheng bingma zhihuisi shulue" 明朝五城兵馬指揮司述略 (On the Warden's Offices of the Five Wards in the Ming dyansty). In *Wenshi ziliao* 文物資料, March issue of 2010, 101–2.

Wang Shuanghuai 王雙懷 and Fang Jun. "Zhongguo Xinan Langren kao" 中國西南狼人考 (The "Wolf People" in Southwest China during the Ming-Qing period). *Beijing shifan daxue xuebao* 北京師範大學學報 (Shehui kexue ban), No. 4 (2013), 77–86.

164   *Bibliography*

Wang Shuanghuai and Jia Yun 賈雲, eds. *Ershiwu shi ganzhi tongjian* 二十五史干支通檢 (The heavenly stems and earthly branches in the Twenty Five Stardard Histories). Xi'an: San Qin chubanshe, 2011.

Wang Shuanghuai, Fang Jun, and Chen Jiarong 陳佳榮 comp. *Zhonghua rili tongdian* 中華日曆通典 (A comprehensive compendium of Chinese-Western calendars). Changchun: Jilin wenshi chubanshe, 2006.

Wang Tianyou 王天有 (1944–2012). *Mingdai guojia jigou yanjiu* 明代國家機構研究 (A study of the state apparatuses of the Ming). Beijing: Beijing daxue chubanshe, 1992.

Wang Yi 王儀. *Mingdai ping Wo shishi* 明代平倭史實 (History of the suppression of Japanese piracy in the Ming). Taibei: Taiwan Zhonghua shuju, 1984.

Wang Yuquan 王毓銓 (1910–2002). *Mingdai de juntun* 明代的軍屯 (Military farming in the Ming). Beijing: Zhonghua shuju, 2009.

Weber, Max (1864–1920). Trans. and ed. Hans H. Gerth. *The Religion of China: Confucianism and Taoism*. Glencoe, IL: The Free Press, 1962.

Wechsler, Howard J. *Offerings of Jade and Silk: Ritual and Symbol in the Legitimation of the Tang Dynasty* New Haven and London: Yale University Press, 1985.

Wei Jianlin 衛建林. *Mingdai huanguan zhengzhi* 明代宦官政治 (Eunuch politics in the Ming dynasty). Taiyuan: Shanxi renmin chubanshe, 1991.

Wei Qingyuan 韋慶遠 (1928–2009). *Mingdai huangce zhidu* 明代黃冊制度 (The Yellow Register system of the Ming dynasty). Beijing: Zhonghua shuju, 1961.

——. *Mingdai de Jinyiwei he Dong Xi chang* 明代的錦衣衛和東西廠 (The Embroidered Uniform Guard and the Eastern and Western Depots during the Ming dynasty). Beijing: Zhonghua shuju, 1979.

——. *Ming Qing shi bianxi* 明清史辨析 (A critical study on the important issues of Ming-Qing history). Beijing: Zhongguo shehui kexue chubanshe, 1989.

Wei Tianfu 韋天富. "Lun Guangxi Langbing zai Mingdai yanhai kang Wo zhanzheng zhong de diwei he zuoyong" 論廣西狼兵在明代沿海抗倭戰爭中的地位和作用 (On the place and role of the Guangxi "Wolf Soldiers" in the coastal anti-pirate war in the Ming). *Guangxi difangzhi* 廣西地方誌, No. 5 (2010), 43–6.

Wei Zhanbin 韋占彬. "Lun Mingdai jingcheng zhian guanli de jigou yu cuoshi" 論明代京城治安管理的機構與措施 (On the agencies and administrative measures of capital management in the Ming). *Handan xueyuan xuebao* 邯鄲學院學報, Vol. 16, No. 4 (Dec. 2006), 95–7.

Wen Gongyi 溫功義 (1915–90). *Mingdai de huanguan he jingji* 明代的宦官與經濟 (Eunuchs and the economy in the Ming). Chongqing: Chongqing chubanshe, 1989.

——. *Mingdai huanguan* 明代宦官 (Eunuchs in the Ming). Beijing: Zijincheng chubanshe, 2011.

Wittfogel, Karl August (1896–1988) and Feng Chia-sheng (1904–70). *History of Chinese Society: Liao (907–1125)*. Philadelphia, PA: The American Philosophical Society, 1948.

Wu Han 吳晗 (1909–69). *Mingshi jianshu* 明史簡述 (A brief account of Ming history). Beijing: Zhonghua shuju, 1980.

——. *Mingchao sanbainian* 明朝三百年 (Three centuries of the Ming dynasty). Beijing: Guojia wenhua chuban gongsi, 2011.

Wu Jihua 吳緝華 (1927–2010). "Lun Mingdai shuiliang zhongxin zhi diyu jiqi zhongshui youlai" 論明代稅糧重心之地域及其重稅由來 (On the major tax grain regions and the origin of heavy taxation in the Ming period). *Zhongyang yanjiuyuan lishi yuyan yanjiusuo jikan* 中央研究院歷史語言研究所集刊, No. 38 (1968), 351–74.

Wu Zhihe 吳智和 (1947–2012). "Mingdai yuhu yu yangzhi shiye" 明代漁戶與養殖事業 (On the fisherman household and the fishing industry in the Ming period). *Mingshi yanjiu zhuankan* 明史研究專刊, No. 2 (1979), 109–64.

Xie Guozhen 謝國楨 (1901–82). *Nan Ming shilüe* 南明史略 (A brief history of the Southern Ming). Shanghai: Shanghai renmin chubanshe, 1957.

——, ed. *Mingdai shehui jingji shiliao xuanbian* 明代社會經濟史料選編 (Selection of source material on the society and economy of the Ming). Fuzhou: Fujian renmin chubanshe, 1981.

Xiao Shaoqiu 蕭少秋. *Zhang Juzheng gaige* 張居正改革 (The Zhang Juzheng reforms). Beijing: Qiushi chubanshe, 1987.

Xin Deyong 辛德勇. *Sui Tang liangjing congkao* 隋唐兩京叢考 (Studies on the two capital systems of the Sui and Tang). Xi'an: San Qin chubanshe, 2006.

Xiong, Victor Cunrui. "Sui Yangdi and the building of Sui-Tang Luoyang." *Journal of Asian Studies*, Vol. 52, No. 1, 66–89.

——. *Sui-Tang Chang'an: A Study in the Urban History of Late Medieval China*. Ann Arbor: Center for Chinese Studies, University of Michigan, 2000.

——. *Emperor Yang of the Sui Dynasty: His Life, Times, and Legacy*. Albany: State University of New York Press, 2006.

Xu Chunyan 徐春燕. "Mingdai tingzhang tanxi" 明代廷杖探析 (A preliminary study of the court beatings in the Ming period). *Liaoning daxue xuebao*遼寧大學學報 (Zhexue shehui kexue ban). Vol. 38, No. 3 (May 2010), 93–100.

Xu Hong 徐泓. "Mingchu Nanjing de dushi guihua yu renkou bianqian" 明初南京的都市規劃與人口變遷 (The urban planning and population changes in early Ming Nanjing). *Shihuo yuekan* 食貨月刊, Vol. 10, No. 3 (June 1980), 12–46.

——. "Ming Beijing xingbu kao" 明北京行部考 (A study of the Beijing Branch ministry). *Hanxue yanjiu* 漢學研究, Vol. 2, No. 2 (December 1984), 569–98.

Yang Guoqing 楊國慶. *Nanjing Mingdai chengqiang* 南京明代城牆 (The Ming walls of Nanjing). Nanjing: Nanjing chubanshe, 2002.

Yang Hongnian 楊鴻年 (1912–2000). *Sui Tang liangjing kao* 隋唐兩京考 (Studies on the two capital system of the Sui and Tang). Wuhan: Wuhan daxue chubanshe, 2005.

Yang Kuan 楊寬 (1914–2005). *Zhongguo gudai ducheng zhidu shi yanjiu* 中國古代都城制度史研究 (Studies on the history of capital systems in pre-modern China). Shanghai: Shanghai renmin chubanshe, 2003.

Yang Shufan 楊樹藩. "Liao Jin difang zhengzhi zhidu zhi yanjiu" 遼金地方政治制度之研究 (A study of the political system of the regional administrations during the Liao-Jin period). In Songshi zuotanhui, ed., *Songshi yanjiu ji* 宋史研究集 Taibei: Guoli bianyiguan, 1979.

Yang Shusen 楊樹森. *Qingdai liutiaobian* 清代柳條邊 (The willow palisade of the Qing dynasty). Shenyang: Liaoning renmin chubanshe, 1978.

Yang Tonggui 楊同桂. *Shengu* 沈故 (The past of Manchuria). Taibei: Wenhai chubanshe, 1967.

Yang Xinhua 楊新華, ed. *Nanjing Ming gugong* 南京明故宮 (The imperial palace of Ming Nanjing). Nanjing: Nanjing chubanshe, 2009.

Yang Zhengtai 楊正泰. *Mingdai yizhan kao* 明代驛站考 (Notes on the Ming postal relay stations). Shanghai: Shanghai guji chubanshe, 2006.

Yang Zhishu 楊之水. *Nanjing* 南京. Beijing: Zhongguo jianzhu chubanshe, 1989.

Ye Xinmin 葉新民. "Yuan Shangdu de guanshu" 元上都的官署 (Governmental offices in the Upper Capital of the Yuan dynasty). *Nei Menggu daxue xuebao* 內蒙古大學學報, No. 1 (1983), 79–92.

166   *Bibliography*

——. *Yuan Shangdu yanjiu* 元上都研究 (Studies on the Upper Capital of the Yuan dynasty). Hohhot: Nei Mengguo daxue chubanshe, 1998.

Yates, Robin. "Saving the Ming through the written text: the case of the loyalist Fan Jingwen." *Ming Studies*, No. 59 (May 2009), 5–20.

Ye Xiaojun 葉驍軍. *Zhongguo ducheng fazhanshi* 中國都城發展史 (A history of urban development in China). Xi'an: Shaanxi remin chubanshe, 1988.

Yu Rongrong 喻蓉蓉. *Xiong Tingbi yu Liaodong jinglüe* 熊廷弼與遼東經略 (Xiong Tingbi and his management of Luiaodong). Yonghe: Huamulan wenhua chubanshe, 2010.

Yu Zhijia 于志嘉. *Mingdai junhu shixi zhidu* 明代軍戶世襲制度 (The hereditary system of military households in the Ming period). Taibei: Taiwan xuesheng shuju, 1987.

Zhang Dexin 張德信 (1940–2009) and Tan Tianxing 譚天星. *Chongzhen huangdi dazhuan* 崇禎皇帝大傳 (A comprehensive biography of the Chongzhen emperor). Shenyang: Liaoning jiaoyu chubanshe, 1993.

Zhang Guihuai 張貴淮 and Lei Changjiao 雷昌蛟. "Bozhou Yangshi xingwang yu ping Bo zhiyi" 播州楊氏興亡與平播之役 (The rise and fall of the Yang family in Bozhou and the Bozhou Campaign). *Guizhou wenshi congkan* 貴州文史叢刊, No. 2 (2001).

Zhang Guoshuo 張國碩. *Xia Shang shidai ducheng zhidu yanjiu* 夏商時代都城制度研究 (A study of capital cities in the Xia and Shang dynasties). Zhengzhou: Henan renmin chubanshe, 2001.

Zhang Weiren 張偉仁, ed. *Zhongguo fazhishi shumu* 中國法治史書目 (A bibliography of Chinese legal history). Taibei: Zhongyang yanjiuyuan lishi yuyan yanjiusuo, 1976.

Zhang Xianqing 張顯清. *Yan Song zhuan* 嚴嵩傳 (A biography of Yan Song). Hefei: Huangshan shushe, 1992.

Zhang Yingpin 張英聘. *Mingdai Nan Zhili fangzhi yanjiu* 明代南直隸方志研究 (Studies on the gazetteers of Nan Zhili in the Ming). Beijing: Zhongguo shehui kexue wenxian chubanshe, 2005.

——. "Mingdai Nanjing qiqing nianbiao jianshu" 明代南京七卿年表簡述 (A chronological table of the Nanjing ministers during the Ming). *Ming Qing luncong* 明清論叢, Vol. 6 (2005), 28–82.

——. "Mingdai Nanjing xingzheng gongneng chutan" 明代南京行政功能初探 (A preliminary study of the administrative functions of Ming Nanjing). *Mingshi yanjiu* 明史研究, Vol. 7 (2001), 39–57.

Zhao Yi 趙毅 and Lin Fengping 林風萍, eds. *Qiqijie Mingshi guoji xueshu taolunhui lunwenji* 第七屆明史國際學術討論會論文集 (Proceedings of the seventh international symposium on Ming history). Changchun: Dongbei shifan daxue chubanshe, 1999.

Zheng Chuanshui 鄭川水 and Chen Lei 陳磊. *Da Qing peidu Shengjing* 大清陪都盛京 (Qing dynasty auxiliary capital Shengjing). Shenyang: Shenyang chubanshe, 2004.

Zheng Liangsheng 鄭樑生 (1929–2007). *Mingdai wokou shiliao* 明代倭寇史料 (Sources on Japanese piracy during the Ming dynasty). Taibei: Wenshizhe chubanshe, 1987.

Zhongguo diyi lishi danganguan 中國第一歷史檔案館 and Liaoningsheng danganguan 遼寧省檔案館. *Zhongguo Mingchao dang'an zonghui* 中國明朝檔案總匯 (Complete collection of the Ming archives). Guilin: Guangxi shifan daxue chubanshe, 2001.

Zhou Baozhu 周寶珠. *Songdai Dongjing yanjiu* 宋代東京研究 (Studies on the Eastern Capital of the Song dynasty). Kaifeng: Henan daxue chubanshe, 1992.

Zhou Liangxiao 周良宵. "Yuandai touxia fenfeng zhidu chutan" 元代投下分封制度初探 (A preliminary study of the appanage system of the Yuan). *Yuanshi luncong*, No. 2, 53–76.

Bibliography   167

Zhou Song 周松. "Mingdai Nanjing de Huihuiren wuguan" 明代南京的回回人武官 (The Muslim military officers in Ming Nanjing). *Zhongguo shehui jingjishi yanjiu* 中國社會經濟史, No. 3 (2010), 12–22.

Zhou Zhibin 周志斌. "Wan Ming Nanjing bingbian erti" 晚明南京兵變二題 (On the military rebellions in late Ming Nanjing). *Xuehai* 學海, No. 3, 2006, 76–80.

Zhu Dongrun 朱東潤 (1896–1988). *Zhang Juzheng dazhuan* 張居正大傳 (A comprehensive biography of Zhang Juzheng). 1957. Reprint. Taibei: Kaiming shudian, 1966.

Zhu Shiguang 朱士光 and Ye Xiaojun. "Shilun woguo lishi shang peiduzhi de xingcheng yu zuoyong" 試論我國歷史上陪都制度的形成與作用 (On the formation and roles of the auxiliary capital system in Chinese history). In Zhongguo guduxuehui, ed., *Zhongguo gudu yanjiu* 中國古都研究. Hangzhou: Zhejiang renmin chubanshe, 1987.

Zhu Xie 朱偰 (1907–68). *Jinling guji tukao* 金陵古跡圖考 (Illustrated studies of the geographical remains of Nanjing). Beijing: Zhonghua shuju, 2006.

——. *Jinling guji mingsheng yingji* 金陵古跡名勝影集 (Collection of photos of Nanjing's geographical remains). Beijing: Zhonghua shuju, 2006.

Glossary

Aizong (Tang) 哀宗

An Lushan 安禄山

Anchashi 按察使

Anlu 安陸

Anning yanjing 安寧鹽井

Anqing 安慶

Anyang 安陽

Archeng 阿城

Bahu 八虎

Bai Ang 白昂 (1435–1503)

Bai Gui 白圭 (1419–74)

Bai Qichang 白啟常 (d. 1519)

Baichengzhi 白城子

Baiguan zhi 百官志

Baihu 百戶

Bailiang 白糧

Baishan 白山

Baishe 擺設

Baiyanjing 白鹽井

Baju 八局

Baliancheng 八連城

Balin zuoqi 巴林左旗

Glossary 169

Banlacheng 半拉城

Bao'an 保安

Baochao tijusi 寶鈔提舉司

Baoding 保定

Baojia 保甲

Baoqing 寶慶

Baotao 豹韜

Baotaozuo 豹韜左

Bazong 把總

Bazuosi 八作司

Bei Zhili 北直隸

Bei'anmen 北安門

Beiliang 北糧

Beiping 北平

Beishi 北士

Beixin 北新

Beixun 北巡

Bianjing 汴京

Biaoxiu 編修

Biao 標

Biaoying 標營

Bingma duzongguan 兵馬都總管

Bingzhangju 兵杖局

Bingzhi 兵志

Bingzi 丙字

Binzhou 並州

Bitieshi 筆帖式

Bo (earl) 伯

Bohai 渤海

Boshi 博士

170　*Glossary*

Boxian 亳縣

Bozhou 播州

Bumen zhi 部門志

Cai Jin 蔡金

Cang 倉

Cangchao 倉鈔

Cangke 倉科

Canjiang 參將

Canyi 參議

Canzan jiwu 參贊機務

Cao Cao 曹操 (155–220)

Cao Jixiang 曹吉祥 (d. 1461)

Cao Pi 曹丕 (187–226)

Caojiang duyushi 操江都御史

Caoliang 漕糧

Cao Rui 曹睿

Caoyun 漕運

Caoyun canjiang 參將

Caoyun zongbingguan 總兵官

Cen Meng 岑猛 (1489–1526)

Cha 察

Chahuang 查黃

Chai Sheng 柴升 (1456–1532)

Chafa 茶法

Chake 茶課

Chan 廛

Chang'an 長安

Chang'anmen 長安門

Changbai 長白

Changde 常德

Changlu 長蘆

Changping 昌平

Changsha 長沙

Changsui 常隨

Changzhou 常州

Chaoguan 朝官

Chaoguan 鈔關

Chaoshi 抄使

Chayin 茶引

Chayin piyansuo 茶引批驗所

Chayou 茶由

Chejiasi 車駕司

Chen Chen 陳琛 (1477–1545)

Chen Dao 陳道 (1436–1504)

Chen Jin 陳金

Chen Jingzong 陳敬宗 (1377–1459)

Chen Ju 陳矩

Chen Kuan 陳寬

Chen Mao 陳懋

Chen Shou (*js* 1472) 陳受

Chen Xi 陳羲

Chen Yu (earl of Pingjiang) 陳豫

Chen Zeng 陳增

Chengdu 成都

Chengtian 承天

Chengwang 成王

Chengyi 誠意

Chengyun 承運

Chenqiao 陳橋

Chi 笞

172   *Glossary*

Chi 尺

Chihe 池和

Chizhou 池州

Chongqing 重慶

Chuanliao 船料

Chunfang 春坊

Chuzhi si 處置使

Chuzhou 滁州

Cui Gong 崔恭 (1409–79)

Cui Wensheng 崔文升 (fl. 1620)

Cui Xian 崔銑 (1478–1541)

Dacha huangce 大查黃冊

Dading 大定

Dadu 大都

Daguanshu 大官署

Dahe 大和

Dai Xian 戴銑 (*js* 1496)

Daji 大計

Dajiang nanbei 大江南北

Dajiaochang 大校場

Dali yi 大禮議

Dalisi 大理寺

Daluhuachi (Daruhuachi) 達魯花赤

Daming 大名

Danei 大內

Daning 大寧

Dao 道

Daolusi 道錄司

Dasheng 大盛

Dashi 大使

Dasinongsi 大司農司

Datengxia 大藤峽

Datong 大同

Daxingcheng 大興城

Daxueshi 大學士

De'an 德安

Deng Maoqi 鄧茂七 (d. 1449)

Dianbu 典簿

Dianji 典籍

Dianzhong yushi 殿中御史

Difang zhenquan 地方政權

Digang 荻港

Ding Xuan 丁瑄

Dingzi 丁字

Dixun 帝訓

Dong'anmen 東安門

Dongchang 東廠

Dongdu 東都

Dongdu liutai 東都留台

Dongge daxueshi 東閣大學士

Dongjing 東京

Dongjingcheng 東京城

Du 都

Dudu 都督

Duiyun 兌運

Dushuisi 都水司

Duyuhoushi 都虞侯使

Duyushi 都御史

Duzhihuishi si 都指揮使司

Duzhijian 度支監

174 *Glossary*

Duzhike 度支科

Duzhishi si 度支使司

Duzhuanyun yanshisi 都轉運鹽使司

Duzhuguan 讀祝官

Ershisi yaman 二十四衙門

Esen 也先 (d. 1455)

Fan Jishi 范濟世

Fang Feng 方鳳 (*js* 1508)

Fang Lian 方廉 (1513–82)

Fang Liangyong 方良永 (1461–1527)

Fang Peng 方鵬 (b. 1470)

Fang Zhenghua 方正化 (d. 1644)

Fang Zongchong 方宗重

Feice 廢冊

Feixiong 飛熊

Feng Bao 馮保 (fl. 1580)

Feng Xi 豐熙 (*js* 1499)

Fengcheng 風城

Fenghua 奉化

Fenghuangcheng 鳳凰城

Fengsi 奉祀

Fengtian 奉天

Fengtiandian 奉天殿

Fengxiandian 奉先殿

Fengxiang 鳳翔

Fengyang 鳳陽

Fengyu 奉御

Fu zongbing guan 副總兵官

Fu Zuozhou 傅作舟

Fu duyushi 副都御史

Fu liushou 副留守

Fu shoubei taijian 副守備太監

Fujun 俯軍

Fujunhou 俯軍後

Fujunyou 右

Fujunzuo 左

Gaidui 改兌

Gaitu guiliu 改土歸流

Gaiyun 改運

Gangzhou 贛州

Gao Gong 高拱 (1514–78)

Gao Hongtu 高鴻圖 (1583–1645)

Gao Qiqian 高起潛

Gao Youji 高友璣 (1461–1546)

Gaodi 高帝

Gaojing 鎬京

Gaoyou 高郵

Gaozong 高宗

Gaozu 高祖

Genben zhongdi 根本重地

Gong 公

Gengcheng 宮城

Gongque lingqin 宮闕陵寢

Gongshi 貢士

Gongying jifang 供應機房

Gu (river) 谷

Gu Dayong 谷大用 (fl. 1516)

Gu Qing 顧清 (1460–1528)

Gu Qiyuan 顧起元 (1565–1626)

Guan 官

176　*Glossary*

Guan 貫

Guan huangce zhushi 管黃冊主事

Guandi 關帝

Guangdezhou 廣德州

Guanghui 廣惠

Guanglu si 光祿寺

Guangou taishi 管勾台事

Guangwenguan 廣文館

Guangwu 廣武

Guangyang 廣洋

Guangying 廣英

Guanling Shangdu qielinkou zhuse renjiang tijusi 管領上都怯鄰口諸色人匠提舉司

Guantun 官屯

Guanxingtai 觀星台

Guanzhong 關中

Guazhou 瓜州

Gui E 桂萼 (1478–1531)

Guiyang 貴陽

Guo Xun 郭勳

Guojiangfei 過江費

Guoxian 椁縣

Guoziguan 國子館

Guozijian 國子監

Guozixue 國子學

Hai Rui 海瑞 (1514–87)

Haibei 海北

Haining wang 海甯王 (r. 1149–61)

Han 漢

Han Bangqi 韓邦奇 (1479–1555)

Han Wen 韓文 (1441–1526)

Han Xuandi 漢宣帝 (74–49 BCE)

Han Yong 韓雍 (1422–78)

Han Yu 韓愈 (786–824)

Hangou 邗溝

Hangzhou 杭州

Hanjun 漢軍

Hanlin bianxiu 翰林編修

Hanlin kongmu 孔目

Haomi 耗米

He Ding 何鼎

He Qian 何簽 (1442–1521)

He Liangjun 何良俊 (1506–73)

He Mengchun 何孟春 (1474–1536)

He Qiaoxin 何喬新 (1427–1502)

He Weibo 何維柏 (1511–87)

Hebosuo 河泊所

Hedong 河東

Heiyanjing 黑鹽井

Heling 和林

Helong 和龍

Henghai 橫海

Hengzhou 衡州

Hetuala 赫圖阿拉

Heyang 和陽

Hexiwu 河西務

Hezhong 河中

Hezhou 和州

Hong Chaoxuan 洪朝選 (1516–82)

Hongguang (Hung-kuang) 弘光

178 *Glossary*

Honglu si 鴻臚寺

Hou 侯

Houhu 後湖

Hu 斛

Hu 戶

Hu Rulin 胡汝霖 (*js* 1535)

Hu Weiyong 胡惟庸 (d. 1380)

Hu Ying 胡瀅 (1375–1463)

Hu Zongxian 胡宗憲 (1511–65)

Huagai 華蓋

Huai En 懷恩

Huai'an 淮安

Huang Bingshi 黃秉石

Huang Fu 黃福 (1363–1440)

Huang Kaihua 黃開華

Huang Ming libu zhi 皇明吏部志

Huang Wei 黃偉

Huang Xiaoyang 黃簫養

Huang Zhongzhao 黃仲昭 (1435–1508)

Huang Zuo 黃佐 (1490–1566)

Huangce 黃冊

Huangcheng 皇城

Huangchuan 黃船

Huangdu 皇都

Huangqi dayingzi 黃旗大營子

Huanyiju 浣衣局

Huben qinjun du zhihuishi si 虎賁親軍都指揮使司

Hubenyou 虎賁右

Hubenzuo 虎賁左

Huichun 琿春

Huiminju 惠民局

Huining 會寧

Huishi 會試

Huizhou 徽州

Huntangsi 混堂司

Huo Tao 霍韜 (1481–1540)

Hushu 滸墅

Huzhou 湖州

Jia 甲

Jia Yingchun 賈迎春 (1485–1565)

Jia Yong 賈詠 (1464–1547)

Jiading 嘉定

Ji'an 吉安

Jiageku (archives) 架閣庫

Jiancha yushi 監察御史

Jianchen 監臣

Jianfu 監副

Jiang Yueguang 姜曰廣 (*js* 1619)

Jiangbei 江北

Jianghai 江海

Jianghu 匠戶

Jianghuai 江淮

Jiangning 江陵

Jiangnan 江南

Jiangning 江寧

Jianguo 監國

Jiangyin 江陰

Jiankang 建康

Jianye 建鄴

Jianzhen 監正

180   *Glossary*

Jiaofang si 教坊司

Jiaojia 腳價

Jiaomi 腳米

Jiaxing 嘉興

Jiazi 甲字

Jichuan 濟川

Jiedushi 節度使

Jiezhi 節制

Jijiu 祭酒

Jiliao 薊遼

Jin 金

Jin 晉

Jin Ying 金英

Jin Lian 金濂 (d. 1454)

Jinbangzhi 金榜紙

Jing 京

Jingcha 京察

Jingcheng 京城

Jingguan 京官

Jingjun 淨軍

Jingli 經歷

Jingkou 京口

Jingshansi 精膳司

Jingshi 京師

Jingwei wuxue 京衛武學

Jingxue zhi 京學志

Jingxun yuan 警巡院

Jingzhou 荊州

Jinhuayin 金花銀

Jining 濟寧

Glossary 181

Jinke 金科

Jinmaoju 巾帽局

Jinshan 金山

Jinshazhou 金沙州

Jinshendian 謹身殿

Jinshi 進士

Jinwuhou 金吾後

Jinwuqian 金吾前

Jinwuyou 金吾右

Jinwuzuo 金吾左

Jinyang 晉陽

Jinyi 錦衣

Jinyiwei 錦衣衛

Jiqing 集慶

Jishizhong 給事中

Jisi 計司

Jiubian 九邊

Jiucumianju 酒醋面局

Jiujiang 九江

Jiuzhou 舊洲

Jixianyuan 集賢院

Jixunsi 稽勳司

Jiyou 給由

Jun 郡

Junchu 軍儲

Junhu 軍戶

Junji chu 軍機處

Junyaoju 軍藥局

Juren 舉人

Kaifeng 開封

182 *Glossary*

Kaiping 開平

Kaizhong 開中

Kangxi 康熙 (r. 1662–1722)

Kanhe 勘合

Kao 考

Kaogongsi 考功司

Kaoman 考滿

Keshen 客省

Khurilitai (Huliletai) 忽里勒台

Kongmu 孔目

Kou 口

Ku 庫

Kuaichuan 快船

Kuang Ye 鄺埜 (1385–1449)

Kuang Zhong 況鍾

Kucang 庫藏

Kuizhou 夔州

Lai Zongdao 來宗道 (1571–1638)

Lan Yu 來宗道 (d. 1393)

Langbing 狼兵

Langdang 蒗蕩

Langshan 狼山

Langzhong 郎中

Li 吏

Li 里

Li Banghua 李邦華 (d. 1644)

Li Biao 李標 (*js* 1607)

Li Fang 李芳 (fl. 1567)

Li Guangpi 李光弼 (708–64)

Li Hualong 李化龍 (1554–1611)

Li Long 李隆 (d. 1447)

Li Mingrui 李明睿

Li Mo 李默 (d. 1556)

Li Rong 李榮

Li Shiqin 李時馨

Li Sui 李遂 (1506–66)

Li Tianchong 李天寵 (d. 1555)

Li Tingji 李廷機 (*js* 1583)

Li Tingxiang 李廷相

Li Xi 李熙 (1465–1524)

Li Xikong 李希孔 (*js* 1610)

Li Yi 李頤

Li Zhen 李震

Li Zhicheng 李自成 (1606–45)

Li Zisheng 李孜省 (fl. 1485)

Liang 兩

Liang Chu 梁儲 (*js* 1478)

Liang Fang 梁芳 (fl. 1470)

Liang Yao 梁瑤

Lianghuai 兩淮

Liangyunshu 良醞署

Liangzhe 兩浙

Liao 遼

Liaodong 遼東

Liaoyang 遼陽

Libu zhigao 禮部志稿

Lidai diwang miao 歷代帝王廟

Li dang ru Beijian 例當入北監

Lifan yuan 理藩院

Lijia 里甲

184　*Glossary*

Limu 吏目

Lin Han 林翰

Lin Fu 林富 (*js* 1501)

Lin'an 臨安

Lingdi (Han) 靈帝

Linghuang 臨潢

Lingtailang 靈台郎

Lingwu 靈武

Linqing 臨清

Linzhang 臨漳

Liu 流

Liu Bang 劉邦 (256–195 BCE)

Liu Hongxun 劉鴻訓 (1561–1639)

Liu Kongzhao 劉孔昭

Liu Ji 劉吉 (1427–93)

Liu Jin 劉瑾 (d. 1510)

Liu Long 劉龍 (1477–1553)

Liu Tianhe 劉天和 (1479–1545)

Liu Tianxu 劉天緒

Liu Xiu 劉秀 (r. 25–57 CE)

Liu Zhong 劉忠 (1452–1523)

Liu Zongzhou 劉宗周 (1578–1645)

Liuguan 流官

Liuke 六科

Liushouhou 留守後

Liushouqian 前

Liushousi 司

Liushouyou 右

Liushouzhong 中

Liushouzuo 左

Liutiaobian 柳條邊

Longchang 龍場

Longhu 龍虎

Longhuzuo 左

Longjiang 龍江

Longjiang yancang piyansuo 鹽場批驗所

Longjiangguan 關

Longjiangyou 右

Longjiangzuo 左

Longquan 龍泉

Longxiang 龍驤

Longxing (route) 龍興

Longyuan 龍原

Lü Daqi 呂大器 (js 1628)

Lu Shen 陸深

Lu Su 盧蘇

Lü Yijian 呂夷簡 (979–1044)

Lubing 陸兵

Lüguan 律館

Luke 蘆科

Luo 洛

Luoyang 洛陽

Luoyi 洛邑

Luozhou 洛州

Luzhou 盧州 (Nan Zhili)

Lu Zhou 瀘州 (Sichuan)

Ma Shiying 馬士英 (d. 1646)

Ma Wensheng 馬文升 (1426–1510)

Ma Xian 馬顯 (*js* 1443)

Ma Zhongxi 馬中錫 (1446–1512)

186 *Glossary*

Ma Yongcheng 馬永成

Machuan 馬船

Maichao yuyin 買鈔餘銀

Mao Hong 毛弘

Mao Zedong 毛澤東 (1893–1976)

Mengtashui 門榻稅

Menguan 門關

Milu 米魯

Min 閩

Mingtang 明堂

Mingzan 鳴贊

Mingzong 明宗

Minhu 民戶

Minke 民科

Mohe 靺鞨

Muchang 牧場

Nan Zhili 南直隸

Nan'an 南安

Nanbei zaixiangfu 南北宰相府

Nan'gan 南贛

Nanchang 南昌

Nandu 南都

Nanhaizi 南海子

Nanhu 南湖

Nanjing guanglu si zhi 南京光祿寺志

Nanjing liangchu 南京糧儲

Nanjing shanglinyuan jian zhi 南京上林苑監志

Nanjing shoubei 南京守備

Nanjing taipu si zhi 南京太僕寺志

Nanjing Xingbu zhi 南京刑部志

Nanjing zhanshi fu zhi 南京詹事府志

Nanjing xietong shoubei 南京協同守備

Nankang 南康

Nanliang 南糧

Nantu zhishi 南土之士

Nanxun 南巡

Nanyong xuzhi 南雍續志

Nanyong zhi 南雍志

Neicheng 內城

Neichengyun 內承運

Neifu 內府

Neige 內閣

Neigong 內宮

Neiguanjian 內官監

Neikeshen 內客省

Neishensi 內省司

Neishoubei 內守備

Neizhiranju 內織染局

Nianli 年例

Ning 寧

Ning'an 寧安

Ningbo 寧波

Ningcheng 寧城

Ningguta 寧古塔

Ningyang 寧陽

Pan Jixun 潘季馴 (1521–95)

Pan Rong 潘榮 (d. 1495)

Panguan 判官

Pei Songzhi 裴松之 (372–451)

Pei-ching (Beijing) 北京

188 *Glossary*

Peng Dehuai 彭德懷 (1898–1974)

Peng Shao 彭韶 (1430–95)

Pingcheng 平城

Pingjiang 平江

Pingshi 評事

Pingzhang zhenshi 平章政事

Pizhou 邳州

Pu'an 普安

Pukouzi 浦口子

Qian duyushi 僉都御史

Qian Longxi 錢龍錫 (1579–1645)

Qian Neng 錢能

Qian Shisheng 錢士升 (1575–1652)

Qianhu 千戶

Qianlong 乾隆 (r. 1736–95)

Qiao 譙

Qiao Yu 喬宇 (1457–1524)

Qin Jin 秦金 (1467–1544)

Qing 卿

Qingce 青冊

Qingjiyin 輕齎銀

Qingming 清明

Qinhuai 秦淮

Qinjunwei 親軍衛

Qintian jian 欽天監

Qishou 旗手

Qiu Ju 丘聚

Qiu Jun 丘濬 (1421–95)

Qiu Ying 仇英 (1498–1552)

Qiujiao 秋醮

Qiuliangmi 秋糧米

Qiyi 起義

Qu Zhi 屈直 (*js* 1484)

Quannongshi 勸農使

Quanzhou 泉州

Quzhou 瞿州

Raozhou 饒州

Renzong 仁宗

Rijiang 日講

Ru Nan 汝南 (*js* 1532)

Sandaying 三大營

Sanfasi 三法司

Sangong 三公

Sangu 三孤

Sanhe 三河

Sanjiang huikou 三江匯口

Sanmenxia 三門峽

Sanqian 三千

Senglusi 僧錄司

Shaanxi sanbian 陝西三邊

Shaanchuan 陝川

Shaanzhou 陝州

Shang Lu 商輅 (1414–86)

Shangbao ju 尚寶局

Shangbaojian 尚寶監

Shangdu bingmasi 上都兵馬司

Shangdu jingxunyuan 上都警巡院

Shangdu liushousi 上都留守司

Shangdu qunmu du zhuanyunsi 上都群牧都轉運司

Shangdu yinye tijusi 上都銀冶提舉司

190 Glossary

Shangdu zhuanyunsi 上都轉運司

Shangjiang 上江

Shangjing 上京

Shanglingyuan jian 上林苑監

Shangqing 上清

Shangqiu 商丘

Shangshanjian 尚膳監

Shangshu 尚書

Shangshui fuyuyin 商稅富餘銀

Shangyang 上陽

Shangyuan 上元

Shangyijian 尚衣監

Shangzhiwei 上直衛

Shanhai 山海

Shanhe zhixian 山河之險

Shao ji wang suiyue, que qian bei yi 稍積望歲月，卻遷北矣

Shao Weizhong 邵惟中

Shaobao 少保

Shaojian 少監

Shaoqing 少卿

Shaowu 紹武

Shaoxin 紹興

Shashi 沙市

Shejitan 社稷壇

Shen Shixing 申時行 (1535–1614)

Shenbotang 神帛堂

Shendu 神都

Shengjing 盛京

Shengjing wubu 盛京五部

Shengongjian 神宮監

Glossary 191

Shenji 神機

Shenlu zhongqiu 審錄重囚

Shenqiang 神槍

Shenshu 神樞

Shenwei 神位

Shenxian 神仙

Shenyang 瀋陽

Shenyangyou 瀋陽右

Shenyangzuo 瀋陽左

Shenyaoku 神藥庫

Shenyueguan 神樂館

Shi (dan) 石

Shi Bangyao 施邦曜 (1585–1644)

Shi Heng 石亨 (d. 1460)

Shi Jixie 史繼偕

Shi Kefa 史可法 (1601–45)

Shi Zhaogong fu Luoyi ru Wuwang yi 使昭公赴洛邑如武王意

Shibo tijusi 市舶提舉司

Shi'erjian 十二監

Shidu xueshi 侍讀學士

Shilang 侍郎

Shiyu 鰣魚

Shiyushi 侍御史

Shoubei 守備

Shoufu 首輔

Shouxi 首席

Shu Yinglong 舒應龍 (*js* 1562)

Shucheng 署丞

Shuguan 書館

Shuibing 水兵

192 *Glossary*

Shuici 水次

Shuijunyou 水軍右

Shuijunzuo 水軍左

Shuike tijusi 稅科提舉司

Shujishi 庶吉士

Shujun 蜀郡

Shumi fushi 樞密副使

Shumishi 樞密使

Shumiyuan 樞密院

Shundi 順帝

Shuntian 順天

Shuwan jia fushang dagu 數萬家富商大賈

Shuzhen 署正

Shuzi 戍字

Si 寺

Sibinshu 司賓署

Si'en 思恩

Silijian 司禮監

Simenguan 四門館

Sishejian 司設監

Sisi 四司

Siwu 司務

Sixiang 司香

Siye 司業

Siyi 四夷

Siyishu 司儀署

Siyuanju 司苑局

Sizheng 寺正

Songjiang 松江

Songpan 松潘

Suanguan 算館

Suanke 算科

Sui Wendi 隋文帝 (r. 581–604)

Sui Yangdi 隋煬帝 (r. 604–18)

Suiji 歲計

Suiyuan 綏遠

Sun Jiao 孫交 (1453–1532)

Sun Yingkui 孫應奎 (*js* 1521)

Suzhou 蘇州

Suzong (Tang) 肅宗

Taibao 太保

Taicang 太倉

Taichang xukao 太常續考

Taichang si 太常寺

Taicang 太倉

Taidingdi 泰定帝

Taijian 太監

Taimiao 太廟

Taiping 太平

Taipu si 太僕寺

Taishou 太守

Taiyi yuan 太醫院

Taiyuan 太原

Taizi taibao 太子太保

Taizu 太祖

Tan Qian 談遷 (1594–1657)

Tangshangguan 堂上官

Tangzhushi 堂主事

Tao Chengxue 陶承學 (1518–98)

Tao Shangde 陶尚德 (*js* 1526)

194   *Glossary*

Tao Yan 陶琰 (1447–1531)

Tezhi 特旨

Tiance 天策

Tianditan sijishu 天地壇祭祀署

Tianshou 天壽

Tianzao dishe 天造地設

Tianzhou 田州

Tidian 提點

Tidu chaojiang 提督操江

Timingji 題名記

Tingzhang 廷杖

Tingzhou 汀州

Tixingshi 提刑使

Tongguan 潼關

Tongji 通濟

Tongshi 通事

Tongyi 同邑

Tongzheng canyi 通政參議

Tongzhengshi 通政使

Tongzhengshisi 通政使司

Tongzhenyuan 通政院

Tongzhi 同知

Tongzhi liushoushi 同知留守使

Toyotomi Hideyoshi 豐田秀吉 (1536–98)

Tu 徒

Tu 圖

Tu Kai 屠楷 (d. 1561)

Tu Qiao 屠僑 (1480–1555)

Tuanshan 團山

Tuanying 團營

Tuiguan 推官

Tumu 土木

Tunliang 屯糧

Tuntiansi 屯田司

Tuoba 拓拔

Tusi 土司

Waicha 外察

Waichai 外差

Waiguocheng 外郭城

Waishoubei 外守備

Wan An 萬安 (d. 1489)

Wan Tang 萬鏜 (*js* 1505)

Wan Yukai 萬虞愷

Wang Cai 王材 (1508–84)

Wang Cheng'en 王承恩 (d. 1644)

Wang Gao 王誥 (1498–1557)

Wang Jun 汪俊 (fl. 1522)

Wang Mang 王莽 (45 BCE-23 CE)

Wang Qiao 王樵 (1521–99)

Wang Qiong 王瓊 (1459–1532)

Wang Shi 王軾 (1437–1506)

Wang Shizhen 王世貞 (1526–90)

Wang Shou 王受

Wang Shu 王恕 (1416–1508)

Wang Ting 王廷

Wang Xian 王憲 (*js* 1490)

Wang Xuekui 王學夔 (*js* 1514)

Wang Yangming 王陽明 (1472–1529)

Wang Yongbin 王用賓

Wang Yue 王嶽

196 *Glossary*

Wang Zhen 王振 (d. 1449)

Wang Zhi 王直 (1379–1462)

Wang Zhi 汪直 (fl. 1477)

Wangjiangjing 王江涇

Wangqi 王氣

Wangwuchadu 旺兀察都

Wanquan 萬全

Waxieba 瓦屑壩

Wei 衛

Wei Ji 魏冀 (1374–1471)

Wei Zhongxian 魏忠賢 (1568–1627)

Weisuo 衛所

Weiyuanbao 威遠堡

Wen 文

Wen Gui 文圭

Wenmiao 文廟

Wensiyuan 文思院

Wenxuansi 文選司

Wenzong 文宗

Wu Wendu 吳文度 (1441–1510)

Wu Yipeng 吳一鵬 (1460–1542)

Wu Yuan 吳遠

Wu Zetian 武則天 (624–705)

Wuchang 武昌

Wude 武德

Wuguanjianhou 五官監候

Wuhu 蕪湖

Wujun 五軍

Wujun dudufu 五軍都督府

Wukusi 武庫司

Wusong 吳淞

Wuxing 五刑

Wuxuansi 武選司

Wuzi 戊字

Wuzong 武宗

Xi Liaozhi jianwujing 襲遼制建五京

Xi Shu 席書 (1461–1527)

Xi'anmen 西安門

Xia Bangmo 夏邦謨

Xiajiang 下江

Xiande 顯德

Xiang 鄉

Xiang Yu 項羽 (232–202 BCE)

Xiang Zhong 項忠 (1421–1502)

Xiangcheng 襄城

Xiangtan 湘潭

Xiangyue 鄉約

Xianqing 顯慶

Xiao 崤

Xiao Xuan 蕭暄 (1396–1461)

Xiaojiaochang 小校場

Xiaoling 孝陵

Xiaoling jinjun 孝陵淨軍

Xiaoling shenggongjian 孝陵神宮監

Xiaoqiyou 驍騎右

Xiaoshan 蕭山

Xiaowendi 孝文帝 (r. 471–99)

Xiaozong shilu 孝宗實錄

Xiashuimai 夏稅麥

Xibo 西亳

198 *Glossary*

Xichang 西廠

Xidu 西都

Xie Bin 謝彬

Xielulang 協律郎

Xigong 西宮

Xiguchengzi 西古城子

Xijing 西京

Xing 興

Xing du zhihuishi si 行都指揮使司

Xinggong 行宮

Xing Gongbu 行工部

Xing Jie 邢玠 (1540–1615)

Xingbu 行部

Xingdu 興都

Xingdu liushousi 興都留守司

Xinghua 興華

Xingjing 興京

Xingliang 行糧

Xingwu 興武

Xingxiang 興襄

Xingyang 滎陽

Xingzai 行在

Xinjiangkou 新江口

Xingzhou 新洲

Xiong Tingbi 熊廷弼 (1573–1625)

Xixinsi 惜薪司

Xu Bida 徐必達 (*js* 1592)

Xu Bin 許彬 (d. 1467)

Xu Daren 徐大任 (*js* 1568)

Xu Hongji 徐弘基

Xu Jin 許進 (1437–1510)

Xu Mu 徐穆 (1468–1511)

Xu Qi 徐琦 (1386–1452)

Xu Youzhen 徐有貞 (1407–72)

Xu Xuemo 徐學謨 (1522–93)

Xuan Ni 軒輗 (fl. 1460)

Xuanfu 宣府

Xuanhuiyuan 宣徽院

Xuanwu 玄武

Xuanzong 玄宗 (r. 712–56)

Xuban 序班

Xuchang 許昌

Xuelu 學錄

Xuezheng 學政

Xun Zhou Han gushi 循周漢故事

Xuncang 巡倉

Xuncao yushi 巡漕御史

Xunfu 巡撫

Xunjiang yushi 巡江御史

Xuzhou 徐州

Yalu 鴨綠

Yamen 衙門

Yan 燕

Yan Shifan 嚴世蕃 (d. 1565)

Yan Song 嚴嵩 (1480–1565)

Yan'an 延安

Yanchang 鹽場

Yanchao 鹽鈔

Yanfa 鹽法

Yang Lian 楊廉 (1452–1525)

200 *Glossary*

Yang Jianchen 楊景辰

Yang Ning 楊寧 (d. 1548)

Yang Pu 楊溥 (1372–1446)

Yang Rong 楊榮 (1371–1440)

Yang Shiqi 楊士奇 (1365–1444)

Yang Su 楊素 (d. 606)

Yang Tinghe 楊廷和 (1459–1529)

Yang Xinmin 楊信民

Yang Yi 楊宜 (*js* 1523)

Yang Yikui 楊一魁 (*js* 1565)

Yang Yinglong 楊應龍 (1551–1600)

Yangwang di 養望地

Yangzhou 揚州

Yanke tijusi 鹽課提舉司

Yanshi 偃師

Yansui 延綏

Yanyin 鹽引

Yanyin piyansuo 鹽引批驗所

Yanyinku 鹽引庫

Yanzhou 嚴州

Yanzhou 兗州

Yao 瑤

Yao Kui 姚夔 (1414–73)

Yao Wenyuan 姚文元 (1931–2005)

Yao Zongwen 姚宗文

Yazhou 雅州

Ye 鄴

Ye Mengxiong 葉夢熊 (*js* 1565)

Ye Xianggao 葉向高 (1559–1627)

Ye Zongliu 葉宗留

Glossary 201

Yiluan ju 儀鸞局

Yin 鄞

Yin 引

Yin Qiu 應秋

Yinghe 迎和

Yingshansi 營膳司

Yingtian 應天

Yingwu 英武

Yingyang 鷹揚

Yinku 銀庫

Yinshoujian 印綬監

Yinzuoju 印作局

Yiren 譯人

Yishi qinzhen 以示親征

Yiwen 懿文

Yizhen 儀真

Yizhi si 儀制司

Yizi 乙字

Yongzhou 雍州

Youbing 遊兵

Youcheng 右丞

Youdu 幽都

Youji 幽薊

Youji 遊擊

Youpingshi 右評事

Youpingzhang zhengshi 右平章政事

Youshuzi 右庶子

Yousilang 右侍郎

Yousi 有司

Youtongzheng 右通政

202 *Glossary*

Youxiang 右相

Youyude 右諭德

Yu Jideng 余繼登 (1544–1600)

Yu Qian 于謙 (1398–1457)

Yu Shenxing 于慎行 (1545–1608)

Yuanpan 院判

Yuanqiu 圜丘

Yuanweilang 員外郎

Yueji 月計

Yueliang 月糧

Yuhengsi 虞衡司

Yuke 魚課

Yulince 魚鱗冊

Yulingqian 羽林前

Yulingyou 羽林右

Yulingzuo 羽林左

Yumajian 御馬監

Yunyang 鄖陽

Yushitai 御史台

Yuwen Kai 宇文愷 (556–612)

Yuyongjian 御用監

Yuzhou 禹州

Zaixiangfu 宰相府

Zangfa 贓罰

Zanwu 贊務

Zaohu 灶戶

Zeng Jun 曾鈞

Zhan Ruoshui 湛若水 (1466–1560)

Zhang 杖

Zhang Bangqi 張邦奇 (1481–1528)

Glossary 203

Zhang Cai 張綵 (fl. 1515)

Zhang Cong 張璁 (1475–1539)

Zhang Feng 張鳳

Zhang Fuhua 張敷華 (1439–1508)

Zhang Huan 章桓

Zhang Jin 張縉

Zhang Jing 張經 (d. 1555)

Zhang Jing 張鯨

Zhang Juzheng 張居正 (1525–82)

Zhang Kai 張楷 (1398–1460)

Zhang Lun 章綸 (1413–83)

Zhang Mao 章懋 (1437–1522)

Zhang Nai 張鼐 (*js* 1547)

Zhang Peng 張鵬 (*js* 1541)

Zhang Pu 張樸

Zhang Sheng 張升 (*js* 1469)

Zhang Shenyan 張慎言 (*js* 1610)

Zhang Shicheng 張士誠 (1321–67)

Zhang Wei 張瑋 (*js* 1619)

Zhang Ying 張瑛 (1375–1436)

Zhang Yixian 張彝憲

Zhang Yong 張永 (1465–1526)

Zhang Zhi 張治 (1488–1550)

Zhangyunshu 掌醞署

Zhangzhou 漳州

Zhangzhu 張渚

Zhanhu 站戶

Zhanshi fu 詹事府

Zhaogong 召公

Zhao Gou 趙構 (1107–87)

204 *Glossary*

Zhao Wenhua 趙文華 (d. 1557)

Zhaomo 照磨

Zhaozong 昭宗

Zhehai 浙海

Zhelin 柘林

Zhending 真定

Zhen Bengong 鄭本公 (*js* 1514)

Zheng He 鄭和 (1371–1433)

Zhen Xiao 鄭曉 (1499–1566)

Zhenfusi 鎮撫司

Zheng Yi 鄭毅

Zhenglan 正藍

Zhengongju 針工局

Zhengqing 正卿

Zhengzhou 鄭州

Zhenjiang 鎮江

Zhennan 鎮南

Zhenshou 鎮守

Zhenshou zhongguan 鎮守中官

Zhenwu 振武

Zhenwuying 振武營

Zheyang 遮洋

Zhi 志

Zhibo 制帛

Zhidianjian 直殿監

Zhifa 知法

Zhifang si 職方司

Zhihui 指揮

Zhike 支科

Zhiyun 支運

Zhongchen 中丞

Zhongdu 中都

Zhongguan 中官

Zhonggusi 鍾鼓司

Zhongjun dudufu 中軍都督府

Zhongshuke 中書科

Zhongshuling 中書令

Zhongshusheng 中書省

Zhongyuan 中元

Zhongzhou 中洲

Zhongzong 中宗

Zhou Chong 周玙

Zhou Daodeng 周道登 (*js* 1598)

Zhou Kengeng 周堪賡

Zhou Lun 周倫 (1463–1542)

Zhu Biao 朱標 (1355–92)

Zhu Chenhao 朱宸濠 (d. 1521)

Zhu Changfang 朱常淓 (1607–46)

Zhu Guozhen 朱國禎 (1557–1632)

Zhu Yong 朱永 (1429–96)

Zhu Yousong 朱由崧 (1607–46)

Zhu Yuanzhang 朱元璋 (1328–98)

Zhuanyunshi 轉運使

Zhuang Yong 莊泳 (*js* 1466)

Zhubu 主簿

Zhujiao 助教

Zhuke si 主客司

Zhumu choufen 竹木抽分

Zhuojun 涿郡

Zhushi 主事

206   *Glossary*

Zichen 自陳

Zijincheng 紫禁城

Zong 總

Zongdu 總督

Zongdu chaoyun 總督漕運

Zongdu hedao 總督河道

Zongdu Nanjing liangchu 總督南京糧儲

Zongguanfu 總管府

Zongli chaoyun jian tidu junwu xunfu 總埋漕運兼提督軍務巡撫

Zongli liangchu 總理糧儲

Zongren fu 宗人府

Zou Yuanbiao 鄒元標 (1551–1624)

Zuo 左

Zuo si 左司

Zuo pingzhang zhengshi 左平章政事

Zuochen 左丞

Zuosi 左司

Zuoxiang 左相

Zuzong zhidi 祖宗之地

Index

aboriginal rebellions in south, suppression of 131–33

administration: army stationed in Nanjing 51; Beijing (Northern Capital) 44, 45, 46, 47, 48–49, 50, 51–52, 53, 54, 55, 56–58; bureaucracy, downsizing of, continuation of 57; bureaucracy, first large-scale reduction of 56; Ceremonial, Directorate of 52–53, 55; civil bureaucracy 44–50; civil offices and staffing levels 46–47; Delicacies, Directorate of 55; Embroidered-Uniform Guard (*Jinyiwei*) 51; eunuch agencies, scale of 54–55; eunuch departments 53; eunuch establishment 52–55; Evaluation Bureau 49; Garden Service 55; governmental departments, substructure of 45; grand commandant, post of 52, 53; imperial guards (*qinjunwei* or *shangzhiwei*) 50–51; Imperial Horses, Directorate of 55; informal collective leadership groups 55–56; Justice Ministry 4, 13, 34, 35, 46, 47, 48, 49, 59n9, 62n85, 68, 75, 82, 90–91n124; leadership 55–56; military apparatuses 50–52; Military Commissions 55–56; military training 51; Nanjing Censorate, power of 50; Nanjing Court of Judicial Review 4, 42n139, 46, 47, 48, 55, 56, 57, 62n81, 63n93, 64, 73, 75, 76, 82, 85, 89n95, 93, 101; Nanjing National University 48; Nanjing (Southern Capital) 44–58; national roles of Southern departments 49–50; Office of Eunuch Grand Commandant 55; Personnel Ministry 8, 33, 46, 47, 49, 60n33, 68, 75, 78, 81, 85, 90n120, 143, 144, 146; political functions 84; ranks and emoluments 45; reduction of offices 56–57; restoration of offices 57–58; Security Offices, power of 50; staffing levels 44–45; Supply Storehouse of Nanjing Palace Treasury 55; territorial jurisdictions 47–48; Twelve Directorates (*shi'er jian*) 52

armies: numbers stationed in Nanjing 51; southern and northern armies, dividing line between 133; *see also* military functions

autumn grain (*qiuliangmi*) tax 94–95

Back Lake [Archives] (Houhu zhi) Gazetteer 110–11

Bai Ang 79

Bai Gang 90n120, 91n130

Bai Gui 132

Bai Qichang 83

Balazs, Etienne 16n46

Ban Gu 19, 37n20

Beijing (Northern Capital) 1–2, 5–6, 7–8, 11, 14n14, 20, 25, 26, 27, 28–29, 30, 31–33, 142–43, 144–45; administration 44, 45, 46, 47, 48–49, 50, 51–52, 53, 54, 55, 56–58; financial functions 92–93, 94–95, 97–98, 99, 100, 101–2, 103, 104, 107, 109–10, 113; military functions 121–22, 126–27, 128–29, 130, 132–33, 134, 135, 136–37; Nanjing and, relationship between 145–46; political functions 64, 65–66, 67–71, 72, 73–74, 75, 77–78, 80, 81, 82, 83, 84–85

Bi Yuan 38n56

Bi Ziyan 93

Bodde, Derk 16n46

208   *Index*

Brook, Timothy 10, 13, 15–16n44, 16n45, 16n50
Brook et al., T. 60n40
bureaucracy: civil bureaucracy 44–50; downsizing of 57; first large-scale reduction of 56; tax grain, administration of 97

Cai Jin 50
Cai Jiude 139n55
Cambridge History of China 9
Cao Cao 20
Cao Erqin 37n17, 37n19
Cao Guoqing 60n42
Cao Jixiang 89n85
Cao Pi 20
Cao Rui 20
Cen Meng 131
Censorate (Beijing and Nanjing) 4, 22, 25, 29, 33, 46, 47, 50, 56, 57, 65, 70, 82, 85, 98, 101, 111, 123
Ceremonial, Directorate of 52–53, 55
Chai Sheng 54, 61n61
Chan Ran 118n120
Chen Chen 90–91n124
Chen Dao 101
Chen Gaohua 39n81, 40n96, 40n105, 41n111
Chen Jingzong 48
Chen Ju 89n86
Chen Kuan 75
Chen Mao 132
Chen Shou 36n13, 36n14, 75, 88n67
Chen Xi 133
Chen Yi 13n2
Chen Yu 132
Chen Zeng 89n85
Chen Zilong 59n16, 60n49, 61n57, 61n62, 119n133
Chen Zuolin 62n80
Chenghua era 53, 64–65, 74, 77, 78, 79, 84, 98, 137n6
Chinggis Khan 28
Chongzhen era 56, 57, 58n4, 62n92, 69, 76, 79, 80–81, 83, 89n87, 123, 126–28, 139n44
Chu, Raymond 87n46
civil bureaucracy 44–50
civil offices and staffing levels 46–47
Collected Statutes of the Ming Dynasty 12, 44
collection of tax grain 94–98
collective leadership groups 55–56
Confucianism 10, 16n48, 30, 34, 35

congratulatory essays *(timingji)* 12
Crawford, Robert B. 61n68
Cui Gong 62n75
Cui Wensheng 77, 89n89
Cui Xian 76

Dai Xian 77
Delicacies, Directorate of 53, 55, 135
Deng Guangming 38n61
Deng Maoqi 132
Ding Haibin 20, 36n7, 36n15, 38n48, 41n137, 42n152, 43n155
Ding Yi 60n46
DMHD (Collected administrative statutes of the Ming dynasty) 46, 47, 58n1, 59n15, 60n34, 61n72, 62n83, 62n85, 63n94, 106, 114n23, 115n27, 115n31, 116n46, 117n74, 118n104, 119n129, 120n158, 138n19, 141n101
Dong Sizhang 117n83
Dreyer, Edward 61n67, 138n25
"*du*" terminology 18–19
Duan Zhijun 91n128
duiyun system, tribute grain delivery and 99

Early Ming Government (Farmer, E.) 6
Elman, Benjamin A. 16n47
Elvin, Mark 116n50
Embroidered-Uniform Guard *(Jinyiwei)* 51
Emperors: Gaozu 22–23; Kangxi 34; Qianlong 34; Renzong 28, 29, 40n94; Shundi 29; Song Taizu 24–25; Suzong 23, 37n39; Taidingdi 29; Wenzong 29; Wuzong 27, 29; Xiandi 20; Xiangqing 22; Xuanzong 23; Yingzong 29; Yuan 28–29; Zhengde 30; Zhongzong 22; *see also* reigns of Ming Emperors
Endicott-West, Elizabeth 40n93
eras *see* reigns of Ming Emperors
Esen, Mongol leader 126
eunuch agencies, scale of 54–55
eunuch departments of state 53
eunuch establishment 52–55
Evaluation Bureau 49

Fairbank, John K. 85n1
Fan Jingwen 59n18, 87n44
Fan Jinmin 14n12, 14n13
Fan Jishi 83
Fang Chaoying 41n123, 85n2
Fang Feng 82

Index 209

Fang Jun 15n32, 16n51, 16n52, 17n54, 17n55, 140n63
Fang Lian 101
Fang Liangyong 68
Fang Peng 82
Fang Zhenghua 89n87
Fang Zhongchong 49
Farmer, Edward L. 6, 14n12, 36n1, 88n58, 90n105, 114n7
Farquhar, David M. 60n32
Fast Ships *(kuaichuan)* 134, 135, 136
Fei Si-yen 14n13
Feng Bao 77, 89n89
Feng Chia-sheng 38–39n68, 39n75
Feng Xi 76, 89n80
financial functions: autumn grain *(qiuliangmi)* tax 94–95; Beijing (Northern Capital) 92–93, 94–95, 97–98, 99, 100, 101–2, 103, 104, 107, 109–10, 113; bureaus which administered tax grain 97; collection of tax grain 94–98; *duiyun* system, tribute grain delivered via 99; fish duty *(yuke)*, collection of 107–8; forest product levy *(zhumu choufen)*, collection of 108–9; *gaidui* system, tribute grain delivered via 100; land tax collection and distribution 95; local business tax *(shangshui)*, collection of 106–7; Nanjing (Southern Capital) 92–113; national revenues, deposits in treasuries of Nanjing administration 109–10; payments for rationed salt *(yanchao)*, collection of 108; reeds tax *(luke)*, collection of 109; regional roles 92–94; salt certificates issued by Nanjing Ministry of Revenue (1549) 104; state salt monopoly, role in 101–4; store franchise fees *(mentanshui)*, collection of 109; summer tax *(xiashuimai)* 94–95; tea revenue *(chake)*, collection of 104–6; transit duties and local business tax collected from seven major customs houses (early Ming) 106; transit duties *(chuanliao)*, collection of 106–7; transport of tribute grain 98–101; Yellow Registers, storage and verification of 110–13
fish duty *(yuke)*, collection of 107–8
Fisher, Carney T. 86n22
Five Dynasties, ephemeral regimes of 23–24

Fontana, Michela 14n17
forest product levy *(zhumu choufen)*, collection of 108–9
Forte, Antonio 37n31
Fu Weiling 138n42
Fu Zuozhou 82–83

gaidui system, tribute grain delivery and 100
Gallagher, Louis J. 14n19
Gao Feng 88n70
Gao Gong 115n40
Gao Hongtu 109, 127
Gao Qiqian 89n87
Gao Shouxian 14n14
Gao Youji 86n29, 101
Gaozu emperor 22–23
Garden Service 55
gazetteers 11–13, 17n54, 44, 81, 107, 110–11, 123
Goodrich, L. Carrington 41n123, 85n2
governmental departments, substructure of 45
Grand Canal *(zongdu hedao)* 7, 21, 64, 72, 100–101, 106, 116n54, 118n106, 133, 136
grand commandant, post of 52, 53
grand coordinatorship, appointments to 73
Grand Ritual Controversy 145
Grand Secretariat *(neige)* 33, 58, 65, 142, 145
grand secretaries *(daxueshi)* 55, 58, 68, 69, 74, 75, 80, 81, 87n39, 93, 130, 146
Great Rites Controversy *(dali yi)* 67, 68, 74–75, 79, 86n22, 90n107
Gu Dayong 75–76, 77, 88n70, 89n89
Gu Qing 76
Gu Qiyuan 14n13, 60n40, 60n54, 87n40, 87n46, 88n72, 137n10, 137n13, 139n51, 141n85, 146n1
Gu Yanwu 19, 36n7, 36n9, 36n13, 118n121
Gu Yingtai 86n22, 88n61, 139n54
Guan Minyi 139n54, 140n72
guard units, transport soldiers from 134
Gui E 68, 75, 145
Guisso, R.W.L. 37n33
Guizhou, female chieftain in Pu'an 131
Guo Xun 50

Hai Rui 15n26, 66, 85n16, 85n17
Han Bangqi 76
Han Guopan 37n18
Han Xuandi 37n20

210 Index

Han Yong 138n42
Han Yu 114n25
Hang Yong 133
Hanlin Academy 17n54, 45, 46, 47,
  59n11, 62n81, 64, 81, 87n39, 89n80, 94
Hartwell, Robert 113n1
Harvard Journal of Asiatic Studies
  113n1
He Ding 89n85
He Jian 83
He Liangjun 59–60n29, 85n9. 85n11
He Mengchun 74
He Qiaoxin 75, 79, 90n111
He Qiaoyuan 85n2, 85n4, 85n6, 85n14,
  86n21, 90n110
He Weibo 75
Hideyoshi Toyotomi 122, 132
History of the Song Dynasty (Songshi)
  25
Ho Ping-ti 8, 15n30, 15n31
Hok-lam Chan 16n48
Hong Chaoxuan 101
Hongguang regime 109, 126–27
Hongwu era 4, 5, 6, 14, 30–31, 51, 71,
  78–79, 108, 112, 114n12, 119n148,
  124, 128
Hongxi era 32, 52, 58n4, 79, 104, 146n3
Hongzhi era 30, 53–54, 59–60n29,
  59n25, 66, 76, 77–78, 79, 84, 117n74,
  131, 137n6
Horse Ships *(machuan)* 134, 136
Hoshi Ayao 116n50, 116n51, 116n54,
  141n87
Hou Fuzhong 139n60
Hsia, Pochia 14n17
Hsu Cho-yun 19, 36n7, 36n8
Hu Mengfei 7, 15n25
Hu Rulin 83
Hu Weiyong 79, 89–90n102
Hu Ying 126
Hu Zongxian 129, 130
Huai En 89n86
Huang, Ray 13, 17n56, 88n62, 94, 95,
  104, 114n9, 114n10, 114n15, 117n75,
  117n77, 117n80, 118n103, 118n110,
  118n117, 119n129, 120n158
Huang Bingshi 66
Huang Fu 49, 62n75
Huang Jin 40n101
Huang Kaihua 7, 66, 85–86n19, 85n18,
  86n20, 86n21
Huang Renyu 114n22
Huang Taiji 42n146
Huang Xiaoyang 132

Huang Xun 120n167
Huang Zhangjian 13, 17n56
Huang Zhongzhao 77
Huang Zongxi 88n69, 90–91n124
Huang Zuo 59n13, 59n21
Hucker, Charles 8, 15n42, 60n46, 61n58,
  85n8, 87n39, 87n46, 88n71, 88n72,
  90n120, 91n129, 114n12, 115n36,
  117n102, 118n110
Huo Tao 78

*Imperial Capital of the Previous
  Dynasties (Gu Yanwu)* 19
imperial guards *(qinjunwei* or
  shangzhiwei) 50–51
Imperial Horses, Directorate of 53, 55, 77
informal collective leadership groups
  55–56

Jia Yingchun 86n29
Jia Yong 67
Jiajing era 15n26, 30, 35, 56–57, 59n9,
  66–67, 68–69, 70, 71, 74–75, 76, 79,
  81–82, 85–86n19, 86n22, 86n35,
  87n42, 90n107, 115n40, 122–23, 129,
  131, 136, 137n9, 145
Jiang Gan 50
Jiang Yonglin 90n105
Jiang Yueguang 139n46
Jiang Zanchu 14n7, 14n11, 38n66
Jiang Zong 77, 89n89
Jianwen era 31, 78–79, 128
Jiao Hong 85n2, 85n3, 85n12, 86n29,
  88n60, 90n110, 90n123, 140n67
Jin dynasty period 18, 23, 25–26, 27, 35,
  127
Jin Lian 132
Jin Ying 89n86, 126
Jin Yufu 41–42n138
"jing" terminology 18–19
Jingtai era 64, 97–98
Joe, Wanne J. 38n46
Jun Fang 59n19, 61n58, 85n13, 88n57,
  141n81
junior officials, training ground for 66–71
Justice Ministry 4, 13, 34, 35, 46, 47,
  48, 49, 59n9, 62n85, 68, 75, 82,
  90–91n124

Kai Filipiak 141n81
Kangxi emperor 34
Khubilai Khan 27, 29
Kierman, Frank 85n1
King Cheng 19

Index 211

King Wu 19
Korea Incident (1592) 122
Kuang Ye 138n41
Kuang Zhong 146n3
Kurt, Johannes 38n64
Kwan-wai So 138n38

Lai Jiadu 138n41
Lan Yu 79, 89–90n102
land tax collection and distribution 95
leadership: administration and 55–56;
  informal collective leadership groups
  55–56
Lei Changjiao 140n78
Lei Li 59n20
Levathes, Louise 61n67
Li Banghua 126
Li Biao 68
Li Denan 61n71
Li Fang 77, 89n89
Li Guang 89n85
Li Guangbi 138n41
Li Guangming 138n24
Li Guangpi 23
Li Guangtao 147n6
Li Hualong 140–41n80
Li Jiantai 126
Li Jiuchang, 36n10, 37n
Li Jiyuan 140n63
Li Long 62n75
Li Longqian 117n77, 118m126,
  118n120, 118n125, 141n100
Li Mingrui 126
Li Mo 69
Li Rong 75
Li Shi 81
Li Shixin 83
Li Sui 89n77
Li Tianchong 129–30
Li Tingji 68
Li Xi 50
Li Xian et al. 14n6, 14n8
Li Xikong 145
Li Xu 41n130
Li Yeming 87n45
Li Yi 101
Li Zhen 132
Li Zhicheng 33, 126
Li Zisheng 78
Liang Chu 69
Liang Fang 77, 89n89
Liang Fangzhong 13, 119n140, 119n141
Liang Yao 132
Liao dynasty period 18, 25–27, 29, 35

Liao Taizong 39n71
Liao Taizu 39n69
Lin Fu 132
Lin Han 59–60n29
Linduff, Katheryn M. 19, 36n7, 36n8
Liu Bang 19
Liu Hongxun 68, 145
Liu Ji 75, 88n67
Liu Jin 50, 54, 60n40, 75–76, 77, 78, 80,
  89n85, 90n106, 90n107
Liu Jinxiang 138n25
Liu Jinzao 41–42n138, 42–43n153,
  42n141, 42n149, 42n151
Liu Kongzhao 139n46
Liu Long 50, 146
Liu Miao 117n73
Liu Ruoyu 53, 61n55, 61n69, 88n71
Liu Tianhe 86n29
Liu Tianxu 137n8
Liu Tianxu Incident (1606) 122
Liu Xiu 19–20
Liu Xu 37n27
Liu Yijie 59n17, 141n95
Liu Zhiqin 88n62
Liu Zhong 80
Liu Zongzhou 127
local business tax *(shangshui)*,
  collection of 106–7
local products, transportation of 134
Long Wenbin 88n76, 115n37
Longqing era 56, 57, 59n9, 77
Lü Daqi 127, 139n46
Lu Shen 76
Lu Su 131–32
Lü Yijian 25
Luan Chengxian 119n141
Luo Fenmei 62n77
Luo Xiang 88n70
Luo Xianglin 140n63
Luo Xiaoxiang 139n52

Ma Huan 61n67
Ma Shiying 127, 139n46
Ma Wensheng 78
Ma Yongcheng 75, 88n70
Ma Zhongxi 76, 89n78
Mao Hong 89n95
Mao Zedong 15n26
*Memorials from the Nanjing Ministry of
  Revenue (Liuji shucao)* 93
Meskill, John 60n41
Military Commissions 41n111, 48, 50–
  51, 52, 53, 55–56, 93–94, 121–22, 123,
  137n5, 143

212 *Index*

military functions: aboriginal rebellions in south, suppression of 131–33; administration of military apparatuses 50–52; administration of military training 51; Beijing (Northern Capital) 121–22, 126–27, 128–29, 130, 132–33, 134, 135, 136–37; Fast Ships *(kuaichuan)* 134, 135, 136; forces under command of the Southern Capital administration 121–24; guard units, transport soldiers in 134; Horse Ships *(machuan)* 134, 136; local products, transportation of 134; military forces under the command of the Southern Capital administration 121–24; Milu rebellion 131; Nanjing Ministry of War, prominence of 121; Nanjing (Southern Capital) 121–37; naval combat training 122–23; non-combat functions 133–37; northward transportation of tribute goods 135–36; piracy along southeast coast, suppression of 128–30; relay transport system 133–34; river-patrol censors *(xunjiang yushi)* 123; shipping vehicles and vessels, construction of 136; southern and northern armies, dividing line between 133; stability at second political center, maintenance of 124–28, 136–37; strength of military forces 124, 125, 128; Tianzhou rebellion 131–32; training divisions *(ying)* 122; tribute articles, delivery of 135–36; tribute grain transportation system 133; Tumu Incident (1449) 64, 85n1, 126, 138n40; "wolf soldiers" *(langbing)* 130, 140n63; Yao tribal revolt of Datengxia (Big Rattan Gorge) 132–33; Yellow Ships *(huangchuan)* 134–35, 136
Miller, Henry 88n62
Milu rebellion 131
Ming dynasty period 2, 7–8, 9, 11–12, 30–33, 44, 66–67, 84, 92, 96, 110, 126, 140n63
Miscellaneous Notes from the Date Grove (Zaolin zazu) 54–55
Miyazaki Ichisada 16n47
Mongol Khans 27–29
Mote, F.W. 7, 14n10, 14n15, 15n28, 15n31, 15n38, 38n67, 85n1, 89–90n102, 89n101, 90n103, 91n128,

114n7, 137n6, 138n25, 138n40, 138n42, 139n54, 146n1
multiple statuses of Nanjing (Southern Capital) 2–6

Nan Bingwen 62n87, 141n81
Nanjing Censorate, power of 50
Nanjing Censorate Gazetteer (Nanjing duchayuan zhi) 12, 13, 17n54, 123
Nanjing Court of Imperial Entertainments Gazetteer (Nanjing guanglusi zhi) 13, 17n54
Nanjing Court of Judicial Review 4, 42n139, 46, 47, 48, 55, 56, 57, 62n81, 63n93, 64, 73, 75, 76, 82, 85, 89n95, 93, 101
Nanjing Directorate of Imperial Parks Gazetteer (Nanjing shanglinyuan zhi) 44
Nanjing Hanlin Academy Gazetteer (Jiujing cilin zhi) 17n54, 81
Nanjing Ministry of Justice Gazetteer (Nanjing xingbu zhi) 13, 17n54
Nanjing Ministry of Personnel Gazetteer (Nanjing libu zhi) 12, 17n54
Nanjing Ministry of Revenue Gazetteer (Nanjing hubu zhi) 12, 13, 17n54, 107
Nanjing Ministry of War, prominence of 121
Nanjing National University 48
Nanjing (Southern Capital): administration 44–58; Beijing and, relationship between 145–46; financial functions 92–113; gazetteers 11–13, 17n54, 44, 81, 107, 110–11, 123; military functions 121–37; multiple statuses of 2–6; political functions 64–85; previous studies 6–9; sources of data on 11–13; state control, auxiliary implement of 142–45; state control, Ming era machinery 9–11; study of, rationale for 1–2; Wang Shu and posting to 64–66, 84; *see also* secondary capital system in Imperial China
national revenues, deposits in treasuries of Nanjing administration 109–10
national roles of Southern departments 49–50
naval combat training 122–23
NJDCYZ (Gazetteer of the Nanjing Censorate) 125, 137–38n14, 137n4, 137n12, 138n15, 141n93
NJHBZ (Gazetteer of the Nanjing Ministry of Revenue) 97, 99, 100, 104,

Index 213

106, 114n2, 114n13, 114n23, 115n31, 116n57, 117n73, 118n103, 119n134, 120n161, 141n83, 146n1
NJLBZ (Gazetteer of the Nanjing Ministry of Personnel) 46, 58n4, 59n10, 59n11, 60n30
nominal capital, symbolic status of 18
non-combat functions of military 133–37
northward transportation of tribute goods 135–36
Nurhachi 42n146

Office of Eunuch Grand Commandant 55
Official History of the Ming Dynasty (Mingshi) 11, 12, 44, 53, 77, 79, 81
officials: junior officials, training ground for 66–71; officials in disfavour, exile of 74–80; promotion patterns of vice ministers 70; ranks and emoluments 45; sinecure for superannuated officials 80–83; specially appointed taskforce central officials, source of 71–74; transfer patterns of ministers 70
Ogodei Khan 28
Ouyang Xiu 36n3

Pan Jixun 138n34
Pan Mingjuan 36n6
Pan Rong 98
Pang Song 13
payments for rationed salt *(yanchao)*, collection of 108
Pei Songzhi 36n13
Peng Dehuai 15n26
Peng Shao 79
personnel management 84–85
Personnel Ministry 8, 33, 46, 47, 49, 60n33, 68, 75, 78, 81, 85, 90n120, 143, 144, 146
Ping-ti Ho 115n32
piracy along southeast coast, suppression of 128–30
political functions: administration 84; Beijing (Northern Capital) 64, 65–66, 67–71, 72, 73–74, 75, 77–78, 80, 81, 82, 83, 84–85; Censorate (Beijing and Nanjing) 4, 22, 25, 29, 33, 46, 47, 50, 56, 57, 65, 70, 82, 85, 98, 101, 111, 123; disfavored officials, place of exile for 74–80; grand coordinatorship, appointments to 73; Grand Secretariat *(neige)* 33, 58, 65, 142, 145; grand secretaries *(daxueshi)* 55, 58, 68, 69, 74, 75, 80, 81, 87n39, 93,

130, 146; junior officials, training ground for 66–71; ministers of administration (1522–66) 67; Nanjing (Southern Capital) 64–85; personnel management 84–85; promotion patterns of vice ministers 70; Revenue Ministry 8, 9, 33–34, 46, 47, 49, 56, 57, 81, 92, 93–94, 95, 96, 97–98, 101–3, 104, 105, 106–7, 109, 110, 111, 113, 136, 142, 144; sinecure for superannuated officials 80–83; specially appointed taskforce central officials, source of 71–74; supreme commandership, appointments to 72; transfer patterns of ministers 70; Wang Shu and posting to Nanjing 64–66, 84
pre-Sui dynasty period 19–20
primary and secondary capitals 18

Qi Chang 85n7
Qi Erguang 141n93
Qian Longxi 68, 69
Qian Neng 65–66, 85n7
Qian Shisheng 68, 69
Qianlong emperor 34
Qiao Yu 67, 128
Qin Jin 68, 81–82
Qing dynasty period 8, 18, 33–36, 41–42n138, 77, 112, 140n63
Qingming Festival 42n147
Qiu Ju 88n70
Qiu Jun 114n25, 142
Qu Zhi 101

ranks and emoluments 45
Records on the Events in the Jiajing Era (Shimiao shiyulu) 81
reduction of offices 56–57
reeds tax *(luke)*, collection of 109
regional roles, financial functions and 92–94
reigns of Ming Emperors: Chenghua 53, 64–65, 74, 77, 78, 79, 84, 98, 137n6; Chongzhen 56, 57, 58n4, 62n92, 69, 76, 79, 80–81, 83, 89n87, 123, 126–28, 139n44; Hongwu 4, 5, 6, 14, 30–31, 51, 71, 78–79, 108, 112, 114n12, 119n148, 124, 128; Hongxi 32, 52, 58n4, 79, 104, 146n3; Hongzhi 30, 53–54, 59–60n29, 59n25, 66, 76, 77–78, 79, 84, 117n74, 131, 137n6; Jiajing 15n26, 30, 35, 56–57, 59n9, 66–67, 68–69, 70, 71, 74–75, 76, 79,

214 *Index*

81–82, 85–86n19, 86n22, 86n35, 87n42, 90n107, 115n40, 122–23, 129, 131, 136, 137n9, 145; Jianwen 31, 78–79, 128; Jingtai 64, 97–98; Longqing 56, 57, 59n9, 77; Taichang 68, 77; Tianqi 58n4, 78, 79, 87n43, 121; Tianshun 54, 64, 74–75, 86n21, 88n63; Wanli 53, 56, 57, 77, 79, 88n62, 131, 136, 145; Xuande 32, 48, 79, 104, 113, 133, 145, 146n3; Yongle 4–5, 6, 11, 31–32, 45, 48–49, 52, 54, 78–79, 113, 122, 124, 125; Zengde 30, 50, 53, 60n40, 60n50, 61n61, 74–80, 86n22, 90n107; Zhengtong 32, 56, 64, 74, 78–79, 81, 108, 115n40, 124, 138n41; *see also* Emperors
relay transport system 133–34
Renzong emperor 28, 29, 40n94
restoration of offices 57–58
Revenue Ministry 8, 9, 33–34, 46, 47, 49, 56, 57, 81, 92, 93–94, 95, 96, 97–98, 101–3, 104, 105, 106–7, 109, 110, 111, 113, 136, 142, 144
Ricci, Matteo 5–6, 14n17
river-patrol censors *(xunjiang yushi)* 123
Robinson, David 140n66
Rossabi, Morris 117n90
Ru Nan 81–82

salt certificates issued by Nanjing Ministry of Revenue (1549) 104
Saywell, William 87n46

The Scholars (Wu Jingzi) 5
Sechin, Jagchid 39n78, 39n80
secondary capital system in Imperial China: "*du*" terminology 18–19; Five Dynasties period 23–24; Jin dynasty period 18, 23, 25–26, 27, 35, 127; "*jing*" terminology 18–19; Liao dynasty period 18, 25–27, 29, 35; Ming dynasty period 2, 7–8, 9, 11–12, 30–33, 44, 66–67, 84, 92, 96, 110, 126, 140n63; nominal capital, symbolic status of 18; pre-Sui dynasty period 19–20; primary and secondary capitals 18; Qing dynasty period 8, 18, 33–36, 41–42n138, 77, 112, 140n63; Song dynasty period 18–19, 24–26, 27, 30–31, 35, 95–96, 127; Sui dynasty period 10, 20–21, 22, 23, 24, 35, 92; Tang dynasty period 10, 18, 21–23, 24, 26, 28, 35, 92, 95; terminology, "*jing*" and "*du*" 18–19;

Yuan dynasty period 7, 18, 27–29, 35, 92, 96
Security Offices, power of 50
Seiwert, Hubert 137n8
Shang Luo 65
Shao Bao 90–91n124
Shen Bang 119n135
Shen Defu 53, 91n125, 137n8
Shen Qi 141n95
Shen Que 67–68, 69
Shen Shixing 75
Shen Zhaoyang 90n109
Shi Bangyao 80–81, 88n63
Shi Heng 75
Shi Jianzhi 139n44
Shi Jixie 68
Shi Kefa 127, 139n46, 139n50
Shi Li 88n73
Shi Weimin 39n81, 40n96, 40n105, 41n111
Shih-shan Tsai 60n46, 61n58, 61n68
shipping vehicles and vessels, construction of 136
Shu Yinglong 101
Shundi emperor 29
Si-yen Fei 91n128
Si Yi 42n152
Sima Guang 37n30, 37n34
sinecure for superannuated officials 80–83
Sohn Pow-key et al. 38n46
Song dynasty period 18–19, 24–26, 27, 30–31, 35, 95–96, 127
Song Taizu emperor 24–25
Song Yubin and Qu Yili 38n48, 38n50
southern and northern armies, dividing line between 133
The Southern Ming (Struve, L.) 8–9
specially appointed taskforce central officials, source of 71–74
Spence, Jonathan 14n17
stability at second political center, maintenance of 124–28, 136–37
staffing levels in administration 44–45
state control: auxiliary implement of 142–45; Ming era machinery 9–11
state salt monopoly, role in 101–4
Statutes of the Ming Dynasty (Da Ming huidian) 11, 107
store franchise fees *(mentanshui),* collection of 109
Struve, Lynn 8–9, 15n39, 61n58, 119n136, 126–27, 139n47, 139n48, 139n50

Index 215

Su Bai 38n49
Su Shuangbi 15n26
Sui dynasty period 10, 20–21, 22, 23, 24, 35, 92; *see also* pre-Sui period
Sui Wendi 21
Sui Yangdi 20–22, 37n19
summer tax *(xiashuimai)* 94–95
Sun Chengze 108n128, 117n101
Sun Jiao 75, 81
Sun Jinghao 118n106
Sun Wenlong 41n118
Sun Yingkui 68
Supply Storehouse of Nanjing Palace Treasury 55
supreme commandership, appointments to 72
Suzong emperor 23, 37n39
Swope, Kenneth 139n44, 140n78
Taichang era 68, 77
Taidingdi emperor 29
Tan Qian 41n117, 44, 53, 54–55, 58n2, 59n23, 61n71, 62n81, 62n82, 62n84, 62n85, 62n90, 63n93, 67, 70, 86n23, 86n29, 86n30, 86n31, 87n45, 115n41, 116n59, 116n65, 119n136, 137n8, 138n43, 147n7
Tan Tianxing 62n92
Tan Xisi 61n64, 141n96
Tang dynasty period 10, 18, 21–23, 24, 26, 28, 35, 92, 95
Tang Gang 141n81
Tang Gaozong 22
Tang Wenji 116n45
Tang Xiaotao 140n63
Tao Chengxue 83
Tao Shangde 12–13
Tao Yan 68
tax grain, collection of 94–98
tea revenue *(chake)*, collection of 104–6
terminology, "*jing*" and "*du*" 18–19
territorial jurisdictions 47–48
Tian Jifang 59n11
Tian Yiheng 118n119
Tianqi era 58n4, 78, 79, 87n43, 121
Tianshun era 54, 64, 74–75, 86n21, 88n63
Tianzhou rebellion 131–32
Tong, James 140n66
Toriyama Kiichi 38n48
Toynbee, Arnold 11, 16n49
training divisions *(ying)* 122
transfer patterns of ministers 70
transit duties and local business tax collected from seven major customs houses (early Ming) 106

transit duties *(chuanliao)*, collection of 106–7
transport of tribute grain 98–101
tribute articles, delivery of 135–36
tribute grain transportation system 133
Tu Du 36n11
Tu Kai 69
Tu Qiao 69
Tu Wanyan 61n68, 141n94
Tumu Incident (1449) 64, 85n1, 126, 138n40
Twelve Directorates *(shi'er jian)* 52
Twitchett, Denis C. 15n31, 15n38, 113n1, 137n6, 138n25, 138n42, 139n54

Veritable Record of the Ming Dynasty (Ming shilu) 11
Veritable Records of the Hongzhi Emperor (Xiaozong shilu) 76
Voices from the Ming-Qing Cataclysm (Struve, L.) 9

Wakeman, Frederic 8, 15n29
Wan An 75
Wan Ming 14n20
Wan Tang 86n30
Wan Yi 14n20
Wan Yukai 137–38n14
Wang An 89n85
Wang Cai 83
Wang Cheng'en 89n87
Wang Chunyu 61n68, 141n94
Wang Fu 37n36
Wang Gao 130
Wang Hon 15n26
Wang Huanbiao 58n3, 59n15, 139n51
Wang Jianying 13n1, 41n116
Wang Jiao 48
Wang Jun 67
Wang Leimin 118n125
Wang Mang 19
Wang Mingsun 38n59
Wang Peihuan 42n152
Wang Qi 118n126
Wang Qiao 59n26, 89n91
Wang Qiju 114n8
Wang Qiong 68
Wang Shi 131
Wang Shizhen 61n59, 87n44
Wang Shou 131–32
Wang Shu 50, 62n75, 64–66, 84, 85n2, 88n67
Wang Shuanghuai 140n63

216   *Index*

Wang Tianyou 6–7, 14n21, 15n22
Wang Ting 115n41
Wang Xian 68
Wang Xuekui 75
Wang Yangming 77, 128, 131–33, 139n54, 140n72, 140n73
Wang Yongbin 81
Wang Yue 75, 76
Wang Yun 40n95
Wang Yuquan 141n81
Wang Zhen 78, 79, 89n85, 90n106
Wang Zhi 49, 65, 77, 78, 79, 81, 89n89, 90n106, 90n107
Wanli era 53, 56, 57, 77, 79, 88n62, 131, 136, 145
Weber, Max 15n41
Wechsler, Howard J. 37n32
Wei Bin 88n70
Wei Ji 81
Wei Jianli 61n68
Wei Qingyuan 8, 15n35, 60n46, 115n26, 119n141, 120n164
Wei Shou 36n15
Wei Tianfu 140n63
Wei Zheng et al. 37n16
Wei Zhongxian 78, 80, 83, 89n85, 90n106
Wen Gui 79
Wenren Quan et al. 13n3, 14n9
Wenzong emperor 29
Wing-Kin Puk 117n73
Wittfogel, Karl 38–39n68, 39n75, 89n101
"wolf soldiers" *(langbing)* 130, 140n63
Wu Han 7, 8, 15n26, 15n27, 15n34
Wu Jihua 115n27
Wu Jingzi 5, 14n16
Wu Tingxie 72, 73, 87n47–52, 116n53, 116n58
Wu Wendu 76, 89n77
Wu Yipeng 67, 68, 75, 76
Wu Yuan 131
Wu Zetian 22–23
Wu Zhihe 118n117
Wuzong emperor 27, 29

Xi Shu 67
Xia Bangmo 69
Xia Xie 90n109
Xiandi emperor 20
Xiang Yu 127–28
Xiang Zhong 65, 132
Xiangcheng Li Long 52
Xiangqing emperor 22

Xiao Shaoqiu 62n87
Xiao Tong 36n4
Xiao Xuan 74
Xiaowendi 20
Xiaoxiang Luo 137n8
Xie Bin 8, 142, 146n1
Xie Guozhen 139n50
Xing Jie 132, 140n78
Xiong Cunrui, Victor 36n2, 36n8
Xiong Mengxiang 40n99
Xiong Tingbi 145, 147n6
Xu Bida 13, 123
Xu Bin 75, 88n63
Xu Chunyan 90n104
Xu Duren 13
Xu Hong 14n12, 41n127, 60n31, 60n35, 88n63, 90n119
Xu Hongji 139n46
Xu Jin 80
Xu Mu 76
Xu Qi 62n75
Xu Tianling 36n11
Xu Xuemo 75, 81, 89n99, 90n116
Xu Youzhen 88n63, 126
Xu Zi 87n41, 139n45, 139n46, 139n49
Xuan Ni 86n21
Xuande era 32, 48, 79, 104, 113, 133, 145, 146n3
Xuanzong emperor 23
Xue Juzheng et al. 38n51

Yadong Xueshe 118n124
Yan Shifan 83
Yan Song 50, 60n42, 80, 83, 129
Yang Ding 48
Yang Fu 56
Yang Lian 112
Yang Ning 82
Yang Pu 79
Yang Rong 79
Yang Sanshou 85n7
Yang Shan 88n63
Yang Shiqi 56, 79
Yang Shunfa 39n75
Yang Shusen 42–43n153
Yang Su 20
Yang Tinghe 68, 69, 74–75
Yang Tonggui 42n150
Yang Xinmin 132
Yang Yi 130
Yang Yikui 101
Yang Yinglong 131, 132, 140–41n80, 140n78
Yang Yiqing 89n92, 145

Yang Zhengtai 146n3
Yangzi River 37n19, 48, 72, 92, 95, 99, 100, 106, 109, 113n1, 122–23, 127–28, 133–34, 135, 145
Yao Kui 75, 88n63
Yao tribal revolt of Datengxia (Big Rattan Gorge) 132–33
Yao Wenyuan 15n26
Yao Zhongwen 145
Ye Mengxiong 132
Ye Xianggao 67, 68, 69
Ye Xiaojun 20, 36n7, 36n15
Ye Xingmin 41n108, 41n111
Ye Zongliu 132
Yellow Registers, storage and verification of 110–13
Yellow Ships *(huangchuan)* 134–35, 136
Yin Shouheng 146n3
Ying Qiu 83
Yingzong emperor 29
Yiwen, Prince of 71, 128, 139n51
Yongle era 4–5, 6, 11, 31–32, 45, 48–49, 52, 54, 78–79, 113, 122, 124, 125
Yu Jideng 59–60n29, 146n4
Yu Qian 126, 138n41
Yu Shenxing 68
Yuan dynasty period 7, 18, 27–29, 35, 92, 96
Yuan emperor 28–29
Yuwen Kai 20

Zeng Jun 50
Zengde era 30, 50, 53, 60n40, 60n50, 61n61, 74–80, 86n22, 90n107
Zhan Ruoshui 71
Zhang Bangqi 82
Zhang Cai 75
Zhang Chunxiu 138n30
Zhang Cong 68, 75, 81, 145
Zhang Dexin 62n92
Zhang Feng 115n37
Zhang Fuhua 101
Zhang Guihuai 140n78
Zhang Guoshuo 19, 36n5, 36n6
Zhang Heng 19, 20, 36n12
Zhang Huan 115n41
Zhang Jin 101
Zhang Jing 89n86, 129–30, 139n60, 145
Zhang Jun 116n62
Zhang Juzheng 50, 57, 75, 79, 80, 82–83, 88n62, 109–10, 145
Zhang Kai 132
Zhang Lun 75
Zhang Mao 77

Zhang Nai 76, 89n79
Zhang Peng 101
Zhang Pu 83
Zhang Sheng 75
Zhang Shenyan 69, 127, 139n46
Zhang Shicheng 115n27
Zhang Wei 76, 89n82
Zhang Weiren 114n11
Zhang Xianqing 60n42
Zhang Yanghao 40n98
Zhang Ying 45
Zhang Yingpin 7, 15n23, 15n24
Zhang Yixian 89n86
Zhang Yong 77, 88n70, 89n89, 89n92, 89n95
Zhang Zhi 69
Zhao Gou 25–26
Zhao Guan 119n147
Zhao Wenhua 129, 130, 145
Zheng Bengong 82
Zheng He 61n67, 89n86
Zheng Liangsheng 139–40n61
Zheng Xiao 62n75, 87n42
Zheng Yi 101
Zhengde emperor 30
Zhengtong era 32, 56, 64, 74, 78–79, 81, 108, 115n40, 124, 138n41
Zhongyuan Festival 42n147
Zhongzong emperor 22
Zhou Baozhu 38n54
Zhou Boqi 40n96
Zhou Cheng 38n56, 38n57
Zhou Chong 130, 139–40n61
Zhou Daodeng 68
Zhou Hui 61n59, 139n55
Zhou Ken 127
Zhou Liangxiao 40n93
Zhou Lun 68
Zhou Song 60n47
Zhou Yingbin 90n114
Zhou Zhibin 137n8, 137n9
Zhu Biao 54, 128
Zhu Changfang 139n46
Zhu Chenhao 128, 139n54
Zhu Dongrun 62n87, 88n62
Zhu Guozhen 87n43, 121, 137n1
Zhu Shiguang 20, 36n7, 36n15
Zhu Tingli 116n70, 117n78
Zhu Ying 76
Zhu Yong 133
Zhu Yousong 139n46
Zhu Yuanzhang 31, 114n7, 115n27
Zhuang Yong 77
Zou Yuanbiao 75